THE FATHERS
OF THE CHURCH

A NEW TRANSLATION

VOLUME 85

THE FATHERS
OF THE CHURCH

A NEW TRANSLATION

CLEMENT OF ALEXANDRIA

STROMATEIS
BOOKS ONE TO THREE

Translated by
JOHN FERGUSON

THE CATHOLIC UNIVERSITY OF AMERICA PRESS
Washington, D.C.

The paper used in this publication meets the minimum requirements of
American National Standards for Information Sciences—Permanence of
Paper for Printed Library Materials. ANSI Z39-48-1984.

∞

LIBRARY OF CONGRESS CATALOGING-IN-PUBLICATION DATA
Clement, of Alexandria, ca. 150–ca. 215.
[Stromata. Libri 1–3. English]
Stromateis. Books 1–3 / Clement of Alexandria: translated by
John Ferguson.
p. cm. — (The Fathers of the Church; v. 85)
Translation of Libri 1–3 of: Stromateis.
Includes bibliographical references and indices.
ISBN-13: 978-0-8132-0085-9 (cl)
ISBN-10: 0-8132-0085-7 (cl)
ISBN-13: 978-0-8132-1433-7 (pbk)
ISBN-10: 0-8132-1433-5 (pbk)
1. Theology—Early church, ca. 30–600. 2. Gnosticism—
Controversial literature—Early works to 1800. 3. Christian life—
Early church, ca. 30–600. 1. Ferguson, John, 1921–1989
II. Title. III. Series.
BR60.F3C56
[BR65.C65S77]
270 s—dc
[239'.1]   90-21352

CONTENTS

FOREWORD

I am grateful for the opportunity of returning to Clement, a richly human and attractive writer, and making one of his outstanding works more accessible to English readers.

I have written about Clement in my *Clement of Alexandria* in the Twayne World Authors Series 289 (1974) as well as in reviews and articles, and have occasionally repeated myself. I express elsewhere my thanks to G. W. Butterworth and C. Mondésert.

Here I must say yet another warm vote of thanks to Lesley Roff for incredibly coping with the typing of one of the messiest MSS even she has ever tamed to tidiness.

JOHN FERGUSON

EDITOR'S NOTE: *Regrettably John Ferguson died on May 22, 1989, before seeing his work in print. Requiescat.*

ABBREVIATIONS

Books in a Series

ANF   Ante-Nicene Fathers. Volume 2. *The Fathers of the Second Century*. Reprint. Grand Rapids, 1979.

CAF   *Comicorum Atticorum Fragmenta*. 3 volumes. Ed. T. Kock. Leipzig, 1880–88.

DK   *Fragmente der Vorsokratiker*. 3 volumes. Ed. H. Diels and W. Kranz. Berlin, 1951–52.

FGrH   *Fragmente der griechischen Historiker*. Ed. F. Jacoby. Berlin, 1923– .

FHG   *Fragmenta Historicorum Graecorum*. 5 volumes. Ed. C. Müller. Paris, 1841–70.

GCS   Die griechischen christlichen Schriftsteller der ersten drei Jahrhunderte. Leipzig, 1897– .

FPG   *Fragmenta Philosophorum Graecorum*. 3 volumes. Ed. F. W. A. Mullach. Paris, 1860–81.

LCC   Library of Christian Classics. Ed. J. Baillie, J. McNeill, and H. P. Van Dusen. Philadelphia, 1953– .

LCL   Loeb Classical Library.

OECT   Oxford Early Christian Texts. Oxford, 1970– .

SC   Sources chrétiennes. Paris, 1942– .

SPCK   Society for Promoting Christian Knowledge. London, 1698– .

SVF   *Stoicorum Veterum Fragmenta*. 4 volumes. Ed. H. F. von Arnim. Reprint. Stuttgart, 1964.

TGF   *Tragicorum Graecorum Fragmenta*. Ed. A. Nauck. Leipzig, 1889.

TU   Texte und Untersuchungen zur Geschichte der altchristlichen Literatur. Berlin, 1882– .

Periodicals

JThS   *Journal of Theological Studies*

HThR   *Harvard Theological Review*

RelStud   *Religious Studies*

RSR   *Recherches de science religieuse*
VigChr   *Vigiliae Christianae*
ZKG   *Zeitschrift für Kirchengeschichte*
ZnW   *Zeitschrift für die neutestamentliche Wissenschaft*
ZwTh   *Zeitschrift für wissenschaftliche Theologie*

Works of Clement of Alexandria

EclProph   *Eclogae ex scripturis propheticis*
ExTheod   *Excerpta ex Theodoto*
Paedagogus *Paedagogus*
Protrepticus *Protrepticus sive cohortatio ad gentes*
Quis dives *Quis dives salvetur?*
Stromateis *Stromata gnosticorum secundam veram philosophiam commentariorum*

SELECT BIBLIOGRAPHY

Texts and Translations

Casey, R. P. *The* Excerpta ex Theodoto *of Clement of Alexandria.* London, 1934.

Hort, F. J. A. and J. B. Mayor. *Clement of Alexandria: Miscellanies Book VII.* New York, 1902.

Le Boulluec, A. *Clément d'Alexandrie: Les Stromates: Stromate V.* SC 278, 279 (1981).

Mondésert, C. and M. Caster. *Clément d'Alexandrie: Les Stromates: Stromate I.* SC 30 (1951).

Mondésert, C. and P. Camelot. *Clément d'Alexandrie: Les Stromates: Stromate II.* SC 38 (1954).

Stählin, O. *Clemens Alexandrinus.* Zweiter Band: Stromata Buch I–VI. GCS (1972).

Secondary Sources

Arnim, H. F. von. *De octavo Clementis Stromateorum libro.* Rostock Progr., 1894.

Bardy, G. "Aux origines de l'école d'Alexandrie." *RSR* 27 (1937) 65–90.

Batey, R. A. *New Testament Nuptial Imagery.* Leiden, 1971.

Bell, Sir H. Idris. *Egypt from Alexander the Great to the Arab Conquest: A Study in the Diffusion and Decay of Hellenism.* Oxford, 1948.

Bigg, C. *The Christian Platonists of Alexandria.* Oxford, 1913.

Broudéhoux, J. P. *Mariage et famille chez Clément d'Alexandrie.* Paris, 1970.

Camelot, P. Th. *Foi et Gnose.* Paris, 1945.

Chadwick, H. *Early Christian Thought and the Classical Tradition.* Oxford, 1966.

———. and J. E. L. Oulton. *Alexandrian Christianity: Selected Translations of Clement and Origen.* LCC 2 (1954).

Daniélou, J. "Typologie et allégorie chez Clément d'Alexandrie." TU 79 (1961) 50–57.

Edsman, C. M. *Le baptême de feu.* Upsala, 1940.

Ernst, W. "De Clementis Alexandrini Stromatum libro octavo qui fertur." Ph.D. Diss. Gottingen, 1910.

Faye, Eugène de. *Clément d'Alexandrie.* Frankfurt, 1967.

Ferguson, John. *Clement of Alexandria*. New York, 1974.
————. *Moral Values in the Ancient World*. London, 1958.
————. "The Achievements of Clement of Alexandria." *RelStud* 12 (1976) 59–80.
Floyd, W. E. G. *Clement of Alexandria's Treatment of the Problem of Evil*. Oxford, 1971.
Hanson, R. P. C. *Allegory and Event*. London, 1959.
Hennecke, E. *New Testament Apocrypha*. Ed. W. Schneemelcher. Tr. R. McL. Wilson. 2 volumes. Philadelphia, 1964.
Heussi, C. "Die *Stromateis* des Clemens Alexandrinus in ihrem Verhältnis zum Protrepticus und Pädagogus." *ZwTh* 45 (1902) 465–512.
Hirner, A. "Die *Stromata* des Clemens von Alexandrien." Ph.D. Diss. Innsbruck, 1970.
Hoek, A. van den. *Clement of Alexandria and His Use of Philo in the Stromateis*. *VigChr* suppl. 3. Leiden, 1988.
Hoyer, R. *De Antiocho Ascalonita*. Ph.D. Diss. Bonn, 1853.
Laistner, M. L. W. *Christianity and Pagan Culture in the Later Roman Empire*. London, 1951.
Lazzati, G. *Introduzione allo studio di Clemente Alessandrino*. Milan, 1939.
Lohmeyer, Ernst. *Die Briefe an die Philipper an die Kolosser und an Philemon, erklärt*. . . . Gottingen, 1930.
Méhat, A. *Etude sur les* Stromates *de Clément d'Alexandrie*. Paris, 1966.
————. "L'Hypothèse des *Testimonia* à l'épreuve des *Stromates*." in *La Bible et les Pères: Colloque de Strasbourg 1ᵉʳ–3 octobre 1969*. Paris, 1971. Pp. 229–42.
————. "Clément d'Alexandrie et les sens de l'Ecriture 1ᵉʳ *Stromate* 176.1 et 179.3." In J. Fontaine and C. Kannengiesser, *Epektasis: Mélanges patristiques offerts au Cardinal Jean Daniélou*. Paris, 1972. Pp. 355–65.
Mondésert, C. "Le symbolisme chez Clément d'Alexandrie." *RSR* 26 (1936) 158–80.
————. Clément d'Alexandrie: Introduction a l'étude de sa pensée religieuse à partir de l'Ecriture. Paris, 1944.
Mondin, Battista. *Filone e Clemente*. Torino, 1969.
Muller, Earl C., S.J. *Trinity and Marriage in Paul*. American University Studies Series 7, Theology and Religion 60. New York, 1990.
Neymeyr, Ulrich. *Die Christlichen Lehrer im Zweiter Jahrhundert*. Leiden, 1989.
Osborn, E. F. *The Philosophy of Clement of Alexandria*. Cambridge, 1957.
————. "Teaching and Writing in the First Chapters of the *Stromateis* of Clement of Alexandria." *JThS* 10 (1959) 335–43.
Pade, B. Λόγος Θεός: *Untersuchungen zur Logos-Christologie des Titus Flavius Clemens von Alexandrien*. Rome, 1939.

Pépin, J. "La vraie dialectique selon Clément d'Alexandrie." *Epektasis: Mélanges patristiques offerts au Cardinal Jean Daniélou.* Ed. J. Fontaine and C. Kannengiesser. Paris, 1972. Pp. 375–84.

Preische, H. *De γνώσει Clementis Alexandrini.* Jena, 1871.

Prestige, G. L. *God in Patristic Thought.* 2d ed. London, 1952.

Prümm, P. K. "Glaube und Erkenntnis im zweiten Buch der *Stromata* des Klemens von Alexandrien." *Scholastik* 12 (1937) 17–57.

Rahner, H. *Greek Myths and Christian Mystery.* London, 1957.

Resch, A. *Agrapha.* TU 30. Leipzig, 1906.

Roberts, L. "The Literary Form of the *Stromateis.*" *Second Century* 1 (1984) 211–22.

———. "The Unutterable Symbols of (Γῆ)-Θέμις." *HThR* 68 (1975) 73–82.

Sanders, E. P. *The Shaping of Christianity in the Second and Third Centuries.* London, 1980.

Schultz, W. "*Stromateis* V 48.4–59.1." *Memnon* 2 (1908) 36–82.

Simon, S. *Clemens Alexandrinus und die Mysterien.* Budapest, 1938.

Smith, M. *Clement of Alexandria and a Secret Gospel of Mark.* Cambridge, MA., 1973.

Steneker, H. Πειθοῦς δημιουργία. Nymegen, 1967.

Tibiletti, C. "Un passo di Clemente Alessandrino su verginità e matrimonio." *Orpheus* 5 (1984) 437–43.

Timothy, Hamilton B. *The Early Christian Apologists and Greek Philosophy.* Assen, Van Gorcum, 1973.

Treu, U. "Etymologie und Allegorie bei Klemens von Alexandrien." TU 79 (1961) 191–211.

Valentin, F. *Clément d'Alexandrie.* Paris, 1963.

Wyrwa, D. *Die christliche Platonaneignung in den* Stromateis *des Clemens von Alexandrien.* Berlin, 1983.

Zahn, T. *Supplementum Clementinum.* Erlangen, 1884.

Zeegers, vonder Vorst, *Les citations des poètes grecs chez les apologistes chrétiens du IIe siècle.* Louvain, 1972.

Gnosticism in Clement

Burkitt, F. C. *Church and Gnosis.* Cambridge, 1932.

Clark, Elizabeth. *Clement's Use of Aristotle: The Aristotelian Contribution to Clement of Alexandria's Refutation of Gnosticism.* New York, 1977.

Cross, F. L., ed. *The Jung Codex.* London, 1955.

Dibelius, O. "Studien zur Geschichte der Valentinianer." *ZnW* 9 (1908) 230–47, 329–40.

Dudon, P. *Le gnostique de saint Clément d'Alexandrie.* Paris, 1970.

Fénelon, François. *Le gnostique de saint Clément d'Alexandrie.* Paris, 1930.

Foerster, W. *Gnosis.* 2 volumes. Oxford, 1972–74.

Grant, R. M. *Gnosticism: An Anthology.* London, 1961.

———. *Gnosticism and Early Christianity.* New York, 1966.

Jonas, H. *The Gnostic Religion.* Boston, 1965.

King, Karen L., ed. *Images of the Feminine in Gnosticism.* Philadelphia, 1988.

Kovacs, Judith L. "Clement of Alexandria and the Valentinian Gnostics." Ph.D. Diss. New York, 1978.

Layton, B. *Rediscovery of Gnosticism. Proceedings of the International Conference on Gnosticism at Yale, New Haven, March 28–31, 1978.* Leiden, 1980.

Lilla, Salvatore R. *Clement of Alexandria: A Study in Christian Platonism and Gnosticism.* London, 1971.

Moingt, P. J. "Le gnose de Clément d'Alexandrie dans ses rapports avec la foi et la philosophie." *RSR* 37 (1950) 195–251, 389–421, 537–64; *RSR* 38 (1951) 82–118.

Pagels, E. *The Gnostic Gospels.* London, 1979.

Puech, H. C. and G. Quispel. "Le quatrième écrit gnostique du Codex Jung." *VigChr* 9 (1955) 65–102.

Quispel, G. *Gnosis als Weltreligion.* Zurich, 1951.

———. *Gnostic Studies.* 2 volumes. Istanbul, 1974–75.

———. "La conception de l'homme dans la gnose valentinienne." *Eranos-Jahrbuch* 15 (1947) 258ff.

Robinson, J. M. *The Nag Hammadi Library in English.* Leiden, 1977. See now the third completely revised edition. Tr. Coptic Gnostic Library Project of the Institute for Antiquity and Christianity. San Francisco, 1988.)

Rudolph, K. *Gnosis.* Edinburgh, 1977.

Sagnard, F. M. *La gnose valentinienne.* Paris, 1947.

Scholer, D. *Nag Hammadi Bibliography 1948–1969.* Leiden, 1971, and annually in *Novum Testamentum.*

Völker, W. *Der wahre Gnostiker nach Klemens von Alexandrien.* TU 57 (1952).

———. *Quellen zur Geschichte der Christlichen Gnosis.* Tübingen, 1932.

INTRODUCTION

INTRODUCTION

Clement

We know little of Clement's youth. His name, Titus Flavius Clemens, is Latin not Greek, and suggests that an ancestor was a freedman of T. Flavius Clemens, a relative of emperors and himself perhaps a Christian convert. Clement must have been born about A.D. 150, in either Athens or Alexandria (Epiphanius, *Adversus lxxx haereses* 32.6). He was a convert, not a Christian by birth (*Paedagogus* 1.1.1, 2.8.62; Eusebius, *Demonstratio evangelica* 2.2.64), and knew the pagan religions from within. Curiously, he tells us little of his conversion; it was perhaps gradual rather than cataclysmic.

(2) He travelled in Magna Graecia, the Near East, and Palestine before settling in Alexandria. Here, in about A.D. 180 he met Pantaenus, and joined him in the catechetical school—not a formal institution, but a group meeting in the teacher's private house. He taught large and small classes alike. He was ordained as elder. We do not know if he was married, although he writes of the married state with understanding. We know nothing of his teaching: his star pupil and successor, Origen, does not mention him.

(3) In A.D. 202–3 persecution descended on the Church in Egypt (Eusebius, *Historia ecclesiastica* 6.1–3) and thousands lost their lives. Clement left Alexandria, never to return. He may have gone to Cappadocia. The persecution eased, but he was not recalled: the formidable Demetrius may have disapproved of his liberalism. We hear of him in a letter of about A.D. 211 (Eusebius, *Historia ecclesiastica* 6.11.6); by A.D. 216 he was dead, one of "those blessed men who have trodden the road before us" (Eusebius, *Historia ecclesiastica* 6.14.8, 6.19.6).

(4) Eusebius called him "practiced in Scripture" (*Historia ec-*

clesiastica 5.11) and he certainly knew his Bible well. Cyril called him "exceptionally expert in Greek history" (*Contra Julianum* 6.215) and Jerome noted his knowledge of secular literature (*De viris illustribus* 38). He cites to our knowledge 348 authors, although he no doubt sometimes draws on anthologies and compendia. He is the supreme example of those who see in Christ the fulfillment of cultural aspirations. "There is only one river of truth, but a lot of streams disgorge their waters into it" (*Stromateis* 1.29 [1–10]).

(5) His philosophy of life centers on God, who is one and beyond one (*Paedagogus* 1.8.71). He sees in Jesus, the eternal *Logos*, the full and perfect revelation of God. He loves God's creation and sees it as good; he gives us a warm, joyous picture of life. He is richly human, sane, and moderate. Charles Bigg said of him: "No later writer has so serene and hopeful a view of human nature."

Alexandria

(6) Three things must be remembered about Alexandria: First, it was one of the only two ancient cities, Rome being the other, that approached the size of a modern city, and might be said to suffer from inner city problems. We may suppose the population to have approached three-quarters of a million people. Strabo (17.1.13) called it "the greatest mart in the world." Theocritus (*Idyll* 15) described its bustle at festival time; 500 years later Bishop Dionysius said that it was easier to traverse the world from east to west than to cross Alexandria. We have from the third century B.C. a set of regulations, preserved on papyrus, prescribing penalties and compensations in different cases of assault.

(7) Second, it was a Greek foundation, Alexander the Great's lasting work. It was not characteristically Egyptian but Greek. The Ptolemaic dynasty that ruled it for three centuries was pure Greek. The Romans, setting it apart, called it *Alexandria ad Aegyptum*, 'Alexandria near Egypt.'

(8) Third, it was cosmopolitan. The original citizens were Greeks, although there was a small Egyptian village called

Rhacotis already on the site. But there were plenty of immigrants from all over the world. In particular the Jews had a quarter of their own; it was here that the Hebrew Scriptures were translated into Greek. The Jews were so Hellenized that they wanted to participate in the athletic festivals. They had their own administration under an *ethnarch* or *alabarch*. At the same time tensions sometimes arose between Greeks and Jews and, at the time of the Jewish War (A.D. 66–70) against Rome, 50,000 Jews died in rioting (Josephus, *Jewish War* 2.487–98). But it was not merely Greeks, Egyptians, and Jews. "I behold among you," says one ancient author, "not merely Greeks and Italians and people from neighboring Syria, Libya, Cilicia, but even Ethiopians and Arabs from more distant regions, and Bactrians, Scythians, Persians, and a few Indians . . ." (Dio Chrysostom, *Oration* 32.40).

(9) It was a striking city, built on the typical Hellenistic grid pattern. A plan was attempted under Napoleon III, and the city walls traced over a circuit of nine and one-half miles. Eleven streets were discovered running east-west, and seven running north-south. The main streets were as much as thirty meters wide, and there was a developed system of street lighting, unusual in antiquity. The houses were built well, having good foundations with cisterns for Nile water in the basement, and stone structures even in the roof, making the city unusually fireproof. The public buildings were distinguished—theaters, baths, gymnasiums, athletic stadiums, and a hippodrome, as well as the palace, the Museum or University, Alexander's tomb, and the celebrated lighthouse.

(10) Alexandria was early a center of scholarship, and the famous museum had a zoo and botanical garden, as well as a library of 700,000 volumes. The driving force behind the foundation was the refugee Aristotelian scholar Demetrius of Phalerum. The great strength of the Aristotelians was in reaching scientific generalizations from the collection and observation of masses of material. The museum (the name had not lost its association with the Muses) was also a center of literary culture, and leading poets—Theocritus, Callimachus, and Apollonius of Rhodes—put down roots there. In medicine, mathematics,

astronomy, and geography too, Alexandria led the world. Eratosthenes was perhaps her greatest scholar, "mathematician,
geographer, astronomer, grammarian, chronographer, historian, philologist, philosopher, and even poet." They nicknamed him "Beta," 'runner-up' to the leader in any field, but
without peer as an all rounder. In the second century B.C., Hip-
parchus established the science of cartography, and discovered
the precession of the equinoxes; in the second century A.D.,
Alexandria welcomed Claudius Ptolemaeus, whose authority
extended to the time of Galileo. In mathematics, Euclid produced the most famous textbook ever written, and Apollonius
developed the understanding of conic sections. About the time
of the coming of Christianity to the city, Soranus was devel-
oping gynecology and Heron inventing a steam engine as a
child's toy.

(11) Alexandria was also a center of religion. Sarapis was a
universal god invented by the Ptolemies as a unifying power
for their universal claims. He had a magnificent temple richly
described in the fourth century A.D. by Ammianus Marcelli-
nus; we know of torchlight processions in his honor. The Egyptian gods and goddesses were in Alexandria in their numbers,
Isis and Osiris and Harpocrates, Hathor and Cnephis, Ra and
Ptah. So were the Greek deities, Zeus and Poseidon, Demeter
and Kore (with an interesting cult of which we have some record), Apollo and Hermes, Hera and Aphrodite, Pan and
Nemesis, and Tyche. Foreign cults infiltrated too. Apart from
the god of the Jews, we find Adonis (whose popular festival is
early recorded by Theocritus, *Idyll* 15), the Thracian Bendis,
the Persian Mithras. On top of all this Alexandria was a natural
center of ruler-cult, and even moderate Roman emperors had
to accept worship in their lifetime, though the humane Claudius deprecated it.

(12) But Alexandria was no great center of orthodoxy (if
such a term is meaningful in ancient religion). For example, a
remarkable Hadrianic coin shows Zeus with the rays of Helios
the sun god, the horizontal ram's horns of Khnemu, the spiral
ram's horns of Ammon, the cornucopia of the Nile, the trident
of Poseidon, and the snake of Asclepius. In another, slightly

later coin of Antoninus Pius, Sarapis is in the center, surrounded by a zodiacal belt and busts of the seven divinities of
the week, which seem to evidence Mithraic influence. Epiphanius, writing in the fourth century A.D., has an extraordinary account of the festival of the New Year in honor of
Demeter's daughter Kore (the Maiden) on January 5–6: "First
at Alexandria, in the Koreion as they call it, a very large temple,
the precinct of Kore, they keep vigil all night long, chanting to
their idol with songs and flutes. At dawn, when they have completed the nocturnal vigil, torchbearers go down into an underground room and bring up a wooden image sitting naked
on a litter, with a mark of a cross in gold on the forehead, two
similar marks on the hands, and two more on the knees—in
all, five marks of gold stamped on it. They carry this image
seven times round the center of the temple to the music of
flutes, drums, and hymns, and then, at the end of the festival,
they replace it in its underground quarters. If asked what is
the meaning of this mystery they reply, 'Today at this hour
Kore'—that is the Virgin—'has given birth to Aion.'" Aion is
the personification of the year. Here the syncretism has taken
in Christianity.

(13) Alexandria also witnessed some of the more brilliant
and some of the more aberrant flights of Gnosticism, with complex systems of salvation; it saw those strange revelations in
which the Egyptian god Thoth is identified with Hermes
Thrice-Greatest, and the wisdoms of Greece, Egypt, and Asia
come together.[1]

Christianity in Alexandria

(14) Alexandria, as we have seen, had a strong Jewish community. It was generally liberal in both religious and social approach. Hebrew and Aramaic seem to have virtually died out,
and Greek was the predominant language. It was not merely a

1. On Alexandria, see now U. Neymeyr, *Die christlichen Lehrer im zweiten Jahr-
hundert* (New York, 1989), 40–105; and A. van den Hoek, "How Alexandrian
Was Clement of Alexandria? Reflections on Clement and His Alexandrian
Background," *Heythrop Journal* 31.2 (1990), 179–194.

matter of language. It was in Alexandria that there developed the attempt to coordinate the Jewish faith with the philosophies of Plato and Zeno, associated above all with the name of Philo (c. 20 B.C.–A.D. 50). There were two aspects of Philo's philosophy important for the understanding of Clement. One is his doctrine of the *logos*, 'word' or 'reason,' in which he brought together the *memra*, 'word,' that God spoke with power in creation (God said, "Let there be light," and there was light), and that came to the prophets, and the *logos*, 'rational principle,' that the Stoics, following Heraclitus, saw at the root of the universe and identified with God. To Philo it was rather an intermediate agent than an immanent power. His thinking was further influenced by the Jewish concept of Wisdom, developed during the Hellenistic Age, and the Platonic concept of Mind or Nous.

(15) The other important side of Philo was his use of allegorical interpretation of Scripture to harmonize it with Greek philosophy. This became an accepted method of interpretation among the Christian thinkers of Alexandria, and, through Ambrose and others, in the Latin West.

(16) The *New Testament* contains nothing specifically about Alexandria. But dwellers from Egypt (no doubt including Alexandria) were present at Pentecost, and the synagogue of the Alexandrians in Jerusalem (also known from the Talmud) was fanatical in the persecution of Stephen: even liberal Jews might not welcome Christianity. However, Apollos, a learned Jew from Alexandria, "mighty in the Scriptures" (Acts 18, 24–25), became a leading Christian convert. Now Apollos was associated with Ephesus. Since it is arguable that Paul's captivity letters were written from Ephesus, and that the *Gospel according to John* was traditionally written there, and since the theology of Philippians 2 and John 1 are closely similar (Lohmeyer has argued that in the former Paul is quoting a hymn, and that John grafts the doctrine of the Logos onto the thought of that hymn), it is reasonable that Apollos brought it to Ephesus.

(17) There is one book of the *New Testament* which is characteristic of the Alexandrian approach—Hebrews. It has been strongly suggested that this was written from Alexandria to

Jewish Christians in Rome. The authorship must remain a matter for speculation. Apollos has been suggested, or possibly his friends Priscilla and Aquila who, not from Alexandria themselves, might have been led there as evangelists.

(18) We know nothing about the foundation of the Church in Alexandria. Eusebius (*Historia ecclesiastica* 2.16) records a tradition that Mark was sent to Egypt to proclaim the gospel he had written, and established churches in Alexandria, where the Christians combined asceticism with philosophy. ("Churches" here means "house-churches"; Alexandria was large enough to support several.) The tradition cannot be pressed, as neither Clement nor Origen mentions it. Eusebius (*Historia ecclesiastica* 3.21, 4.1) tells us that the first bishop was Anianus, who laid down office in A.D. 83–4; Abilius followed until A.D. 96–7, then Cerdo until A.D. 108–9, followed by Primus. Beyond these shadowy figures we hear from Justin (*Apologia* 1.29) of an Alexandrian Christian, who, like Origen later, wanted to take literally Jesus' words about those who made themselves eunuchs for the sake of the kingdom. Any other evidence for Christianity in Egypt during the first century, as Sir Idris Bell has commented sagely, is too slight to justify any positive conclusion, although, even without evidence, we can hardly doubt that the gospel reached Alexandria well before the end of the century.

(19) In truth we know little before A.D. 180, although we can work backwards a little from that date: There was a bishop, and it is possible that Demetrius (c. A.D. 188–231) was the first bishop in the modern sense with extensive and authoritative jurisdiction. Besides the bishop we learn from Clement of presbyters and deacons, and of widows as a recognized group in the churches. Second, Clement tells us that the Church spread among all classes, rich and poor, educated and uneducated. Third, Alexandrian Christianity had a notable concern for education. The origin of the famous catechetical school is lost, but it is possible that it went back to the first century A.D. (Eusebius, *Historia ecclesiastica* 5.10; Jerome, *De viris illustribus* 36). Certainly it was well established by the time of Pantaenus, a famous teacher whom Clement described as "the true, the Sicilian bee gathering the spoil of the flowers of the prophetic

and apostolic meadow." Pantaenus possibly came from Athens, and was a convert to Christianity from Stoicism; he had made a missionary journey to India. He was flourishing by A.D. 180, with a reputation which attracted pagans as well as Christians. (20) Fourth, there was a particular concern for the written word (although Pantaenus himself was not a writer). There was a local version of the gospel, the *Gospel according to the Egyptians*. An Alexandrian provenance has been claimed for a number of early Christian writings, apart from Hebrews, notably the *Epistle of Barnabas*, 2 Peter, the *Didache*, the *Preaching of Peter*, and the *Apostolic Canons*. None of this can be proved, but a literary tradition is certain. In addition, there were close links with the churches of Palestine, which looked to Alexandria rather than to Antioch for a lead.

(21) Finally, as we have already noticed, in such a cosmopolitan environment, it was almost inevitable to find some freedom of speculation. Of the great Gnostic leaders, Valentinus was educated in Alexandria and Basilides preached there (Epiphanius, *Adversus lxxx haereses* 31.2, 24.1).

The Stromateis

The Title

(22) The word translated "miscellanies" is *strōmateis*. The full title is *Miscellanies of Notes of Revealed Knowledge in Accordance with the True Philosophy*. It is not a common word in earlier Greek, and is probably best taken to mean a patchwork quilt; a secondary usage applied to a variegated fish (Athenaeus, 7.322 A) is an easy derivation. There is evidence enough of its application to miscellaneous writings: Eusebius (*Praeparatio evangelica* 1.7.16) applies it to such a work by Plutarch, and Aulus Gellius (*Noctes Atticae*, pref. 6–8) cites it as a familiar title for works of this kind. Clement himself [*Stromateis* 6.2(1)] describes his work as a somewhat unorganized collection of flowers or trees which have grown together naturally.

(23) The word translated "notes" is *hypomnemata*, 'memory aids.' It can be used of any memorandum, the minutes of a committee, a note in a banker's ledger, a doctor's clinical notes,

a historical sourcebook. But it has a special philosophical use: Arrian uses the word for his reminiscences of the Stoic Epictetus. He means that they are unelaborated, but a serious contribution to philosophy and factually accurate. Further Plato (*Phaedrus* 249 C) uses the word of his view that knowledge is a recollection of things apprehended before birth, and Clement, a devout Platonist, will not have been averse to those overtones.

(24) *Gnostic* means 'pertaining to knowledge.' Here there is a problem both of translation and of comprehension. Gnosticism may be approximately understood as the doctrine whereby salvation depends on revealed knowledge. It was first perhaps a tendency or emphasis, already discernible in the first generation of Christians, as when Paul counters it by saying that knowledge will pass away, whereas love never ends (1 Cor 13.8). Later it became a more defined philosophical and religious movement, associated with outstanding thinkers such as Valentinus and Basilides, often with a complex mythology. These schools tended to see the world of matter as evil. To the mainstream body of the Church they were heretical. Clement is concerned to refute and criticize them. I have referred to them as "Gnostics" with a capital *G*. But Clement, somewhat confusingly, is concerned with *gnosis* as 'Christian revelation.' In the attempt to avoid confusion, I have usually rendered *gnosis* as 'revealed knowledge' or sometimes 'true knowledge'; and the person who achieves it as a 'Christian Gnostic,' 'Gnostic Christian,' or 'true Gnostic.'

Its Place in the Writings of Clement

(25) There is a major question of where and how the *Stromateis* fits into the succession of Clement's works. At the outset of the *Paedagogus,* the *Tutor* (1.1), he identified three aspects of human experience—character, action, emotion. Character comes first: if that is right the rest follows. So while the *Paedagogus* was directed to action, the *Protrepticus,* the *Exhortation to the Greeks,* was directed to the formation of character. The triptych was to have its climax in the *Didaskalos,* the 'Teacher.' But there is no work of Clement's with that title or scope. The suggestion that the *Stromateis* is the climactic work is nonsense:

it does not fit the plan at all. More probably, then, Clement himself was unsure of what should have been his masterpiece. He had in his scrapbooks a lot of miscellaneous material, but he decided to deal with important questions elsewhere (*Stromateis* 2.37, 6.4.168).

(26) Not merely did Clement not write the *Didaskalos*, he did not complete the *Stromateis*. Book Eight as we have it would have been a most unsatisfactory conclusion. Our single primary manuscript has eight books followed by *Excerpta ex Theodoto, Excerpts from Theodotus* and *Eclogae ex scripturis propheticis, Selections from the Prophets.* The Byzantine patriarch and man of letters Photius, however, records manuscripts of the *Stromateis* that pass from Book Seven to the little treatise *Quis dives salvetur? Who Is the Rich Man That Is Being Saved?* This has led some to suppose that Book Eight is not authentic. On the other hand, it bears all the marks of Clement. More likely, the present book and the two collections of excerpts were raw material waiting to be added to the patchwork that show Clement as philosopher, theologian and Biblical commentator. The alternative view that they are fragments of a completed but lost last book is less plausible.

(27) Eusebius gives us an account of the *Stromateis* in his *Historia ecclesiastica* 6.13.4–8: "In the *Stromateis* he has composed a patchwork, not only from holy Scripture, but from the writings of the Greeks, recording anything that seems useful in their views, expounding generally held opinions alike from Greek and non-Greek sources, and correcting the false doctrines of the leaders of heresy. He unfolds a wide area of research, and provides a project of considerable erudition. With all this he includes the theories of philosophers, so that he has made the title *Stromateis* appropriate to the contents. He uses in this work evidence from the disputed Scriptures, the so-called *Wisdom of Solomon,* the *Wisdom of Jesus Son of Sirach,* the *Epistle to the Hebrews,* the letters of Barnabas, Clement, and Jude. He mentions Tatian's *Oratio ad Graecos,* Cassian, the author of a chronological history, and the Jewish writers Philo, Aristobulus, Josephus, Demetrius, and Eupolemus, all of whom may show in their works that Moses and the Jewish peo-

ple antedate Greek antiquity. This writer's works mentioned here are packed with a great deal of useful learning. In the first volume he speaks of himself as very close in succession to the apostles, and promises in the work a commentary on Genesis." So too in the *Praeparatio evangelica* 10.1.461 D–2.463 D Eusebius quotes at some length from Book Six to demonstrate the borrowings of the Greeks from the Jews.

Structure

(28) The structure of Clement's wide-ranging work may be summarized, although, perhaps, at the expense of the richness of the whole:

BOOK ONE: THE RELATIONSHIP BETWEEN PHILOSOPHY AND CHRISTIAN TRUTH—True philosophy is found in Jesus Christ; the Greeks offer a *propaedeutic*, a 'preparatory exercise.' God is the origin of all good things, including philosophy. A long historical analysis argues for the priority of the Jews to the Greeks.

BOOK TWO: FAITH AND THE HUMAN GOOD—Faith is the way to truth. It is an assent in the field of religion. Clement sets the true Gnostic in firm contrast to the heretics Basilides and Valentinus. Fear has its place in leading to repentance, hope, and love. Clement discusses moral responsibility. Our aim is restoration to sonship. The book ends with a preview of the next.

BOOK THREE: MARRIAGE—Ought we to marry? Yes. Fornication and adultery are condemned in the Law and in the gospel. He attacks the permissiveness of some heretics and the asceticism of others. His own treatment is not wholly consistent, and he finds some texts difficult, but has a beautiful exposition of "two or three gathered together" as husband, wife, child. Birth is not evil; celibacy may, but need not, be chosen; Christian marriage is a partnership.

BOOK FOUR: THE MARTYR AND THE PERFECT GNOSTIC CHRISTIAN—The true Gnostic is not afraid of death. The martyr is a witness to the sincerity of his faith. To deny the Lord

from fear of death is to deny oneself. God was suffering to
change the world. Christian perfection lies in love of humankind. It may be approached by different paths, but the one full
instance is Jesus. The true Gnostic is one with Christ.

BOOK FIVE: THE KNOWLEDGE OF GOD AND SYMBOLISM—
There is no knowledge without faith or faith without knowledge. Clement treats hope briefly and passes to the reasons for
veiling the truth in symbols. God cannot be expressed in words.

BOOK SIX: PHILOSOPHY, REVELATION, AND HUMAN
KNOWLEDGE AS A PREPARATION FOR THE TRUE GNOSTIC—
The Greeks are indebted to the Jews. True philosophy is not
sectarian; it is solid knowledge. The true Gnostic must be
something of a polymath, and takes his knowledge into realms
which others find intractable. Clement discusses number mysticism, and different approaches to knowledge.

BOOK SEVEN: THE TRUE GNOSTIC—The last full book is a
defense and glorification of the Gnostic Christian, buttressed
by passages from Plato and Scripture. He attacks the anthro-
pomorphic gods of the Greeks and defends the true Gnostic
against charges of atheism and impiety. He then passes to a
positive evaluation of the true Gnostic, a laborer in God's vineyard, who gives help to all in need. He attacks various heretics
and ends with an account of the *Stromateis*.

BOOK EIGHT: INVESTIGATION—Truth is attained by seeking; the search should be peaceable. Define your terms clearly;
examine your propositions in the light of your definitions.
Everything is not demonstrable; we need first principles. Clement attacks the Sceptics, and discusses the methodology of investigation, the subject matter of speech, and causality. These
are unorganized jottings, based on Plato and Aristotle.

EXCERPTA EX THEODOTO—We know nothing of the Theodotus whom Clement excerpts. He was a Gnostic with a typi-
cally complex system. Mostly Clement merely transmits. Occasionally he is critical, as he would have been in a fully worked-
out response.

ECLOGAE EX SCRIPTURIS PROPHETICIS—These are not the *Old Testament* prophets, but the prophetic trend in all Scripture. There are four well-marked sections: 1–26 baptism; 27–37 the Gnostic; 38–50 and 51–63 are very miscellaneous scriptural commentaries.

Textual Tradition

(29) The *Stromateis* survives in an eleventh-century manuscript from Florence (L = *Laurentianus* V 3), which has been supposed to have belonged, like *Parisinus* 451 (preserving *Protrepticus*) to Arethas, Archbishop of Caesarea. It is carelessly written, with errors of names and numbers, phrases omitted and the like. The only other manuscript is the sixteenth-century *Parisinus Supplementum Graecum* 250, which is in the direct line of descent from the earlier manuscript and of no independent value. Both manuscripts were collated by Otto Stählin for his Berlin edition, and this remains the basis for all future work. A modern edition is under way in Sources chrétiennes. As I developed my work, only Book One, Book Two, and Book Five were available. In addition, there is a useful edition of Book Seven by F. J. H. Hort and J. B. Mayor. I have referred to all of these for their record of conjectural emendations. Where I have accepted these I have generally recorded them, unless they were very slight. Occasionally [e.g., *Stromateis* 1.155(2)] I have ventured a suggestion of my own, though I do not profess to be a textual critic. There are one or two places where the meaning is clear, but there are several plausible possibilities for the Greek wording: at these points I have put in a sensible translation without suggesting what the original Greek was. In some of the faulty quotations from other authors I have not followed other editors in correcting the text: Clement quoted often, freely, carelessly, and from memory.

(30) In making the translation I have had open before me the French versions in Sources chrétiennes where these are available. They have sometimes saved me from error, for which I am grateful; sometimes I have temerariously ventured a different view of the Greek; sometimes I have borrowed felicitous

phrases; sometimes I find we have arrived at similar phrases independently; sometimes I may unconsciously have followed the French. For Book Three and Book Seven I have gained greatly from H. Chadwick and J. E. L. Oulton, *Alexandrian Christianity* (London, 1954), and for the *Excerpta ex Theodoto* from R. P. Casey (London, 1934). I have referred to W. Wilson's version in the Ante-Nicene Fathers (Reprint. Grand Rapids, 1979), only after completing my own version. Although he was working from an unsatisfactory text, his translation has hitherto been the only complete English version available, and we cannot be too grateful to the man who for over a century has kept this major work before English readers.

(31) It has proved to be impossible to be wholly consistent in translating a particular word. I have explained above my treatment of *gnosis*. *Epistēmē* I have most often rendered 'scientific knowledge,' although sometimes 'knowledge' has seemed adequate. *Logos* is always difficult in Clement, since he plays on the meanings 'reason,' 'word,' 'the Word,' and others: it is at times impossible to represent this in English and I have had to be content with a note. It is sometimes impossible to tell which idea is uppermost, and I have had to make a choice that others might not accept. Other verbal elements, such as the relation between philosophy and wisdom (*sophia*) have gone by the board, though I have tried where possible to convey a wordplay in translation.

(32) For the notes I am deeply indebted to the Sources chrétiennes editors, who have saved me a great deal of labor. This edition is far more thoroughly equipped with basic factual information about Clement's references than any previously. The edition of Book Five is especially copiously supplied. The debt extends to Sagnard's edition of *Extraits de Théodote*. Stählin's references are also useful, as are the notes of Hort and Mayor.

Interpretation of Scripture

(33) One topic must be more fully explored, even if briefly. This is the different ways in which Scripture may be interpreted. At *Stromateis* 1.179(3) Clement notes four different

criteria for interpreting the Law—typological, symbolic (allegory), ethical, and prophetic.

(34) In *Allegory and Event* R. P. C. Hanson begins by showing that the Jews held a doctrine of the plenary inspiration of Scripture. The Rabbis began from the literal meaning, and Christian critics charged them with overliteralism. But there was also a simple typology, certainly in deliverance—Noah from the flood, Abraham from paganism, Lot from Sodom, the Israelites from Egypt, Jonah from the sea monster, the three young men from the fire, Daniel from the lions, some of which were taken up by the Christians. Further the *Habbakuk Commentary*, one of the Dead Sea Scrolls, writes on the fulfillment of prophecy in a way that spills over into allegory: thus the "beasts" of 2.17 are "the simple ones of Judah, the doers of the Law."

(35) The Greeks of the Hellenistic Age practiced allegorical interpretation. The chief surviving exponent is the unknown Heraclitus, who defined allegory as "saying one thing and meaning something other than what it says" (*Quaestiones Homericae* 22). Heraclitus uses allegory to protect Homer. Apollo's arrows are an allegory of pestilence; Athena pulling Achilles' hair to check him is an allegory of the hero's state of mind; the gods' plot to bind Zeus is an allegory of the interaction of air and water.

(36) The other major strand, and a great influence on Clement, is Philo, the learned Hellenistic Jew from Alexandria. Philo insists that there is nothing superfluous or accidental in Scripture. He is not consistent in accepting literal historicity, but does so more often than not. He is always looking for allegorical meanings, sometimes willfully and wantonly. Abraham's migrations, which he accepts historically, show a soul that loves virtue searching for the true God. If Lot's daughters lie with their father (Gen 19.30–8), that is Counsel and Consent making Mind drunk with folly and producing illegitimate offspring. Egypt is the country of the body, Pharaoh the atheistic and pleasure-loving disposition. Circumcision is "an outward symbol of the duty of excising passion from our lives";

but there is still an obligation to take it literally. But Philo does use allegory to get free from the shackles of literalism. As far as we know he had in this no successors in Judaism, only in Christianity.

(37) Typology, the use of example or prefiguring figures, is a commonplace of early Christian thought, and is found in the *New Testament*. Thus Jesus uses Jonah's escape as a type of his own resurrection (Matt 12.39–41). Paul found the Israelites' crossing of the Red Sea as a type of baptism (1 Cor 10.1–6) and the author of Hebrews saw Melchizedek as a type of Christ (7.1–19).

(38) The great exponent of allegory in the early Church was Clement's protégé, Origen. Scripture yields three meanings: literal (corporeal), moral (corresponding to the *psyche*), and intellectual or spiritual. Thus in the healing of the two blind men at Jericho by Jesus (Matt 20.29–34), the literal interpretation is the historical event. In the spiritual interpretation the beggars are Israel and Judah, Jericho is the world. The moral interpretation is directed to his hearers or readers: we must come out of our Jericho to be given sight by God's Word. Again in the story of Lot's daughters lying with their father (Gen 19.30–8), Origen does not explain away the literal story, although he seeks to exculpate the daughters. He has a long discussion about the spiritual meaning, eventually settling for Lot as the Torah, the daughters Jerusalem and Samaria, and the wife the people that fell in the wilderness. The moral interpretation gives Lot as the mind, the wife as the flesh, the daughters as vainglory and pride, and the whole as a lesson for contemporary Christians.

(39) Clement was not as systematic as his follower Origen, but he had a firm belief in allegorical symbolism. In Book Five he says that all who have written of the ultimate have used allusions, symbols, allegories, etc. He identifies four reasons for this. The first is *ethical*: the object is to conceal the truth from those who might profane it; the second is *didactic*: veiled truths need interpreters, they need training, and the result is to ensure that the underlying truths are not lost; the third is *psychological*: indirect statements make more impression than direct

ones; the fourth relates to *complexity*: symbolic interpretations allow more than one layer of meaning. For specific examples of Clement at work on symbolism see his exposition of the furnishings of the Temple (*Stromateis* 5.32) or of numbers (*Stromateis* 6.84ff.); but he uses the practice throughout.

STROMATEIS

OR

*MISCELLANIES OF NOTES
OF REVEALED KNOWLEDGE
IN ACCORDANCE WITH
THE TRUE PHILOSOPHY*

BOOK ONE

1[1]

Guidelines on the Publication and Dissemination of the Stromateis

1(1) . . .[2] "for you to read them readily and to be able to keep them."[3] Ought the writings not to be generally available, or only to some people? If the former, what is the point of the writings? If the latter, are they for the worthy or the unworthy? It would be plainly ridiculous to reject the writing of worthwhile authors and accept those who are very different in the quality of their composition. (2) Are we to give the right to write this disgraceful stuff to Theopompus and Timaeus with their slanderous fictions, and on top of them Epicurus, prince of atheism, and, besides, Hipponax and Archilochus,[4] and to prevent the preacher of truth from leaving to posterity beneficial work? I imagine it is a fine thing to leave good children to posterity. Children are our physical offspring, writings are our spiritual offspring;[5] (3) further, we call our religious instructors fathers.[6] Wisdom is open to all, and loves humankind.[7] Anyway, Solomon says, "My son: if you accept my words of instruction and keep them deep within you, your ear will

1. See also E. F. Osborn, "Teaching and Writing in the First Chapter of the *Stromateis* of Clement of Alexandria," *JThS* n.s. 10 (1959), 335–44.
2. The first page is lacking; cf. Plato, *Phaedrus* 257 D.
3. Hermas, *Shepherd*, Visions 5.4.
4. Theopompus (c. 400–370 B.C.) was an Athenian comic dramatist; Timaeus is unknown; Epicurus (341–270 B.C.) was an Athenian philosopher who believed in non-intervening gods, and seemed to exalt pleasure, although he was personally highly abstemious; Hipponax (c. 540 B.C.) was a poetical satirist; Archilochus (c. 700–650 B.C.) was a highly original poet, personal and mordant.
5. See Plato, *Phaedrus* 278 A; *Symposium* 209 A–D; *Theaetetus* 150 D.
6. See 1 Cor 4.15; Phlm 10; but also, in contrast, Matt 23.9.
7. For φιλανθρωπία see Titus 3.4 and J. Ferguson, *Moral Values in the Ancient World* (London, 1958).

listen to wisdom."⁸ This means that the word is sown and kept deep in the soul of the learner as if in the ground. This is spiritual growth.

2(1) So he adds, "You shall direct your heart to understanding and direct it towards instruction for your son."⁹ For in my view, the union of soul with soul and spirit with spirit in accordance with the sowing of the word brings growth to the seed sown and produces life. Everyone who is educated in obedience to his educator becomes a son. "My son," says Solomon, "do not forget my ordinances."¹⁰ (2) But if revealed knowledge is not for all, then to put the writings before the man in the street is, in the proverbial phrase, "the donkey and the lyre."¹¹ Pigs "prefer mud"¹² to clean water. (3) "That is why I speak to them in parables," says the Lord, "because they see without seeing and hear without hearing or understanding."¹³ The Lord is not responsible for their ignorance—a blasphemous thought!—but like a prophet shows up the ignorance already there, and indicates that they will fail to understand his words.

3(1) And now the Savior appears in person out of his superabundance. He distributes his goods among his servants, proportionately to the capacity of the recipient (and this ought to be increased by disciplined practice). He returns and demands an account from them. Those who have increased his money and have "been faithful in a small matter," he welcomes and promises "to give wide responsibilities," telling them to enter "their master's joy." (2) But one who conceals the money entrusted to him for lending out at interest and restores the money he has received, without growth, is told, "Wicked, idle servant, you ought to have invested my money with the bankers, and on my return I should have received my due." At this, the useless servant will be thrown "into the darkness outside."¹⁴

---

8. Prov 2.1–2.   9. Prov 2.2.

10. Prov 3.1.

11. Menander, *Misoumenos* 18, fr. 527; Aulus Gellius, *Attic Nights* 3.16.3; Diogenian 7.33; Apostolius 12.91a.

12. Apostolius parallels the donkey's incomprehension of the lyre with the pig's of the trumpet, but Clement is thinking of Plato, *Republic* 7.535 E.

13. Matt 13.13.

14. Matt 25.14–30; Luke 19.12–28.

(3) Paul also says, "So be strong in the grace which is in Christ Jesus. Hand on to people of faith, who will be competent to teach others, all that you have heard from me before plenty of witnesses."[15] (4) And again: "Do your best to present yourself to God in a state fit for approval, a worker who has no call to be ashamed, treating the word of truth properly."[16]

4(1) If two people preach the word, one in writing, one orally, receive them both: they have made the faith operative by their love.[17] Responsibility rests with the person who does not choose the best course, not with God.[18] Some people have the task of putting out the word at interest, others of examining it and deciding whether to choose it or not. Their judgment is a judgment upon them. (2) This[19] knowledge presented in preaching is in some sense the work of a messenger of God; however it operates, whether through the hand or through the tongue, it brings benefit, "since anyone who sows for the Spirit shall harvest eternal life from the Spirit. Let us not grow weary in doing good works."[20] (3) The greatest gifts are piled up for those who are by God's providence ready for them—the foundation of faith, enthusiasm for right conduct, an impulse towards truth, a drive for investigation, the traces of revealed knowledge. In a word, he grants the starting-point of salvation. Those who are genuinely nourished by the words of truth take the viaticum of eternal life and wing their way to heaven.[21] (4) The Apostle puts it brilliantly: "Commending ourselves as God's servants through and through, as beggars yet enriching many people, as having nothing and yet possessing all things, our mouth is open for you."[22] "I charge you," he says in his letter to Timothy, "before God and Christ Jesus and the chosen angels to keep these things without favor, doing nothing in partiality."[23]

5(1) It is essential that both examine themselves. The one

---

15. 2 Tim 2.1–2.
16. 2 Tim 2.15.
17. See Gal 5.6.
18. Plato, *Republic* 10.617 E; reading ἡ δὲ αἰτία with Bywater.
19. Reading ἥδε with Mayor.
20. Gal 6.8–9.
21. See Plato, *Phaedrus* 248 B.
22. 2 Cor 6.4,10–11.
23. 1 Tim 5.21.

must see if he is fit to speak and to leave behind written records, the other if he has the right to listen or read. It is just as in the distribution of the eucharist; in the normal practice, they leave it to each member of the congregation to decide whether to take a portion. (2) Conscience is the best guide for determining accurately whether to say Yes or No. The firm foundation of conscience is an upright life joined to appropriate learning. The best means towards the understanding of truth and the performance of the commandments is to follow those others who have already been through the test with flying colors. (3) "So whoever eats the bread or drinks the cup of the Lord in an unworthy manner will be guilty of the Lord's body and blood. Let a person examine himself or herself and only then eat of the bread and drink of the cup."[24]

6(1) It follows that the person who is set on the service of his neighbor should consider carefully to be sure that he has not leaped into teaching hastily or out of jealousy of others; that he is not spreading the word out of personal ambition; that the sole reward he is securing is the salvation of his hearers. Anyone who speaks on the basis of written rites is free thereby from currying favor by his discourse, and from the charge of venality. (2) "As you know, we were never engaged in flattering words," says the Apostle, "or in words as an excuse for profiteering—God is my witness. We never pursued glory from human beings, from you or anyone else, though we could have brought pressure as Christ's apostles. But we were gentle with you, like a nurse tending her children."[25] (3) In the same way, those who want to take up a share of the oracles of God must watch out that they are not engaging in the question out of idle curiosity, like visitors to public buildings in the cities, and that they are not coming for a share in worldly goods, in the knowledge that those dedicated to Christ share in daily provisions. They are hypocrites; forget about them. If anyone "wants to possess the reality rather than the semblance of justice,"[26] he had better have only the highest principles in his conscience.[27]

24. 1 Cor 11.27–8.   25. 1 Thess 2.5–7.
26. Aeschylus, *Seven against Thebes* 592.
27. Reading συνειδέναι with Arcerius and Canter for συνιέναι.

7(1) If "the harvest is plentiful, the laborers few,"[28] then it really is appropriate to pray that we may have as many workers as possible. The farming is of two kinds: one uses writing, the other does not. But whichever method the Lord's worker uses to sow the good grain, to help the stalks to grow, and to reap the harvest, he will be clearly seen as God's true farmer. (2) "Work," says the Lord, "for the food which lasts to eternal life, not for the food which perishes."[29] There is a nourishment taken in food and another in words and thoughts. In very fact, "Blessed are the peacemakers,"[30] those who teach a different way to those who are warred upon by ignorance here on earth in a life of error, and who lead them instead towards peace which is found in the logos[31] and the life which follows God, and who nourish those who hunger for righteousness[32] by the distribution of the bread.[33] (3) There are souls too with their own particular diets, some growing through knowledge and scientific understanding, others pastured in accordance with Greek philosophy, though, as with nuts, not all of that is edible. (4) "He who plants and he who waters"—being servants of the One who grants growth—"are one" with respect to their service, "and each will receive his appropriate wages in the light of his own labor. We are fellow workers with God. You are God's field. You are God's building." So the Apostle puts it.[34]

8(1) It is not right to entrust the Word[35] to hearers to make a test of it on the basis of comparison or to hand it right over for investigation to those who have been brought up to all kinds of sophisticated arguments and who vaunt[36] the power of their intellectual proofs, those whose souls are already determined beforehand instead of being emptied of prejudgments. (2)

---

28. Matt 9.37; Luke 10.2.   29. John 6.27.
30. Matt 5.9.
31. Throughout Clement the word *logos*, 'word,' 'reason' or 'thought,' is liable to be used ambiguously with *Logos* (John 1.1) as a title of Jesus, perhaps the primary meaning here.
32. Matt 5.6.
33. Plainly with reference to the Eucharist, but perhaps not solely: the preaching of Jesus is the distribution of the bread of life (John 6.32–5).
34. 1 Cor 3.8–9.   35. See nt. 31.
36. Reading ὠγκωμένοις with Münzel for ὀγκωμένων.

When anyone elects out of faith to go to the banquet, he has faith as a reasonable criterion of judgment, and is strong to receive the words of God. From that point, conviction pursues him out of his superfluity. This is the real meaning of the prophet's words: "If you do not have faith, you cannot understand."[37] "So then, as we have opportunity, let us do good to all, and particularly those who belong to the household of faith."[38] (3) Each of these should follow the blessed David in chanting with gratitude:[39] "You will purge me with hyssop and I shall be clean; you will wash me and I shall be whiter than snow. You will make me hear joy and gratitude; my bones in humiliation will rejoice. Turn away your face from my sins, and wipe out my illegal acts. (4) God, create a clean heart in me, and renew a right spirit in my inward parts. Do not throw me out from your presence; do not remove your Holy Spirit from me. Give me back the joy of your deliverance, and strengthen me by the guidance of your Spirit."[40]

9(1) The person who addresses people who are present uses time as a test and judgment to come to a verdict. He distinguishes the one who is capable of hearing from the rest. He keeps an eye on their words and ways, their character and life, their impulses and attitudes, their looks, their voice, the parting of the ways, the rock, the well-trodden path, the ground that bears fruit, the countryside that is thick with trees, the land which is fertile, excellent, praised, the soil which is capable of multiplying the seed.[41] (2) The person who uses the written word for communication hallows it before God in proclaiming in writing that he is not writing[42] for profit or vainglory; that he is not overpowered by emotion, a slave to fear, or exulting in pleasure; that his sole delight is in the salvation of those who encounter his writings. In that salvation he does not claim any present share. He receives in hope the change that will be

---

37. Isa 7.9.
38. Gal 6.10.
39. Possibly "at the Eucharist."
40. Ps 51.7–12.
41. In Clement's time the philosopher was a kind of chaplain: how much more the Christian lover of wisdom. The parting of the ways is a Pythagorean symbol of choice: Y (cf. Matt 7.13–14); it is not necessary to pick out all the allusions, but see Luke 8.5–8 and Plato, *Phaedrus* 275 D–E.
42. Reading ⟨γράφειν⟩ with Stählin.

granted, come what may, by the one who has promised to reward his workers according to their worth. (3) But anyone enrolled as a fully grown Christian ought not even to have the desire for recompense. Anyone who boasts of his good actions has his reward already through his reputation.[43] Anyone who performs any of his duties for the sake of his recompense, whether he is eager to secure the reward of doing well or to evade the consequences of doing wrong, is surely in the grip of this world's practice. He ought to imitate the Lord as far as possible. (4) The person who does this is serving God's will to the full; he receives a free gift, and offers a free gift. He accepts a magnificent payment in his citizenship. Scripture says: "The wages of a prostitute shall not enter the holy places."[44]

10(1) Anyway, it is forbidden to bring "a bitch's price" to the altar. Anyone who does not[45] have "the eye of the soul"[46] darkened in the face of the light which is his own by false nurture and teaching, should walk towards the truth which shows through Scripture things which cannot be written in Scripture. "You who are thirsty, come towards water," says Isaiah,[47] and Solomon advises, "Drink the water from your own cistern."[48] (2) Anyway, in the *Laws*, Plato, the philosophic pupil of the Hebrews, tells the farmers not to irrigate or take water from their neighbors unless they have first dug their own soil down to the so-called virgin bedrock and found the land to be without water.[49] (3) It is[50] an act of righteousness to rescue destitution but there is nothing noble in sustaining laziness. It is precisely the situation in which[51] Pythagoras used to say that it is reasonable to help a man up who has a burden but that there is no obligation to help him down.[52] (4) Scripture helps to kindle the fire in our soul, it directs our natural sight to contemplation, it is swift to implant something new (like a farmer grafting), it rouses to new life our natural endowment. (5) In the

43. See Matt 5.1–2, 23.1.   44. Deut 23.18.
45. Reading ⟨μὴ⟩ with Münzel.   46. Plato, *Republic* 7.533 D.
47. Isa 55.1.   48. Prov 5.15.
49. Plato, *Laws* 8.844 A–B in free allusion.
50. Reading [οὐ] with Potter.
51. Reading ἠ with Wilamowitz for εἰ.
52. Pythagoras, *FPG* 1.505.

divine Apostle's words: "There are many weak and without strength" among us, "and some have fallen asleep. But if we judged ourselves properly, we should not be judged."[53]

11(1) This work is not a writing rhetorically shaped for exhibition.[54] It is a collection of memoranda, a treasure for my old age, a remedy against forgetfulness, a mere reflection, a sketch of vividly alive originals, words I was thought worthy to hear, and blessed and genuinely memorable men from whom I heard them. (2) One of these, an Ionian, came from Greece, the remainder from the Greek Dispersion; one from Coele-Syria, one from Egypt, others from the East, one from among the Assyrians, one a Jew by birth, from Palestine. I fell in with a final one—supreme in mastery. I tracked him down to his hiding-place in Egypt and stayed with him. He was[55] the true Sicilian bee, culling out of the flowers from the meadow of prophets and apostles a pure substance of true knowledge in the souls of his hearers.[56] (3) But they preserved the true tradition of the blessed doctrine in direct line from Peter, James, John, and Paul, the holy apostles, son inheriting from father (only few sons are like their fathers) and came with God's help to plant in us those seeds of their apostolic progenitors.

12(1) I am quite sure that they will be delighted—I do not mean pleased with this exposition of mine, but simply by the preservation of the tradition in following my adumbrations. In my view, the sketch of a soul which yearns to preserve the blessed tradition without losing a single drop runs something like this: "When a man loves wisdom, his father's heart will be warmed."[57] (2) Wells which are constantly baled out provide a clearer water; wells which no one draws from turn to rottenness. Use keeps iron brighter, disuse produces rust in it. In general, exercise produces fitness in souls and bodies. (3) "No

53. 1 Cor 11.30–1.   54. See Thucydides 1.22.4.
55. Reading ἦν with Münzel for ἡ.
56. As Caster says, we cannot be certain who are these saintly masters: the Ionian might be Melito of Sardis; the Assyrian Bardesanes or Tatian; the Jew, Theophilus of Caesarea or Theodotus; there is general agreement that the Sicilian bee is Pantaenus, now dead, founder of the catechetical school in Egypt. The account of the last echoes Euripides, *Hippolytus* 73–81.
57. Prov 29.3.

one lights a lamp and puts it under a bushel"[58] but on a stand
to give light to those thought worthy to share in the same banquet. What is the use of a wisdom which does not bring wisdom
to the person who is capable of listening? Again, the Savior is
always engaged in saving. He is always at work, as he sees his
father always at work.[59] As one teaches, one learns more and
more.[60] As one speaks, one is often listening in company with
one's class. "There is only one teacher,"[61] whether of lecturer
or student, and he is the source of understanding and the word
spoken.

13(1) The Lord did not hold us back from doing good because of[62] the sabbath laws. He agreed that "those who were
capable of receiving"[63] should share in the mysteries of God
and in that holy light.[64] (2) Further, he did not reveal to the
people in the street what was not for them; only to a few, to
whom he knew it to be apposite, those who could accept the
mysteries and be conformed to them. The secrets, like God
himself, are entrusted not to writing but to the expressed
word.[65] (3) If anyone says that it is written in Scripture: "There
is nothing hidden which shall not be revealed, nothing veiled
which shall not be unveiled,"[66] he must listen to us too when
we say that in this pronouncement he foretold that the hidden
secret shall be revealed to the one who listens in secret, and all
that is veiled, like the truth, shall be shown to the one who is
capable of receiving the traditions under a veil, and that which
is hidden from the majority shall become clear to a minority.
Since everyone is capable of receiving the truth,[67] why does
everyone not know the truth? (4) If righteousness is for everyone, why is righteousness not loved? No, the mysteries are

58. Matt 5.15.   59. John 5.17,19.
60. So writes Seneca, *Epistles* 7.8: *homines dum docent discunt,* 'while people
are teaching they are learning.'
61. Matt 23.8.
62. Reading ⟨διὰ τὸ⟩ with Stählin.
63. See Matt 16.11.
64. The mysteries at Eleusis were for initiates only: the climax of revelation
involved a brilliant light.
65. There is ambiguity between 'oral discourse' and the *logos* (see nt. 31).
66. Matt 10.26.
67. A lacuna must be filled with some such words.

transmitted mysteriously, so that they may be on the lips of speaker and listener—or rather not in their voices at all, but in their minds. (5) "God has granted" to the Church "some as apostles, others as prophets, others as evangelists, others as pastors and teachers, to equip the members of the Church for the work of ministry, for building up the body of Christ."[68]

14(1) So I am well aware of the weakness of this compilation of notes compared with the grace of the Spirit whom we have been deemed worthy to sit under as auditors. It can only be a likeness, a reminder of the original for the one who has been struck by the thyrsus.[69] "Speak to a wise man," says Scripture, "and he will be wiser,"[70] and "To the possessor, more shall be given."[71] (2) There is a promise, not to give a full interpretation of the secrets—far from it—but simply to offer a reminder, either when we forget, or to prevent us from forgetting in the first place. I am very well aware that many things have passed away from us into oblivion in a long lapse of time through not being written down. That is why I have tried to reduce the effect of my weak memory, by providing myself with a systematic exposition in chapters as a salutary[72] aide-mémoire; it has necessarily taken this sketchy form. (3) There are things which I have not even recorded—these blessed men were endowed with great power. There are others which remained with me with no need of noting, but with the passage of time[73] have now escaped me. Others were growing faint to the point of extinction in my mind, since service of this kind is not easy for those who are not qualified experts. These I took good care[74] to rekindle by making notes. Some I am deliberately putting to one side, making my selection scientifically out of fear of writing what I have refrained from speaking—not in a spirit of grudging (that would be wrong), but in the fear that my companions

---

68. Eph 4.11–12.
69. The staff carried by worshippers of Dionysus, tipped with a pine cone and garlanded with ivy, used to communicate ecstasy.
70. Prov 9.9.   71. Matt 13.12.
72. There is a double meaning: 'helpful' and 'pertaining to salvation.'
73. Reading [ἃ] with Dindorf.
74. Reading δὴ with Münzel for δὲ.

might misunderstand[75] them and go astray and that I might be found offering a dagger to a child (as those who write proverbs put it). (4) "Once a thing is written there is no way of keeping it from the public,"[76] even if it remains unpublished by me, and in its scrolls it employs no voice except the one single writing forevermore. It can make no response to a questioner beyond what is written.[77] It cannot help needing support either from the writer or some other person following in his footsteps. 15(1) Sometimes my manuscript will make allusive references. It will insist on some things, it will make a simple statement of others. Sometimes it will try to say something unobtrusively or to reveal something without uncovering it or to demonstrate it without saying anything. (2) It will expose the dogmas of the notable heresies. It will oppose these in everything which ought to be provided in advance within the revealed knowledge which follows visionary[78] contemplation. This revealed knowledge will be advantageous to us in accord with "the glorious, majestic norm of tradition."[79] We set out from the creation of the world, laying out the things that[80] necessarily involve a prior account of the contemplation of nature and eliminating all that stands in the path of coherent thought. We want to have attention ready to receive the tradition of revealed knowledge, once the ground has been cleared of thorns and all weeds by scientific farming for the plantation of a vineyard.[81] (3) The prelude to a contest is a contest. The prelude to mysteries is a mystery. Our notes will not hesitate to use the highest examples from philosophy, and all the other educational preliminaries. (4) As the Apostle puts it, it is reasonable to become a Jew by reason of the Hebrews and those subject to the Law; it is also reasonable to become a Greek for the sake of the Greeks. We want to gain them all.[82] (5) In the letter to

75. Reading ⟨ἐκδεξάμενοι⟩ with Münzel; cf. 6.126.1.
76. Plato, *Epistles* 2.314 C. If we follow his text we must read μὴ ⟨οὐκ⟩.
77. See Plato, *Phaedrus* 275 D–E.
78. Literally "epoptic," with reference to the higher grades of initiation at Eleusis.
79. Clement of Rome, *First Epistle to the Corinthians* 7.2.
80. Reading ⟨τὰ⟩ with Markland.
81. See e.g., Isa 5.1–2, 27.2–5; Ezek 19.10; Mark 12.1–9; John 15.1–8.
82. 1 Cor 9.20–1.

the Colossians he writes "We admonish every one; we instruct them in all wisdom, so that we may produce every single human being perfect in Christ."[83]

16(1) Furthermore, my notebook sketches fit in well with the elegance of intellectual contemplation. The immense quantity of good instructional material acts as a kind of savory spice mixed in with an athlete's diet, one who does not go in for luxury but has the sensible appetite which is higher endeavor. Anyway, as we make our music we slacken anything which has too much tension in the search for majesty to make it tuneful.[84] (2) Just as those who wish to address the public often do so through a herald so that their words will be better heard, so here (as the words we need to speak before turning to the tradition are addressed to the people in the street) we have to lay before them their familiar[85] views and the voices which speak loudly to them on the several points, voices which are more likely to attract the hearers' attention. (3) In sum, just as in a quantity of small pearls one stands out, and in a large catch of fish the most beautiful fish stands out,[86] so, with time and hard work, and with adequate help, the truth will shine out. For God grants the majority of his benefits through human intermediaries.

17(1) So all of us who use our eyes, use them to examine things which come into view, but we use them in different ways. A cook and a shepherd do not have the same view of a sheep: One is interested only in the richness of its flesh, the other keeps an eye on its breeding; if A wants nourishment, he can take the sheep's milk, if B[87] wants clothes, he can shear off the fleece. (2) In this way, I can profit from the fruit of the Greek educational system. I do not think that anyone would reserve the title fortunate to a work which no one contradicts, but you can reasonably apply it to one which no one will reasonably

---

83. Col 1.28.
84. Clement is not afraid of mixing or varying metaphors.
85. Omitting διό.
86. See Matt 13.45–8. For the particular fish see Athenaeus 7.282. It is probably *Labrus* or *Serranus Anthias* (see D'Arcy W. Thompson, *A Glossary of Greek Fishes* [London, 1947], 14 and 98).
87. Reading ⟨ὁ δὲ⟩ with Mondésert.

contradict. And in fact,[88] the behavior and doctrine one should approve is not one which finds no criticism, but one which no one will have rational grounds for criticizing. (3) It does not follow that if a person who has planned carefully fails to bring a task[89] to an immediate conclusion, he is thereby acting under force of circumstances. If he disposes it according to God's wisdom, adapting himself to his environment, he will achieve his end. The man already endowed with virtue has no further need of the path that leads to virtue; the man who enjoys good health has no need of convalescence. (4) Farmers water the soil in advance. Similarly, we use the pure water of Greek philosophy to water in advance the earthly part of our readers, to make them fit to receive the sowing of the spiritual seed and enable it to grow without difficulty

18(1) My *Stromateis* will embrace the truth which is mixed in with the dogmas of philosophy—or rather which is covered in and hidden within them, as the edible part of the nut is covered by the shell. In my view, only the farmers of faith are fit to protect the seeds of truth. (2) I am well aware of the repeated comments of certain people who suffer from ignorant fears. They say that we ought to concentrate on essentials involving the faith, and ignore external superfluities which cause us useless worries and confine us to matters totally irrelevant to our destiny. (3) These people think that philosophy comes[90] from an evil source, that it drifted into our life at the hands of some evil deviser to do damage to human beings. (4) Throughout the whole of the *Stromateis* I shall show that vice is naturally vicious and could never sustain the part of farmer of a healthy crop. In so doing, I shall suggest that philosophy too is in some manner a work of divine providence.

---

88. Reading ἄρα with Markland for ἅμα.
89. Reading ⟨τι⟩ with Stählin.
90. Reading ⟨οὖσ⟩αν with Stählin.

2

The Value of Greek Philosophy as an Introduction to Knowledge:
The Stromateis *Are Purposefully Obscure*

19(1) On the subject of my notes which embrace the opinions
of the Greeks at the appropriate essential moments, I have
something to say to those petty critics. In the first place, if philosophy were useless, and it were useful to establish its uselessness, then it would be useful.[91] (2) Secondly, it is not possible
to vote against the Greeks on the basis of a mere mention of
their doctrines without embarking on a detailed *exposé* leading
to full knowledge. (3) Refutation combined with experience
certainly deserves credence because knowledge of the things
condemned is found to be the most fully convincing demonstration. (4) There are many things which do not contribute to
the final goal but which help to improve the expert's image. In
particular, wide learning which is evidenced by expounding
the most important philosophic views contributes to the confidence of the audience; creating astonishment in candidates
for church membership, it disposes them towards the truth.

20(1) To guide souls in this way deserves confidence. Those
who are eager to learn receive the truth under a veil.[92] In consequence, they do not imagine[93] that philosophy is a deviser of
false facts and evil acts, damaging to our life, as some allege;
rather they see it as a clear likeness of truth, a gift granted to
the Greeks by God. (2) A further consequence is that we are
not drawn away from the faith as if tricked by some magic, but,
you may say, we are using a broader circuit, and providing
some sort of joint exercise for the demonstration of faith. (3)
Yes, and contact[94] with the views of philosophers is a way of
wooing the truth by contrast. It is from truth that revealed
knowledge follows. Philosophy did not come on the scene according to some *a priori* principle, but because of the harvest
which comes from true knowledge. We take hold of a strong

91. I.e., philosophy is needed to prove that it is not needed.
92. Reading κεκαλυμμένην with Wilamowitz for κακουμένην.
93. Reading αὐ⟨τοὺς δοκεῖν⟩ with Wilamowitz.
94. Reading ⟨ἡ⟩ with Mayor.

propensity to grasp the truth through the scientific understanding of hidden meanings. (4) I do not need to say that my *Stromateis* are given bodily substance by breadth of learning and aim at the skilled concealment of the seeds of true knowledge.

21(1) The lover of the chase catches his prey by a process of hunting, searching, tracking, and using the speed of hounds. Similarly, truth is clearly a desirable object[95] of a hunt, secured by hard work. (2) Why on earth have we judged it right for our notebooks to be organized like this? Because there is a considerable danger in betraying the secret formula, which truly belongs to the real philosophy,[96] to those who[97] have an immeasurable desire to contradict everything without any justification and throw away words and phrases of all kinds in complete disorder, deceiving themselves and deceiving those who cling to them.[98] (3) As the Apostle says, "The Hebrews demand miracles, whereas the Greeks seek wisdom."[99]

3
The Dangers of Sophistical Subtleties

22(1) There is a large mob of people like that. Some of them are slaves to pleasures and have a will to disbelieve, and laugh at a truth which merits all reverence; they make play with their lack of culture. (2) There are some others who, in their exaltation of themselves, force themselves to find calumnies against our words. They produce argumentative investigations, they track down petty phrases, they are mad about trivialities, they are "wranglers and thimble-riggers" in the words of the famous writer from Abdera.[100] (3) We have the words:

95. Reading γλυκύ τι with Heinsius for γλυκύτητι.
96. I.e., Christianity.
97. Reading ⟨τού⟩τοις ⟨οἳ⟩ with Stählin.
98. Reading . . . ους with Höschel for . . . οις.
99. 1 Cor 1.22.
100. Democritus (fourth century B.C.) published his work on atomic theory in 405 B.C. (see DK 68 B 150); Abdera in Thrace was on the edge of the Greek world.

Human tongues are glib, and have many a speech.
There is a rich pasture of words of all kinds everywhere.

adding

The original statement determines the response.[101]

(4) The damnable sophists[102] are proud of their skill; they twitter in their subtleties; they labor throughout their lives over distinctions between words and the appropriate combination and grouping of expressions; they are shown[103] to be more continuous in their cooing than turtledoves. (5) They tickle and titillate the ears of those who are eager to be titillated, effeminately, in my view—a literal torrent of words and a drop of sense. They are like old shoes. The rest of them has weakened or admits water; only the tongue is left.

23(1) Solon of Athens has a magnificent exposition when he says:

Watch the tongue, the words of a flatterer.
Each one of you is moving on the fox's tail.
And when you are all together your mind is a gaping void.[104]

(2) This is of course allusively linked with the Savior's words: "Foxes have lairs, but the son of man has nowhere to lay his head."[105] I suppose it is only on the faithful, absolutely distinguished from those others whom Scripture calls wild animals,[106] that the head of the universe finds rest, the gentle, upright Logos, (3) "who catches the wise in their craftiness. For the Lord alone knows the futility of the ratiocinations of the wise."[107] Scripture, of course, applies the term "wise" to

---

101. Homer, *Iliad* 20.248–50.

102. The term *Sophist* originally meant an expert; it was then applied to adult educators of the fifth century B.C. and to their trivializing successors; then it encompassed the Second Sophistic, adult educators of the second century A.D., whom Clement undervalues.

103. Reading ⟨ἀναφαίνον⟨ται⟩ with Stählin.

104. Solon, fr. 11.7,5,6 (see Plutarch, *The Life of Solon* 30). Solon (early sixth century B.C.) was a moderate Athenian statesman whose reforms paved the way to democracy. Editors correct Clement's text from Solon's original, but Clement's citations are not perfect.

105. Matt 8.20; Luke 9.58.   106. E.g., 2 Pet 2.12.

107. 1 Cor 3.19–20 quoting Job 5.13; Ps 94.11.

the sophists in their excessive concern for language and technique.

24(1) As a result, the Greeks themselves have called those who spend too much time on a single object sages or sophists indifferently, the words being related. (2) Anyway, Cratinus in the *Archilochuses* ends a catalogue of poets with

What a swarm of sophists you have been groping after.[108]

(3) Similarly Iophon, like[109] the comic dramatist in *The Satyr-Flutists,* says of rhapsodes and others:

Yes, there arrived
a great mob of sophists all at the ready.[110]

(4) It is of these and those like them who practice idle discourse that God's Scriptures say superbly: "I will destroy the wisdom of the wise and bring to nothing the cleverness of the clever."[111]

4

Wisdom in the Practical Skills and Philosophy Acquires a Spiritual Sense from Christian Instruction

25(1) Homer even calls an artisan wise, and writes something as follows about Margites (if the poem is Homer's):

The gods did not make him a digger or ploughman,
or wise in any other field; he missed out on every skill.[112]

(2) Hesiod said that Linus the lutenist was "expert in every form of wisdom," and does not hesitate to call a sailor wise, writing, "not endowed with wisdom in navigation."[113] (3) The

---

108. Cratinus, fr. 2. He was one of the greatest comic dramatists of the mid-fifth century B.C.; this dates from c. 440.

109. Reading ὁμοίως ⟨ὡς⟩ with Schwartz.

110. Iophon, fr. 1. He was a tragic poet, son of the great Sophocles.

111. 1 Cor 1.19 quoting Isa 29.14.

112. [Homer] *Margites* fr. 2.

113. Hesiod, fr. 193, *Works and Days* 649. Hesiod (seventh century B.C.) was a Boeotian poet; Linus was in myth either the son or victim of Apollo or the music teacher of Heracles whose name was formed from the cry "Ailinon."

prophet Daniel says, "The mystery the king asks. No power
of wise men, magi, weavers of spells, or Gazarenes can proclaim it to the king, but there is a God in heaven who reveals
mysteries."[114] In fact, he is calling the people of Babylon wise.
(4) Scripture applies the same word "wisdom" to every form
of worldly knowledge or skill—and there are plenty[115] of
those, thought up by human calculation and accumulated. It
also asserts that intellectual skill and wisdom come from God.
This will be clear from a consideration of the following text:
(5) "The Lord spoke to Moses, saying, 'See, I have called Be-
zalel, son of Uri, grandson of Hur, of the tribe of Judah. I
have filled him with the divine spirit of wisdom, understanding, and scientific knowledge in work of all kinds—inventing,
constructing, working gold, silver, and bronze, precious stone,
purple and scarlet porphyry, shaping building stone, carpen-
try and woodwork, work of every description.'"[116]

26(1) Then a word of really general application is added:
"To everyone with understanding in the heart I have granted
understanding"[117]—that is to say, to everyone capable of receiving it through labor and discipline. Once again it is expressly written in the Lord's name: "And you shall speak to
all those wise in understanding, whom I have filled with spiritual perception."[118] (2) Those who are "wise in understanding" have a certain natural personal gift, but they receive
"spiritual perception" from sovereign wisdom, in two forms,
when they show themselves ready for it. (3) For those who go
in for practical skills enjoy exceptionally acute sense perception: the musician (in the popular sense)[119] with hearing, the
sculptor with touch, the singer with voice, the perfumer with
smell, the engraver of figures on sealstones with sight. (4)
Those engaged in education are granted an inward perception, which directs the poets' choice of meter, the sophists'

114. Dan 2.27; the magi were priestly astrologers, the Gazarenes, fortune-
tellers.
115. Reading πολλαὶ with Schwartz for ἄλλαι.
116. Exod 31.1–5.   117. Exod 31.6.
118. Exod 28.3.
119. The Muses covered many forms of cultural activity.

choice of language, the dialecticians' choice of syllogisms, and the philosophers' of doctrine. (5) This inward perception is an instrument of discovery and invention. It persuades us to plausible experiments. Discipline directed to scientific knowledge helps to increase our willingness to experiment.

27(1) The Apostle had good reason to call God's wisdom "variegated,"[120] "working in many forms and many ways"[121] through technical skill, scientific knowledge, faith, prophecy; it shows us its power to our benefit, because "all wisdom comes from the Lord and is with him to all eternity," as the wisdom of Jesus puts it.[122] (2) "For if you call for practical wisdom and perception at the top of your voice, if you seek it as you would a treasure of silver, and if you track it down ardently, then you will realize the meaning of reverence for God and you will grasp the perception of God."[123] The prophet spoke to distinguish this from the philosophic approach to perception. He is teaching us with great dignity and solemnity to search it out in order to progress towards reverence for God. (3) So he opposed to it perception made in reverence for God, alluding to revealed knowledge in these words: "For God grants wisdom from his mouth together with perception and practical wisdom, and stores up help for the righteous."[124] When people are made righteous by philosophy, they have stored help for themselves, and inward perception which leads to reverence for God.

5

Philosophy, a Preparatory Science for Christianity

28(1) So, before the Lord's coming, philosophy was an essential guide to righteousness for the Greeks. At the present time, it is a useful guide towards reverence for God. It is a kind of preliminary education for those who are trying to gather faith through demonstration. "Your foot will not stum-

120. Eph 3.10. 121. Heb 1.1.
122. Sir 1.1.: Jesus is here the son of Sirach.
123. Prov 2.3–5. 124. Prov 2.6–7.

ble," says Scripture,[125] if you attribute good things, whether
Greek or Christian, to Providence. (2) God is responsible for
all good things: of some, like the blessings of the Old and New
Covenants, directly; of others, like the riches of philosophy,
indirectly. (3) Perhaps philosophy too was a direct gift of God
to the Greeks before the Lord extended his appeal to the
Greeks. For philosophy was to the Greek world what the Law
was to the Hebrews, a tutor escorting them to Christ. So philosophy is a preparatory process; it opens the road for the
person whom Christ brings to his final goal. (4) Solomon says,
"Surround Wisdom with a stockade, and she will exalt you;
she will shield you with a rich crown,"[126] since[127] once you have
fortified her with a fence by means of the true riches of philosophy, you will keep her inaccessible to the sophists.

29(1) There is only one way of truth, but different paths
from different places join it, just like tributaries flowing into
a perennial river. (2) So these are really inspired words: "Hear,
my son, and accept my words, to have many paths of life. I
am teaching you the ways of wisdom, so that its springs may
never fail you"[128]—that is, those which spurt from the same
soil. (3) He is not merely affirming that there is more than
one path of salvation for a single righteous person. He adds
that there are plenty of righteous people and plenty of routes
for them. He explains this as follows: "The paths of the righteous shine like light."[129] The commandments and the preliminary stages of education would seem to be paths, starting-
points for life. (4) "Jerusalem, Jerusalem, how often have I
wished to gather your children together to me like a bird with
her fledgelings!"[130] "Jerusalem" means 'vision of peace.' He is
showing us prophetically that those who have grasped the vision of peace have had a large variety of different tutors leading to their calling. (5) All right. He wished but could not.
How often? Where? Twice: through the prophets and through
his own coming. Therefore the phrase "How often?" indicates

125. Prov 3.23.   126. Prov 4.8–9.
127. Reading κἂν with Schwartz for καὶ.
128. Prov 4.10–11.21.   129. Prov 4.18.
130. Matt 23.37.

the varieties of wisdom. It offers salvation in individual ways, qualitatively and quantitatively, universally, in time and in eternity, "since the spirit of the Lord has filled the world."[131] (6) If anyone forces the passage "Pay no attention to a loose woman, for honey drips from the lips of a prostitute"[132] to refer to Greek education, he should hear what follows: "She picks the right moment to apply oil to your throat." Philosophy does not flatter. (7) Then whom does Scripture allude to as the whore? It adds expressly: "The feet of Folly lead those who attach themselves to her down to Hades in the company of death, and her steps are not firm. So make your journey far from foolish Pleasure, and do not stand before the doors of her house for fear of giving your life to others."[133] (8) It gives further evidence: "Then in old age you will have regrets, when your bodily flesh is worn out."[134] This is the end point of foolish pleasure. (9) So much for that. When Scripture says, "Do not keep going steady with a foreign woman,"[135] it is advising us to make use of secular education but not to settle there permanently. Each generation received beneficial gifts at the appropriate points, but they were in preparation for the Word of the Lord. (10) "There are some people who have been charmed by potions produced by attendant women and have grown old in neglect of the lady of the house, Philosophy:"[136] some in music, some in geometry, some in grammar, most of all in rhetoric.

30(1) Just as the educational curriculum[137] conduces to its lady Philosophy, so Philosophy herself contributes to the acquisition of wisdom. Philosophy is a form of the practice of wisdom;[138] wisdom is the scientific understanding of things

---

131. Wis 1.7.   132. Prov 5.3.
133. Prov 5.5,8.   134. Prov 5.11.
135. Prov 5.20.
136. See A. van den Hoek, *Clement of Alexandria and His Use of Philo in the Stromateis, VigChr* Suppl. 3 (Leiden, 1988); Philo, *On the Preliminary Studies* 77. Philo (first century B.C.) was a Hellenistic Jewish writer from Alexandria, to whom Clement is much indebted.
137. The Seven Liberal Arts (as Martianus Capella called them) were inherited from Plato and Isocrates, the *quadrivium* of arithmetic, astronomy, geometry, and music, and the *trivium* of grammar, rhetoric, dialectic.
138. Reading ⟨σοφίας⟩ from Philo (see nt. 136).

divine, things human, and their causes. Thus wisdom is in authority over philosophy, as philosophy is over the preliminary stages of education. (2) For if philosophy advertises control of the tongue, the belly, and the parts below the belly, and is desirable for its own sake, then it will appear more majestic and more authoritative if it is practiced for the glory and true knowledge of God. (3) Scripture will provide evidence of what I am saying in the following examples. Sarah, Abraham's wife, had long been barren. As Sarah did not give birth, she entrusted her maidservant, Hagar by name, from Egypt, to Abraham to produce children.[139] (4) So Wisdom, who makes her home with the man of faith—Abraham was accounted faithful and righteous[140]—was still barren and without child in that generation and had not yet conceived a child of virtue for Abraham. She sensibly thought it best that the man who had at the time a suitable opportunity for progress should begin by going to bed with secular education (Egypt is an allegory of the secular world), and later come to her to father Isaac in accordance with divine Providence.[141]

31(1) Philo[142] interprets Hagar as 'resident in a foreign land' (it is written: "Do not keep going steady with a foreign woman"),[143] and Sarah as 'my sovereignty.' So it is possible to go through a preliminary education before reaching sovereign Wisdom, from whom the race of Israel will multiply. (2) From this we have a demonstration that wisdom is teachable.[144] Abraham went in search of it when he passed from the spectacle of heavenly things to faith and righteousness in God's sight. (3) Isaac represents the 'self-taught'; that is why he is identified as a type of Christ.[145] He was the husband of one

139. Gen 11.30, 16.1–16; Gal 4.22–31.

140. Gen 15.6; Rom 4.3,9, 22–3; Gal 3.6.

141. Gen 17.15–21, 21.1–7; this is a typical piece of Alexandrian allegorical interpretation.

142. Philo, *On the Preliminary Studies* 20, 34–7 (see nt. 136).

143. Prov 5.20 (see nt. 135).

144. Philo, *On the Preliminary Studies* 34–7; see Aristotle, *Nicomachaean Ethics* 6.1139 B 25, and the Platonic discussion on whether virtue is teachable, e.g., *Meno* 71 A, *Protagoras* 328 C, *Euthydemus* 274 E.

145. Typology is another important tool of interpretation.

wife, Rebecca, who signifies 'patience.' (4) Jacob is recorded in association with several women, and is interpreted as 'man of discipline.' Measures of self-discipline involve a number of different dogmas. As a result, he has the alternative name "Israel," 'the genuine visionary,' with his wide experience and practice of discipline. (5) Something else becomes clear from these three forefathers; that the seal of true knowledge is sovereign, and it comprises nature, learning, and disciplinary practice.[146] (6) You could have another image of what I have been saying in Tamar sitting at a crossroads and passing for a prostitute, so that Judah, eager to learn (the name means 'capable'), the man who never left anything unconsidered or uninvestigated, considered her and "turned to her," while maintaining his confession of faith in God.[147]

32(1) That is why Abraham, when Sarah was jealous at Hagar's comparatively honorable status, choosing only the utilitarian element from secular philosophy, said to her, "Look, your maid is in your power; treat her as you want,"[148] meaning, "I welcome liberal education as young and fresh, and as your servant, but I revere and honor your scientific knowledge as mistress in the fullest sense. (2) "And Sarah treated her harshly"—that is equivalent to "disciplined her, rebuked her." At least it is well said, "My son, do not despise education from God; when he shows you up, do not try to escape. The Lord educates the object of his love, and whips everyone he accepts as son."[149] (3) The passages of Scripture I have quoted yield other mysteries to our understanding if we investigate them under different headings. (4) So from this we make the simple assertion that philosophy includes questions concerning truth and the nature of the universe (the truth of which the Lord himself says, "I am the truth");[150] I also assert that the stage of education preliminary to resting in Christ exercises the mind, awakens the understanding, and produces a sharpness

---

146. I.e., Abraham, Isaac, Jacob.
147. Gen 38.15–16.   148. Gen 16.6.
149. Prov 3.11–12.   150. John 14.6.

of intellect which uses true philosophy for its investigations. Those who discover this, or rather who have received it from Truth herself and hold on to it, are the true initiates.

6

Philosophy Is Excellent Training

33(1) Our readiness to see what we ought to see is largely due to this preliminary training. This training must be in perceiving intelligible objects with the mind.[151] Their nature is of three kinds, considered in number, size, and definition. (2) Definition on the basis of demonstrations implants in the soul of one who follows the argument a faith which is precise and incapable of coming to any other conclusion about the subject of the demonstration; such a definition does not allow us to succumb to those who seek to deceive and undermine us. (3) In the course of these studies, the soul is purified from its sense perceptions and rekindled with the power of discerning the truth. (4) "For the preservation of a good diet of education forms virtuous natures, and those naturally excellent latch on to education of this sort and grow even better than they were before, particularly in the production of offspring, as with the rest of the animal creation."[152] (5) That is why Scripture says, "Go to the ant, you sluggard, and become wiser than he."[153] The ant at the time of harvest lays up an ample and varied store of food against the threat of winter. (6) "Or go to the bee and learn her diligence."[154] For she feeds over the whole meadow to produce a single honeycomb.

34(1) If you pray in your inner room, as the Lord taught,[155] in a spirit of adoration, then your domestic economy would no longer be confined to your domicile, but would extend to your soul. What should it feed on? How? In what quantity? What should we store in its treasury? When should these treasures be produced? For whom? Those who live by virtue

---

151. This is very Platonic.
152. Plato, *Republic* 4.424 A, though the received text is different.
153. Prov 6.6.   154. Prov 6.8.
155. Matt 6.6.

emerge, not naturally but by education, like doctors or pilots. (2) We all alike can see a vine or a horse. Only the cultivator will know whether the vine is good for bearing grapes or not; only the groom will readily distinguish a sluggish from a speedy horse. (3) Admittedly some people are naturally more inclined to virtue than others; this is shown by the practices of those so endowed compared with the rest. (4) But this by no means proves perfection in virtue on the part of those better endowed, since those less inclined to virtue by nature have been known through the enjoyment of appropriate education to achieve personal excellence in every regard, and again by contrast, those favorably endowed become wicked through neglect. God has created us sociable and righteous by nature.

35(1) It follows that we may not say that righteousness appears simply by a divine dispensation. We are to understand that the good of creation is rekindled by the commandment, when the soul learns by instruction to be willing to choose the highest. (2) But just as we say that it is possible to have faith without being literate, so we assert that it is not possible to understand the statements contained in the faith without study. To assimilate the right affirmations and reject the rest is not the product of simple faith, but of faith engaged in learning. (3) Ignorance involves a lack of education and learning. It is teaching[156] which implants in us the scientific knowledge of things divine and human. (4) It is possible to live uprightly in poverty. It is also possible in wealth. We admit that it is easier and quicker to track down virtue if we have a preliminary education. It can be hunted down without these aids, although even then those with learning, "with their faculties trained by practice,"[157] have an advantage. (5) "Hatred," says Solomon, "stirs up strife, but education guards the paths of life."[158] There is no possibility of being deceived or kidnapped by those who engage in evil artifices to injure their listeners. (6) "Education without refutation goes astray," he

156. Reading ἐντίθησιν ἡ διδασκαλία with Jackson for ἐντίθησι τῇ διδασκαλίᾳ.
157. Heb 5.14.   158. Prov 10.12.

says.[159] We must claim our share in the pattern of refutation in order to repress the false views of the sophists.

36(1) Anaxarchus the Eudaemonist wrote well in his book *On Sovereignty*: "Wide learning is both of great advantage and great disadvantage to its possessor. It benefits the person of skill, it damages the person who lightly says anything in any company. You must know the limits of the appropriate moment. That is the definition of wisdom. Those who make speeches at the wrong[160] moment, even if they are full of sense, are not counted wise and have a reputation for folly."[161] (2) Hesiod too says,[162]

> The Muses who make one rich in thoughts,
> inspired, vocal.

By "rich in thoughts" he means one who is fluent in the use of words; by "inspired" and "vocal" he means one who is skilled, wise, and knowing of truth.

7

Each Philosophical Sect Has Some Elements of Truth

37(1) It is clear that the Greek preliminary education combined with philosophy itself has come from God to human beings, not as an ultimate goal, but rather as rainstorms bursting on fertile soil, manure heaps, and houses alike. Grass and wheat sprout alike, figtrees and other less respectable trees grow on top of graves, and these growths emerge in the pattern of the genuine articles, because they enjoy the same power of the rain; but they do not have the same charm as those which grow in rich soil; they either wither or are torn up. (2) Yes, and the parable of the seed as explained by the Lord has its place here too.[163] There is only one cultivator of

159. Prov 10.17.
160. Reading ⟨ἔξω⟩ καιροῦ ῥῆσιν with Hense for καὶ θύρησιν.
161. Anaxarchus was a follower of Democritus, also from Abdera, who accompanied Alexander the Great (see DK 72 B 1).
162. Hesiod, fr. 197 (see nt. 113).
163. Matt 13.1–23; Mark 4.1–20; Luke 8.4–15.

the soil within human beings. It is the one who from the first, from the foundation of the universe, has been sowing the seeds with potential growth, who has produced rain on every appropriate occasion in the form of his sovereign Word. Differences arise from the times and places which receive the Word. (3) Besides, the farmer does not confine his sowing to wheat (and there are plenty of varieties of that), but sows other seeds as well—barley, beans, peas, vetches, seeds of vegetables and of flowers. (4) Care of plants is part of the same process of cultivation—all the operations appropriate to nurseries, parks, orchards, and, in general, the growth and nurture of trees of all kinds. (5) Similarly, pastoral care involves more than sheep—all the skills needed for cattle, horses, hounds, bees, and, in general, the maintenance of flocks and herds, and the nurture of life, differ from one another to a greater or smaller extent, apart from the fact that they are all helpful to life. (6) When I speak of philosophy, I do not mean Stoic, Platonic, Epicurean or Aristotelian.[164] I apply the term philosophy to all that is rightly said in each of these schools, all that teaches righteousness combined with a scientific knowledge of religion, the complete eclectic unity. I do not know how I could call divine, likenesses made from human calculations.

38(1) Let us now consider this. However admirably people live, if they do so without real knowledge of what they are doing, their good actions go for nothing.[165] They have stumbled into doing good works by accident, whereas there are

164. The four main schools of Greek philosophy, with chairs established at Athens. The Stoics went back to Zeno (335–263 B.C.) and taught public and private duty, pantheism, and a comprehensive world picture. The Platonists or Academy derived from Plato (427–347 B.C.) looking to a world beyond this one; they had later espoused a doctrine of knowledge based on probability. The Aristotelians, Peripatetics, or Lyceum were scientists, originating with Aristotle (384–322 B.C.). These three schools tended to draw together in religion, ethics, and politics. The Epicureans or the Garden, from Epicurus (341–270 B.C.), believed in gods remote from humankind, pleasure as the ultimate aim (but in no cheap sense), atomism, a retired life free from hopes and fears, and friendship.

165. The last three words are not in the Greek; something is missing, but what, is mere guesswork.

people who hit the target of the Word of truth by means of understanding. "Abraham was accounted just for his faith, not his actions."[166] (2) So whatever good actions they perform today will be of no benefit to them after life's close, unless they have faith. (3) This is why the Scriptures were translated into the language of the Greeks, so that the latter could never offer a plea of ignorance; they are perfectly capable of hearing all that we have to say if they are only willing. (4) Someone talking about truth and Truth giving an account of herself are very different matters. The first is a shot at truth, the second is truth. The first is a likeness, the second the actuality. The first survives by learning and discipline, the second by power and faith. (5) Instruction in religion is a gift, faith is a grace. We know the will of God by doing the will of God. "Open the gates of righteousness," Scripture says, "for me to go in by them and make my confession before the Lord."[167] (6) God offers salvation in many different ways (for he is good) and the roads to righteousness are many and various and lead to the master road and master gate. If you are looking for the authentic royal entrance, you will hear this: "This is the Lord's gate; righteous people will enter by it." (7) "Many gates are open. This one is in righteousness, that is in Christ. Blessed are all those who enter by it, keeping a straight course in holiness and revealed knowledge.[168] (8) Paul, in his letter to the Corinthians, expounds the differences between those of repute in the Church. I am quoting: "Let one be noted for faith, another capable of explaining revealed knowledge, another wise in distinguishing between arguments, another energetic in his actions."[169]

---

166. Rom 4.2–3,16; cf. Gen 15.6.   167. Ps 118.19.
168. Ps 118.20.
169. Clement of Rome, *First Epistle to the Corinthians* 48.4–5, but the quotation is free.

8

The Arts of Sophistry Are Deceitful

39(1) Skill in sophistry, an enthusiasm of the Greeks, is a power operating on the imagination, using arguments to implant false opinions as if they were true. It produces rhetoric for persuasion, eristic for controversy.[170] If the skills lack philosophy, then anyone at all would find them damaging. (2) Plato opposed sophistry, calling it "immoral practice,"[171] and Aristotle in his turn showed it to be "skill in banditry,"[172] in that it uses persuasion to filch the whole practice of wisdom and promises a wisdom that it has never practiced. (3) To put it briefly, just as persuasiveness is the starting-point of rhetoric, argument its practice, and persuasion its goal, so with eristic the starting-point is opinion, its practice contention, its goal victory. (4) Similarly with sophistry, the starting-point is the world of the senses. Its practice is twofold: one, derived from rhetoric, is expository;[173] one, from dialectic, is interrogatory. Its goal is to shock. (5) Dialectic, which the schools of philosophy are always preoccupied about, is revealed as a philosopher's exercise in the field of conjecture, to acquit the power of refutation. Truth does not lie in any of these.

40(1) So, the admirable Apostle was right to play down these appalling[174] excesses in language skills when he says, "If anyone does not agree with these sound words, but with some other doctrine, he is proud and ignorant; he has a morbid craving for asking questions and for verbal disputation. From these emerge strife, jealousy, slander, wicked suspicions, and altercations between men who are intellectually depraved and have lost all contact with truth."[175] (2) You see how worked-up he is, how he calls their skill in arguments a disease, although the sophists, Greek and non-Greek alike, pride them-

---

170. A Platonic distinction, e.g., *Sophist* 226 A, 236 C, 239 C, 240 D.
171. Not in fact Plato but Sextus Empiricus, *Against Mathematicians* 2.12.
172. See [Aristotle], *Topics* 4.126 A 30.
173. Reading [φαινόμενον] with Potter.
174. Clement puns on Paul's name.
175. 1 Tim 6.3–5.

selves on it and love this twittering immoral practice. (3) The tragic dramatist Euripides put it excellently in the *Women of Phoenicia*:

> The unjust argument
> is ill; it needs the medicine of wisdom.[176]

(4) In this the Word of salvation is called "healthy," since it is itself truth. That which is healthy forever remains immortal. That which distances itself from the healthy and divine is godlessness and death-dealing disease. (5) These people are ravaging wolves concealed in the fleeces of sheep;[177] they are kidnappers, plausible seducers of souls, secret robbers whose brigandage is unmasked, directing their efforts to capturing us by guile or violence, with our simplicity and inferior oratorical skills.

> 41(1) Often a man caught without readiness of speech,
> although his words are just, fares worse than the ready-
> tongued.[178]
>
> Today they steal the truth with torrents of eloquence
> so that appearances become deceptive.[179]

So says tragedy. (2) That is the nature of these contentious fellows, whether they follow a sect or whether they practice dialectical craft. These are people who, in the words of Scripture, stretch the warp without weaving anything.[180] They set their hearts on useless labor, which the Apostle called human cunning and craftiness "directed to leading people astray."[181] (3) "There are many people," he says, "who refuse to take instructions, talk nonsense and spread false ideas."[182] So everyone was not being addressed in the words "You are the salt of the earth."[183] (4) Some of the hearers of the Word are like

---

176. Euripides, *Women of Phoenicia* 471–2.
177. Matt 7.15.
178. Euripides, fr. 56 from *Alexander.*
179. Euripides, fr. 439 from *Hippolytus Veiled.*
180. Not in the Bible but a saying attributed to Jesus from other sources (see A. Resch, *Agrapha*, TU 30 [1906] 38).
181. Eph 4.14, reading ἀνθρωπίνην with Dindorf for αὐτήν.
182. Tit 1.10.   183. Matt 5.13.

fish of the sea. They have grown up in saltwater from birth and even so need salt in their preparation. (5) I am totally in agreement with the words of tragedy:

> My son, well-spoken words may still be false
> and use beauty of language to win a victory
> over the truth. But that is not what counts for most.
> Rather it is an upright nature. A victory won
> by eloquence shows cleverness. But I think
> that actions always speak louder than words.[184]

(6) So never set your sights on pleasing the crowd. We do not practice what delights them. Our knowledge is a long way away from their disposition. "We must not seek for an empty reputation," says the Apostle. "We must not provoke or be jealous of one another."[185]

42(1) Plato loves truth and was virtually inspired in some similar words. He says, "My nature is incapable of assenting to any other argument than the one that, after due consideration, is clearly the best."[186] (2) At any rate, that is a criticism of those who give thoughtless and ignorant credence to opinions: it is not right to lose hold of the Word of health and uprightness and trust words tainted with falsehood. To be deceived over the truth is an evil; to hold to the truth and have opinions conformable to reality is good. (3) Human beings do not like being deprived of good things, but they do suffer such deprivation through theft, trickery, violence or a failure in faith. (4) The person who fails[187] in faith is already being willingly led astray. The person who allows himself to be persuaded contrary to his better judgment, or[188] simply forgets, is suffering theft; arguments or time expropriate him and he does not realize it. Violence is often grief, or pain, or sometimes ambition, or wrath leading to a change of outlook.

---

184. Euripides, fr. 206 from *Antiope*.
185. Gal 5.26.
186. Plato, *Crito* 46 B; a slight difference in text is probably due to Clement's memory or illegible notes.
187. Reading ⟨μὴ⟩: my proposal.
188. Reading ⟨καὶ ὁ⟩ with Jackson.

The universal instruments of trickery are the charms of pleasure or the terrors of fear. All these methods are involuntary.
None of them has the power to dislodge scientific knowledge.

9

Faith Grounded in Reason Is Preferable to Simple Faith

43(1) There are some people who imagine they are fully
equipped by nature, and do not consider it right to have anything to do with philosophy or dialectic—more, they refuse
to engage in the consideration of the natural world at all. All
they ask for is simply and solely faith. It is as if they expected
to gather grapes from the very first without taking any care
of the vine. (2) The vine is allegorically the Lord.[189] From him,
with care and an agricultural skill that follows the Word, we
can harvest the fruit. We have to prune, dig, fasten, and all
the rest. We need the pruning-knife, the mattock, and all the
other tools of agriculture for the care of the vine, if we want
it to produce edible fruit for us. (3) In farming or[190] medicine,
the expert[191] is the person who has grasped a wide variety of
lessons to enable him to become a better farmer or doctor. (4)
So here I affirm that the expert is the one who brings everything to bear on the truth. He culls whatever is useful from
mathematics, the fine arts, literary studies, and, of course,
philosophy, and protects the faith from all attacks. No one
bothers about the athlete whose only contribution to the community is his physical strength.[192]

44(1) We approve of the sea-captain who has had plenty of
experience and has visited "the cities of many peoples,"[193] and
the doctor who has treated many patients. This is how some
people form the idea of "the empirical doctor."[194] (2) Anyone

189. John 15.1.
190. Reading [οὕτω] with Stählin.
191. *Chrestomathes*, 'expert,' puns on 'disciples of Christ.'
192. Reading ἐκτὸς ῥώμης οὐδὲν ἀλλ' with Stählin for ὡς προείρηται ἀλλ';
in general see Plato, *Republic* 3.413 A–C.
193. Homer, *Odyssey* 1.3.
194. The empirical school of medicine, one of the three main approaches

who brings every experience to bear on right action, taking models from Greeks and non-Greeks alike, is a highly skilled hunter of truth. He really is "many-wiled."[195] Like the testing stone (a stone from Lydia that was believed to distinguish genuine from false gold),[196] our "man of many skills,"[197] our Christian Gnostic, is also competent to distinguish sophistry from philosophy, superficial adornment from athletics, cookery from pharmacy, rhetoric from dialectic,[198] and then[199] in Christian thought, heresies from the actual truth. (3) The person who yearns to touch the fringes of God's power must of necessity become a philosopher to have a proper conception about intellectual objects. He must be able also to distinguish the ambiguities and nominally similar terms in the two Testaments. (4) It is in fact by an ambiguity that the Lord outwits the devil at the time of the temptation,[200] and I no longer understand how the inventor of philosophy and dialectic can be deceived by the method of ambiguity and led astray, as some people suppose.

45(1) Admittedly the prophets and apostles had no knowledge of the techniques which clarify philosophical exercises. The intelligence of the Spirit of prophecy and instruction speaks obscurely because everyone does not have the capacity to listen with understanding; for clarity it demands the techniques of teaching. (2) The prophets and the Spirit's disciples have learned to know this intelligence without stumbling. For by faith they realized that the Spirit did not speak simply and that it was impossible to receive its words in their true sense without a period of learning.[201] (3) Scripture says, "Write my

---

to medical science, was reputedly founded in the third century B.C. by Serapion of Alexandria and Philinus of Cos, rejecting dogmatism and using experience as their ground.

195. Homer, *Iliad* 1.311 and often.

196. A siliceous stone used to assay gold (see Plato, *Gorgias* 486 D).

197. Homer, *Odyssey* 15.459.

198. Plato, *Gorgias* 465 C.

199. Reading μετὰ . . . ⟨καὶ⟩ τὰς with Stählin for ματὸ ... τῆς.

200. Matt 4.4: "Not on bread alone is man to live, but on every utterance that comes from the mouth of God."

201. The text and meaning are uncertain; I have accepted the elimination of the second ὡς with Schwartz, and the movement of οἷόν τε from the first clause to the second with Stählin.

commandments twice, according to your wishes and your true knowledge, so as to answer words of truth to those who pose you questions."[202] (4) What is the true knowledge of answering questions? The same as the true knowledge of asking questions. This is of course dialectic.[203] (5) Well then. Is not speech an action? Does action not arise from speech? If we are not acting according to the rational Word, we would be acting irrationally. The action in accordance with the rational Word is brought to fulfillment in accord with God. "And nothing came into being without him," says Scripture of the Word of God.[204] Did the Lord not do everything by his Word? (6) Animals work when they are driven by pressure of fear. Are we not to say that the so-called orthodox are drawn to good works without knowing what they are doing?

10

Excess in Speech Should Be Avoided

46(1) This is why the Savior took bread and began by speaking words of thanks.[205] He then broke the bread and offered it for us to eat in the spirit of the Logos, and, in knowledge of the Scriptures, to work out our citizenship in obedience. (2) Wicked words are not different from wicked actions. Slander is a servant of the sword; calumny creates distress; both subvert life; they are the actions of wicked words. Similarly, the use of good language is close to the practice of noble actions. (3) After all, it is the Word who offers the soul resurrection and encourages it to nobility. Blessed is the ambidextrous! The skilled speaker must not calumniate the person of good works. The man equipped for right action must not throw mud at one who has the capacity for right speech. Each must act in accordance with his nature. (4) The speaker utters what the Word reveals. It is as if he is preparing the way[206]

202. Prov 22.20–1.
203. Important in Plato's philosophy, e.g., *Republic* 7.534 E.
204. Clement, as often, is playing on *Logos,* a title of Jesus, and the meanings 'word' and 'reason.'
205. Matt 26.26; Mark 14.22; Luke 22.19; 1 Cor 11.24.
206. Matt 3.3; Mark 1.3; Luke 3.4; Isa 40.3.

for doing good works and leading his hearers to beneficial acts. There is a word of salvation and an act of salvation. Righteousness, at any rate, does not exist without reason.[207]

47(1) If we remove benefaction, benefit is at an end. If we do not receive the commandment and its explanation, faith and obedience are no more. As it is, by mutual interaction we are rich in words and actions. (2) On all grounds we must deplore eristic and sophistic skills, since the actual sentences of the sophists steal away ordinary people by enchantment, and[208] sometimes use violence to win a Theban victory.[209] (3) The familiar psalm is very very true: "The righteous man shall survive to the end, because he will not see corruption, although he sees wise men in death."[210] Whom does he mean by "wise men"? Listen to words from the *Wisdom of Jesus*:[211] "Knowledge of wickedness is not wisdom." He means by this of course the sort of thing dreamed up by the handbooks of speech and argument. (4) "So you will seek for wisdom among the wicked without finding it."[212] If you still ask, "What sort of wisdom?" Scripture will tell you: "The mouth of a righteous man will distill wisdom."[213] It is a truth of wordplay only to call sophistic technique philosophic wisdom.

48(1) I think it is a reasonable aim for me to live in the light of the Word, to have in my mind his ordinances, and to be content simply with references to my understandings without ever having pretensions to eloquence. I do not care what the technical term is for revealing what I wish to present. I am quite certain that what matters most of all is to have found salvation and to share in helping those with a desire for salvation, rather than composing elegant but valueless phrases. (2) In Plato's the *Statesman* the Pythagorean says, "If your eye is fixed on the refusal to become excited about mere words, you will be clearly seen to be richer in practical wisdom in old

207. 'Word' and 'reason' are both *logos*.
208. Reading ⟨καὶ⟩ with Mayor.
209. Literally "Cadmean" from Cadmus, founder of Thebes—a victory in which neither side wins: Eteocles successfully stemmed the attack on Thebes by his brother Polyneices, but died in the fighting.
210. Ps 49.9–10.　　　　　211. Sir 19.19 (see nt. 122).
212. Prov 14.6.　　　　　213. Prov 10.31.

age."[214] (3) Again in the *Theaetetus* you can find: "Casualness over words and phrases, and a failure to pick them out precisely is in general not ignoble, but its opposite is sometimes necessary but illiberal."[215] (4) Scripture conveys this as briefly as possible saying, "Do not go to excess in speech."[216] Speech is like the clothes on a body, actions are the flesh and sinews. It is wrong to place the care of clothing above the health of the body.[217] (5) The person who has chosen the life of truth must practice an economical way of life combined with a speech which avoids the extravagant and recondite, that is, if we are really deploring luxuries as uncontrolled dangers, as the Spartans of old proscribed perfume and purple, rightly judging dyed clothing and unguents as dangerous, and saying as much.[218] A dish of food which contains more spices than nourishment is no good. A style of language, however cultured, which is able to produce more pleasure than profit for the listeners is of no use either. (6) Pythagoras advises us to take more pleasure in the Muses than in the Sirens, teaching the practice of all forms of wisdom without pleasure, and exposing any other form of spiritual guidance as deceitful.[219] Enough for one person to have sailed past the Sirens,[220] and for a different one to have found the answer to the Sphinx—in the latter case you may think one was too many.[221]

49(1) You must not "make your phylacteries broad"[222] in

214. Plato, *Statesman* 261 E.

215. Plato, *Theaetetus* 184 B–C.

216. Job 11.2.   217. Matt 6.25.

218. For ancient Spartan legislation against luxury cf. Athenaeus 15.686F; Seneca, *Natural Questions* 4.13.9.

219. Pythagoras (see DK 14) was a thinker who emigrated from Samos to Italy in the sixth century B.C. and founded a community based on mysticism and mathematics; the Muses, daughters of Zeus and Memory, inspired the arts; the Sirens were bird-women, spirits of death (see *FPG* 1.400).

220. Odysseus (see Homer, *Odyssey* 12.39–54, 165–200) who stopped his crew's ears and had himself fastened to the mast.

221. Oedipus. The Sphinx was a lion-woman monster ravaging Thebes. Her riddle was: "What goes on four legs and two legs and three legs, and when it has most it is weakest?" In finding the answer "Man" he destroyed the Sphinx and won the kingdom. But the queen he married was his mother, and disaster followed.

222. Matt 23.5; the phylactery consisted of strips of parchment inscribed in Hebrew, placed in purses worn round the forehead.

eagerness for empty repute. The Christian Gnostic is satisfied with finding an audience of one. (2) At least you can listen to Pindar the Boeotian when he writes:

Do not divulge the traditional words to all and sundry.
There are times when the paths of silence bring most persuasion.
The word victorious becomes a spur to strife.[223]

The blessed Apostle is urgent in his admirable warning "to avoid disputing about words, an unprofitable activity which only harms the listeners, and to keep away from irreligious gossip. It will lead people into more and more ungodliness, and the words will start battening like gangrene."[224]

11

Studies Should Be Pursued with the Sole Intention of
Better Understanding the Divine Writings

50(1) This "worldly wisdom is folly in God's eyes" and "the Lord knows the emptiness of the thoughts of these wise people."[225] No one should glory in his superiority in human intelligence. (2) There is an excellent passage in Jeremiah: "The wise man should not glory in his wisdom, or the strong man in his strength, or the rich man in his riches. Anyone who glories should glory in this, that he understands and knows that I am the Lord and that I practice mercy, judgment, and righteousness in the world, because my pleasure lies in those, says the Lord."[226] (3) "To induce us to trust, not in ourselves, but in the God who raises the dead," says the Apostle, "who delivered us from that grim death"[227] "so that our faith might rest, not in men's wisdom, but in God's power."[228] "The spiritual man judges all things; he is judged by none."[229] (4) I also hear him saying, "I say this so that no one may set your thinking astray by plausible words,"[230] and that no "pillager" may

---

223. Pindar, fr. 170 B; Pindar was the leading lyric poet of the early fifth century B.C.
224. 2 Tim 2.14,16–17.
225. 1 Cor 3.19–21.
226. Jer 9.23–4.
227. 2 Cor 1.9–10.
228. 1 Cor 2.5.
229. 1 Cor 2.15.
230. Col 2.4.

find his way in. (5) Again, "See to it that no one becomes a pillager on you by means of philosophy or vain deceit, following human tradition, following the elemental spirits of the universe rather then Christ."[231] (6) He does not mean all philosophy, but the Epicurean variety[232] (which Paul mentions in the *Acts of the Apostles*,[233] criticizing it for rejecting Providence and making a god of pleasure) and any other form which honors the elements without a scientific knowledge of their creative cause, and without any notion of the creator.[234]

51(1) The Stoics too, of whom he also speaks, say wrongly that God is corporeal and moves through matter of the most disreputable kind. (2) "Human tradition"[235] is his term for this intellectual nonsense. That is why he also gives instructions: "Shun immature investigations."[236] Such rivalries are childish. "Morality is not a matter for young children," says the philosopher Plato[237] (3) and, according to Gorgias of Leontini, our "contest requires two[238] virtues—boldness and wisdom. Boldness means facing danger; wisdom means understanding hidden meanings. My word, like the proclamation" at the Olympic Games "is an invitation to any with the desire but gives the prize only to those with the ability."[239] (4) The Word does not want the man of faith to be indifferent to truth, and in fact lazy. For he says, "Seek and you shall find"[240] but sets a limiting point to the search—discovery. He banishes idle chatter and approves only the sort of investigation that strengthens our faith. (5) "I say this so that no one may set you thinking astray by plausible words,"[241] says the Apostle. He is

231. Col 2.8.   232. See nt. 164.
233. Acts 17.18.
234. Clement uses the Platonic word, properly applied to a craftsman working on preexistent material.
235. Col 2.8.
236. 2 Tim 2.22–3 conflated.
237. Not in our texts of Plato.
238. Reading [δὲ] with Wilamowitz.
239. Gorgias (fifth century B.C.) was a leading theorist and practitioner of rhetoric from Leontini in Sicily (see DK 82 B 8); the Games, in honor of Olympian Zeus, were held in Olympia from 776 B.C. to A.D. 393 every four years, and open to all Greeks.
240. Matt 7.7.
241. Col 2.4, as in nt. 230.

clearly addressing those who have learned to discriminate between the things these people say, and who have been taught to repel their attacks.

52(1) "Therefore, as you have received Jesus Christ our Lord, walk in him, rooted and built up in him and established in the faith."[242] The power that establishes faith is persuasion. "See to it that no one pillages you," taking you away from faith in Christ "by means of philosophy or vain deceit" which rejects Providence, "following human tradition."[243] (2) Philosophy which follows divine tradition gives Providence a firm place. Take Providence away and God's plan for the Savior appears a legend leading us on "according to the elemental spirits of the universe and not according to Christ."[244] (3) Teaching that follows Christ recognizes God in the creator.[245] It brings Providence in, even to matters of detail. It shows that the elements are by nature subject to birth and change. It teaches us, so far as we can,[246] to exercise our citizenship in likeness to God, and to accept God's plan as the directive power for the whole of our education. (4) Some make the elements objects of reverence: Diogenes with air, Thales with water, Hippasus with fire; as well as those who hypothesize the atoms as first principles, wearing covertly the name of philosophy, but really being godless, all too human and pleasure-loving.[247]

53(1) "For this reason I pray," says the Apostle, "that your

242. Col 2.6 with one of Paul's most mixed metaphors.

243. Col 2.8, as in nt. 231.

244. Col 2.8.

245. Unlike some Gnostic sects to whom the creator was a kind of anti-God.

246. Plato, *Theaetetus* 176 B, a famous passage.

247. Not quite right since the early scientists were seeking a material basis, not a divinity, although the upper air was thought to be from the divine "mind-stuff" outside of the world we know: Thales of Miletus (early sixth century B.C.) postulated a basis in water, which freezes into a solid and boils into a gas and nurtures life; Diogenes of Apollonia (mid-fifth century B.C.) followed Anaximenes in opting for air; Hippasus of Metapontum (c. 500 B.C.) was a Pythagorean, who, like Heraclitus, chose fire; Atomism was devised by the shadowy Leucippus and more famous Democritus towards the end of the fifth century B.C. and taken up a century later by Epicurus (see nts. 100 and 164).

love may abound to a yet greater and greater extent, with
knowledge and all perceptivity, so that you may approve the
things that are exceptional,"[248] since, as the same Apostle says,
"when we were children we were enslaved to the elemental
spirits of the universe. The child, even if he is an heir, is no
different from the slave until the occasion predetermined by
his father."[249] (2) So the philosophers too are children, if they
have not been brought to maturity by Christ. For if "the son
of the maidservant shall not inherit along with the son of the
free woman,"[250] he is still the seed of Abraham, and his own
blessing was not a result of the promise but was received as a
free gift. (3) "Solid food is for grownups, for those who have
their faculties trained and conditioned to distinguish good
from evil. Everyone who takes milk is inexperienced in the
word of righteousness."[251] He is a child and does not yet have
any real knowledge of the Word who is the basis of his faith
and action, and is incapable in himself of giving an explanation. (4) "Test everything," says the Apostle, "and hold firmly
onto that which is good."[252] He is addressing spiritual hearers
who use truth as the criterion for judging whether everything
that is said[253] has a mere semblance to, or a genuine grasp of,
truth.

54(1) "Education without criticism goes astray; beatings and
criticisms give an education in wisdom."[254] He means of
course criticisms offered in love. "For an upright heart seeks
true knowledge"[255] because "he who seeks God will find true
knowledge accompanied by righteousness. Those who seek in
the right way find peace."[256] (2) "I shall," says the Apostle,
"come to know the power, not just the words, of the con-
ceited."[257] He is writing to cudgel those who wear the appearance of wisdom—in their own eyes too—without the
reality. (3) "For the kingdom of God is not to be found in
word" (that is, in the word which uses hypothesis to induce

248. Phil 1.9–10.
250. Gal 4.30; Gen 21.10.
252. 1 Thess 5.21.
254. Prov 10.17, 29.15.
256. Prov 16.8.

249. Gal 4.2,3.
251. Heb 4.13,14.
253. Reading ⟨τὰ⟩ with Stählin.
255. Prov 27.21.
257. 1 Cor 4.19.

persuasion, rather than the true Word), "but in power," he said.[258] Truth alone has real power. (4) And again, "If anyone imagines that he has acquired some knowledge, he does not yet know as he ought."[259] Truth is never a matter of opinion. It is the presumption of knowledge which puffs up and swells with pride. "Love is constructive."[260] It moves in the field of truth, not opinion. That is why it is said, "If anyone loves, God recognizes him."[261]

12

The Stromateis *Are Permitted to Enter into the Highest Truths with Extreme Discretion*

55(1) Since our tradition is not held in common or open to all, least of all when you realize the magnificence of the Word,[262] it follows that we have to keep secret "the wisdom which is imparted in the context of a mystery,"[263] taught by God's Son. (2) Already the prophet Isaiah had his tongue purified by fire to enable him to recount his vision.[264] We too ought to be purified in hearing as well as tongue, if we are to try to have a share in the truth. (3) These thoughts obstructed my writing. Even now I am careful (in the words of Scripture) about "throwing pearls down in front of pigs, in case they trample them underfoot and turn to attack you."[265] (4) It is difficult to present arguments which are really pure and lucid, and concern the true light,[266] to people who are like pigs in their lack of education. There is almost nothing which seems more ridiculous to the man in the street than these addresses, or more marvellous and divinely inspired to those of noble natures.[267]

56(1) "The unspiritual person does not receive the gifts of God's Spirit; they are folly to him."[268] "The wise do not pro-

258. 1 Cor 4.20.   259. 1 Cor 8.9.
260. 1 Cor 8.1.   261. 1 Cor 8.3.
262. Or "the teaching," ambiguous as usual (see nt. 31).
263. 1 Cor 2.7.   264. Isa 6.1–8.
265. Matt 7.6.   266. John 1.9.
267. See nt. 12.   268. 1 Cor 2.14.

duce in public the things which they discuss in council."[269] (2) But "announce from the housetops what you hear whispered in your ear," says the Lord.[270] He is telling us to receive the secret traditions of revealed knowledge, interpreted with outstanding loftiness and, as we have heard them whispered in our ears, to pass them on to appropriate people, not to offer them to all without reserve, when he only pronounced thoughts in parables to them. (3) But in fact, my present outline of memoranda contains the truth in a kind of sporadic and dispersed fashion,[271] so as to avoid the attention of those who pick up ideas like jackdaws. When it lights on good farmers, each of the germs of truth will grow and show the full-grown grain.

13

Greek and Non-Greek Philosophies Contain Germs of the Truth

57(1) Truth is one.[272] Error has countless ways of going astray. The philosophic sects, whether Greek or not, are like the Maenads scattering the limbs of Pentheus,[273] each boasting their own limited claim as the whole truth. Everything is illuminated when the true light rises. (2) So all who stretched out towards the truth, Greeks and non-Greeks alike, could be shown to possess some portion of the Word of Truth—some a considerable part, others a fraction, as it falls out. (3) Eternity holds together in a single moment the whole of time: future, present, and past as well. But truth is far more potent than eternity in bringing together its own seeds, even if they have fallen into alien soil. (4) We could discover that very many of the opinions voiced among the sects (those that have not been rendered totally deafened or cut off from following

---

269. See Prov 24.7.   270. Matt 10.27.
271. Something is wrong with the text! I have ventured ὡς for ὅσα and ἔχει for ἔχουσι.
272. A proverbial saying.
273. In Euripides, *Bacchae*, Pentheus, king of Thebes, opposed the worship of Dionysus, and was torn to pieces by his mother and others of the Maenads or Bacchants, the god's women followers.

nature, so that they cut off Christ's head as the pack of women did with the man),[274] even if they seem mutually inconsistent, do in fact accord with their own kind and with truth in general. They follow one another to make a whole, like members of a body, parts of a total, species, or genus. (5) The high note is opposed to the low note, but both form a single chord. In numbers, odd and even are different, but both form an integral part of arithmetic, just as circle, triangle, rectangle, and other figures differ from one another in form. In the universe too, all the parts, even if they differ from one another, preserve a family relationship to the whole. (6) So in the same way, philosophy, Greek and non-Greek, has made of eternal truth a kind of dismembering, not in the legends of Dionysus but in the theological understanding of the eternal Word. If anyone brings together the scattered limbs into a unity, you can be quite sure without risk of error that he will gaze on the Word in his fullness, the Truth.

58(1) It is written in Ecclesiastes: "I have wisdom above all those who were in Jerusalem before me, and my heart has had great experience of wisdom and revealed knowledge. I have come to know allegorical and scientific knowledge. This is the choice of the Spirit, since in copious wisdom there is copious true knowledge."[275] (2) Anyone skilled in all aspects of wisdom is a Christian Gnostic in the full sense of the word. Again it is written: "The advantage of the knowledge of wisdom is that it gives life to the person who has it."[276] (3) Again, here is a quotation to give clearer confirmation to my words: "All this is accessible to those who have intelligence" ("all" means both Greek and non-Greek, since one without the other would no longer be all), "as is clear to those who are willing to acquire perceptivity. (4) Prefer my instruction to silver, and revealed knowledge to tested gold; prefer perceptivity to pure gold. For Wisdom is better than precious stones; all the objects you value cannot compare with her."[277]

---

274. I.e., Pentheus.
276. Eccl 7.10.

275. Eccl 1.16–18.
277. Prov 8.9–11.

14

Filiation of Greek Philosophies

59(1) The Greeks say that after Orpheus and Linus[278] and their oldest poets, the first to acquire a high reputation for wisdom were the so-called Seven Sages.[279] Four came from Asia: Thales of Miletus, Bias of Priene, Pittacus of Mytilene and Cleobulus of Lindos; two from Europe: Solon of Athens and Chilon of Sparta. For the seventh, some adduce Periander of Corinth, some Anacharsis of Scythia, (2) others Epimenides of Crete,[280] whom the apostle Paul mentions in his letter to Titus in the words: "One of their own number, a prophet of theirs, has said,

> Cretans are always liars, evil beasts, lazy gluttons,

and his evidence is true."[281] (3) Do you see how he grants a measure of truth to the prophets of Greece as well and is not ashamed, in a discussion designed to build them up and direct them to self-examination, to use Greek poems? (4) At any rate, in writing to the Corinthians—not only in the example just quoted—when speaking of the resurrection of the dead, he uses an iambic verse from tragedy, saying, "What use is it to me? If the dead are not raised, let us eat and drink, since we die tomorrow. Do not be deceived:

278. Clement embarks on an analysis of early Greek philosophy (see W. K. C. Guthrie, *History of Greek Philosophy* (Cambridge, 1962–1981) and G. S. Kirk, J. E. Raven, and M. Schofield, *The Presocratic Philosophers* (Cambridge, 1983); Orpheus was the legendary musician torn to pieces by Maenads; on Linus see nt. 113.

279. The fullest ancient account is in Diogenes Laertius 1.13.41; Thales was a genuine scientist and philosopher; several were statesmen—Bias, Pittacus, Cleobulus, Solon, Chilon; some of them were dictators. Their wisdom was mostly gnomic, and phrases such as "Avoid excess" and "Know yourself " were attributed to them. Anacharsis is different again, a shaman-like figure; Epimenides is shadowy; Mytilene (the official spelling) is actually on the island of Lesbos, as Lindos is on Rhodes.

280. Omitting with Wilamowitz ὃν Ἑλληνικὸν οἶδε προφήτην, an obvious gloss.

281. Titus 1.12 quoting Epimenides (see DK 3 B 1).

Bad company corrupts good character."[282]

(5) Others list Acusilaus of Argos among the Seven Sages, others Pherecydes of Syros. Plato omits Periander as unworthy of the name sage through being a political dictator and lists in his place Myson of Chenae.[283]

60(1) I shall show a little later that the Greek sages were somewhat after the date of Moses.[284] We must at the moment pay attention to the Hebraic and allusive nature of their philosophy. (2) Certainly they embraced gnomic brevity as most helpful. Plato tells us that this mode was enthusiastically[285] embraced in the past, generally among the Greeks, but particularly by the Spartans and Cretans who enjoyed the best laws.[286] (3) The phrase "Know yourself " was attributed by some to Chilon, to Thales in Chamaeleon's treatise *On the Gods,* to the Delphic oracle by Aristotle.[287] (4) It can be taken as an encouragement to pursue true knowledge. It is not possible without the substance of the whole to have knowledge of the parts. We really must be concerned with the origin of the universe; through that, it will be possible to understand human nature.

61(1) Again the words "Avoid excess" are attributed to Chilon of Sparta. But Strato in his book *On Discoveries* attributes the epigram to Sodamus of Tegea; but Didymus attributes it to Solon and he attributes "Moderation is best" to Cleobulus.[288]

282. 1 Cor 15.31–2 quoting either Euripides (as he thinks: "tragic"), fr. 1024 or Menander, fr. 218 (*Thais*).

283. Plato, *Protagoras* 343 A; Acusilaus (pre-fifth century B.C.) (see *FGrH* 1.47); Pherecydes (c. 550 B.C.) was a mythographer; Syros is one of the Cyclades; Myson is otherwise unknown; Chenae (or Chen) was a village of Thessaly.

284. This is certain, for they mostly belong to the sixth century B.C.; Moses was not later than the thirteenth century B.C., but Clement's wording shows some of the difficulties of ancient chronology.

285. Omitting τὸ with Stählin.

286. Plato, *Protagoras* 343 B; *Laws* 1.641 E.

287. Aristotle, fr. 3. The words appeared over the temple of Apollo at Delphi. They are often quoted by Plato, e.g., *Phaedrus* 229 E; *Protagoras* 343 B; Chamaeleon, fr. 36, was an uncritical but learned follower of Aristotle.

288. Strato (287–269 B.C.) was head of the Peripatetics; Sodamus is known only in one epigram; Didymus (first century B.C.) was an Alexandrian voluminous polymath.

(2) Cleomenes in his book *On Hesiod* suggests that the epigram "Make a pledge and disaster is near" was anticipated by Homer in the words,

The pledges of the worthless are worthless pledges.

Aristotle's school think it was Chilon's; Didymus says that it was advice from Thales.[289] (3) Next we have "All human beings are bad" or "Most human beings are bad" (the same epigram is recorded in both forms). The school of Sotades of Byzantium[290] say this belongs to Bias and want "Practice cleans up everything" to belong to Periander and similarly to make "Know the right moment" a piece of advice from Pittacus. (4) Solon gave Athens its laws, Pittacus Mytilene. Later Pythagoras, pupil of Pherecydes, was the first to call himself a philosopher.[291]

62(1) After the individuals I have just mentioned, there were three schools of philosophy named after the places where they operated: the Italian deriving from Pythagoras, the Ionian from Thales, the Eleatic from Xenophanes.[292] (2) Pythagoras came from Samos and was son to Mnesarchus, as Hippobotus says. But Aristoxenus, in his *Life of Pythagoras*, Aristarchus, and Theopompus say he came from Tyre, Neanthes from Syria or Tyre, so that the majority agree that Pythagoras was racially non-Greek.[293] (3) Thales too was a Phoenician in the

289. Homer, *Odyssey* 8.351; Cleomenes is not otherwise known, unless he is the Cynic philosopher of the same name.

290. Sotades of Byzantium is cited in the *Suda*, but otherwise unknown.

291. Pythagoras (see nt. 219) was hardly a pupil of Pherecydes. He said that none was wise except God; a human could be only a lover of wisdom or "philo-sopher" (see Diogenes Laertius 1.12).

292. A standard analysis of the *diadochai*, 'successions' or 'schools' of philosophy: The chronological order was Thales, Pythagoras, Xenophanes.

293. Hippobotus (late third century B.C.) was a historian of philosophy; Aristoxenus (fourth century B.C.), fr. 1, was a pupil of Aristotle, philosopher and musicologist; Aristarchus is perhaps a mistake for Aristotle, fr. 190, and it recurs in Theodoret, *Curatio* 1.24, borrowed from Clement; Aristarchus (second century B.C.) of Samothrace was librarian of Alexandria; Theopompus of Chios (fourth century B.C.) was a leading historian, fr. 67; Neanthes of Cyzicus (third century B.C.) was a voluminous but unreliable historian, fr. 17; Samos is agreed upon by most modern scholars, but the name is odd, and some have even made it *pitta-guru*, 'father-teacher'—he was familiar with Indian thought.

accounts of Leander and Herodotus, though others assume
from Miletus.[294] (4) Thales seems to have had contact with
none except the prophets of Egypt. He is not recorded as
anyone's pupil, not even of Pherecydes, with whom Pythagoras
studied.[295]

63(1) The Italian school of philosophy which followed Pythagoras settled in Metapontum and lasted there a long time.
(2) Anaximander of Miletus, the son of Praxiades, succeeded
Thales, and was succeeded by Anaximenes of Miletus, the son
of Eurystratus, and he by Anaxagoras of Clazomenae, the son
of Hegesibulus. It was he who transferred the school from
Ionia to Athens.[296] (3) His successor was Archelaus, and Socrates heard him lecture.

> In fact, the stone polisher, the law-champion, the enchanter
> of the Greeks, moved away from them,

wrote Timon in his *Silloi,* owing to Socrates moving from natural philosophy to ethics.[297] (4) Antisthenes was a disciple of
Socrates and became a Cynic. Plato moved to the Academy.[298]
(5) Aristotle studied philosophy with Plato, then moved to the
Lyceum and founded the Peripatetic school. He was succeeded by Theophrastus, then in turn Strato, Lycon, Crito-

294. Leander (or Maeandrius), historian of his native Miletus, fr. 2; Herodotus 1.170.

295. Reading μόνοις with Potter for μόνος (see 15.66[2]); Thales had certainly visited Egypt and seen the effect of the Nile floods (see DK 11 A 11);
on Pherecydes see nt. 283.

296. This is imposing a later pattern on the past: Before Pythagoras there
were not schools with heads, but the three Milesians worked closely together.
Anaxagoras, an associate of Pericles, was independent, and more than a century later, but he was, in some sense, following in their steps.

297. Archelaus (fifth century B.C.) was a philosopher from Athens, a disciple of Anaxagoras, and perhaps an influence on Socrates; Timon of Phlius
(third century B.C.) was a Sceptic philosopher: His *Silloi* were poetic lampoons
on dogmatism; Socrates' move is recorded in Plato, *Phaedo* 96A–100A.

298. Socrates' claim to draw out from his associates rather than mold them
(Plato, *Theaetetus* 149A–151D) is nowhere clearer than in these two—the
down-to-earth Antisthenes and the intellectual, otherworldly Plato (427–347
B.C.); Antisthenes however, though of similar outlook, was not a Cynic (this
suggestion was due to the Stoics seeking a link with Socrates); the Academy
was the area of Athens where Plato established his "school" after 387 B.C.

laus, Diodorus.[299] (6) Plato was succeeded by Speusippus, then in turn Xenocrates and Polemo. Polemo had as disciples Crates and Crantor, under whom the Old Academy as Plato had founded it came to an end. Arcesilaus took over from Crantor, and from his time to Hegesinus, the Middle Academy flourished.[300]

64(1) Then Carneades and his successors took over from Hegesinus. Zeno of Citium, founder of the Stoic school, was a disciple of Crates. Cleanthes was his successor, followed by Chrysippus and the others.[301] (2) Xenophanes of Colophon founded the Eleatic school. Timaeus says that he lived at the time of the Sicilian dictator Hiero and the poet Epicharmus. Apollodorus places his birth in the fortieth Olympiad, saying that he lived until the reigns of Darius and Cyrus.[302] (3) Par-

299. Aristotle (384–322 B.C.) was at the Academy 367–347 B.C., then left for Asia Minor; he became Alexander's tutor and he established the Lyceum on his return in 335 B.C. The building had a *peripatos* or 'covered walk.' Theophrastus of Eresus in Lesbos (c. 370–285 B.C.) was Aristotle's successor, and a justly reputed scientist; on Strato see nt. 288; Lycon (c. 300–226 B.C.) was the pupil and successor of Strato, a man of the world; Critolaus of Phaselis (second century B.C.) was head of the Peripatetics who visited Rome in 156—155 B.C.; Diodorus of Tyre (c. 110 B.C.) was successor to Critolaus.

300. Speusippus (c. 407–339 B.C.) was Plato's nephew and outstanding successor; Xenocrates of Chalcedon, head of the Adademy 339–314 B.C., was a man of gentle austerity; Polemo, an Athenian, converted from a dissolute youth to succeed Xenocrates from 314 to 270 B.C.; Crates, an Athenian, was successor to Polemo; Crantor of Soli (c. 335–275 B.C.) was an academic philosopher and a commentator on Plato's *Timaeus*; Arcesilaus (c. 315–242 B.C.), a convert of Crantor and head of the Academy, fostered skepticism and the withholding of judgment; Hegesinus of Pergamum was an early second-century head of the Academy.

301. Carneades (c. 214–129 B.C.), head of the Academy from c. 160 and founder of the New or Third Academy, fostered the withholding judgment but assented to probability; Zeno (335–263 B.C.) was not a student of the Platonist Crates but of the Cynic of the same name; Cleanthes (331–233 B.C.) was a religious genius; Chrysippus (c. 280–201 B.C.) was a polymath who systematized the school: "If there had been no Chrysippus there would have been no Porch" (i.e., Stoics).

302. Xenophanes (c. 570–478 B.C.), emigré from Ionia to Magna Graecia, was a religious philosopher-poet; Colophon was a city of Asia Minor (see Kirk-Raven-Schofield, *Presocratic Philosophers*, 163); Timaeus (c. 356–260 B.C.) was a learned historian of Sicily; Hiero was the ruler of Syracuse 478–467 B.C. with a cultured court; Epicharmus (early fifth century B.C.) was a Sicilian writer of comedy; Apollodorus (second century B.C.) was an Athenian scholar; the fortieth Olympiad was 616–613 B.C.; Darius (521–486 B.C.) and Cyrus (559–529 B.C.) were kings of Persia (Clement has them in the wrong order).

menides studied under Xenophanes, Zeno under him, then came Leucippus, and then Democritus.[303] (4) Protagoras of Abdera and Metrodorus of Chios studied under Democritus, Diogenes of Smyrna under Metrodorus, Anaxarchus under him, and so to Pyrrho, and from him to Nausiphanes. There are those who say that Epicurus was his disciple.[304] (5) Such in summary form is the succession of Greek philosophers. I must next expound in order the chronology of the founders of philosophic schools, so that we may show by a process of comparison that Hebrew philosophy is many generations older.

65(1) I have already explained that Xenophanes was the founder of the Eleatic school. Eudemus, in his *Researches into Astronomy*, says that Thales predicted an eclipse of the sun which took place at the time of the battle between Media and Lydia during the reign of Cyaxares, father of Astyages in Media, and Alyattes, father of Croesus in Lydia. Herodotus in his first volume agrees with this. The period is *circa* the fiftieth Olympiad.[305] (2) Pythagoras is placed in the dictatorship of Polycrates around the sixty-second Olympiad.[306] (3)

303. Parmenides of Elea (c. 515–445 B.C.) was a philosophical poet of monism; Zeno of Elea (fifth century B.C.) (not to be confused with Zeno of Citium) was a follower of Parmenides, buttressing his views with acute paradoxes; Leucippus (fifth century B.C.) was the shadowy founder of atomism; Democritus (c. 450–360 B.C.) was a leading atomist and ethical exponent of happiness.

304. Protagoras (fifth century B.C.), like Democritus, came from Abdera in the far north, but was older: he was the leading sophist; Metrodorus of Chios (fourth century B.C.) was a disciple of Democritus; Diogenes of Smyrna is mentioned half a dozen times, but the references add nothing; Anaxarchus of Abdera, a follower of Democritus with skeptical tendencies, accompanied Alexander the Great; Pyrrho of Elis (c. 364–275 B.C.) was the founder of Greek skepticism; Nausiphanes of Teos (c. 360–300 B.C.), an atomist, was a friend of Pyrrho, a link between Democritus and Epicurus; Epicurus (see nt. 164) did not owe indebtedness to any, but used the atomic theory.

305. Eudemus of Rhodes (second half of the fourth century B.C.) was an astronomer and philosopher, a friend and pupil of Aristotle; Thales' prediction of an eclipse was famous, although it has been questioned: it must have been 28 May 585 B.C. in the forty-eighth Olympiad (the four-year period beginning in 776 B.C.); Cyaxares, according to Herodotus, was the third king of Media, but there are dating problems; Alyattes (c. 610–560 B.C.) was the fourth king of Lydia; Herodotus of Halicarnassus (fifth century B.C.) was the first great historian (see *Stromateis* 1.73–4, 103–6).

306. Polycrates was dictator of Samos: Pythagoras may well have left in reaction in c. 532–529 B.C.

Solon is recorded as having an enthusiastic follower named
Mnesiphilus, with whom Themistocles was associated. Solon
was thus at the height of his powers in the forty-sixth Olym-
piad.[307] (4) Heraclitus, Blyson's son, persuaded the dictator
Melancomas to abdicate. He scorned an invitation from king
Darius to come to Persia.[308]

15

Non-Greek Thought Is Older than That of the Greeks

66(1) This is the chronology of the older Greek sages and
philosophers. I hardly need to say that the majority of them
were non-Greek by birth and educated by non-Greeks, when
Pythagoras has been shown Tyrrhenian or Tyrian; Antisthenes, Phrygian; and Orpheus, Odrysian or Thracian. The
majority make Homer an Egyptian.[309] (2) Thales was said to
be Phoenician by birth, and to have consorted with the prophets of Egypt, just as Pythagoras did with the same prophets
who induced him to undergo circumcision in order to enter
their shrines and learn from the Egyptians their mystic philosophy. He also was found with the best of the Chaldaeans
and the Magi; his common table was an allusive prefiguration
of our Church.[310] (3) Plato does not deny importing from
abroad the best parts into his philosophy, and admits a visit
to Egypt.[311] In the *Phaedo* he says that the philosopher can
profit from all sources: "Cebes," he said, "Greece is populous

307. On Solon see nt. 104; Mnesiphilus was an Athenian statesman who
influenced Themistocles over the battle of Salamis, but cannot have known
Solon; Themistocles (c. 528–462 B.C.) was the Athenian statesman responsible
for creating the navy in c. 596–593 B.C.

308. Heraclitus of Ephesus (c. 500 B.C.) was certainly politically involved.
Melancomas and the episode are not known (see DK 22 A 3); on Darius see
nt. 302.

309. An extraordinary statement, although Homer's birthplace was disputed among the Greek cities of the Asia Minor coast. Clement is forcing his
evidence.

310. Pythagoras certainly travelled, and may have encountered Indian
thinkers in Babylon.

311. This is not in surviving works, although references to Egypt in the
Laws have been taken to imply it.

and there are men of perfect virtue there, but foreign peoples are virtuous too."[312]

67(1) So Plato thinks that there are philosophers among foreigners too, contrary to Epicurus who supposes that only Greeks are capable of philosophy.[313] (2) In the *Symposium* Plato praises the foreigners as outstanding in the practice of laws: "different people in many different places both among Greeks and foreigners, with many shrines established through such fine children."[314] (3) The non-Greeks are famous for the exceptional honor they pay their legislators and teachers, calling them gods. (4) According to Plato, they suppose that good souls leave "the place beyond the heavens"[315] and submit to coming to this Tartarus of ours, taking bodily form, and sharing in all the evils of birth in their care for the race of humankind; it was they who laid down laws and proclaimed philosophy: "No greater blessing ever came to humankind from the gods or ever will."[316]

68(1) I think that it was in the realization of the great benefit accruing from the sages that all the Brahmans, the Odrysae, the Getae, and the people of Egypt honored these men and made philosophy a public institution and examined their words as sacred texts, together with the Chaldaeans and the inhabitants of Arabia Felix (as it is called), and of Palestine, and a considerable section of the Persian people, and countless other peoples in addition.[317] (2) Plato's continual respect for non-Greeks is clearly revealed: he recalls that he, like Pythagoras, learned the majority of his finest theories among foreigners.[318] (3) So he spoke of "foreign peoples" because he

312. Plato, *Phaedo* 78 A.
313. Epicurus, fr. 226.
314. Plato, *Symposium* 209 D–E. The words before are contorted: I read νόμους, ἄλλοι with Potter for μόνους ἀληθῶς, but without certainty; the "children" are virtues.
315. Plato, *Phaedrus* 247 C, but the rest of the thought does not appear there. It may refer to the Myth of Er (see *Republic* 10.314B–321D).
316. Plato, *Timaeus* 47 A–B.
317. Brahmans comprise the highest caste in India; Odrysae and Getae are peoples of Thrace; Arabia Felix is the peninsula rather than the desert and the area round Petra.
318. Plato, *Phaedo* 78 A.

knew foreign peoples who were philosophers. In the *Phaedrus* he shows us that the king of Egypt is wiser than Thoth (whom he knew as Hermes).[319] In the *Charmides* too he shows his knowledge of some Thracians who are said to believe in the immortality of the soul.[320]

69(1) Pythagoras is recorded as the disciple of Sonchis, highest prophet of the Egyptians, Plato of Sechnuphis of Heliopolis, Eudoxus the Cnidian of Chonuphis, another Egyptian. (2) In his work *On the Soul* Plato. . . .[321] Again he shows his knowledge of prophecy when he introduces the character who proclaims Lachesis' dictum to the souls casting lots, so as to predict the future.[322] (3) In the *Timaeus* he introduces Solon, in all his wisdom, learning from the foreigner. Here is a quotation: "O Solon, Solon, you Greeks are always children. There is no old man in Greece. You have no learning grown grey with age."[323] (4) Democritus appropriated[324] the ethical teachings of the Babylonians. He is said to have included an interpretation of the stele of Acicarus[325] in his own writings, as can be recognized from his writing: "These are Democritus' words." (5) Yes, and actually[326] boasting of his wide learning, he says somewhere, "I travelled over more of the earth than any human beings of my day, made the most extensive researches, viewed more climates and countries, listened to more intellectuals. No one has ever surpassed me in the composition of geometrical figures accompanied by a demonstration, not even the Egyptians called Arpedonaptae with whom . . . I spent in all eighty years abroad."[327] (6) He travelled to Baby-

---

319. Plato, *Phaedrus* 274 E. Theuth or Thoth was a moon god, a power of learning and helper of the dead. The equation with Hermes is not in Plato but see Cicero, *On the Nature of the Gods* 3.56, and the *Suda* s.v., *Thoth*.

320. Plato, *Charmides* 156 D.

321. A lacuna; *On the Soul* is *Phaedo*; on Chonuphis see Diogenes Laertius 8.90.

322. Plato, *Republic* 10.617 D; Lachesis is one of the Fates.

323. Plato, *Timaeus* 22 B.

324. Reading ⟨ἰδίους⟩ with Cobet; on Democritus see nt. 100.

325. See DK 68 B 299. Acicarus is unknown, but Theophrastus wrote a book *Acicharus* (see Diogenes Laertius 5.50); Strabo (10.762) has a mystical Achaicarus; see also Tobit 1.21–2.

326. Reading δὴ with Schwartz for ἤ.

327. See DK 68 B 299; Arpedonaptae is not known—we must assume a

lon, Persia, and Egypt and studied with magi and priests. Pythagoras was enthusiastic about Zoroaster, the Persian Magus, and the followers of Prodicus' heretical claim to have obtained secret books of this writer.[328]

70(1) Alexander, in his work *On Pythagorean Symbols*, records that Pythagoras was a pupil of the Assyrian Zaratus (whom some identify with Ezekiel, wrongly, as I shall show presently), and claims in addition that Pythagoras learned from Gauls and Brahmans.[329] (2) Clearchus the Peripatetic says that he knew a Jew who studied with Aristotle.[330] (3) Heraclitus claims that the Sibyl's discernment of the future was not humanly achieved but divinely inspired.[331] At any rate, they say that a rock can be seen near the council chamber at Delphi on which the first Sibyl is said to have sat; she had been brought up by the Muses and came down from Helicon. Some say she came from Malis and was daughter to Lamia and granddaughter to Poseidon.[332] (4) Sarapion in his epic says that the Sibyl does not cease prophesying even after death, and that after death part of her passes into air, and it is that which provides the prophetic element in prophecies and omens. Her body is changed to earth and out of it,[333] as you would expect, a grass

---

lacuna; eighty years must be wrong, though Clement may not have thought so: perhaps we should read πέντε, 'five'; eighty was expressed as π'.

328. Zoroaster or Zarathustra used to be dated to the sixth century B.C., but has now been pushed back to somewhere about the eighteenth century B.C.; he was a religious genius, whose work was revised in Persia under Cyrus and Darius; Prodicus was a Gnostic leader (see also *Stromateis* 3.30, 7.41, 103).

329. Alexander Polyhistor (early first century B.C.) was an encyclopedist from Miletus who came to Rome as a prisoner (see *FGrH* 3 A 273); Zaratus or Zaratas, of whom little is known but his name; Pythagoras must have got his doctrine of reincarnation from Indians whom he might have met in Babylon.

330. Clearchus of Soli (c. 340–250 B.C.) was a learned ascetic, and the author of *Ways of Life*, and a work in praise of Plato.

331. See DK 22 B 92; reading τὸ μέλλον with Mayor for μᾶλλον; there were many Sibyls, inspired female seers.

332. The rock can still be seen; Helicon, the mountain of the Muses, is not far away; Malis is a small area of northern Greece; Lamia was the daughter of Poseidon, and mother of the Sibyl Herophile by Zeus (see Pausanius 10.12.1).

333. Reading ⟨ἐκ⟩ from the text of Plutarch, *Moralia* 398 C–D on which this passage is based; Sarapion was an Athenian poet.

grows, and all the animals who browse on that grass at that particular spot show human beings a precise delineation of the future through their entrails (so he writes). He thinks her soul is the face which appears in the moon.

71(1) So much for the Sibyl. Numa, king of the Romans, was a Pythagorean but it was thanks to Moses that he prevented the Romans from making images of God in the form of human being or animal. At any rate, in the first 170 years when they built temples, they did not make images in sculpture or painting at all.[334] (2) Numa showed them in a mystery that it is not possible to touch the highest good except through the mind. (3) So philosophy reached a climax long ago among non-Greeks as something precious, and shone brightly through the peoples and later reached the Greeks. (4) Its main authorities were the prophets of the Egyptians, the Chaldaeans among the Assyrians, the Druids among the Gauls, the Samanaeans in Bactria, among the Celts their own philosophers, the Magi among the Persians (who by their magic[335] powers actually foretold the Savior's birth, arriving in the land of Judaea led by a star), the Gymnosophists in India, and other non-Greek philosophers.[336] (5) There are two classes of these, called Sarmans and Brahmans. Among the Sarmans, the so-called forest dwellers do not occupy cities or have roofs over their heads. They wear tree bark, take their food from berries and drink water from their hands. They do not recognize marriage or the procreation of children, like our present day so-called Encratites.[337] (6) Among the Indians are some who follow the precepts of Buddha, whom for his exceptional sanctity they have honored as a god.[338]

334. Numa Pompilius, traditionally the second king of Rome (715–673 B.C.), was a religious reformer, unhistorically associated with Pythagoras.

335. Reading μαγείᾳ with Schwartz for μέν γε.

336. Of those not previously mentioned the Druids were priests; Bactria was roughly northern Afghanistan; the Samanaeans are not known, but perhaps thought to mean 'those who make plain'; the Celts are really not separate from the Gauls; for the Magi see Matt 2.1–12; *gymnosophists* simply means 'naked fakirs.'

337. The Brahmans were the upper-caste Indian priests (see Strabo 15.1.60 who reads Garmans for Sarmans and describes their way of life); the Encratites were an ascetic Christian sect.

338. The reference to the Buddha is exceptionally interesting: Pantaenus

72(1) Anacharsis was a Scythian, and is considered the superior of many Greek philosophers.[339] (2) Hellanicus says that the Hyperboreans live beyond the Rhipaean mountains. They learn justice, and eat no meat but live from berries. They take their sexagenarians outside the gates and eliminate them.[340] (3) Among the Germans there are those called "holy women" who watch the stirrings of streams and discern and proclaim the future by the intricate patterns and sounds of flowing waters. At any rate, it was these who would not let them join battle with Caesar before the appearance of the new moon.[341] (4) The Jewish people are by far the oldest of these. Philo the Pythagorean (not to mention Aristobulus the Peripatetic and lots of others, without taking time to name them all) demonstrates that they had a written philosophy long before Greek philosophy.[342] (5) The clearest evidence comes from Megasthenes, the historian who was contemporary with Seleucus Nicator. He wrote in the third volume of his *History of India*: "However, all that has been said by the ancients about nature is also said by philosophers outside Greece, the Brahmans in India, and the people called the Jews in Syria."[343]

73(1) Some people with a taste for legend say that the first sages were found among those named the Dactyls of Ida. They attribute to them the invention of the so-called Ephesian letters and musical rhythms. That is how the dactyls in musical circles have got their name. The Dactyls of Ida were non-

---

may have travelled in the East. But the veneration of the Buddha does not give him the title of a god, although he is the Lord.

339. See nt. 279.

340. Hellanicus of Lesbos (fifth century B.C.) was a historian; the Rhipaean ('gusty') mountains were dimly conceived in the far North; the Hyperboreans have associations with Apollo, and are taken as standards of justice.

341. The Germans were in northern and central Europe east of the Rhine River (see Plutarch, *Life of Caesar* 19).

342. Sozomen, *Ecclesiastical History* 1.12; but this was perhaps Philo of Alexandria (c. 30 B.C.–A.D. 45), the Hellenizing Jewish philosopher; Aristobulus (late second century B.C.) was an Alexandrian Jew, the reputed author of a commentary on the Pentateuch.

343. Megasthenes (c. 350–290 B.C.) was ambassador of Seleucus I to India, and author of *History of India* (see *FGrH* 3 C 715); Seleucus I Nicator (c. 358–281 B.C.) was one of the successors of Alexander the Great, and the founder of the Asian kingdom.

Greek Phrygians.[344] (2) Herodorus records that Heracles was a seer devoted to natural philosophy and received the columns of the world from Atlas, a Phrygian. The legend is an allegory of the acquisition, by learning, of the knowledge of the sky.[345] (3) Hermippus of Berytus calls Chiron the Centaur wise. The author of the *Titanomachy* says of him that he was the first

> to lead the race of mortals to righteousness, revealing
> oaths and sacred sacrifices and the constellations of Olympus.[346]

(4) He was tutor to Achilles, who fought against Troy. Hippo, the Centaur's daughter, married Aeolus, and taught him research into nature, her father's scientific knowledge.[347] (5) Euripides gives evidence about Hippo as follows:

> She was the first to foretell the will of the gods
> in clear oracles after the risings of stars.[348]

(6) After the capture of Troy, it was this Aeolus who welcomed Odysseus as a guest.[349] Note these dates for comparison with the time of Moses and the oldest period of philosophy, contemporary with him.

---

344. Ida was the mountain dominating Troy (also a mountain in Crete); Dactyls were mythical magicians and technicians from Phrygia or Crete, attached to worship of Rhea Cybele.

345. Herodorus (fifth century B.C.) from Heracleia on the Black Sea was the author of a large work on Heracles; Atlas (personifying the mountain range in North Africa) supported the sky: Heracles took it over while Atlas secured him the apples of the Hesperides. The allegorical interpretation of myth is typical of the Stoics and of the Alexandrian Christians.

346. Hermippus (early second century A.D.) was a grammarian; Berytus is not Beirut but an inland village; the Centaurs were wild men-horses, but Chiron was the wise and gentle tutor of Achilles; the *Titanomachy* was the eighth-century B.C. epic of the battle of gods and giants attributed to Arctinus or Eumelus; reading ἱερὰς with Köchly for ἱλαρὰς and σήματ' with Teuffel for σχήματ'.

347. *Hippo*, 'mare,' elsewhere called *Hippe*.

348. Reading σάφεσιν . . . ἐπ' ἀντολαῖς for ἠδ' . . . ἐπαντολάς from Cyril; Euripides, fr. 482 from *Melanippe*.

349. Homer, *Odyssey* 10.1.

16

Non-Greeks Invented Most of the Skills of Civilization

74(1) Non-Greeks invented not only philosophy but practically every form of technical skill. (2) At any rate, the Egyptians together with the Chaldaeans were the first people to produce astrology for humankind. The Egyptians also were the first to show how to light lamps, to divide the year into twelve months, to forbid sexual intercourse in holy places, even proscribing entry into temples after contact with a woman without purification by water. The same[350] people again invented geometry. (3) There are some who say that Carians[351] first thought of divination of the future through the stars. (4) The Phrygians were the first to observe the flight of birds, and the Etruscans, neighbors of Italy, made precise use of sacrifice.[352] (5) The Isaurians and Arabs worked out auspices, as the Telmissians also did with augury from dreams.[353] (6) The Tyrrhenians invented the trumpet, and the Phrygians the recorder: Olympus and Marsyas were Phrygians.[354]

75(1) Cadmus was a Phoenician who invented the Greek alphabet, as Ephorus says. That is why Herodotus writes that the characters were called Phoenician. Others say that Phoenicians and Syrians invented the alphabet simultaneously.[355] (2) Tradition has it that Apis, an indigenous Egyptian, invented medicine before Io reached Egypt, and Asclepius later

350. Reading ⟨οἱ αὐτοὶ⟩ from Eusebius.
351. Omitting a second οἱ with Eusebius; the Carians were in southwest Asia Minor.
352. The Phrygians were in northwest Asia Minor; the Etruscans were on the west coast of Italy, north of Rome: their origin is in dispute and their divination famous (a model liver carefully marked out was found in Piacenza).
353. Reading ⟨ἀμέλει⟩ from Eusebius; the Isaurians were from a wild mountain area of central Asia Minor; the Telmissians or Telmessians were from Lycia.
354. Reading ⟨δὲ⟩ from Eusebius; the Tyrrhenians were Etruscans from northwest Italy; Olympus and Marsyas were legendary flute or recorder players from Asia; Marsyas challenged Apollo and upon losing was flayed alive.
355. Cadmus was a legendary king of Thebes; the Phoenicians simplified the syllabary at the cost of ambiguity by omitting vowels; the Greeks perfected the alphabet by adding vowel signs; Ephorus of Cyme (c. 405–330 B.C.) was a leading historian (see Herodotus 5.58).

developed the science.[356] (3) Atlas in Africa was the first to build a boat and sail on the sea.[357] (4) The Dactyls of Ida, Celmis and Damnameneus, were the first to find iron on Cyprus. Delas, another from Ida, found the alloy of bronze: Hesiod says he was a Scythian.[358] (5) Yes, and the Thracians were the first to invent the so-called cutlass (a curved blade) and the first to use light shields on horseback. (6) Similarly, the Illyrians invented the round shield called *parma*. (7) It is also said that the Etruscans thought of sculpture, and Itanus, a Samnite, first devised the long shield.[359] (8) Cadmus the Phoenician invented stone-cutting and thought of mining gold in the area of Mount Pangaeum.[360] (9) It was another people, the Cappadocians, who first invented the instrument called *nabla*, just as the Assyrians did with the two-stringed lyre.[361] (10) The Carthaginians were the first to build a quadrireme: the actual ship was built by a man of the country called Bosporus.[362]

76(1) Medea from Colchis, daughter of Aeetes, first invented hair dye.[363] (2) The Noropes (from Paeonia, now called Noricum) were the first to work bronze and to refine iron.[364] (3) Amycus, king of the Bebryces, invented boxing-gloves.[365]

---

356. Apis was a sacred bull of Egypt, sometimes confused with the legendary king of Argos; Io was a mythical Argive identified with Isis who was loved by Zeus, turned into a heifer, wandered far, and gave birth in Egypt; Asclepius was a demigod and, after Apollo, the god of healing: he was perhaps originally a historical doctor.

357. On Atlas see nt. 345.

358. On Dactyls see nt. 344.

359. Samnites were a people of central Italy; Itanus is not otherwise known.

360. Pangaeum was a mountain of Thrace: the gold was the basis of Macedonian power later.

361. Cappadocia was the large plateau of central and eastern Asia Minor; the *nabla* was a musical instrument of ten or twelve strings, a semitic word.

362. Reading αὐτόχθων from Eusebius for αὐτοσχέδιον; a quadrireme was a warship (probably with four men to an oar) that was ousted by triremes and quinqueremes.

363. Medea was the famous witch, Jason's lover, from the east end of the Black Sea.

364. Noricum was a Roman Alpine province south of the Danube River.

365. Amycus was a boxer defeated by Polydeuces: the "gloves" were really thongs wrapped around his hands; the Bebryces were a people of Bithynia.

(4) In music, Olympus from Mysia loved playing the Lydian scale. The so-called Troglodytes invented the musical instrument, the sambuca.[366] (5) It is said that the transverse flute was the invention of Satyrus from Phrygia. Similarly Agnis, another Phrygian, invented the three-stringed lyre and the diatonic scale.[367] (6) Similarly, it was the Phrygian Olympus who was responsible for use of the plectrum, and Marsyas for the Phrygian, Mixophrygian and Mixolydian scales, a man of the same nationality as the others, whereas Thamyris from Thrace devised the Dorian mode.[368] (7) We have been told that the Persians were the first to make chariots, beds, and footstools, and the people of Sidon were the first to build a trireme.[369] (8) The Sicilians, bordering on Italy, first invented the *phorminx* (not much inferior to the lyre)[370] and devised castanets. (9) To the reign of Semiramis in Egypt, historical records assign the invention of linen clothes.[371] (10) Hellanicus attributed the gathering of dispatches to Atossa, queen of the Persians.[372]

77(1) These historical facts are recorded by Scamon of Mitylene, Theophrastus of Eresus, Cydippus of Mantinea, Antiphanes, Aristodemus and Aristotle as well as Philostephanus,

366. On Olympus see nt. 354; Mysia was in northwest Asia Minor; the Lydian scale, normally understood as C to C was thought to be relaxed; Troglodytes (Trogodytes) were from northern Sudan; the sambuca was a triangular instrument with four strings.

367. The diatonic scale used tones and semitones; this last sentence is added from Eusebius.

368. Phrygian mode was a scale from C to C (our major); mixophrygian is not a term in normal use; Phrygian D to D, inspirational, and Hypophrygian G to G, austere, are found; Mixolydian, B to B, was passionate; Dorian, E to E, majestic; Thamyris was the legendary blind bard from Thrace (see Homer, *Iliad* 2.594).

369. Sidon was on the coast of Palestine; a trireme was a warship with three rowers to a bench pulling individual oars.

370. The distinction is not wholly clear: the *phorminx* is an early sacred lyre, normally with four strings; the *kithara*, larger and stronger, had seven to twelve strings.

371. Semiramis (Sammuramat) was regent of Assyria 810–805 B.C. who, in Greek legend, was daughter to a goddess, a ruler, a soldier, and a builder who became a sacred dove.

372. On Hellanicus see nt. 340; Atossa was queen to Xerxes in the early fifth century B.C.

and Strato the Peripatetic in his work *On Inventions*.[373] (2) I
have quoted a few facts from them to establish the natural
ability among non-Greeks for inventions useful to life. The
Greeks have gained from them in their daily life. (3) If anyone
casts aspersions on the speech of those who are not Greeks,
Anacharsis says, "I think that all the Greeks speak like Scythians."[374] (4) He was much admired by the Greeks for his
words: "My clothes consist of a cloak, my dinner of milk and
cheese."[375] Do you see how non-Greek philosophy offers actions, not words?

78(1) The Apostle says, "So with you. If you speak in languages words which are unintelligible, how will anyone know
what you are saying? You will be addressing the air. There are
in fact plenty of families of language in the world, and none
is without significance. So if I do not know the meaning behind the sound, I shall be a foreigner to the speaker and the
speaker a foreigner to me. Anyone who speaks in tongues
should pray for the power of interpretation."[376] (2) Yes, and
the skills in oral instruction and the written word were late in
reaching the Greeks. (3) At any rate, Alcmaeon from Croton,
son of Perithus, was the first to compose a treatise on natural
philosophy.[377] (4) Others record that Anaxagoras of Clazomenae, son of Hegesibulus, published the first written book.[378]
(5) The first person to set poems to music was Terpander of
Antissa who produced music in the Spartan songs.[379] Lasus of
Hermione invented the dithyramb; Stesichorus of Himera, the
hymn; Alcman of Sparta, the dance; Anacreon of Teos, the

373. On Scamon see *FGrH* 3 B 475; on Theophrastus see nt. 299; Cydippus is not otherwise known; Antiphanes is probably the writer from Berga
in Thrace who specialized in curiosities; on Aristodemus see *FGrH* 3 B 383;
on Aristotle see nt. 164; Philostephanus of Cyrene (third century B.C.) was
an antiquarian and friend of Callimachus; on Strato see nt. 288.

374. Anacharsis (see nt. 279), *Ep.* 1.

375. Anacharsis, *Ep.* 5.

376. 1 Cor 14.9–11,13.

377. Alcmaeon (sixth century B.C.) was a physician and scientist, influenced by Pythagoras.

378. On Anaxagoras see nt. 296.

379. Terpander (seventh century B.C.) was a poet and musician from Lesbos; *nomoi* were rigid Spartan 'song structures.'

love song; Pindar of Thebes, the song and dance; and Timotheus of Miletus was the first to set airs for lyre and chorus.[380]

79(1) Yes, and Archilochus of Paros invented iambic poetry; Hipponax of Ephesus, the "limping iambic"; Thespis of Athens, tragedy; Susarion of Icaria, comedy.[381] (2) The grammarians present us with the dates of these people, but it would be a lengthy business to present them in detail in a comparative table, especially as Dionysus himself, in whose honor the Dionysiac spectacles are presented, is demonstrably later than Moses or of much the same period.[382] (3) People say that it was Antiphon of Rhamnus, son of Sophilus,[383] who invented oratory directed to moral exhortation and the idioms of rhetoric, and that he was the first person to compose a legal plea for money, which he wrote and then sold. So says Diodorus. Apollodorus of Cyme was the first person to introduce the title "grammarian" in place of[384] "critic," and was consequently known as the Grammarian. Others say that this applied to Eratosthenes of Cyrene when he had published two volumes with the title *On Grammar.* In our sense of the word, the first to be called grammarian was Praxiphanes of Mitylene, son of Dionysophanes.[385] (4) Zaleucus of Locri is re-

---

380. Lasus (sixth century B.C.) was a scholar and poet in Athens; Stesichorus (sixth century B.C.) was a lyric poet from Sicily; Alcman (seventh century B.C.) was a lyric poet from Sparta; Anacreon (sixth century B.C.) was a lyric poet of love and politics from Teos; Pindar (518–438 B.C.) was a Boeotian lyric poet; Timotheus (c. 450–360 B.C.) was a dithyrambic poet and musical revolutionary from Miletus.

381. On Archilochus see nt. 4; iambic is a line of three measures in either 6/8 or 7/8; on Hipponax see nt. 4; the limping iambic, with inverted rhythm at the end, was used for lampoons; Thespis was the first in the history of tragedy to separate actor from chorus, and he won the prize at the first tragic Dionysia 535–533 B.C.; Susarion the Megarian is mentioned on the Parian Marble as the inventor of comedy c. 581–560 B.C.

382. Dionysus was the god of Tragedy and Comedy.

383. Reading ⟨Σω⟩φίλου with Potter; Antiphon (c. 480–411 B.C.), one of the Attic orators, was a right-wing politician; Rhamnus was near Athens. In Greek trials the defendant had to deliver his speech, but might get a professional to compose it.

384. Reading ⟨τοῦ γραμματικοῦ ἀντὶ⟩ with Meier; Diodorus (first century B.C.) was a world historian from Sicily, fr. 19; on Apollodorus see Pliny, *Natural History* 7.37 who comments on his fame: we know little else.

385. Eratosthenes of Cyrene (c. 275–194 B.C.) was one of the greatest of

corded as the first legislator. Others name Minos, Zeus' son, in the period of Lynceus.[386] (5) Lynceus is later than Danaus, in the eleventh generation after Inachus and Moses, as I shall show a little lower down.[387] (6) Lycurgus was born many years after the fall of Troy, and legislated for the Spartans a century before the Olympic era.[388] We have already spoken of Solon's dates.[389]

80(1) Dracon, another legislator, has his birth recorded about the thirty-ninth Olympiad.[390] (2) Antilochus spent some time in the study of scholars and estimates in all 312 years from the time of Pythagoras to the death of Epicurus, which took place on the tenth of the month of Gamelion.[391] (3) It is said that Phanothea, wife to Icarus, invented the heroic hexameter: others attribute it to Themis, one of the daughters of Titan.[392] (4) Didymus in his book *On Pythagorean Philosophy* records that Theano of Croton was the first woman philosopher and writer of poetry.[393] (5) Greek philosophy in the view of some teaches the truth in one way or another by accident, but obscurely and without the whole truth. Others would have

---

all polymaths, and head librarian at Alexandria; Praxiphanes (c. 300 B.C.) was a Peripatetic philosopher; the word "grammarian" originally covered the broad spectrum of literary criticism.

386. Zaleucus (c. 650 B.C.) was a lawgiver of Italian Locri who prescribed precise penalties; Minos was the legendary king of Crete, son of Zeus and Europē, later judge over the dead; Lynceus, son of Aegyptus, was the only one to escape murder by the daughters of Danaus.

387. Danaus, the brother of Aegyptus, was a refugee in Argos who planned for his daughters to marry and murder their cousins; Inachus was the river god of Argos and ancestor of the kings.

388. Omitting πεντήκοντα with Tatian and Eusebius, Clement's date is thus c. 876 B.C.; Lycurgus was the traditional founder of the constitution of Sparta in the eighth or seventh century B.C.

389. On Solon see nts. 104 and 279.

390. I.e., 524–621 B.C.; Draco was an Athenian legislator noted for severity.

391. On Antilochus (some would read Antiochus) see *FHG* 4.306: He is not otherwise known but the dates might reasonably be 582–271 B.C.; Gamelion was the seventh month of the Attic year, roughly our January.

392. This attribution to women is fascinating: Phanothea's husband Icarius was given the vine by Dionysus and murdered by guests who thought he had poisoned them with wine; Themis was the daughter of Uranus and Ge.

393. On Didymus see nt. 288; Theano was a disciple (more probably than wife) of Pythagoras.

it as set in motion by the devil. Some have supposed that all philosophy is inspired by inferior powers. (6) But even if Greek philosophy does not grasp the magnitude of the truth, and further, is too weak to fulfill the Lord's commandments, still it prepares the way for the supremely royal teaching; in one way or another it produces a sense of discipline, foreshadows right character, and prepares the[394] person who has an inkling of Providence to receive the truth.

17

Philosophy Is a Form of Theft but Nonetheless Beneficial

81(1) But, people say, it is in Scripture: "All those before the Lord's coming are robbers and bandits."[395] To understand all those covered by the quotation as all who existed before the incarnation of the Logos is too comprehensive an interpretation. (2) Certainly the prophets, sent and inspired by the Lord, were servants, not robbers. (3) Scripture says, "Wisdom has sent out her servants, summoning people with trumpets to the mixing bowl of wine."[396] (4) Philosophy was not sent out by the Lord, but came, says Scripture, either as an object of theft or a robber's gift. Some power, some angel learned a portion of the truth, but did not remain within the truth, and stole these things and taught them to human beings by way of inspiration. The Lord has known the outcome of the future from before the foundation of the world and[397] of individual beings: he knew all about this but did not stop it. (5) For the transmission of the theft to human beings did bring some advantage at the time—not that the thief had the advantage in view!—but Providence straightened out the result of the crime and turned it to our advantage.

82(1) I know that many people are relentlessly pressing on us and saying that not to prevent something is to be responsible for it. They say that a person who does not keep proper

394. Reading ⟨τόν⟩ with Mayor.
395. John 10.8.
396. Prov 9.3–5.
397. Reading ⟨κόσμου καὶ τοῦ⟩ with Schwartz.

guard to prevent a theft is responsible for that theft, just as much as a person who does not put out the beginning of a dangerous fire is responsible for the fire, or a pilot who has not furled the sail is responsible for the shipwreck. (2) Further, those responsible in these cases are punishable by law. Responsibility for an event attaches to anyone who had the power to prevent it. (5) The result takes place because the power of prevention does not act to prevent.[398] (3) We make them the emphatic answer that responsibility lies in action, accomplishment, and intention to perform; in those terms, failure to prevent is no part of the action. (4) Furthermore, the responsibility lies in the performance, as the shipbuilder is responsible for the existence of the boat, or the builder for the completion of the house. Non-prevention is quite different from bringing into being. What act does the person who fails to prevent perform? (6) Their argument is now passing into absurdity if they really charge that the wound is caused, not by the weapon, but by the failure of the shield to impede the passage of the weapon. That is to exempt the thief from criticism and pile the blame on the person who fails to prevent the theft.

83(1) We might as well say that it was not Hector who burned the Greek ships but Achilles by his failure to prevent Hector when he could have done so.[399] (2) In point of fact, Achilles did perhaps share the responsibility in his failure to put out the fire because of his anger (it being in his power whether or not[400] to succumb to anger). The devil is responsible for his actions. He was capable of changing his mind or of committing the theft. It is he who bears responsibility for the theft, not the Lord who did not prevent him. But the gift was not even harmful enough to call for intervention. (3) If we have to present the matter to them more precisely, they must know that the failure to prevent (which we agree took place in relation to the theft) is not a cause at all and carries no responsibility. It is an act of prevention which is included

398. Transferring this § from after (4) with Mayor.
399. Homer, *Iliad* 16.112 ff.
400. Omitting καὶ μὴν with Stählin after καὶ μὴ.

in the category of responsible causes. (4) The person who shields his companion is responsible to the one he shields for saving him from wounds by preventing him from being wounded. Socrates' guardian spirit was responsible, not by its failure to prevent action, but by turning him aside from wrong action even if it never worked positively.[401] (5) Praise, blame, rewards, and punishments are not just if the soul lacks the power to say Yes or No and the wrong act is involuntary.

84(1) It follows that a person who takes preventive action carries responsibility. The one who takes no preventive action has the right to judge the soul's free choice, so that God carries no responsibility for our sin.[402] (2) Since sins have their origin in our free choice and desire, and since erroneous assumptions often rule us, which in our ignorant failure to learn we make no effort to escape from, God would be justified in punishing us. (3) Fever is involuntary, but when a person suffers from fever through his own intemperance, we fault him. Similarly with sin too, even if it is involuntary. (4) No one chooses evil *qua* evil. He is led astray by the accompanying pleasure, supposing it good, and he thinks it right to choose. (5) In these circumstances it rests with us to deliver ourselves from ignorance and from the choice that is attractive but sinful, and, rather than this, not to assent to those corrupting fantasies. (6) The devil is called a bandit and robber. He mixes false prophets among the prophets like weeds among the grain. (7) So "all before the Lord's day were robbers and bandits"[403] does not apply simply to all human beings but to all the false prophets and all who were not sent out by his authority.

85(1) The false prophets also have committed theft. They have stolen the name of prophets. They are prophets, but prophets of the Deceiver. (2) The Lord says, "You come from your father the devil and your will is to perform your father's

401. Plato, *Apology* 31 D; *Theages* 128 D; Socrates had an inner sense turning him away from wrong; but he did treat its absence as a positive encouragement.
402. Plato, *Republic* 10.617 E (cf. nt. 18).
403. See nt. 395.

desires. His design from the beginning was to kill human beings. He has nothing to do with the truth because there is no truth in him. When he utters lies, he is speaking from his heart since he is a liar and the father of lies."[404] (3) The false prophets utter occasional truths among their lies. They were really taken out of themselves when they prophesied as ministers to the Rebel. (4) "The Shepherd, the angel of repentance" says to Hermas about the false prophet, "He speaks some words of truth. For the devil fills him with his own spirit, to see if he will be able to break down any of the righteous."[405] (5) So everything is organized from on high[406] for good "so that through the Church the whole spectrum of God's wisdom may be made known according to the foreknowledge of all the ages which he established in Christ."[407] (6) Nothing can oppose God; nothing can stand in his path; he is Lord and ruler of all.

86(1) But the plans and actions of the rebel angels are partial only, and spring from a rotten disposition, like bodily diseases. But the Providence who directs the universe directs them to a healthy conclusion even if the original cause is disease ridden. (2) At any rate, the supreme example of God's Providence lies in his not allowing the evil which springs from that freely chosen rebellion to lie in unprofitable uselessness, still less to become totally baneful. (3) It is the work of divine wisdom, excellence, and power not only to create good (this is, so to speak, God's nature, as it is the nature of fire to warm, and light to illuminate) but above all to bring a course of action devised through some evil intentions to a good, valuable conclusion, and to make beneficial use of things which seem bad, like the emergence of martyrdom from a time of trial.

87(1) So there is in philosophy, stolen as it were by Prometheus, a little fire which blazes up helpfully into a useful light; a trace of wisdom, an impulse about God.[408] (2) In this

---

404. John 8.44.
405. Hermas, *Shepherd*, Mandates 11.3.
406. Or "from the beginning."
407. Eph 3.10–11 condensed and misquoted.
408. Prometheus stole a spark of fire from heaven, which he hid in a reed.

way only could the Greek philosophers be called "robbers and bandits," taking[409] from the Hebrew prophets fragments of the truth before the Lord's coming, but without full knowledge, rather appropriating them as personal doctrine, defacing some, twisting others in an ignorant excess of enthusiasm, while actually discovering some fully. Perhaps they did have "a spirit of perceptivity."[410] (3) Aristotle agreed with Scripture when he called sophistry "the skill in stealing wisdom,"[411] as I indicated previously. (4) The Apostle says, "We express this, not in words we have learned from human wisdom, but in words learned from the Spirit."[412] (5) Scripture says of the prophets, "We have all received from his fullness"[413]—that is, Christ's. So the prophets are not thieves. (6) And the Lord says, "My teaching is not mine, but my father's and he sent me."[414] About the robbers he says, "Anyone who speaks on his own authority is seeking his own glory."[415] (7) Such are the Greeks, "lovers of self, arrogant."[416] Scripture in calling them wise is not attacking the real sages but those masquerading as sages.

18

Everybody Is Called to Wisdom

88(1) And, says Scripture, with these "I shall destroy wisdom of the wise, and reduce to nothing the understanding of the understanding."[417] The Apostle adds, "Where is the wise man? Where is the scribe? Where is our contemporary worldly debater?"[418] He is setting up the contemporary worldly debaters, the gentile philosophers, in distinction from the scribes. (2) "Has not God turned worldly wisdom to folly?"[419] This is equivalent to saying "showed it to be foolish" rather than true, as they supposed. (3) If you ask the cause of their false as-

---

409. Omitting χαὶ with Wilamowitz.
410. Exod 28.3.
411. On Aristotle see nt. 172.
412. 1 Cor 2.13.
413. John 1.16.
414. John 7.16.
415. John 7.18.
416. 2 Tim 3.2.
417. Isa 29.14; 1 Cor 1.19.
418. 1 Cor 1.20.
419. 1 Cor 1.20.

sumption of wisdom, he will answer, "It is due to their hardness of heart."[420] "Since in the wisdom of God"—that is, as proclaimed through the prophets—"the world by means of wisdom"—the wisdom which speaks through the prophets— "did not recognize him"—plainly God—"this very God thought it right through the folly of what we preach"—folly in the eyes of the Greeks—(4) "to save those who have faith. Since Jews," he goes on, "demand signs"—to induce faith—"and Greeks look for wisdom"—clearly their so-called irrefutable arguments and the rest of the syllogisms—"but we preach Jesus Christ nailed to a cross, a stumbling-block to Jews"—since despite their knowledge of prophecy they have no faith in its fulfillment—"and folly to Greeks."[421] (5) Those with a false assumption of wisdom think it a myth that a son of God should speak through a human being, or that God should have a son at all, and particularly that this son should have suffered. That is why their presumptuous prejudice induces their failure in faith. (6) For the coming of the Savior has made fools of understanding, teachable, and yes, faithful people as well as the hardhearted and faithless. (7) As a result of this voluntary adherence of those who responded, those who refused to be persuaded were demonstrably in a different category—foolish, faithless, and lacking understanding. (8) "But to those who have been called, Jews and Greeks together, Christ is the power and wisdom of God."[422]

89(1) Clearly then, we ought not to think the words "God did not turn worldly wisdom to folly?" as negative (even if it seems better) and equivalent to "He did not turn it to folly" to avoid the imputation that God was clearly responsible for their hardness of heart by turning their wisdom to folly.[423] On the contrary, for all their wisdom they were the more responsible themselves if they did not respond with faith to the message preached. Their choice to turn from the truth[424] was

---

420. Eph 4.18.   421. 1 Cor 1.21–3.
422. 1 Cor 1.24.
423. 1 Cor 1.20. The point, difficult to convey in written, though not in spoken English, is that the same words with a different inflection may be a question expecting the answer Yes or a negative statement.
424. Reading ἐκτροπή with Reinkens for ἐκλογή.

voluntary. (2) In the words "I shall destroy the wisdom of the wise"[425] he is speaking of outshining when the scorned and[426] despised non-Greek philosophy is placed in comparison, just as the lamp when outshone by the sun is said to have gone out because it cannot bring to bear a comparable power of light. (3) Out of all the human beings who have been invited, the term "called" is applied only to those who have shown their willingness to respond. There is no "injustice on God's part."[427] Those who have shown faith from both nations are "a people of God's very own."[428] (4) And in the *Acts of the Apostles* you can find, "So those who accepted his words were baptized";[429] clearly those who refused to respond set themselves apart.

90(1) Prophecy addresses these people: "If you are willing and obedient, you shall eat the good of the land,"[430] proving that choice and refusal rest with us. The Apostle applies the words "wisdom of God"[431] to teaching in conformity with the Lord, so as to show true philosophy as transmitted through the Son. (2) Even the person with a false assumption of wisdom has words of encouragement from the Apostle, telling him "to put on the new human nature created after the likeness of God in true righteousness and holiness. So put falsehood to one side. Speak truth. Give the devil no room. Stop stealing; instead, work hard at an honest job."[432] (3) The job is to labor in the pursuit of truth, supported by the gracious help of the Word, "so that you may be able to share with those in need,"[433] both worldly wealth and divine wisdom. (4) He wants the Word to be the subject taught. He wants the silver to have been exactly assayed before being deposited with the bankers as an investment. (5) So he adds, "Do not let any rotten language proceed from your mouth"—rotten language being the product of presumption—"but anything good for

425. See nt. 425.   426. Reading ⟨καὶ⟩.
427. Rom 9.14.   428. Titus 2.14.
429. Acts 2.41.   430. Isa 1.19.
431. 1 Cor 1.21,24, transferring σοφίαν from the later in the sentence with Stählin.
432. Eph 4.24–5, 27–8.   433. Eph 4.28.

edification as needed, to bring grace to the hearers."[434] The word of a good God cannot help being good. One who saves has to be good.

19

The Greek Philosophers Attained Partial Truth

91(1) So there is evidence that the Greeks too hold some true doctrines. There are other grounds too from which this can be seen. Paul in the *Acts of the Apostles* is recorded as addressing the people on the Areopagus: (2) "I observe that you are somewhat religious. As I passed through investigating your objects of worship, I found an altar on which was inscribed TO AN UNKNOWN GOD. I am proclaiming to you the god you worship in ignorance. (3) The god who made the world and everything in it is Lord of heaven and earth, and does not live in temples built by human hands. He does not need anything, to be served by human hands. He gives to all life, breath, and all else. (4) He has made every race of human beings to live on all the face of the earth. He has set prescribed times and boundaries to their lives, for them to seek the divine in the hope of feeling for him or finding him. And yet he is not far from each one of us. We live and move and exist in him, as some of your own poets have said:

> For we are in fact his family."[435]

(5) From this it is clear that by using poetic examples from the *Phaenomena* of Aratus he approves the best statements of the Greeks. Besides, he refers to the fact that in the person of the unknown god the Greeks are indirectly honoring God the creator, and need to receive him and learn about him with full knowledge through the Son.

92(1) "I sent you to the gentiles for this purpose," says Scripture, "to open their eyes, for them to turn from darkness to light and from the power of Satan to God, for them to receive

---

434. Eph 4.29.
435. Acts 17.22–8, quoting Aratus, *Phaenomena* 5; Aratus of Soli (c. 315–240 B.C.) was a Stoic poet.

release from sins and an inheritance among those who are sanctified by faith in me."[436] (2) So these are "the opened eyes of the blind,"[437] which means the clear knowledge of the Father through the Son, the direct grasp of the thing to which the Greeks indirectly allude. "To turn from the power of Satan" means to go right away from sin, the source of their slavery. (3) However, we do not accept every form of philosophy without qualification, only that about which Socrates speaks in the pages of Plato: "As they say in the mysteries, 'Many carry the thyrsus, few become Bacchants,'"[438] alluding to the fact that many are called but few chosen.[439] (4) Anyway, he makes it clear when he adds, "These last are to my way of thinking simply those who have practiced philosophy properly. So far as I could in my whole life, I never neglected these people, but made every effort to be of their number. Whether I really did make an effort and achieved something, I shall know for sure a little later, when I reach my destination, God willing."[440]

93(1) Do you not think that he has been convinced[441] out of the Hebrew Scriptures to show this clear hope in justice after death? Again in the *Demodocus* (if it is an authentic work of Plato) he says, "Do not imagine philosophy is spending one's life stooped over practical skills or in the pursuit of wide erudition. No; that is in my view a scandal."[442] (2) I suppose he knew with Heraclitus the truth: "Much learning does not teach intelligence."[443] (3) In the fifth book of the *Republic* he says, "'Are we to rank as philosophers all these and others engaged in similar studies and those[444] concerned with minor practical skills?' 'No,' I replied, 'only caricatures of philosophers.' 'Whom do you call the true philosophers?' he asked.

---

436. Acts 26.17–18.   437. Isa 42.7.

438. Plato, *Phaedo* 69 C (I see no reason to alter the text to conform with Plato); the thyrsus is the sacred wand of the followers of Dionysus: the Bacchants are the full initiates.

439. Matt 22.14.

440. Plato, *Phaedo* 69 D.

441. Reading πεισθεὶς with Münzel for πίστεως.

442. [Plato] *Amatores* 137 B (not *Demodocus*).

443. See DK 22 B 40.   444. Reading ⟨τοὺς⟩ from Plato.

'Those whose joy is in the contemplation of truth,' I responded."[445] (4) For philosophy does not consist in geometry with its postulates and hypotheses, or in music, which operates by approximation, or in astronomy which is stuffed full of arguments which have to do with physical nature, arguments which are fluid and depend on probability. Philosophy operates through knowledge of the Good in its own being, and through the truth, which are not identical with the Good, but more like paths to it. (5) Socrates does not grant that the educational curriculum finds its outcome in the Good either; it rather contributes to the soul's awakening and its practice in the direction of intelligible objects.

94(1) So if people say that it was by accident that the Greeks delivered a slice of true philosophy, the accident was a part of the divine dispensation (no one is going to deify Spontaneity out of regard for us); but if it was by coincidence, the coincidence was governed by Providence. (2) Again, if anyone were to say that the Greeks have grasped an innate notion of nature, nature is the work of a single creator, as we know, just as we have declared righteousness natural.[446] If it is said that they possess only the common human mind, let us consider who is the father of that common human mind and of the righteousness that accords with its widespread existence. (3) If anyone speaks of a gift of prediction or lays the responsibility on telepathy, he is talking about forms of prophecy. Yes, and others claim that the philosophers made some statements to reflect the truth. (4) The divine Apostle writes of us: "At present we see as in a mirror."[447] We know ourselves by reflection from it. We contemplate, so far as we may, the creative cause on the basis of the divine element in us. (5) It is written: "You have seen your brother; you have seen your God."[448] I think it is the Savior who has now at last been named to us as God. (6) But after we have got rid of our flesh it will be "face to face,"[449] definitively, with a firm grasp, once our heart is

445. Plato, *Republic* 5.475 D–E.   446. See 34(4) above.
447. 1 Cor 13.12.
448. Not in our Scriptures; J. B. Bauer, "*Vidisti fratrem vidisti dominum tuum* (*Agraphon* 144 Resch und 126 Resch)," *ZKG* 100 (1989), 71–6.
449. 1 Cor 13.12.

pure. (7) Those among the Greeks with the most precise grasp of philosophy discern God through a reflection or through a transparent medium. Such are the images of truth our weakness admits, like an image perceived in water or seen through transparent or translucent bodies.

95(1) Solomon put it well when he said, "Anyone who sows righteousness is helping faith to grow. Those who sow their own seeds are the people who make them grow in quantity."[450] And again, "Take care of your pastures in the plain and you will have grass to cut. Harvest your fodder when it is ripe so as to have sheep to give you clothes."[451] (2) You see how you have to think of covering from outside as well as protection. "Know the characters of your flock with real knowledge."[452] (3) "When gentiles who do not have the Law fulfill by nature the demands of the Law, even if they do not have the Law, they are their own law";[453] that is, "when a man who is uncircumcised keeps the precepts of the Law,"[454] in the Apostle's words, before the time of the Law and also before the coming of Christ. (4) The Word makes a sort of comparison between those whose basis is philosophy and the so-called heretics with utter clarity in saying, "Better a neighbor at hand than a brother living at a distance."[455] "Anyone who relies on falsehoods is shepherding winds and chasing birds on the wing."[456] (5) I do not think that the Word is speaking of philosophy here, although in many cases philosophy puts its hand to reasonable hypotheses and makes out a case for them. He is giving the heresies a drubbing. (6) He goes on thus: "He has abandoned the paths of his own vineyard; he is lost in the tracks of his own farm."[457] These are the heresies that, from the first, abandon the Church. (7) Anyone who falls into heresy "is crossing a waterless desert."[458] He has left behind the God who really exists; he is without God; he is seeking a water that is no water: "he is reaching an uninhabited, thirsty land, gathering in his hands barrenness."[459]

450. Prov 11.21–4.
451. Prov 27.25–6.
452. Prov 27.23.
453. Rom 2.14.
454. Rom 2.26.
455. Prov 27.10.
456. Prov 9.12.
457. Prov 9.12.
458. Prov 9.12.
459. Prov 9.12.

96(1) "I offer an invitation to those who lack intelligence" (clearly those attached to the heresies), says Wisdom. "Touch the mystic loaves in gladness, and delicious stolen water."[460] Scripture sets down bread and water in clear reference simply to the heresies that use bread and water in their offertory contrary to the rules of the Church. There are some who actually celebrate the Eucharist with plain water. (2) "Jump up; do not linger in her place."[461] Scripture is using the ambiguous word "place" to designate the synagogue as opposed to the Church. (3) Then it adds, "In this way you will be crossing a foreign water," regarding heretical baptism as foreign and improper, (4) "and traversing a foreign river"—one which takes you astray and dumps you in the sea, where everyone who allows himself to be led away from the firm ground of the truth is deposited, flowing again into the undisciplined pagan rollers of life.

20

Philosophy's Contribution to the Attainment of Truth

97(1) When a crew of men haul on their boat, we do not say that they constitute a large number of causes. There is one cause comprising several elements. Each individual is not the cause of the boat's being hauled except in cooperation with the others. In the same way, philosophy makes a contribution to grasping the truth—it is a search for truth. It is not of itself the cause of the grasp. It is a contributory cause together with the others, though perhaps a contributory cause is a cause of sorts. (2) Blessedness is a single thing; its causes, the virtues, are multiple. Warmth is produced by sun, fire, baths, clothes. In the same way, truth is one; there are many contributory factors to its investigation; its discovery depends on the Son. (3) Consider this: virtue is single in power, but the fact is that when it is realized in one form of action it is called practical wisdom, in another, disciplined moderation,

460. Prov 9.16–17.   461. Prov 9.19.

in others, courage or justice.[462] (4) So by analogy, truth is one, but there is a truth of geometry found in geometry, of music in music; there is no reason why there should not be a Greek truth in the best philosophy. But it is only this unreachable sovereign truth in which we are educated by God's Son.

98(1) It is in this way that when one and the same coin is given to a sea-captain we speak of money to pay for passage, to a tax-collector, tax, to the property owner, rent, to the teacher, tuition, to the salesperson, deposit. Each virtue, each truth, while carrying a common name, is responsible solely for the result that accords with its character. (2) A life of blessedness results from a blend of these (Do not imagine that blessedness depends on words!), when we apply the word "blessed" to an upright life and to the person who has ordered his soul in accordance with virtue. (3) Even if philosophy contributes from a distance to the discovery of truth,[463] as it reaches out with different efforts towards a knowledge that is closely linked to such truth as[464] lies in our scope, still it is a genuine contribution for the person who is committed to the effort to grasp true knowledge with the help of the Logos.[465] (4) The truth vouchsafed to the Greeks is not the same as ours, even if it does share the same name; it is separated by the grandeur of revealed knowledge, by more authoritative demonstration, by divine power, and so on. We are "God-taught."[466] We have been educated in a course which is really holy by God's Son. The Greeks do not develop their souls in the same way at all; their process of learning is different.

99(1) Captiousness may require us to go on making distinctions. In saying that philosophy[467] is a joint and contributory cause to the grasp of truth, because it is a search for

462. The fourfold division of what Ambrose was to call the cardinal virtues goes back to Plato, *Republic* 4.427 E.

463. Reading πρὸς τὴν ἀληθείας εὕρεσιν with Stählin for τῇ πρὸς τὴν ἀλήθειαν εὑρέσει.

464. Reading τῆς with Stählin for τὴν.

465. Or "of reason."

466. 1 Thess 4.9.

467. Reading ⟨τὴν⟩ with Sylburg and Stählin.

truth, we shall be accepting it as a kind of preparatory education for the Christian Gnostic. We do not regard a joint cause as a simple cause or a contributory cause as having a comprehensive grasp of its object. We do not regard philosophy as a *sine qua non*. Almost all of us, without going through the full curriculum of Greek philosophy, sometimes even without literacy, under the impulse of non-Greek philosophy coming from God, have "in power"[468] grasped through faith the teaching about God. Our education was under the sole charge of Wisdom. (2) Anything which operates in conjunction with something else and is incapable of achieving results on its own, is termed a conjoint and contributory cause from the fact that its causality is shared with another cause, or[469] because it receives the name of cause only when it comes together with something else, and of itself is incapable of producing results which accord with truth. (3) And yet philosophy on its own did bring the Greeks to righteousness, though not to perfect righteousness (we have seen it as a contributor to this, rather as the first two steps make a contribution to a prospective ascent to the loft or the elementary teacher to the prospective philosopher). It does not mean that its removal entails any elimination or destruction of the truth for the universal Word, since sight, hearing, and speech contribute to truth, but it is mind alone that recognizes it. (4) The contributory causes vary in their efficacity. Clarity contributes to the transmission of truth, dialectic to escaping from the attacks of the heresies.

100(1) The Savior's teaching is sufficient without additional help, for it is "the power and wisdom of God."[470] The addition of Greek philosophy does not add more power to the truth; it reduces the power of the sophistic attack on it.[471] It turns aside the treacherous assaults on truth, and is rightly called the wall of defense for the vine. (2) Truth following faith is as

---

468. 1 Thess 1.5.
469. Reading ⟨ἤ⟩ with Schwartz.
470. 1 Cor 1.24.
471. Compare David Russell's comment: "The task of the Christian intellectuals is that of the navy during the war. They cannot win the war, but they can lose it."

essential to life as bread. The preliminary education is like a savory accompaniment or dessert.

> At the end of a meal a rich dessert,

says the Theban poet Pindar.[472] (3) Scripture declares outright: "The innocent man will be more ready for anything if he keeps me company; the wise man will receive knowledge."[473] Also the Lord says, "Anyone who speaks on his own authority is seeking his own glory. Anyone who is seeking the glory of the one who sent him is true; there is no unrighteousness in him."[474] (4) Once again, it is dishonest to appropriate ideas from foreign people and proudly put them forward as one's own, puffing up one's own reputation and playing false with the truth. This is the person whom Scripture calls "robber."[475] At least it is said, "My son, do not tell lies; lies lead to theft."[476] (5) The robber really does hold what he holds as a result of theft, whether it be gold, or silver, or ideas, or doctrines. There is partial truth within their stolen material, but their knowledge of it is guesswork, entangled in chains of logic. It follows that with proper instruction they will have a firm grasp of knowledge.

21

Chronology of the Ancient World

101(1) Somewhat later I shall discuss the way the philosophers have plagiarized their doctrines from the Hebrews.[477] Before that, to preserve the sequence, I must speak of the chronology of Moses. This will show unambiguously that Hebrew philosophy is the oldest of any form of wisdom. (2) Tatian, in his *Against the Greeks,* offers a meticulous account of this; so does Cassian in Book One of his *Expositions.*[478] All the

---

472. Pindar, fr. 111 B (see nt. 380).
473. Prov 21.11.
474. John 7.18; reading λαλῶν for λαβών as at 1.87(6) with John.
475. See nt. 404.   476. *Didache* 3.5.
477. See Book Five.
478. Tatian (second century A.D.) was a Christian Apologist. See M. Whit-

same, my summary demands that I run over the same ground. (3) The grammarian Apion (nicknamed the Champion) was ill-disposed to the Hebrews, being Egyptian by birth, and even wrote a book called *Against the Jews*. In volume four of his *Egyptian Researches* he is writing of King Amosis of Egypt and the achievements of his reign, citing Ptolemy of Mendes as evidence. (4) Here is the exact passage: "Amosis who excavated Lake Avaris was a contemporary of Inachus of Argos, as Ptolemy of Mendes says in his *Chronology*."[479] (5) This Ptolemy was a priest. He set out the achievements of the kings of Egypt in three complete volumes. He says that the journey of the Jews from Egypt under the leadership of Moses took place in the reign of Amosis in Egypt. This is how he arrives at the conclusion that Moses was in his prime in the time of Inachus.[480]

102(1) The history of Argos (from the time of Inachus, I mean) is the oldest portion of Greek history, as Dionysius of Halicarnassus teaches us in his *Chronology*.[481] (2) Attic history dating from Cecrops (who was born of the earth and had two natural forms) was four generations younger,[482] Tatian explic-

---

taker, ed., *Tatian: Oratio ad Graecos and Fragments*, OECT (1982); Cassian was an early Christian writer of whom nothing is known for sure.

479. Apion (first-century A.D.) was a learned Greek of Alexandria whom Josephus wrote against; Amosis (I'ḥms) was the first king of the eighteenth dynasty (see H. H. Wolfgang, *Lexikon der Ägyptologie*, Band 1 (Wiesbaden, 1975), s.v., *Ahmose*, column 99); Ptolemy of Mendes (early first century A.D.) was an Egyptian priest and historian of Egypt (see *FGrH* 3 C 611); Avaris (ḥwt w'rt) was the Egyptian town associated in the Kamose stela with the residence of the Hyksos (see J. van Seters, *The Hyksos* [New Haven, 1966], 149–51).

480. Amosis (see nt. 479), founder of the eighteenth dynasty, ruled from 1580 to 1558 B.C. Scholars today are more likely to date the Exodus to the nineteenth dynasty and the reign of Ramses II (c. 1290–1224 B.C.), although all proposed dates involve problems (see Arthur T. Droge, *Homer or Moses? Early Christian Interpretations of the History of Culture* [Tübingen, 1989]), 94, 145.

481. Reading παλαίτατα with Christ for παλαίτερα; Dionysius of Halicarnassus (late first century B.C.) was a literary critic and historian of Rome (see *Roman Antiquities* 1.74.2).

482. Reading τέσσαρσι with Hervet and Lagarde for τεσσαράκοντα; Attica is the country around Athens; Cecrops was a legendary founding king, partly snake in form.

itly states; Arcadian history from Pelasgus (also by tradition earthborn) was nine generations younger.[483] (3) The history of Phthia from Deucalion is two generations younger still.[484] From Inachus to the time of the Trojan War is estimated at twenty or twenty-one generations,[485] that is, about 400 years or more. (4) And if, on the evidence of Ctesias, the history of Assyria began many years anterior to the history of Greece, it will become clear that the departure of Moses from Egypt in the times of Amosis of Egypt and Inachus of Argos took place in the four hundred and second year of the kingdom of Assyria and the thirty-second of the reign of Beluchus VIII.[486] (5) In Greece, it was at the time of Inachus's successor, Phoroneus, that we find the Flood of Ogygus and the monarchy of Sicyon, first of Aegialeus, then Europs, then Telchin, and that of Cres in Crete.[487] (6) Acusilaus describes Phoroneus as the first human being. This is why the poet of the *Epic of Phoroneus* called him "father of mortals."[488]

103(1) This is Plato's starting-point when he writes in his *Timaeus* following Acusilaus: "On occasions, wanting to encourage them to talk about the past, he endeavors to speak of the prehistory of the city, about Phoroneus (called the first mortal) and Niobe, and of the events that followed the Flood."[489] (2) "Actaeus was a contemporary of Phorbas: Attica

483. Arcadia was the rural area of southern Greece; Pelasgus was a pre-Greek mythical prince of Arcadia or Argos or Thessaly.

484. Phthia was in Thessaly; Deucalion was the legendary survivor of the Flood, the Greek Noah.

485. Reading ⟨μιᾷ⟩ from Eusebius.

486. Some of these details, missing from our MSS, are taken from Eusebius. Ctesias (late fifth century B.C.) was a Greek doctor in Persia, whose history he wrote; Who is this Beluchus? the first dynasty of Babylon goes back to the second millennium; early Assyrian history is obscure: Enlil-nasir I was contemporary with Amosis (see nts. 479 and 480); I know of no dynasty with eight kings of the same name.

487. Phoroneus was the legendary Argive ancestor and son of Inachus; Ogygus was a primeval ruler of Boeotia or Lycia or Egypt who experienced the first flood; Sicyon was an important city adjoining Corinth; Aegialeus was the son of Inachus and founder of the Sicyon monarchy; Europs was the son of Aegialeus; Telchin was the son of Europs; Cres was the eponymous ancestor of the Cretans and the son of Zeus and a nymph.

488. On Acusilaus see nt. 283.

489. Plato, *Timaeus* 22 A; Niobe the wife of Amphion of Thebes was an archetype of the sorrowing mother.

was named Actaea after him. Contemporary with Triopas were Prometheus, Atlas, Epimetheus, Cecrops with his two natural forms, and Io.[490] Contemporary with Crotopus was the Great Fire in the time of Phaethon and the[491] flood in the time of Deucalion.[492] (3) Contemporary with Sthenelus was the monarch of Amphictyon, the arrival of Danaus in the Peloponnese, the[493] establishment of Dardania by Dardanus,

> the first-born of cloudgathering Zeus,

in Homer's words,[494] and the transportation of Europē to Crete from Phoenicia.[495] (4) Contemporary with Lynceus was the rape of the Maid, the foundation of the shrine at Eleusis, the discovery of agriculture by Triptolemus, the coming of Cadmus to Thebes, the monarchy of Minos.[496] (5) Contemporary with Proetus was the war of Eumolpus against Athens. Contemporary with Acrisius was the emigration of Pelops to Athens from Phrygia, and the arrival of Ion in Athens, and the reign of Cecrops II, the exploits of Perseus and Dionysus, as well as Orpheus and Musaeus."[497]

490. Actaeus was in some versions the first king of Attica; Phorbas was the mythical Lapith from Thessaly; Triopas was the son of Phorbas; *Prometheus*, 'Forethought' (though perhaps derived from *pramantha*, 'firestick') was a trickster, craftsman, and demigod, linked with fire and the creation of humans; on Atlas see nt. 345; *Epimetheus*, 'Afterthought,' was the brother of Prometheus; on Cecrops see nt. 482; on Io see nt. 356.

491. Reading ⟨ἢ⟩ from Tatian and Eusebius.

492. Crotopus was a legendary king of Argos; Phaethon was the son of the sun god who drove his chariot too near the sun; on Deucalion see nt. 484.

493. Reading ⟨ἡ⟩ from Tatian and Eusebius.

494. Homer, *Iliad* 20.215.

495. Sthenelus was the name of several heroes, none of whom seems quite to fit the chronology; Amphictyon was the son of Deucalion who usurped the kingdom of Attica; on Danaus see nt. 387; Dardanus was the son of Zeus and ancestor of the Trojans; Europē (the Latin is Europa) was a Phoenician princess, the mother of Minos, who was loved by Zeus in the form of a bull; the name is added from Tatian.

496. On Lynceus see nt. 386; the Maid Persephone was raped by Pluto, the underworld god, and doomed to spend part of the year underground (a myth of the seed corn). Demeter's sorrow and subsequent joy were at the root of the Eleusis Mysteries; Triptolemus was a young hero of Eleusis, the inventor of agriculture; on Cadmus see nt. 209; on Minos see nt. 386.

497. Proetus was a mythical king of Argos, the grandson of Danaus; Eu-

104(1) Troy was captured in the eighteenth year of Agamemnon's reign, and the first year of the reign of Theseus'
son Demophon at Athens.[498] According to Dionysius of Argos
it took place on the twelfth of Thargelion; (2) according to
Agias and Dercylus in their third volume, on the twenty-third
of Panemus; according to Hellanicus, on the twelfth of Thargelion; according to some local historians of Attica, on the
twenty-third of that month, in the last year of Menestheus'
reign, at the full moon. The poet of the *Little Iliad* writes:

It was midnight and the moon was shining brilliantly.

Others[499] place it on the same day of Scirophorion.[500] (3) Theseus, Heracles' rival, is one generation before the Trojan War.
At any rate, Homer mentions Tlepolemus, Heracles' son, as
having fought at Troy.

105(1) It is[501] definitely shown that Moses is 604 years anterior to the apotheosis of Dionysus if the latter was divinized
in the thirty-second year of the reign of Perseus, as Apollodorus states in his *Chronology*.[502] (2) From Dionysus to Heracles
and the heroes who sailed with Jason in the *Argo* is reckoned

---

molpus was a mythical ancestor of the aristocracy of Eleusis who was admitted
to the mysteries by Demeter; Acrisius was a brother of Proetus and the grandfather of Perseus; Pelops, a mythological son of Tantalus, was the husband
of Hippodameia and king of Pisa; Ion was the eponymous ancestor of the
Ionians, the son of Creusa and Apollo or Xuthus; Cecrops II was the son of
Erechtheus; Perseus, a mythical hero, was the son of Zeus and Danae and
the killer of the Gorgon; on Dionysus see nt. 382; on Orpheus see nt. 278;
Musaeus was a mythical singer, dedicated to the Muses.

498. Agamemnon, a king of Mycenae or Argos, was the commander in
the Trojan War; Theseus was a national hero and a king of Athens.

499. Demophon was the son of Theseus and Phaedra.

500. Reading ⟨δὲ⟩ from Eusebius; on Dionysius of Argos see *FGrH* 3 B
308; Thargelion was the eleventh month of the Attic calendar, roughly our
May; Agias and Dercylus were historians of Argos before Callimachus (see
FGrH 3 B 305); Panemus was the name of a month in Argos and Boeotia,
about our September; on Hellanicus see nt. 340; Menestheus was a king of
Athens who led them against Troy; *Little Iliad* was one of the Epic Cycle,
telling the end of the War; Scirophorion was the second month of the Attic
calendar, roughly our June.

501. Heracles was a mythological hero, a son of Zeus, and perhaps a historical king of Tiryns near Argos; on Tlepolemus see Homer, *Iliad* 2.657.

502. On Perseus see nt. 497; on Apollodorus see nt. 385.

at sixty-three years in all. Asclepius and the Dioscuri sailed
with them, as Apollonius of Rhodes records in his *Argonautica*.[503] (3) From the reign of Heracles in Argos to the apotheosis of Heracles and Asclepius is estimated at thirty-eight
years according to the annalist Apollodorus.[504] (4) From there
to the divinization of Castor and Polydeuces was fifty-three
years which takes us to somewhere about the capture of
Troy.[505] (5) If we can believe the poet Hesiod, let us listen to
him:

> Maia, daughter of Atlas, bore to Zeus far-famed Hermes,
> herald to the gods, once she had entered his sacred bed.
> Semele, daughter of Cadmus, after engaging in love,
> bore a brilliant son, Dionysus radiant with joy.[506]

106(1) Cadmus, Semele's father, came to Thebes in the time
of Lynceus and invented the Greek alphabet. Triopas was contemporary with Isis in the seventh generation after Inachus
(Isis is also called "Io" through her 'going' wandering over all
the earth). Istrus in his book *On the Migration of the Egyptians*
says that she was daughter to Prometheus.[507] (2) But Prometheus was a contemporary of Triopas in the seventh generation after Moses. It follows that Moses is seen to have existed
before the creation of human beings in Greece.[508] (3) Leon,
the expert on the gods of Egypt, says that Isis was called De-

503. Jason sailed in the *Argo* to Colchis with a company of heroes, including Asclepius (see nt. 364), Heracles, and the Dioscuri (Castor and Polydeuces). The Hellenistic epic poet Apollonius of Rhodes (third century B.C.) told the story.

504. Clement regards them as "exalted humans" rather than "decayed gods," perhaps rightly; in myth both were sons of gods, divinized for their services to humankind.

505. Sons of Zeus and Leda.

506. Hesiod, *Theogony* 938–41; on Atlas see nt. 345; on Cadmus see nts. 209 and 355.

507. On Lynceus see nt. 386; on the alphabet see nt. 355; on Io see nt. 356: The supposed derivation is from *ienai*, 'go.' She was identified with Isis, the Egyptian goddess and consort of Osiris, who also wandered in search of her husband's scattered limbs; on Triopas see nt. 490; Istrus was a slave and friend of Callimachus who also wrote on Athens (see *FGrH* 3 B 334).

508. Prometheus (see nt. 490) in myth not merely brought fire to humans, but formed them from clay.

meter by the Greeks, and she was a contemporary of Lynceus in the eleventh generation after Moses.[509] (4) Apis, king of Argos, founded Memphis, says Aristippus in volume one of his *History of Arcadia*.[510] (5) Aristeas of Argos says that he was named Sarapis and it is he whom Egyptians worship.[511] (6) Nymphodorus of Amphipolis in volume three of his *Practices of Asia* says that Apis is the bull who dies and is embalmed and placed in a grave (*soros*) within the temple of the divinity honored, and from this is called Soroapis and later Sarapis by local habit. Apis is the third generation from Inachus.[512]

107(1) Leto is certainly contemporary with Tityos:

For he raped Leto, Zeus' glorious bedfellow.[513]

(2) Tityos was contemporary with Tantalus. So Pindar of Boeotia is justified in writing: "Apollo was born in course of time." Nothing surprising in that, since we find him as servant to Admetus in company with Heracles "for a full year."[514] (3) Zethus and Amphion, inventors of music, belonged to the age of Cadmus.[515] (4) If anyone tells us that the first oracle was delivered by Phemonoe to Acrisius, he had better know that twenty-seven years after Phemonoe we have Orpheus, Mu-

509. Leon of Pella in Macedonia (fourth century B.C.) *qui res Aegyptias conscripsit* (see Hyginus, *Astronomy* 2.20) to whom the gods were exalted kings (see *FGrH* 3 C 659); the equation with Demeter, the earth mother or corn mother, another Lady of Sorrows, was also made.

510. On Apis see nt. 356; Memphis was a major city of lower Egypt; on Aristippus see *FGrH* 3 B 317 and Diogenes Laertius 2.83.

511. On Aristeas see *FHG* 4.323; Sarapis was probably a creation of Ptolemy I as a universal god for his empire; the name was formed from Osiris + Apis.

512. On Nymphodorus see *FHG* 2.375 where he is identified with the fourth-century B.C. historian of Syracuse, fr. 20; Apis in Egypt is certainly the bull: The clause refers to Apis of Argos; on Inachus see nt. 387.

513. Homer, *Odyssey* 11.580; Tityos was a son of Earth, punished in Hades; Leto was the mother of Apollo and Artemis; Clement's aim is to bring the gods into history.

514. Pindar, fr. 134 B (with a slight error): Apollo was banished from Olympus for killing the Cyclopes, and became shepherd to Admetus, king of Pherae, who treated him well, and for whom he found a wife.

515. Zethus and Amphion were sons of Zeus and Antiope: Zethus was a herdsman, Amphion a musician.

saeus, Linus (Heracles' tutor) and the rest.[516] (5) Homer and Hesiod were appreciably later than the Trojan War. The Greek legislators, Lycurgus and Solon, were long after them, as were the Seven Sages, and Pherecydes of Syros, the famous Pythagoras and their followers, *circa* the introduction of the Olympiads as we have shown.[517] (6) So we have proved Moses earlier than the majority of the Greek gods, as well as those they call sages and poets.

The Sibyl and Her Oracles

108(1) Not only Moses. The Sibyl too antedates Orpheus. Many accounts of her and the oracles attributed to her are recorded: that she came from Phrygia, was called Artemis, came to Delphi, and gave utterance:

(2) People of Delphi, servants of far-shooting Apollo,
   I am come to proclaim the mind of aegis-bearing Zeus, ˉ
   in anger against my brother Apollo.[518]

(3) There is another Sibyl at Erythrae, called Herophile. Both are mentioned by Heraclides of Pontus in his work *On Oracular Shrines*. I omit the Sibyls of Egypt and Italy (living in the Cermalus at Rome, mother of Evander who established the shrine of Pan in Rome called the Lupercal).[519]

The Prophets after Moses and the Judges

109(1) At this point, it is useful to examine thoroughly the chronology of the other Hebrew prophets after Moses. (2) After the end of Moses' life, Joshua took over the leadership

516. Phemonoe (her name combines speech and intelligence) was the daughter of Apollo and priestess at Delphi, the mythical poetess who invented hexameter verse; on Acrisius, Orpheus, and Musaeus see nt. 497; on Linus see nt. 113.
517. On Sages see nt. 279; on Solon see nt. 104; on Lycurgus see nt. 388; on Pherecydes see nt. 283; on Pythagoras see nt. 219.
518. See Hesychius s.v., Σίβυλλα; on the Sibyl see nt. 331; on Phrygia see nt. 352; Artemis was the sister of Apollo, the god of Delphi.
519. Erythrae was a coastal city of Asia Minor; Heraclides of Pontus (fourth century B.C.) was a Platonic philosopher and writer; Cermalus was part of the Palatine hill; Evander was a semi-divine figure who migrated from Arcadia to Italy, settled on the Palatine, and became an ally of Aeneas; the Lupercal was supposedly the cave where the she-wolf nurtured Romulus and Remus; Pan was an Arcadian shepherds' god.

of the people. He spent six[520] years in war, and remained in the land of goodness for another twenty-five. (3) According to the account in the book of Joshua, the hero of whom we have been speaking held the succession from Moses for twenty-seven years. (4) Then the Hebrews fell into sin and were handed over to Chusachar king of Mesopotamia for eight years, as the book of Judges records.[521] (5) Later they prayed to God and were given as their leader Gothoniel, Chaleb's younger brother, of the tribe of Judah; he killed the king of Mesopotamia and ruled the people for another fifty years.[522] (6) They fell into sin again and were handed over to Eglom, king of Moab, for eighteen years. Then they repented, and were led by an ambidextrous man of the tribe of Ephraim name Aod for eighty years.[523]

110(1) After Aod's death they fell into sin again and were handed over to Jabin, king of Canaan, for twenty years. It was at that point that Deborah, Lappidoth's wife of the tribe of Ephraim, began to prophesy. The high priest was Ozius, son to Rhiesu. (2) It was under her influence that Barak, son to Benner, of the tribe of Naphthali, took command of the army, took up position against Jabin's commander-in-chief, Sisera, and was victorious. From then on, the people were governed by Deborah's judgments for forty years.[524] (3) After her death, the people again fell into sin and were handed over to the Midianites for seven years.[525] (4) In this situation, Gideon, son to Joash, of the tribe of Manasseh, in command of 300 men, killed 120,000 Midianites, and remained in authority for forty years, being succeeded by his son Abimelech for three years.[526] (5) He was succeeded by Boleas, son of Bedan and grandson of Charran, of the tribe of Ephraim, who was in authority for

520. A simple correction.

521. Judg 3.8, where he is called Cushan-rishathaim.

522. Judg 3.9, where he is called Othniel.

523. Judg 3.12–30, where they are called Eglon and Ehuel. The lefthandedness made the assassination possible.

524. Judg 4–5, where the high priest is not named, and Barak's father is Abinoam.

525. Judg 6.1.

526. Judg 6–9.

twenty-three years. After him, the people fell into sin again and were handed over to the Ammonites for eighteen years.[527]

111(1) They repented again and found a leader in Jephtha, son to Gilead, of the tribe of Manasseh, who was in charge for six years; after him, authority passed to Abatthan of Bethlehem, of the tribe of Judah, for seven years, then to Hebron of Zebulun for eight years, then to Eglom of Ephraim for eight years. Some authorities add Hebron's eight years to Abatthan's seven.[528] (2) After him, the people fell into sin again and were subject to foreigners, the Philistines, for forty years. Then they repented and Samson of the tribe of Dan became leader and defeated the foreigners in battle. He was in authority for twenty years.[529] (3) After him, there was no ruler, and Eli, the priest, was judge over the people.[530] (4) He was succeeded by the prophet Samuel who held sway for twenty-seven years, including those of Saul's reign; he also anointed David king.

The Judges Are Succeeded by the Kings

112(1) Samuel died two years before Saul when Abimelech was high priest. It was Samuel who anointed Saul king, the first king of Israel after the Judges, whose total span up to and including Samuel was 460 years seven months. (2) Then, to the end of the first book of Kings[531] there were twenty years of Saul, when he was restored and took the throne. (3) After Saul's death, David, Jesse's son, of the tribe of Judah, was the second king in Hebron, and reigned for forty years, as the second book of Kings[532] narrates, with Abiathar, son of Abimelech of Eli's family as high priest. Gad and Nathan were prophets in his reign. (4) From Joshua, son of Nave, to David's attaining the throne was 450 years in some accounts, but, as the chronology I have outlined demonstrates, comprises 523 years seven months to David's death.

527. Judg 10.1–9, where he is called Tola, son of Puah and grandson of Dodo, a man of Issachar.

528. Judg 12.7–15, which has Jephtha (six years), Ibzan of Bethlehem (seven years), Elon of Zebulun (ten years), Abdon of Pirathon (eight years).

529. Judg 13–16.   530. Judg 21.25; 1 Sam 4.18.

531. I.e., 1 Sam.   532. I.e., 2 Sam.

113(1) After this, Solomon, David's son, reigned for forty years. Nathan continued in the office of prophet, and further encouraged him in the building of the Temple. Similarly, Achias from Selom was a prophet, and both kings, David and Solomon, were themselves prophets. (2) Zadok was the first high priest to sacrifice in the temple which Solomon built, he was eighth in line from Aaron, the first high priest. (3) From Moses to the time of Solomon, there were 595 or 576 years according to different reckonings. (4) If you add to the 450 years from Joshua to David the forty years when Moses was in command, and the further eighty years he had lived before the exodus of the Hebrews from Egypt, and add to those the forty years of David's reign, the grand total will be 610.

114(1) My chronology will be more precise. If you add to the 523 years seven months up to the death of David, 120 years of Moses and forty years of Solomon, the grand total will be 683 years seven months. (2) Hiram gave his daughter to Solomon at the time of Menelaus' arrival in Phoenicia after the capture of Troy, according to Menander of Pergamum and Laetus in his *History of Phoenicia*.[533] (3) After Solomon, his son Rhoboam[534] reigned for seventeen years, Zadok's son Abimelech being high priest. (4) During his reign the kingdom split. Jeroboam of the tribe of Ephraim, Solomon's servant, ruled in Samaria. Achias the Selonite was still prophet (together with Samaias, Alami's son) and came from Judah to Jeroboam and prophesied by the altar.[535]

115(1) After him, Abium his son reigned for three years,[536] and similarly, his son Asa for forty-one years. He suffered from gout in old age.[537] In his reign, Iu,[538] son to Ananias,

---

533. Hiram was king of Tyre and ally of Solomon; Menelaus was the husband of Helen and brother of Agamemnon, but the dates do not coincide; Menander of Pergamum (or Ephesus) was a historian of Phoenicia (see *FGrH* 3 C 783); Laetus (or Laïtus) was a historian of Phoenicia (see *FGrH* 3 C 784).

534. Rehoboam.

535. See 1 Kgs 11.26–40, 13.1–2, where he is called Ahijah the Shilonite.

536. Omitting εἴκοσί with Potter from 1 Kgs 15.2; Jeroboam's son is there Abijam.

537. 1 Kgs 15.23.

538. Jehu.

was prophet. After him, his son Josaphat reigned for twenty-five years.[539] Prophets of his days were Elias the Thesbite, Michaias son to Iebla, and Abdias son to Ananias.[540] (2) Contemporary with Michaias was a false prophet from Canaan named Zedekias. (3) Next followed the reign of Josaphat's son Joram for eight years, during which Elias was prophet and in succession to Elias, Elissaeus, son to Saphat.[541] (4) During his reign, the Samaritans were driven to eat pigeon dung and their own children.[542] The period of Josaphat extends from the latter part of the third book of Kings into the fourth. (5) In Joram's reign, Elias was taken up to heaven,[543] and Elissaeus, son to Saphat, began six years of prophecy at the age of forty. Next Ochozias was king for one year; in his reign Elissaeus was still prophet, as was Abdadonaeus.[544]

116(1) After him, Ozias' mother Gotholia reigned for eight years after assassinating her nephews. She belonged to Achaab's family. Ozias' sister Josabaea stole away Ozias' son Joas and later secured him the throne. (2) Elissaeus was still prophesying under Gotholiah. After her, as already indicated, Joash came to the throne as a result of his rescue by Josabaea, wife to the high priest Jodae.[545] This adds up to forty years in all. (3) So, putting it all together, from Solomon to the death of the prophet Elissaeus comes in total to 105 or 102 years in different reckonings, but as the dated account above makes clear, really 180 in years from Solomon's accession.

117(1) From the fall of Troy to Homer's birth was 180 years according to Philochorus, which takes us past the Ionian colonization.[546] (2) But Aristarchus in his *Notes on Archilochus* says

539. Corrected from 1 Kgs 22.42, Jehoshaphat.
540. Elijah the Tishbite, Micaiah, son of Imla (1 Kgs 22.8), and Jehu, son of Hanani, appear in Scripture.
541. Elisha, son of Shaphat.
542. 2 Kgs 6.24–31.
543. 2 Kgs 2.11.
544. The king, named differently in this and the next section, is Ahaziah, his mother, Athaliah, his daughter (not sister), Jehoshabeath, his son, Joash; Athaliah's reign is six years, not eight (2 Chr 22.10–12), but the errors may be Clement's carelessness; the prophet may be Azarias, son of Adad or Oded.
545. Jehoiada.
546. Homer is now generally placed in the eighth century B.C. Philochorus

that Homer's place was contemporary with the Ionian colonization 140 years after the war with Troy.[547] (3) Apollodorus places him a century after the Ionian colonization, when Agesilaus, son of Doryssus, was king of Sparta so that the legislator Lycurgus as a young man was contemporary with him.[548] (4) Euthymenes in his *History* suggests that Homer's maturity coincided with that of Hesiod when Acastus was in power in Chios, about two centuries after the fall of Troy.[549] (5) Archemachus in volume three of his *History of Euboea* is of the same opinion. If so, Homer and Hesiod are later than the prophet Elissaeus.[550] (6) If anyone wants to follow the grammarian Crates and date Homer's birth to the period of the return of Heracles' sons, eighty years after the capture of Troy, he will still be found to be after Solomon, seeing that Menelaus reached Phoenicia in his reign, as I have already said.[551] (7) Eratosthenes places Homer's life a century after the fall of Troy.[552] (8) Yes, and Theopompus in volume forty-three of his *History of Philip* records Homer's birth 500 years after the expedition against Troy.[553] (9) Euphorion in his *History of the Aleuadae* puts his birth in the time of Gyges, whose reign began in the eighteenth Olympiad, calling him also the first dictator.[554] (10) Sosibius of Sparta in his *Chronological Table* puts

(c. 340–260 B.C.) was an Athenian religious official and historian (see *FGrH* 3 B 328); by tradition, the Ionians were driven by the Dorians from mainland Greece to Asia Minor c. 1000 B.C.

547. Aristarchus of Samothrace (c. 217–145 B.C.) was a scholarly commentator and head librarian at Alexandria; on Archilochus see nt. 4.

548. On Apollodorus see nt. 385; Argesilaus was an early king of Sparta whose dates and lengths of reign are conflicting (see Pausanius 3.2.3); on Lycurgus see nt. 388.

549. Euthymenes is not otherwise known (see *FGrH* 2 B 243); Hesiod was a Boeotian poet c. 700 B.C.; Acastus is not otherwise known; Chios was a large island of the northeastern Aegean, which claimed Homer's birth.

550. Only a few fragments of Archemachus remain (see *FGrH* 3 B 424); Euboea was a large island off the east coast of Greece.

551. Crates of Mallos (second century B.C.), a scholar, was head of the Pergamum library, and a Stoic who lectured at Rome in 168 B.C.

552. On Eratosthenes see nt. 385.

553. Theopompus of Chios (fourth century B.C.) was a historian, author of the *Hellenica* and the *Philippica* (a vast general history).

554. Of Euphorion of Chalcis in Euboea little is known (see *FGrH* 3 B 383, 738); the Aleuadae was a leading family of Thessalian nobility; Gyges was king of Lydia c. 685–657 B.C., a mystic and magical figure to the Greeks.

Homer in the eighth year of the reign of Charillus, son to Polydectes. Charillus reigned for sixty-four years, followed by his son Nicander for thirty-nine years. If so, Homer lived about ninety years before the establishment of the Olympic Games.[555]

118(1) After Joash, his son Amasias succeeded to the throne for thirty-nine years, followed by his son Ozias who died of leprosy after a reign of fifty-two years. Prophets during his reign were Amos, his son Esaias, Osee son of Beeri, and Jonas son of Amathi; Jonas came from Geth Chober, preached to the people of Nineveh, and escaped from the sea monster.[556] (2) Next Jonathan, Ozias' son, reigned for sixteen years which saw the prophecies of Esaias continuing and Osee and Michaias the Morasthinite and Joel, son to Bathuel.[557]

119(1) He was succeeded by his son Achaz for sixteen years. In his fifteenth year Israel was deported to Babylon, and Salmanazar, king of Assyria, settled the inhabitants of Samaria in Media and Babylon.[558] (2) Next Achaz was succeeded by Osee for eight years, then by Ezekias for twenty-nine. In the light of his piety, towards the end of his life, God granted him, through Esaias, to live a further fifteen years; this was confirmed by the sun reversing course.[559] (3) The prophecies of Esaias, Osee, and Michaias extended into this reign. They are said to be after the time of the Spartan legislator Lycurgus.[560] (4) Dieuchidas in volume four of his *History of Megara* puts the *floruit* of Lycurgus *circa* 290 years after the fall of Troy.[561] (5) We have seen Esaias still at work as a prophet three cen-

555. Sosibius (c. 200 B.C.) was a Spartan historian (see *FGrH* 3 B 595); Polydectes was a brother of Lycurgus; Charillus was a soldier king, in some traditions an autocrat; Nicander was noted for his pithy sayings.

556. Amaziah (twenty-nine years in 2 Chr 25.1); Uzziah (for the leprosy see 2 Chr. 26.21); Amos; Isaiah son of Amoz; Hosea son of Beeri; Jonah son of Amittai (see 2 Kgs 14.25 from Gath-hepher).

557. On Jonathan or Jotham see 2 Chr 27; Micah of Moresheth; Joel, son of Pethuel.

558. On Ahaz or Shalmaneser see 2 Kgs 17.3–6.

559. On Hoshea or Hezekiah see 2 Kgs 20.8–11.

560. On Lycurgus see nt. 388.

561. Dieuchidas (fourth century B.C.) was a historian (see *FGrH* 3 B 485); Megara was an important city on the isthmus of Corinth.

turies[562] after Solomon's reign (the period when, as I have shown, Menelaus reached Phrygia), together with Michaias, Osee, and Joel son to Bathuel.

120(1) After Ezekias, his son Manasses reigned for fifty-five years, then his son Amos for two years, and after him his son Josias, noted for his dedication to the Law, for thirty-one. He piled the limbs of the humans onto the limbs of the idols, as is established in writing in Leviticus.[563] (2) In the eighteenth year of his reign, the Passover was celebrated for the first time since Samuel, with no intervening celebration.[564] At this time too, Chelkias the priest, father of the prophet Jeremias, chanced to find the book of the Law lying in the temple and died after reading it. Prophets during his reign were Olda, Sophonias and Jeremias.[565] (3) Contemporary with Jeremias was a false prophet named Ananias. This Josias ignored the warnings of Jeremias, the prophet, and was killed by Nechao, king of Egypt, by the river Euphrates, meeting him on his expedition against the Assyrians.[566]

121(1) Josias was succeeded by his son, Jechonias, also called Joachas,[567] who reigned for three months ten days. Nechao, king of Egypt, took him in fetters to Egypt after putting his brother Joachim on the throne in his place, charged with paying tribute for the land. He lasted eleven years. (2) After him, a king of the same name, Joachim, ruled for three months, then Sedekias for eleven years.[568] (3) Jeremias continued as a prophet into his reign, together with Buzi, Urias, the son of

562. Following Bentley, where the MS L had "two centuries."

563. Manasseh or Amon; for Josiah's reforms see 2 Kgs 23; for the gory treatment of the priests of Baal see 2 Kgs 23.14,20; 2 Chr 34.4–5; and cf. Lev 26.30.

564. 2 Kgs 23.21–3; the reading is uncertain, the meaning clear.

565. On Hilkiah see 2 Kgs 22; Huldah (a prophetess); Shaphan (the secretary, not a prophet); Jeremiah.

566. 2 Kgs 23.28–30; Necho or Niku II, who marched north in 508 B.C. to immediate success and eventual defeat; reading Ἰωσίας with Stählin for Ἰωσίου.

567. Reading ⟨δ⟩ with Potter.

568. In 2 Kgs the succession is Jehoahaz (three months); Eliakim, also called Jehoiakim (eleven years); Jehoiachin (eight years); Zedekiah, formerly Mattaniah (eleven years).

Samaeas, and Ambakum.[569] This was the end of the Hebrew kings. (4) So the period from the birth of Moses to this deportation was 972 years in some accounts, but a precise chronology gives 1085 years six months and ten days. From the outset of David's reign to the Babylonian Captivity, some make 452 years six months, but our precise calculation of the time makes the total 482 years six months ten days.

The Captivity in Babylon

122(1) In the twelfth year of king Sedekias, seventy years before the dominance of the Persians, king Nabuchodonosor campaigned against the Phoenicians and Jews, as Berossus says in his *Researches on the Chaldaeans*.[570] (2) Juba, writing *On the Assyrians*, admits that he took his account from Berossus, testifying to his accuracy.[571] (3) Nabuchodonosor blinded Sedekias and removed him to Babylon, deporting the whole people except a few who escaped to Egypt. The Captivity lasted for seventy years.[572] (4) Jeremias and Ambukum continued to prophesy under Sedekias, and in the fifth year of his reign Iezekiel was prophesying in Babylon. After him came the prophet Nahum, then Daniel, and again after him, Angaeus and Zacharias prophesied for two years under Darius I, and after him, one of the twelve, the Herald.[573]

123(1) After Angaeus and Zacharias, Nehemias, senior wine steward to Artaxerxes, son of Acheli the Israelite, rebuilt the city of Jerusalem and restored the Temple.[574] (2) To this captivity are assigned Esther and Mardochaeus; they have a book

569. Buzi (Ezek 1.3); Uriah, son of Shemaiah (Jer 26.20); Habbakuk.

570. Nabuchodonosor is more familiar as Nebuchadnezzar or Nebuchadrezzar. The dating is slightly odd: his campaigns were 597 B.C. and 586 B.C. and Persian dominance began in 538 B.C.; Berossus (c. 290 B.C.) was a priest of Bel, historian of Babylon (*FGrH* 3 C 680).

571. Juba II (c. 50 B.C.–A.D. 23) was king of Mauretania and a learned writer (see *FGrH* 3 A 275).

572. 2 Kgs 25.7,11–12,26.

573. The prophets are Ezekiel, Nahum, Daniel, Haggai, Zechariah and (the Herald) Malachi; the twelve are the "Minor Prophets" from Hosea to Malachi; Darius I reigned 521–486 B.C.

574. Neh 1.1 calls his father Hacaliah; Artaxerxes I was king of Persia 464–424 B.C.

to themselves, like the book of the Maccabees.[575] (3) During this captivity, Misael, Ananias, and Azarias refused to worship the idol, were thrown into a blazing furnace and rescued through the appearance of an angel.[576] (4) At that time, Daniel, because of a snake, was thrown into a den of lions, was nourished by the Providence of God through the hand of Ambakum, and was rescued six days later.[577] (5) Here also came the miracle of Jonas; Tobias, guided by the angel Raphael, took Sarah as his wife when the demon had destroyed her seven former husbands, and after his marriage, Tobias' father Tobit regained his sight.[578]

124(1) At this point Zorobabel overcame his antagonists by wisdom and succeeded in obtaining from Darius the restoration of Jerusalem in recompense for his work, and returned with Esdras to his homeland. (2) He was the instrument in the redemption of his people, and the recognition and restoration of the Scriptures inspired by God; he introduced the Passover of salvation, and put an end to marriages with foreigners.[579] (3) Further, Cyrus had proclaimed the restoration of the Hebrews to their country. The promise was fulfilled under Darius, and the Festival of Consecration was celebrated as well as the Festival of Tabernacles.[580] (4) The total period, including the Captivity, from the birth of Moses to the restoration of the people, comprises 1155 years six months ten days, and from David's reign 552[581] years in some versions, but more precisely 572 years six months ten days.

125(1) So from the Captivity in Babylon in the time of the Prophet Jeremias, the words of the prophet Daniel began to be fulfilled. They run as follows: (2) "Seventy weeks of years

575. Esther; Mardochaeus = Mordecai; the analogy with Maccabees (the account of the struggle against Greek oppression in the second century B.C.) is odd but not wrong.
576. Dan 3.
577. A story in the Greek text of Daniel, today printed in the Apocrypha.
578. Jonah; Tobit.
579. Zerubbabel; Ezra; on Darius I see nt. 573; see also Ezra 6.19, 10.17.
580. See Ezra 3.2–6, 6.16; the Festival of Tabernacles or Booths (Succoth) was a pilgrimage festival commemorating the period after the Exodus and celebrating the grape harvest.
581. With Lowth, correcting the MS 300.

have been set aside for your people and for the holy city to
complete their transgression, to put the final seal on their sins,
to wipe out their iniquities, to atone, to bring an eternal righteousness, to affix the seal to vision and prophet, to anoint the
Holy of Holies. (3) You are to know and understand that from
the utterance of a word of response, an order for the building
of Jerusalem to the coming of an anointed leader, there will
be seven weeks and sixty-two weeks; you will turn again, and
street and wall shall be rebuilt, and the times will be frustrat-
ing. (4) After the sixty-two weeks, an anointed one will be
slaughtered; the judgment is not with him. The judgment,
together with the commander who comes, will destroy the city
and holy place. They will be overwhelmed in a flood, and this
will go on until the end of a war whose end is determined by
annihilation. (5) A single week will make a strong agreement
with many peoples. For half of that week sacrifices and libations will be stopped, and the abomination of desolation shall
rest upon the sanctuary, and everything, absolutely everything, shall be given over to desolation until the time is fulfilled. (6) In the middle of the week, the incense of sacrifice
shall come to an end, until the total destruction of the wing
of the altar. It will be a vigorously organized process of annihilation."[582]

126(1) It is clear that the temple was built in seven weeks:
it is so written in Esdras.[583] In this way, it was an anointed
king who came into a position of leadership among the Jews
when the seven weeks were up in Jerusalem. In the sixty-two
weeks the whole of Judaea was at peace and free from wars,
(2) and our Lord, the Anointed One,[584] "holy of holies," came
and fulfilled "the vision and the prophet," and was anointed
in the flesh by the Spirit of the Father himself in the course
of "these sixty-two weeks," as the prophet said. (3) As for the
"one single week," the reign of Nero took up half, and set up
the "abomination" in the holy city of Jerusalem, and in the

582. Dan 9.24–7, a corrupt and difficult passage.
583. Ezra 6.15 gives the date of completion but not the period of building.
584. The Anointed One = Messiah = Christ: here perhaps the High
Priest Onias III.

"half-week" he was taken away, as were Otho, Galba and Vitellius, and Vespasian secured the power and destroyed Jerusalem and laid the holy place desolate. To anyone capable of understanding, it is clear that this is so, just as the prophet has said.[585]

127(1) So, when the eleventh year was completed, at the beginning of the following year, when Joachim was on the throne, the Captivity in Babylon came about at the hands of King Nabuchodonosor in the seventh year of his reign over the Assyrians, and the second year of Vaphris' rule in Egypt. Philip was senior magistrate at Athens. It was the first year of the forty-eighth Olympiad.[586] (2) The Captivity lasted seventy years and ended in the second year of the reign of Darius, son of Hystaspes, over Persia, Assyria, and Egypt. In his reign, as I have already said, prophecy was coming from Angaeus, Zacharias, and one of the Twelve, the Herald. The high priest was Jesus, son of Josedek.[587] (3) Darius was the king who put an end to the power of the Magi, as Herodotus says.[588] It was also in the second year of his reign that Zorobabel, Salathiel's son, was sent to raise and make beautiful the Temple in Jerusalem.

128(1) So here is the full chronology of the kings of Persia: Cyrus ruled for thirty years; Cambyses for nineteen; Darius for forty-six; Xerxes for twenty-six; Artaxerxes for forty-one; Darius for eight; Artaxerxes for forty-two; Ochus for eight; Arses for three. . . .[589] (2) This makes a total of 235 years for

585. Nero (reigned A.D. 54–68) saw the start of the Jewish War; but the reference to the abomination is a confusion with Caligula. On his death the empire fell into chaos, and Galba, Otho, and Vitellius (in that order) were briefly on the throne until Vespasian established a new dynasty, confirmed by the sack of Jerusalem in 70 A.D. The prophecies in Daniel have continually evoked fresh interpretations.

586. I.e., 588 B.C., not quite right (see nt. 570); Vaphris or Apries (see Herodotus 2.161) or Hophra (see Jer 44.30) was Pharaoh 588–568 B.C.; Philip is otherwise unknown.

587. See nt. 573. Ezra 3.2 calls the high priest Jeshua (the same name), son of Jozadak.

588. Herodotus 3.79.

589. There must be a lacuna, as the sums do not match; we need Darius III, six, and Alexander, six.

the kings of Persia. Alexander of Macedon supplanted this last Darius and began to reign for the years stated. (3) Similarly, the chronology of the Macedonian kings runs: Alexander ruled for eighteen years; Ptolemy, son of Lagus, for forty; Ptolemy Philadelphus for twenty-seven; Euergetes for twenty-five; Philopator for seventeen; Epiphanes for twenty-four, (4) succeeded by Philometor who ruled for thirty-five; followed by Phryscon for twenty-nine; Lathurus for thirty-six; and the one named Dionysus for twenty-nine years.[590]

129(1) After all these, Cleopatra ruled for twenty-two years; after her, the reign of her children lasted eighteen days.[591] (2) So the periods of the Macedonian kings add up in the same way to 312 years eighteen days. (3) So we can demonstrate that the prophets contemporary with Darius, son to Hystaspes, in the second year of his reign were Angaeus, Zacharias, and one of the Twelve known as the Herald. They were prophesying in the first year of the forty-eighth Olympiad, and were consequently further in the past than Pythagoras, who is placed in the sixty-second Olympiad, and the oldest of the Greek sages, Thales, who was born somewhere around the fiftieth.[592] (4) Those who share the title of sage with Thales were his contemporaries, as Andron says in the *Tripod*. Heraclitus was certainly posterior to Pythagoras as he mentions him in his treatise.[593]

130(1) From this it cannot be denied that the first Olympiad (407 years after the Trojan War, as we have shown) must be well before the age of the prophets of whom I have been speaking as well as the so-called Seven Sages. (2) So it is quite easy to see at a glance that Solomon (a contemporary of Me-

590. They were all called Ptolemy, and rulers of Egypt (not Macedonia), although they were certainly of Macedonian blood; Cleopatra (sometimes claimed as African) was a Greek.

591. The remarkable Cleopatra VII (69–30 B.C.) was lover of Julius Caesar and wife to Mark Antony; the children were Alexander Helios and Cleopatra Selene.

592. This gives 532–529 B.C. for Pythagoras (see nt. 306) and 580–577 B.C. for Thales (see nt. 305).

593. Andron of Ephesus (c. 400 B.C.), see *FHG* 2.347; cf. Diogenes Laertius 1.30): the title comes from a prize offered to the wisest.

nelaus, and therefore the Trojan War) was many years anterior to the Greek Sages. In what has gone before, we have shown how many more years Moses goes back than Solomon. (3) Alexander, called Polyhistor, in his treatise *On the Jews* included letters from Solomon to Vaphris, king of Egypt, and to the king of Tyre in Phoenicia, and letters from them to Solomon. These show that Vaphris sent 80,000 men to construct the Temple, and the other king a further 80,000 with an architect from Tyre, whose mother was a Jewess of the line of David. His name is recorded in the book as Hyperon.[594]

The Most Ancient of the Writers of Greece

131(1) Onomacritus of Athens, the reputed author of the poems attributed to Orpheus, is to be found in the reign of the Pisistratides *circa* the fiftieth Olympiad.[595] (2) Orpheus sailed with Heracles and was a pupil of Musaeus.[596] Amphion lived two generations before the Trojan War. Demodocus and Phemius were famous lyre singers after the Trojan War (one among the Phaeacians, the other with the suitors).[597] (3) It is said that the oracles attributed to Musaeus were composed by Onomacritus, Orpheus' *Mixing-Bowl* by Zopyrus of Heraclea, the *Descent to Hades* by Prodicus of Samos.[598] (4) Ion of Chios in his *Triads* records that Pythagoras attributed some of his work to Orpheus.[599] (5) Epigenes in his work *On Poetry Attributed to Orpheus* says that the *Descent to Hades* and the *Sacred*

594. On Alexander Polyhistor see nt. 329; the king of Tyre is Hiram; the letters and their contents are of course inauthentic; Vaphris (see nt. 586), is of a different era.

595. I.e., 580–577 B.C.; Onomacritus (fourth century B.C.) was an Athenian poet; on Orpheus see nt. 278; Pisistratus was an Athenian dictator 561–556 B.C., 546–527 B.C. who established a cultural court.

596. Heracles sailed on the *Argo*; on Musaeus see nt. 497; some editors emend "pupil" to "teacher," but Clement is capable of error.

597. On Amphion see nt. 515; on Demodocus see Homer, *Odyssey* 8.54 etc.; on Phemius see Homer, *Odyssey* 1.154 etc.

598. Of Zopyrus of Heraclea not much is known; see Kern, *Orphica* 179, 189, 222–3; Prodicus of Samos is otherwise unknown, but see Kern, *Orphica* 200, 222.

599. Ion of Chios (c. 490–422 B.C.) was a tragic poet and a man of letters prominent in Athens; there are similarities between Pythagorean and Orphic thought.

Doctrine are works of the Pythagorean Cercops and the *Robe* and the *Works of Nature,* writings of Brontinus.[600] (6) Yes, and some people place Terpander among the older writers. Hellanicus records his birth at the time of Midas, but Phanias puts Lesches of Lesbos before Terpander and later than Archilochus, and says that Lesches competed victoriously against Arctinus.[601] (7) Xanthus of Lydia records the foundation of Thasos *circa* the eighteenth Olympiad (Dionysius says the fifteenth). It is clear from this that Archilochus was already known after the twentieth. At any rate, he records the destruction of Magnesia as recent.[602] (8) Simonides is traditionally a contemporary of Archilochus, Callinus not much older, since he mentions Magnesia as flourishing, whereas Archilochus speaks of it as wiped out. Eumelus of Corinth must have been older to have met Archias, founder of Syracuse.[603]

132(1) I have been particularly keen to say all this because people place the poets of the epic cycles among the oldest.[604] Traditionally, the Greeks had plenty of oracle-mongers, like those called Bacis, one from Boeotia, and another from Ar-

600. Epigenes was a grammarian of the Hellenistic period; Cercops was a Pythagorean poet of whom little is known; Brontinus or Brotinus of Metapontum was the father or husband of the Pythagorean Theano (see Kirk-Raven-Schofield, *Presocratic Philosophers,* 220).

601. Terpander (c. 650 B.C.) was a leading musician and poet from Lesbos; on Hellanicus see nt. 340; Midas was the historical king of Phrygia 738–696 B.C. to whom legends of wealth accrued; Phanias is not known but was perhaps a poet who is also called a grammarian (see the *Palatine Anthology* 17.537); Lesches of Mytilene (seventh century B.C.) was an epic poet, to whom the *Little Iliad* is attributed; on Archilochus see nt. 4; Arctinus of Miletus (eighth century B.C.) was an epic poet.

602. Xanthus of Lydia (fifth century B.C.) was a romantic historian of Lydia; Thasos was an island of the north Aegean, colonized from Paros c. 680 B.C.; Dionysius is unidentified among the hundreds of that name; Magnesia on the Maeander was a city of Asia Minor destroyed by the Cimmerians and rebuilt; the dates are 18th, 708–705 B.C.; 15th, 720–717 B.C.; 20th, 700–697 B.C.

603. Simonides (c. 556–468 B.C.) from Ceos was a leading lyric and elegiac poet, not a contemporary of Archilochus; Callimachus of Ephesus (seventh century B.C.) was an elegiac poet; Eumelus (c. 725 B.C.) was an aristocratic epic poet from Corinth; Archias (c. 734 B.C.) was a noble Corinthian emigrant.

604. This is, of course, right: bardic traditions of oral poetry antedate most other forms.

cadia, who offered many people many predictions.[605] (2) Pisistratus owed the strong power of his dictatorship to the advice of Amphilytus, who showed him the right moment to step in.[606] (3) This is to say nothing on Cometes of Crete, Cinyras of Cyprus, Admetus of Thessaly, Aristaeus of Cyrene, Amphiaraus of Athens, Timoxenus of Corcyra, Demaenetus of Phocaea, Epigenes of Thespiae, Nicias of Carystus, Ariston of Thessaly, Dionysius of Carthage, Cleophon of Corinth, Hippo (Cheiron's daughter), Boio, Manto, all the Sibyls (of Samos, Colophon, Cumae, Erythrae, Macedon, Thessaly, Thesprotia, as well as Phyto and Taraxandra), as well as Calchas and Mopsus (the elder, since he sailed with the Argonauts) during the Trojan War.[607]

133(1) It is said that Battus of Cyrene composed the work called the *Prophetic Power of Mopsus*. Dorotheus in volume one of his *Universal Encyclopaedia* records that Mopsus received instruction from a kingfisher and a raven.[608] (2) The great Pythagoras applied himself ceaselessly to acquiring knowledge of the future: so did Abaris the Hyperborean, Aristeas of Proconnesus, Epimenides of Crete (who moved to Sparta),

605. Bacis was a generic term for seers, misunderstood here as a proper name (see Herodotus 8.20).

606. On Pisistratus see nt. 595; Amphilytus was a seer from Acarnania (Herodotus 1.62) or Athens (Plato, *Theages* 124 D).

607. Cometes is not known for certain; Cinyras was a legendary king, musician, seer, and founder of the cult of Aphrodite; on Admetus see nt. 514; Aristaeus was a semi-divine figure, a guardian of flocks, who was linked with North Africa among other places; Amphiaraus was a legendary semi-divine hero from Argos, one of the Seven Against Thebes, who was swallowed up in the earth and venerated at Oropus; Timoxenus is not known; Demaenetus is not known, but it was a name of Asclepius; Epigenes is not known; Nicias is not known; Ariston is not known; Dionysius is not, I think, otherwise known; Cleophon is not known; on Hippo see nt. 347; Boio was a poetess from Delphi; Manto was a prophetess of Thebes, the daughter of Teiresias; on Sibyls see nt. 331: their *loci* include Aegean, Asia Minor, Italy, northern Greece, Epirus; the last two are proper names; Michelangelo used them in the Sistine Chapel. Calchas was a seer with the Greek army at Troy; Mopsus was a rival seer from Claros, but Mopsus the Argonaut was different.

608. Battus was the father of the poet Callimachus; several authors of the name Dorotheus are known so we cannot guess which wrote this; the book title was also used by Cicero's freedman Tiro (see Aulus Gellius 13.9), the kingfisher was a mourning bird whose child Apollo stole; the raven was sacred to Apollo.

Zoroaster the Mede, Empedocles of Acragas, Phormio of Sparta and, of course, Polyaratus of Thasos and Empedotimus of Syracuse and finally, above all, Socrates of Athens.[609] (3) He remarks in the *Theages*: "From childhood I have had by divine fate assigned to me a spiritual sign, in the form of a voice. When it occurs, it is to inhibit me from what I am intending to do, never to encourage me."[610] (4) Execestus, dictator of Phocis, wore two enchanted rings. He could tell the favorable moments for action by the sound of their contact. All the same, he died as the result of a treacherous assassination despite the warning sound, according to Aristotle in his *Constitution of Phocis*.[611]

134(1) Among the Egyptians also we find former human beings deified by human delusion: Hermes of Thebes, Asclepius of Memphis, and again in Thebes, Teiresias and Manto, as Euripides says. In Troy there are Helenus, Laocoön, and Oenone (daughter to Cebrenus).[612] (2) Tradition records Crius[613] (one of the children of Heracles) as a noteworthy seer, together with Iamus (founder of Iamidae) in Elis, and Polyidus in Argos and in Megara, who is mentioned in tragedy.[614] (3)

609. On Pythagoras see nt. 219; on Abaris see nt. 340; Aristeas of Proconnesus was a legendary shaman in Apollo's service; Epimenides was a religious teacher from Crete who attracted legendary accretions (see DK 3); on Zoroaster see nt. 328; Empedocles (c. 493–433 B.C.), philosophical pluralist, poet, and mystagogue, was from Acragas in Sicily (see DK 31); Phormio was associated with the Dioscuri; Polyaratus was not known; Empedotimus was a visionary appearing in a dialogue by Heraclides Ponticus; Socrates (469–399 B.C.) was a charismatic Athenian who raised ethical issues and had a profound influence.

610. Plato, *Theages* 128 D.

611. Execestus is not known (see Aristotle, fr. 599 R); Aristotle (384–322 B.C.) with his students made a collection of constitutional histories, of which the one on Athens survives.

612. The Greek gods Hermes and Asclepius were identified with the Egyptian Thoth and his son: a dialog between them on God, man, and the universe survives in the late mystical Hermetic literature; Teiresias was a blind seer of Thebes who became both man and woman; on Manto see nt. 607; Helenus was a Trojan prince, the son of Priam and a prophet (see Vergil, *Aeneid* 3.294); Laocoön was a Trojan prince and priest, who denounced the wooden horse; Oenone was the daughter of a river god, the wife of Paris.

613. Reading κριός with Schwartz for κρῆνος.

614. Crius, a seer, was the son of Theocles (see Pausanias 3.13.3); Clement

Is there need to extend the list to Telemus (seer to the Cyclopes, who prophesied to Polyphemus the episodes associated with Odysseus' wanderings), or Onomacritus at Athens, or Amphiaraus, who was traditionally one generation before the capture of Troy and joined with the Seven in their expedition against Thebes, or Theoclymenus in Cephallenia, or Telmessus in Caria, or Galeus in Sicily?[615] (4) We could adduce others in addition to these: Idmon (who accompanied the Argonauts), Phemonoe at Delphi, Mopsus (son of Apollo and Manto) in Pamphylia and Cilicia, Amphilochus (son to Amphiaraus) in Cilicia, Alcmaeon in Acarnania, Anius on Delos, Aristandrus of Telmessus (an associate of Alexander). Philochorus in volume one of his work *On Divination* records the fact that Orpheus was a seer.[616]

135(1) Theopompus, Ephorus and Timaeus write of a seer named Orthagoras. So too Pythocles of Samos in volume four of his *History of Italy* names Caius Julius Nepos.[617] (2) But "all these robbers and brigands" (in the words of Scripture)[618] made most of their forecasts on the basis of intelligent obser-

---

has read carelessly; Iamus was a legendary son of Apollo and Evadne, ancestor of the Iamidae, prophets of Olympia; Polyidus was a seer of Corinth who found Glaucus' body about whom Sophocles and Euripides wrote lost plays.

615. Telemus was the prophet who told the Cyclops that Odysseus would blind him (see Homer, *Odyssey* 9.507); on Onomacritus see nt. 595; on Amphiaraus see nt. 607; Theoclymenus was a descendant of Melampus, seer and murderer (see Homer, *Odyssey* 15.256 etc.); Telmessus is not known, but there may be some confusion with the town: also Apollo was called Telmisseus; Galeus was the son of Apollo and the Hyperborean Themisto, ancestor of Sicilian seers.

616. *Idmon*, 'the knowing one,' was a seer with the Argonauts (see Apolloniaus Rhodes 1.139); on Phemonoe see nt. 516; on Mopsus see nt. 607; Amphilochus was the brother of Alcmaeon, a seer at Troy (although not in Homer), and a temple founder; Alcmaeon was a legendary avenger of his father on his mother Eriphyle, a subject of lost tragedies; Anius was a mythical king of Delos and priest of Apollo; Aristandrus was a seer in the court of Alexander the Great; on Philochorus see nt. 546; on Orpheus see nt. 278.

617. On Theopompus see nt. 553; Ephorus of Cyme (fourth century B.C.) was an author of a universal history; on Timaeus see nt. 4; Orthagoras was also called Satyrus (see Plutarch, *The Life of Timoleon* 4); Pythocles of unknown date was the author of *History of Italy, Concord*, and *Agriculture* (see *FGrH* 3 C 833); C Julius Nepos is not known, but C. Oppius Severus (second-century A.D.) a senator, was named.

618. John 10.8.

vation and guesswork, just like the doctors who set up as diviners on the basis of physiognomy. Some were activated by spiritual powers or brought to ecstasy by water, inhalation, or by a quality of air. (3) By contrast, among the Hebrews the prophets spoke by the power and inspiration of God. Before the Law there was Adam who used a power of prophecy over the woman and over the naming of animals; Noah, preaching repentance; Abraham, Isaac, and Jacob offering a clear foreshadowing of a large number of events future or imminent.[619] (4) With the Law come Moses and Aaron. Prophets after their time were: Jesus the[620] son of Naue, Samuel, Gad, Nathan, Achias, Samaias, Iu, Elias, Michaias, Abdiu, Elissaeus, Abdadonai, Amos, Esaias, Osee, Jonas, Joel, Jeremias, Sophonias, Buzi, Iezekiel, Urias, Ambakum, Nahum, Daniel, Misai, the author of the *Song of Blessings*, Angaeus, Zacharias, and the one of the Twelve called the Herald.[621]

136(1) This makes thirty-five prophets in all. Among the women (there were prophetesses as well) were Sarah, Rebecca, Miriam, Deborah and Olda.[622] (2) Then, at much the same time, John prophesied about the baptism of salvation, and after the birth of Christ, Anna and Simeon. Zacharias, John's father, is recorded in the Gospels as being a prophet before his son.[623] (3) So now we are going to put together Greek chronology, starting from Moses. From the birth of Moses to the Exodus of the Jews from Egypt was eighty years, followed by another forty up to his death. The Exodus took place in the time of Inachus since Moses left Egypt more than 345

619. On Adam see Gen 2.19–20,23; Noah is not in Genesis, but see 2 Pet 2.5; Abraham was called a prophet (Gen 20.7), but although God gives him foreknowledge, he does not make predictions; so too Isaac and Jacob.

620. Joshua, reading ⟨ὁ⟩ with Wilamowitz.

621. See the fuller historical account above with notes. But the list is not quite identical, which suggests that Clement is using a different handbook; the *Song of Blessings*, reading εὐλογισμούς with Stählin for συλλογισμούς.

622. Sarah was Abraham's wife; Rebecca was Isaac's wife; Miriam was Moses' sister; on Deborah see Judg 4.4; on Huldah see 2 Kgs 22.14; some editors mark a lacuna on the assumption that Clement would include Elizabeth and Mary, especially in the light of the next words.

623. Mark 1.4–8; Luke 2.25–38; Luke 1.67–79.

years before the Sothiac Cycle.[624] (4) From Moses' taking up command (i.e. from Inachus) to Deucalion's flood (I mean the second deluge) and the great fire caused by Phaethon which took place in the time of Crotopus adds up to eight[625] generations; three generations make up a century.[626] (5) From the flood to the great fire of Ida, the discovery of metal, and the Dactyls of Ida, seventy-three years according to Thrasyllus. From the great fire of Ida to the rape of Ganymede, sixty-five years.[627]

137(1) From there to the expedition of Perseus, the time also when Glaucus founded the Isthmian Games in honor of Melicertes, fifteen years. From the expedition of Perseus to the foundation of Troy, thirty-four years. From there to the sailing of *Argo*, sixty-four years.[628] (2) From there to Theseus and the Minotaur, thirty-two years; then to the Seven Against Thebes, ten years; to the establishment of the Olympic Games by Heracles in honor of Pelops, three years; to the expedition of the Amazons against Athens and the rape of Helen by Theseus, nine years.[629] (3) From there to the apotheosis of

624. Sothis is our Sirius. The cycles, approximately 1460 years, began when the heliacal rising of Sothis coincided with the start of the civil year: 4231 B.C., c. 2775 B.C., c. 1320 B.C.

625. Christ's emendation of the MS 40 (η´ for μ´).

626. On the date of Moses see nt. 480; on Deucalion see nt. 484; on Phaethon see nt. 492; on Crotopus see nt. 492.

627. The Great Fire of Ida: the mountains in Phrygia and Crete were associated with the discovery of iron working, perhaps originally through a forest fire (see Lucretius, *On the Nature of Things* 5.1241–4; Seneca, *Epistles* 90.12; Athenaeus, 6.233 D–E of Alps); on Dactyls see nt. 344; Thrasyllus is not otherwise known (see *FGrH* 2 B 253); Ganymede was a handsome prince of Troy who was kidnapped by Zeus to be cupbearer on Olympus: the word *catamite* is derived from him.

628. On Perseus see nt. 497; Glaucus was the son of Sisyphus, who is more usually the founder; the Isthmian Games were contests at Corinth in honor of Poseidon to commemorate Melicertes; Melicertes was thrown into the sea by his mother Ino, deified as Palaemon; on the *Argo* see nt. 503.

629. On Theseus see nt. 498; the Minotaur was a bull-man, the son of Pasiphae, queen of Crete, who was hidden in a labyrinth and killed by Theseus; on the Seven Against Thebes see nt. 607; the Olympic Games start with a firm date of 776 B.C.; on Pelops see nt. 497; Amazons were female warriors on the borders of the known world who besieged Theseus in Athens, who, nonetheless, repelled them and captured Hippolyte; on the abduction of Helen as a child see Plutarch, *The Life of Theseus* 31.

Heracles, eleven years; then to the abduction of Helen by Alexander, four years. Then to the capture of Troy, twenty years.[630] (4) From the capture of Troy to the arrival of Aeneas and the founding of Lavinium, ten years; and to the reign of Ascanius, a further eight; to the return of the children of Heracles, sixty-one; to the Olympiad of Iphitus, 338 years.[631]

138(1) Eratosthenes reckons the chronology as follows. From the capture of Troy to the return of the children of Heracles, eighty years. From there to the founding of Ionia, sixty years. Then, in order, to the acceptance of responsibility by Lycurgus, 159 years.[632] (2) Then to the[633] initial year of the first Olympiad, 108 years. From that Olympiad to Xerxes' sea expedition, 297 years; from there to the start of the Peloponnesian war, forty-eight years;[634] (3) then to the defeat and dissolution of the Athenians, twenty-seven years; and to the battle of Leuctra, thirty-four years; thereafter to the death of Philip, thirty-five years; after that to the death of Alexander, twelve years.[635] (4) Again, from the first Olympiad to the foundation of Rome is estimated by some at twenty-four years. From there to the end of the monarchy,[636] when[637] consuls were established, 243 years, and from the expulsion[638] of the kings to the death of Alexander, 186 years.[639]

---

630. Inserted by Müller; the apotheosis of Heracles was on Mt. Oeta; Alexander or Paris, prince of Troy, who stole Helen from Menelaus; 732 B.C. is far too late for the capture of Troy.

631. Aeneas was the Trojan prince who migrated to Italy and became ancestor of the Romans; Ascanius was his son, otherwise Iulus; the Dorians made a legend of the return of the children of Heracles for their own conquest of the Peloponnese; Iphitus was a restorer of the Olympic games (see Pausanius 5.4.5).

632. On Eratosthenes of Cyrene see nt. 385; on Lycurgus see nt. 388.

633. Reading ⟨τὸ⟩ with Jacoby.

634. Xerxes, king of Persia, came against Greece in 480 B.C. (not 479 B.C.): the Peloponnesian War which divided Greece began in 431.

635. The defeat of Athens was in the battle of 404 B.C.; that of Leuctra (between Thebes and Sparta) in 371 B.C.; Philip II of Macedon died in 336 B.C.; Alexander III the Great died in 323 B.C.

636. Reading Βασιλέων with Scaliger for Βαβυλῶνος.

637. Reading ὅτε with Bywater before the phrase for ἐπὶ after it.

638. Reading ἐλάσεως with Bywater for ἁλώσεως.

639. For the foundation of Rome there are various traditional dates including 753 B.C.; for the end of the monarchy 509 B.C.; and for the death of Alexander 323 B.C.

139(1) From there to Augustus' victory and Antony's suicide at Alexandria, when[640] Augustus was consul for the fourth time, 294 years.[641] (2) From this point to the establishment of games in Rome by Domitian, 114 years; and from the first of these games to the death of Commodus, 111 years.[642] (3) Some people reckon from Cecrops to Alexander of Macedon 1228 years;[643] from Demophon 850,[644] and from the fall of Troy to the return of the children of Heracles, 120 or 180 years. (4) From then to the date when Euaenetus was magistrate (the date when Alexander crossed into Asia), 715 years according to Phanias, 735 according to Ephorus, 820 according to Timaeus and Cleitarchus, 770[645] according to Eratosthenes. Duris allows 1000 years from the fall of Troy to Alexander's invasion of Asia.[646] (5) From there to Hegesias[647] holding office at Athens (the year of Alexander's death), eleven years. From there to the reign of Germanicus Claudius Caesar, 365 years. From that period, the number of years to the death of Commodus is clear.[648]

140(1) After Greek history, we have to take evidence from non-Greek[649] chronologies in accordance with their major divisions. (2) From Adam to the Flood comprises 2148 years four days; from Shem to Abraham, 1250 years; from Isaac to the grant of the promised inheritance, 616 years. (3) Then

---

640. Reading ⟨ὅτε⟩ with Lowth.

641. He was suffect consul in 43 B.C., consul in 33 B.C., and 30–23 B.C. Antony's suicide however was in 30 B.C.

642. Domitian (ruled A.D. 81–96) enjoyed *ludi* (Suetonius, *Domitian* 4). He completed the Colosseum, dedicated by Titus in A.D. 80, and celebrated the *ludi saeculares* in A.D. 87; Commodus (A.D. 161–192), worthless son and heir to Marcus Aurelius, was emperor A.D. 180–192.

643. With Stählin for MS 1828.

644. With Stählin for MS 1250.

645. With Müller for MS 774.

646. Euaenetus was an Athenian archon 335–4 B.C. and magistrate who gave a dating structure; on Phanias see *FHG* 2.294; on Ephorus see nt. 617; on Timaeus see nt. 4; Cleitarchus was a historian from Alexandria (see *FGrH* 2 B 137); on Eratosthenes see nt. 385; Duris was a historian from Samos (see *FGrH* 2 A 76).

647. With Potter for MS Euaenetus.

648. Hegesias was an Athenian archon 342–3 B.C.; Claudius was emperor A.D. 41–54, a slightly unexpected point of reference.

649. Reading ⟨βαρ⟩βάρους with Victorius.

from the Judges to Samuel, 463 years seven months. (4) After the Judges 572 years six months ten days of monarchy. (5) After this period, 235 years of Persian monarchy, and then 312 years eighteen days of Macedonian monarchy up to the removal of Antony. (6) After that period, the Roman empire to the death of Commodus, 222 years. (7) To go back again, from the seventy-year-long captivity and the restoration of the people to the land of their fathers to the captivity under Vespasian comprises 410 years, finally from Vespasian to the death of Commodus is found on investigation to be 121 years six months twenty-four days.[650]

141(1) Demetrius[651] in his book *On the Kings of Judaea* says that the tribes of Judah, Benjamin, and Levi were not taken captive by Senacherim,[652] and moreover, from that captivity when Nabuchodonosor deported them from Jerusalem, the period was 128 years six months. (2) From the time when the ten tribes were taken as prisoners from Samaria to Ptolemy IV, 573 years nine months, and from the deportation from Jerusalem, 338 years three months. (3) Philo too has written of the kings of Judaea but his figures are at variance with those of Demetrius.[653] (4) Again, Eupolemus in a work of similar scope says that the total number of years from Adam to the fifth year of king Demetrius (= the twelfth year of Ptolemy's reign in Egypt) comes to 5149 years.[654] (5) From the point when Moses led the Jews out of Egypt to the same point comprises in all 1580 years.[655] From that date to Cnaeus Domitius and Asinius holding the office of consul at Rome comprises 120 years.[656]

---

650. Vespasian (ruled A.D. 69–79) was responsible for the sack of Jerusalem in A.D. 70.

651. Demetrius (third century B.C.) was a Hellenistic Jew and historian of the Jews under Ptolemy IV.

652. Sennacherib was an Assyrian ruler 705–681 B.C.; in the Bible the Assyrian deportations are earlier (2 Kgs 17.6, 18.11).

653. Philo (c. 30 B.C.–A.D. 45) was a Greek Jewish philosopher and writer.

654. Eupolemus was a historian of Judaea (see *FGrH* 3 C 723); Demetrius I (336–283 B.C.) became king in Macedon in 294 B.C. Ptolemy I (c. 367–283 B.C.) became king in 304 B.C.

655. With Clinton for MS 2580.

656. I.e., 40 B.C., from when Herod the Great dated his reign; Asinius

142(1) Ephorus and a lot of other historians say that there are seventy-five nations and languages, following the words of Moses: "All the souls of Jacob's house who went down to Egypt numbered seventy-five."[657] (2) But by a correct calculation there seem to be seventy-five natural dialects (as our Scriptures record) and very many others emerging from the synthesis of two, three or more dialects. (3) A dialect is a form of speech which shows the peculiar characteristic of a particular place, or a form of speech which shows a peculiar or common ethnic characteristic. (4) The Greeks say that they have five dialects: Attic, Ionic, Doric, Aeolic, and the fifth the *koinē*; foreign languages are impossible to grasp; they are not even dialects, but are to be called tongues.[658]

143(1) Plato assigns a kind of dialect to the gods, taking his evidence particularly from dreams and oracles, and especially from those possessed by spirits who speak no known language or dialect but that of the spiritual beings which possess them.[659] (2) He thinks that irrational animals also have dialects, comprehensible to those of the same species. (3) Certainly if an elephant falls into a marsh and cries out, another arrives, surveys the whole scene, retraces his steps, and shortly after brings with him a herd of elephants and rescues the one who has had the accident. (4) They say too that in Africa[660] a scorpion which fails to sting a human goes away and comes back with several others. These then fasten on to one another like a chain, and in this way make an effort to succeed in their design. Irrational animals do not, I think, use some imperceptible movement; they do not communicate by gesture; they have, I believe, a language of their own. (5) Some people say

Pollio, a great patron, had Jewish connections: we know of a Pharisee called Pollio.

657. Gen 46.27, but our texts give 70: see the next section which adds Joseph's two sons born in Egypt.

658. Attic was spoken in Attica, and is close to the Ionic of some islands and Asia Minor towns; Doric belongs to the Peloponnese and Magna Graecia, Aeolic to Lesbos; in the Hellenistic Age they developed a common (*koinē*) form of expression, which is the language of the *New Testament*.

659. Not in any surviving work of Plato.

660. Aelian, *On the Nature of Animals* 6.23.

that if a fish escapes in the very moment of being caught because the line breaks, no fish of the same species will be found at the same spot again that day. (6) The original ethnic dialects were non-Greek, but their words arose naturally, since human beings admit that prayers have greater power when uttered in a language other than Greek.[661] (7) Plato in the *Cratylus*, wanting to give an interpretation of "fire," calls it a foreign word; he gives evidence that the Phrygians use the same word with a slight modification.[662]

144(1) I fancy that it is no less important to introduce alongside these the chronology of the emperors of Rome to establish the date of the Savior's birth. (2) Augustus ruled for twenty-three years; Tiberius for twenty-one; Gaius for four; Claudius for fourteen; Nero for fourteen; Galba for one; Vespasian for ten; Titus for three; Domitian for fifteen; Nerva for one; Trajan for nineteen; Hadrian for twenty-one; Antoninus for twenty-three; the second Antonius and Commodus for thirty-two.[663] (3) The total from Augustus to the death[664] of Commodus, 222, from Adam to the death of Commodus, 5784 years two months twelve days. (4) Some people give the following account of Roman chronology: Gaius Julius Caesar three years four months six days; Augustus for forty-six years four months one day; then Tiberius for twenty-six years six months nineteen days; his successor Gaius Caesar for three years ten months ten days; Claudius for thirteen years eight months twenty-eight days; Nero for thirteen years eight months twenty-eight days; Galba for seven months six days; Otho for

661. That language is a natural phenomenon is an Epicurean view, although not on these grounds.

662. Plato, *Cratylus* 410 A.

663. Augustus may be from 29 B.C. (formal end to war) to A.D. 14; Tiberius from A.D. 14 to 37; Gaius (Caligula) from A.D. 37 to 41; Claudius from A.D. 41 to 54; Nero from A.D. 54 to 68; Galba from A.D. 68 to 69; Otho A.D. 69; Vitellius A.D. 69; Vespasian from A.D. 69 to 79; Titus from A.D. 79 to 81; Domitian from A.D. 81 to 96; Nerva from A.D. 96 to 98; Trajan from A.D. 98 to 117; Hadrian from A.D. 117 to 138; Antoninus Pius from A.D. 138 to 161; Marcus Aurelius Antoninus from A.D. 161 to 180; Commodus from A.D. 180 to 192; it is curious that some of the figures here and in the next section should be at fault.

664. Reading ⟨τελευτῆς⟩ with Usener.

five months one day; Vitellius for seven months one day; Vespasian for eleven years eleven months twenty-two days; Titus for two years two months; Domitian for fifteen years eight months five days; Nerva for one year four months ten days; Trajan for nineteen years seven months fifteen days; Hadrian for twenty years ten months twenty-eight days; Antoninus for twenty-two years three months seven days; Marcus Aurelius Antoninus for nineteen years eleven days; Commodus for twelve years nine months fourteen days. (5) So from Julius Caesar to the death of Commodus produces 236 years six months.[665] The sum total from Romulus the founder of Rome to the death of Commodus, 943 years six months.

145(1) Our Lord was born under Augustus in the twenty-eighth year, when they first gave authority for a census. (2) That this is true is written in the *Gospel of Luke*: "Under Tiberius Caesar in the fifteenth year the word of the Lord came to John, Zacharias' son," and again in the same gospel: "Jesus came to baptism at the age of thirty."[666] (3) That his preaching could not have lasted more than a year is written in the following passage: "He sent me to preach the year of the Lord's favor."[667] These are the words alike of prophet and gospel. (4) So fifteen years of Tiberius and fifteen of Augustus make up the thirty years leading towards the Passion.[668] (5) From the Passion to the disaster of Jerusalem occupied forty-two years and three months,[669] from the disaster of Jerusalem to the death of Commodus, 121 years[670] ten months and thirteen days. So from the Lord's birth to the death of Commodus comprises 194 years one month and thirteen days. (6) There

665. Mathematics was not his strong point: his figures (allowing a thirty-day month) add up to 235 years two days. The modern figure would be 235 years nine months.

666. Luke 3.1–3,23 is misquoted.

667. Luke 4.19 quoting Isa 61.1–2, but the year is the subject, not the duration, of the preaching.

668. There is no calculation of the ministry, which in John lasts about three years.

669. This suggests a date of A.D. 28 for the Crucifixion, which some people accept.

670. Correcting the MS figure for the total, and also Usener's, which does not add up.

are some people who are more meticulous about the Savior's nativity and adduce the day as well as the year, the twenty-fifth of Pachon in the twenty-eighth year of Augustus.[671]

146(1) The followers of Basilides also celebrate the day of his baptism, spending the previous night in readings.[672] (2) They place it in the fifteenth year of Tiberius Caesar on the fifteenth (or according to others the eleventh) of the month of Tubi.[673] (3) Making a precise calculation, there are some who place his Passion in the sixteenth year of Tiberius Caesar on the twenty-fifth of Phamenoth; others say the twenty-fifth of Pharmouthi, and others still place the Savior's Passion on the nineteenth of Pharmouthi.[674] (4) Further, some of them place his nativity on the twenty-fourth or twenty-fifth of Phar-mouthi.[675] (5) We have to make these extra additions to our chronology: I am referring to the number of days allusively referred to by Daniel from the desolation of Jerusalem.[676] . . . seven years eleven months of Vespasian.[677] Two years are added to the seventeen months and eight days of Otho, Galba, and Vitellius (6) making three years six months, which is the prophet Daniel's "half a week."[678] (7) He has said that there were 2300 days from the infliction of the abomination upon the holy city by Nero to its disastrous end.[679] (8) The following passage shows this in this way: "How long will the vision last, the abolition of the sacrifice and[680] the setting up of the sin

671. Pachon is the ninth Egyptian solar month (varying by our calendar from year to year) placing the birth on 20 May. The Armenian Church celebrated it on 6 January. The festival on 25 December dates from A.D. 336. There is no month in which the birth has not been placed.

672. Reading ⟨ἐν⟩ with Mayor; Basilides (second century A.D.) was a Syrian Gnostic who taught in Alexandria. He had an acute mind, and expounded the *via negativa*.

673. Tubi was the fifth Egyptian solar month.

674. Phamenoth was the seventh Egyptian solar month; Pharmouthi was the eighth Egyptian solar month.

675. 10 or 11 April.

676. Dan 9.27.

677. Something must be missing: Clement is fiddling frantically with his figures.

678. Very approximately!

679. See nt. 585.

680. Reading ⟨καὶ⟩ from Daniel, and ἐρημώσεως for ἐρημωθήσεται.

of desolation, how long will the power and the holy place be trampled down? And he answered, '2300 evenings and mornings and the holy place shall be destroyed.'"[681] (9) These 2300 days, then, make six years four months, half of which was in the grip of Nero's monarchy, making up half of the "week." The other half was taken up by Vespasian, together with Otho, Galba, and Vitellius. (10) This is why Daniel says, "Blessed is he who succeeds in coming to the 1335 days."[682] The war lasted that number of days before its conclusion.

147(1) This number is also revealed by the following verse understood like this: "From the time that the continuity of sacrifice is abrogated and the abomination of desolation set up is 1290 days."[683] (2) Flavius Josephus, the Jew, who compiled *Researches into Jewish History,* says in his chronology that from Moses to David is a period of 585 years, from David to the second year of Vespasian's reign 1179 years.[684] (3) Then from there to the tenth year of Antoninus, seventy-seven years, making 1883 from Moses to the tenth year of Antoninus.[685] (4) Others, counting from Inachus and Moses to the death of Commodus, have spoken of 1842 or 1921 years.[686] (5) In the *Gospel of Matthew* the genealogy from Abraham concludes in the Lord's mother Mary: "There are," he says, "fourteen generations from Abraham to David, fourteen generations from David to the deportation to Babylon (6) and similarly a further fourteen generations from the deportation to Babylon to Christ"—three mystical periods fulfilled by six sets of seven generations.[687]

---

681. Dan 8.13–14.   682. Dan 12.12.
683. Dan 12.11–12.

684. Flavius Josephus (c. A.D. 37–100) was the author of *Antiquities of the Jews* and *The Jewish War,* soldier in the war, and later pro-Roman; the second year of Vespasian (A.D. 70) was the year in which Jerusalem fell.

685. Even simple addition goes wrong: the figures total 1841 (curiously Caster gives a wrong figure).

686. With Bywater for MS 2842 and 2921.

687. Matt 1.17 somewhat loosely quoted. The genealogy in fact ends with Mary's husband Joseph. The number mysticism is important. Odd numbers have a special significance, and seven is important in Jewish and pagan religion. Two proximate numbers, even and odd, give special power, and 6 = 2 × 3, the first number (in ancient thought), and the first odd number.

22

The Septuagint Translation of the Scriptures

148(1) So much for chronology, the many different records of others, and my own exposition. It is said that the translation of the Scriptures, meaning the Law and the prophets, from Hebrew into Greek took place in the reign of Ptolemy Lagus or, according to others, Ptolemy called Philadelphus. The king showed the greatest enthusiasm for the undertaking, and Demetrius of Phalerum paid close attention to the whole business of the translation.[688] (2) The Macedonians were still in control of Asia when the king, in his ambition to adorn the Library he had founded in Alexandria with everything written, thought that the people of Jerusalem should translate their prophecies into Greek.[689]

149(1) They, being Macedonian subjects, chose from among their most reputed people seventy experts in the Scriptures who were familiar with the Greek language, and sent them to him with their sacred books. (2) Each translated every individual prophecy separately. When they were compared, all the translations agreed in both sense and diction! It was God's will to achieve a result for Greek ears.[690] (3) Nothing strange that the inspiration of the God who granted the original prophecy should direct the translation to make it a kind of Greek prophecy. In the captivity under[691] Nabuchodonosor, the Scriptures were destroyed. In the time of Artaxerxes, king

688. Ptolemy I Lagus (c. 367–283 B.C.) ruled Egypt from 323 B.C., as king from 304 B.C.; Ptolemy II Philadelphus (308–246 B.C.) ruled from 285 B.C.; Demetrius of Phalerum (c. 350–280 B.C.) was an Aristotelian philosopher and politician; the translation by seventy scholars, hence called *Septuagint* (LXX), attracted much legend.

689. Alexander's empire, after jockeying for power, split into a northern part ruled from Macedon, a southern part ruled from Egypt, and an eastern part ruled from Antioch: Palestine oscillated between the latter two; the Library founded by Ptolemy I with encouragement by Demetrius was huge, and is said to have reached 700,000 volumes.

690. The story is fantastic: note "ears" not "eyes," since all reading was aloud.

691. Reading ⟨ἐπὶ⟩ on the basis of Irenaeus, *Against Heresies* 3.21.2, to which this passage is indebted.

of Persia, the Levite and priest Esdras was inspired to a prophetic restoration of all the old documents.[692]

150(1) Aristobulus, in volume one of his *To Philometor,* wrote: "Plato too was a follower of our system of law, and it is obvious that he had spent a lot of time on each of its precepts. (2) There had been a translation by others before Demetrius, before the domination of Alexander or the Persians, recording the events concerning the exodus from Egypt of our fellow citizens the Jews, the realization of all that happened to them, the conquest of their own land, and the exposition of the whole system of law. (3) It is clear enough that the philosopher I mentioned, a man of wide learning, took a great deal from it, much as Pythagoras borrowed a great deal from us to form his own philosophic system."[693] (4) The Pythagorean philosopher Numenius wrote directly: "What is Plato but Moses speaking Greek?"[694] This Moses was a theologian and prophet and, in the eyes of some, an interpreter of sacred laws. (5) The actual Scriptures—and they merit our full confidence—record his birth, actions, and life. However, we too must speak of him as briefly[695] as may be.

23

The Life of Moses

151(1) So[696] Moses, originally Chaldaean by race, was born in Egypt; his ancestors had emigrated from Babylon to Egypt owing to a long period of famine. He was born in the seventh generation and brought up in the royal household. This is what happened to him. (2) The population of the Hebrews had grown enormously in Egypt. The king of the land feared that the numbers might lead to revolution. He gave orders

692. Probably referring to 1 Esdr 8.23, 9.39–41.

693. Aristobulus (second century B.C.) was an Alexandrian Jew interested in Greek philosophy.

694. Numenius (second century A.D.) was a Pythagorean of Apamea, fr. 9.

695. "Briefly" is not in the Greek, but must be restored in one of several possible phrases.

696. Reading ⟨οὖν⟩ with Stählin.

that when children were born to the Hebrews, they should
bring up the females (women being too weak for war) and kill
the males. He was suspicious of youth and strength. (3) Moses
was a child of noble birth, and his parents brought him up
for three whole months in secret. Their natural affection out-
weighed the tyrant's cruelty. Later on, they were afraid that
they might be executed with the child. They made a kind of
basket from the local papyrus, put the child in it, and left it
by the banks of the river where it was marshy. The child's
sister stood a little way off and watched what would happen.

152(1) Then the king's daughter, who had been barren for
a long time and longed for children, came to the river that
very day for washing and bathing, heard the child's howls,
gave orders for him to be brought to her, took pity on him,
and called for a nurse for him. (2) Then the child's sister ran
up, and said that she could produce a Hebrew woman who
had given birth not long before to be his nurse if the princess
approved. The princess assented and asked for the nurse. The
girl produced the child's mother to be his nurse as if she were
a stranger working for an agreed wage. (3) Then the princess
gave the child the name Moses, an etymological derivation
from the fact that she had rescued him from water into which
he had been put to die: the Egyptian word for water is *moü*.
In fact, they call anyone who dies by drowning Moses.[697]

153(1) So it is clear that previously at his circumcision, his
parents had given him a name and he was called Joachim.
According to the mystics, he had a third name in heaven after
his assumption—Melchi.[698] (2) When he came of age, he studied with the leading Egyptian savants and learned arithmetic,
geometry, rhythm, harmony, meter,[699] music, and symbolic
philosophy expressed in hieroglyphic script. Greeks in Egypt
taught him the rest of the normal educational curriculum, as
a royal child. So Philo says in his *Life of Moses*. (3) In addition,

697. Clement is drawing on Philo, *Life of Moses* 1.16–17; see also Exod
2.1–11, where the derivation is from Hebrew not Egyptian.

698. From the apocryphal *Assumption of Moses*.

699. Reading μετρικὴν from Philo for ἰατρικὴν, 'medicine' (see Philo, *Life
of Moses* 1.23).

he learned from Chaldaean and Egyptian teachers Assyrian script and knowledge of the heavenly bodies. This is why he is said in Acts "to have been educated in all the wisdom of the Egyptians."[700] (4) Eupolemus in his work *On the Kings of Judaea* says that Moses was the first sage and the first person to transmit to the Jews the science of writing, which passed from the Jews to the Phoenicians, and from the Phoenicians to the Greeks.[701] (5) When he reached the age of manhood[702] he developed his practical wisdom, being zealous for his national, ancestral educational traditions, to the point of striking down and killing an Egyptian who was unjustly attacking a Hebrew.[703]

154(1) The mystics say that he eliminated the Egyptian simply by speaking, as later in Acts Peter is said to have killed by his words those who had kept for themselves part of the price of the land and had told lies.[704] (2) Anyway Artapanus, in his treatise *On the Jews*, records that Moses was put in prison by Chenephres, king of Egypt, because he pleaded for the liberation of his people from Egypt. The prison opened in the night by God's will; he emerged, went to the palace, found the king asleep and awakened him.[705] (3) The king was shattered by what had happened and commanded Moses to tell the name of the God who had sent him. Moses stooped down and whispered in his ear. When the king heard, he fell down unable to speak. He was revived by Moses' power.

155(1) On Moses' education we shall have supporting evidence from Ezekiel the Jewish tragic poet in the play entitled *Exodus*, when he wrote the following passage for the character of Moses.[706]

700. Acts 7.22.
701. On Eupolemus see nt. 654; the Phoenicians reduced a syllabary to the initial consonants, simplifying at the cost of ambiguity; the Jews and Greeks took over from there: the Greeks by adding signs for vowels produced the first full alphabet.
702. Reading ἀνδρῶν from Philo for αὐτῶν.
703. Exod 2.11–15.
704. Acts 5.1–11.
705. Artapanus was a historian of Jews, known mainly from Eusebius (see *FGrH* 3 C 26); Chenephres was presumably Chephren, but he is Fourth Dynasty and far too early.
706. See R. G. Robertson, *Ezekiel the Tragedian: A New Translation and In-*

(2) Pharaoh the king has seen our race
    grown to great size, and organized against us
    many subtle plans, insulting the men
    in making bricks and heavy building-programs
    and fortifying[707] cities. Unfortunate people!
    Then he decreed that we, the Hebrew people,
    should throw our sons into the deep waters of the rivers.
(3) Then my mother who bore me hid me
    for three months, she used to tell me.
    She exposed me, in beautiful clothes,
    by the river's brim in a thick overgrown marsh.
(4) Mariam my sister watched from nearby.
    Then came the king's daughter there to cleanse
    her young body delicately in the waters.
    Straightaway she saw me, seized me, picked me up, and
    knew me for a Hebrew. My sister Mariam
    ran up to the princess and spoke these words:
    "Do you want me to find a nurse for the child
    from the Hebrews, without delay?" She encouraged[708] the girl
(5) who ran and told her mother, and she came quickly
    and took me[709] up in her arms, she my real mother.
    The king's daughter said: "Woman, breast-feed
    this boy, and I will pay your wages."
    She called my name Moses, because she
    had drawn me up from the bank of the flowing stream.
(6) When the time of infancy had passed me by,
    my mother took me to the princess' palace.
    She had first shared with me the whole story
    of my forefathers' line and the gifts of God.
(7) As long as I was still a boy,
    in royal upbringing and royal education
    the princess offered all, as if I were a child of her own body.[710]
    But when the full cycle of days had come,
    I went out from the royal palace.

---

troduction in J. H. Charlesworth, ed., *The Old Testament Pseudepigrapha* (New York, 1983), 2.803–819; and H. Jacobson, *The Exagoge of Ezekiel* (Cambridge U Press, 1983), pp. 36–37.

707. Reading πόλεων τε πύργοις for πόλεσί τε πύργους.
708. Reading ⟨ἐπ⟩έσπευσεν *metri causa* from Eusebius.
709. Reading ⟨μ'⟩ *metri causa* from Eusebius.
710. It is probably right to read ἑῶν from Eusebius, though ἕνα makes sense.

156(1) Then he tells the story of the fight between the Hebrew and the Egyptian, the burial of the Egyptian in the sand, and he speaks of the second fight[711] in these terms:

> (2) "Why are you hitting one weaker than you?"
> He said, "Who sent[712] you to be a judge over us?
> An umpire here? Are you going to kill me
> as you did the man yesterday?" I was afraid
> and said, "How did that get about?"

(3) He ran away from there and began shepherding flocks, an apprenticeship for leadership in the shepherding of people. Shepherding is a training for royalty for anyone who is going to have authority over the tamest of all flocks, the human, just as hunting is the natural training for warfare. God was leading him from there to the command of the Hebrews.

157(1) Then the Egyptians received repeated warnings and repeatedly failed to understand. The Hebrews became spectators of evils suffered by others while they remained unharmed, and learned clearly the power of God. (2) The Egyptians still refused to listen to and accept the full conclusions of God's power, fools unconvinced because of their folly, so at that time, in the familiar words, the fools came to know the facts.[713] Subsequently, the Hebrews in their exodus left, carrying a great deal of Egyptian spoil, not out of love of material goods as their detractors suggest (God forbade them even to covet the possessions of others) (3) but, in the first place, taking their proper pay for all the time of service they had given the Egyptians, and secondly, protecting themselves by a kind of retributive act against the money-changing Egyptians by carrying off spoil, since they had mistreated the Hebrews by enslaving them. (4) So, as anyone might speak of it as an act of war, they thought they were justified in carrying off their enemy's property by the law of conquest, stronger over weaker. (This was the cause of the war. The Hebrews came to the Egyptians as suppliants because of famine. The

711. Exod 2.13.
712. Reading ἀπέστειλε⟨ν⟩ *metri causa*.
713. Homer, *Iliad* 17.32, 20.198.

Egyptians enslaved the foreigners and forced them into service just like prisoners of war, not even paying them wages.) If on the other hand we think of them as at peace, then they simply took the spoil as wages from unwilling hands which had for a long time robbed them by failing to pay them.

24

Moses as General

158(1) So there is Moses—prophet, legislator, organizer, general, statesman, philosopher. We shall treat his prophetic gifts later, when we discuss prophecy.[714] Organization is a part of generalship, generalship part of the equipment of a king. Again, legislation is part of the equipment of a king; so is skill as a judge. (2) Part of the equipment of a king comes directly from God; it consists in following God and his holy Son, who accord to us the earth's good gifts, external goods, and complete blessedness. "Ask for great things," says Scripture, "and you will receive the small things in addition."[715] (3) There is a second aspect of kingly authority which follows the rational disposition coming from God and uses the spirited element of the soul for kingly rule. Heracles, king of Argos, and Alexander of Macedon were rulers of this sort.[716] (4) A third aspect aims singlemindedly at conquest and the reduction of enemies without any attention to directing the victory to good or evil purposes. The Persians practiced this in their expedition against Greece.[717] (5) The singleminded love of victory is characteristic of the spiritual element, which establishes autocracy simply for power's sake. Love of the high and noble is shown when the soul directs the spirit to the high and noble.

159(1) The fourth type of kingship is the worst of all; it regulates itself to follow the desires. Such was the monarchy

714. See *Stromateis* 4.2(2), 4.93(1), 5.88(4).

715. Matt 13.12, 25.29; Mark 4.25; Luke 8.18, 19.26 (see Resch, *Agrapha* 41).

716. On Heracles see nt. 501; on Alexander see nt. 635; Plato in the *Republic* divided his ruling class between those who are governed by wisdom—the rulers proper—and their auxiliaries, governed by the spirited element.

717. Under Xerxes in 480 B.C.

of Sardanapallus and of all who make their goal the greatest
possible gratification of their desires.[718] (2) Organizational
ability is the instrument of royal power whether winning its
victories by virtue or violence. But it varies according to the
nature and material of its object. (3) If it is a matter of weapons or living creatures engaged in combat, it is the soul and
intelligence that produce organization by means of instruments either living or lifeless. If we are talking of passions
within the soul which we overpower by virtue, then the organizing power rests with the faculty of reason. It sets its seal
on self-control and self-discipline combined with piety and on
true knowledge of the good combined with truth. It directs
the goal to reverence for God. (4) For those who practice[719]
virtue in this way, the organizing power is practical wisdom;
in its divine dimension, wisdom; in its human dimension,
statesmanship; and together, the quality of a king. (5) A king
is one who rules in accordance with law and knows how to
rule willing subjects. Such is the Lord, who attracts those who
through him have faith in him. (6) For God has handed over
everything to be subject to the authority of Christ our king
"that at the name of Jesus every knee should bend, the knee
of things in heaven, things on earth, and things under the
earth; and every tongue should confess that Jesus Christ is
Lord to the glory of God the Father."[720]

160(1) Skill as a general is contained in three forms: care
for safety, enterprise, and the combination of the two. Each
of these comprises three elements: operating by words, actions, or the simultaneous combination of the two. (2) It will
be possible to realize all this by persuasion or violence or unjust actions used in self-defense or just actions when circumstances allow, the use of false statements or true statements,
or a simultaneous use of some of these methods on the same
occasion. (3) The Greeks benefitted by taking all these and

718. Sardanapallus was the last legendary, luxurious king of Assyria; his
character does not correspond with the historical Sin-shar-ishkan but rather
to Plato's dictator or tyrant.
719. Reading χρωμένοις with Victorius for χρώμενοι.
720. Phil 2.10–11.

their individual uses from Moses. (4) To establish the pattern I will mention one or two examples of skill as a general. When Moses led the people out of Egypt, he suspected that the Egyptians would pursue him, so he left the short cut and turned aside to the desert and, for the most part, marched by night. (5) He had another practical aim in mind. The Hebrews would be educated through a long period of deep deprivation and disciplined patience to be in the habit of simply having faith in the existence of God.

161(1) This stratagem of Moses teaches us that before the appearance of danger we ought to survey advantageous courses along those lines. (2) In fact, it happened just as he suspected. The Egyptians did pursue him with horses and chariots, but were wiped out when the sea was suddenly divided and swamped them with their chariots and horses so that not a trace of them was left. (3) After that, following a column[721] of fire (which went before them to show the way), he led the Hebrews by night through the wilderness, exercising them in courage and endurance through laborious journeys as he transported them, so that after the experience of seeming dangers they might see clearly the richness of the land to which he was bringing them after their uphill journey.

162(1) Yes, and he routed and exterminated the enemies who had previously settled in that land by assailing them from the rough road in the desert—this showed the quality of his generalship. Capturing enemy territory is always a task for experienced generalship. (2) It was in careful consideration of this that Miltiades, the commander of the Athenians, defeated the Persians in the battle of Marathon.[722] He copied Moses as follows. He led the Athenians by night, marching through trackless terrain and leading the Persian scouts astray. Hippias, the renegade Athenian, was guiding the foreigners into Attica and captured the most likely points and put them under

721. Reading στύλῳ with Caster for στῦλος.
722. At Marathon in 490 B.C. the Athenians repulsed a punitive force from Persia. Miltiades was not commander-in-chief but was the grand strategist. There is not the slightest reason to suppose that he had ever heard of Moses.

guard, using his familiarity with the ground.[723] (3) So the task was to evade Hippias, which is why Miltiades had the sense to use trackless land and attack the Persians under Datis' command by night, and with his troops brought off the whole battle successfully.

163(1) Again, when Thrasybulus was leading back the exiles from Phyle, and wanting to do so unperceived, a column was his guide as he travelled away from the roads. (2) The restoration took place on a moonless night in bad weather. Thrasybulus saw a fire going in front of him. It led them in safety and left them near Munychia, where the altar to the Goddess who Brings Light now stands.[724] (3) The Greeks ought to learn from this to have confidence in our traditions, when they say that it really is possible for God Almighty to make a column of fire for the Hebrews to lead them by night, since the same column showed them the way too. (4) Further, an oracular writing says,

> Dionysus, god of joy, is a pillar to the Thebans.

That is taken from Hebrew history.[725] (5) Again, Euripides says in his *Antiope,*

> In the oxherds' room
> is a column of the god Euius with head covered in ivy.[726]

(6) The column shows the impossibility of making an image of God. In addition to showing this impossibility, the column of light reveals God's stable permanence and his unchanging light, which no form can catch.

164(1) The people of old set up pillars and honored them

723. Hippias was an ex-dictator in exile, hoping for restoration; Attica was the country around Athens.

724. Thrasybulus (d. 388 B.C.) was an Athenian democratic statesman who overthrew the Thirty Tyrants who had taken over Athens after her defeat in 404 B.C. His base was the frontier fortress of Phyle: his first goal was Munychia (the citadel of Peiraeus, the port); the Goddess who Brings Light was Artemis; the story is in Xenophon, *Hellenica* 2.4.7 (see Diodorus Siculus 14.33).

725. *Oracles,* fr. 207 H.

726. Euripides, fr. 263; *Euius* was the name of Dionysus/Bacchus, after the cry in his honor.

as representations of God before going into detail over the form of statues. (2) At any rate, the author of the *Phoronis* writes,

> Callithoe, who holds the keys for the Queen of Olympus,
> Hera of Argos, was the first to adorn
> with garlands and fillets the Queen's mighty pillar.[727]

(3) Further, the author of the *Story of Europē* records that the image of Apollo at Delphi was a pillar. These are his words:

> To suspend the tithe and the firstfruits in the god's honor
> from the sacred posts and lofty pillar.[728]

However, Apollo, mystically understood in terms of the absence of plurality, is the one and only God.[729] (4) Finally, this fire in the likeness of a column and the fire in the tree are symbols of the holy light which crosses from earth and runs up again to heaven by means of the Word, through which it is granted us to see with understanding.[730]

25

Plato's Laws Indebted to Moses

165(1) The philosopher Plato gained from the teachings of Moses material on his legislation. He criticized the constitutions of Minos and Lycurgus as looking no further than courage, but praised as superior the constitution directed to a single end and always directed to a single viewpoint.[731] He is in fact saying that it is more appropriate for us to philosophize

727. Fr. 4 K; reading ἐκόσμησε⟨ν⟩ *metri causa*; *Phoronis* is a lost epic about Phoroneus (see nt. 487); Callithoe was the first priestess of Hera of Argos.

728. *The Story of Europē* (see nt. 495) is another wide-ranging lost epic, attributed to Eumelus.

729. Apollo derives supposedly from *a* (negative) *polloi* (plural).

730. Exod 3.2; John 1.9, 9.5, 12.46; Clement has a complex wordplay between *dia batou*, the 'tree' or 'bush,' and *diabainontos*, the 'passage of the light,' and the wood (= the Cross) as something which catches and transmits fire.

731. Plato, *Laws* 1.626 A, 3.688 A, 4.705 D; on Lycurgus see nt. 388; on Minos see nt. 386; there is no reason to suppose that Plato had heard of Moses.

with power, solemnity, and practical sense, looking to the values of heaven and using without reserve the same opinion[732] on the same subjects. (2) Can you not see that his interpretation accords with the Law; that he is telling us to keep our eyes fixed on the unique God and to act righteously? (3) He is saying that there are two forms of political science: one has to do with law, the other with the politics after which it is named. When he speaks of the statesman in his book of that name, in the most authoritative sense he is referring to the Divine Craftsman,[733] and calls those who keep their eyes fixed on him, living in the active practice of righteousness combined with contemplation, statesmen as well.[734] (4) Political science, which has its name on equal terms to legal science, he divides into the high intelligence directing the universe, and particular organization, to which he applies the names order, fitness, and disciplined control, which is when rulers care for their subjects,[735] and subjects obey their rulers. This is the object towards the realization of which Moses' political practice was vigorously directed.

166(1) Further, Plato, benefitting from the knowledge that legal science has to do with the world of becoming,[736] and political science with fellowship and concord, added to the *Laws* the philosopher in the *Epinomis,* who knows the course of the whole process of becoming, under the influence of the planets.[737] He introduces in an appendix to the *Republic* another philosopher, named Timaeus, an astronomer contemplatively researching into the coordination of the movement of the heavenly bodies and their mutual relationship.[738] Then. . . .[739] (2) For contemplation is, I think, the goal alike of the statesman and of the person who lives in accordance with the Law.

---

732. Omitting καὶ with Mayor.   733. Plato, *Statesman* 307 B.
734. Plato, *Republic* 4.430 E.
735. Reading περιέπωσι τοὺς ἀρχομένους with Tengblad for πρέπωσι τοῖς ἀρχομένοις.
736. The material world as against the unchanging world of being.
737. Plato, *Epinomis* 977 B.
738. Plato, *Timaeus* 27 A. Timaeus is a Pythagorean from Locri, not otherwise known.
739. Lacuna.

At any rate, right-minded statesmanship is essential, but best of all is the practice of philosophy. (3) A person of intelligence would live in the direction of all his powers to true knowledge, keeping his life straight by the practice of goodness, turning his nose up at the opposite sort of behavior, pursuing studies which are directed to truth. (4) Law does not consist in things done in obedience to law, any more than sight consists in objects seen. Law does not consist in any judgment (certainly not in a pernicious judgment). Law is a judgment governed by excellence, and that means truth, and that means the discovery and attainment of reality, that which is. "He who is has sent me," says Moses.[740] (5) Some, no doubt following that excellent judgment, have defined law as right reason,[741] prescribing what is to be done and proscribing what is not.

26

The Greeks Confronted with the Law of Moses

167(1) So it is reasonable to say that the Law was given through Moses[742] and is a measure of what is just and unjust. We could authoritatively call the Law given by the Deity through Moses our duty.[743] At any rate, it leads us towards the divine. (2) Paul too says, "The Law was introduced because of offenses, until the promised offspring should appear."[744] Then, as if elaborating on the thought, he adds, "Before faith came, we were confined in prison under law"—clearly meaning by fear as a result of sins—"until the future revelation of faith. So the Law was our tutor escorting us to Christ, that we might be justified by faith."[745] (3) The true lawgiver is the one who makes the appropriate assignment to each part of the soul and its activities.[746] In a word Moses was law incarnate in that he was governed by the goodness of the Word.[747]

740. Exod 3.14.
741. On the Stoics see *SVF* 3.332.
742. John 1.17.
743. Clement plays on *theos* 'God,' and *thesmos*, 'ordinance.'
744. Gal 3.19.
745. Gal 3.23–24.
746. Plato, *Republic* 9.580 D ff.; Philo, *Life of Moses* 1.162.
747. Or "sound reason."

168(1) Anyway, he provided an excellent constitution—that is, a noble nurture for human beings on the basis of a shared society. He further put his hand to the science of verdicts, a branch of knowledge designed to put wrongs right for justice's sake. (2) Partner to this is the science of punishment, which consists in knowledge of the right proportion to be observed in punishing. Punishment is a method of setting the soul straight. (3) It is pretty well true to say that the whole educational practice of Moses was for those capable of becoming outstanding men and tracking down others like them, a form of generalship. Skill in the appropriate treatment of those captivated by reason would seem to be legislative wisdom. To secure and treat such people is the peculiar quality of this, which is truly fitted to a king. (4) At any rate, the philosophers say that the only wise man is the king, legislator, commanding officer; that he alone is just, pious, and a friend to God.[748] If we were to find these qualities in Moses, as can be shown from the actual Scriptures, then with full conviction we could call Moses a truly wise man.

169(1) So, just as we say skill in shepherding is care for the sheep, for "the[749] good shepherd lays down his life for his sheep,"[750] so we shall say that skill in legislation is the[751] provision of virtue in human beings, awakening as far as possible what is good in human beings in the process of directing and caring for the human flock. (2) And if the flock of the Lord's parable is simply a human herd, the same person will be a good shepherd and a good legislator for the single herd, the sheep who know his voice; he will be the single one caring for them, seeking the one who is lost,[752] and finding him thanks to the Law and the Word, if in fact "the law is spiritual"[753] and leads to blessedness. (3) This is the real legislator, who not only promises things of excellence but has a true understanding of them. The law of this man who has such a sci-

---

748. On the Stoics see *SVF* 1.223 a, 3.332.
749. Reading ὁ γὰρ with Lowth for οὕτω γὰρ ὁ.
750. John 10.11.
751. Reading ⟨τὸ⟩ with Stählin.
752. Luke 15.4.   753. Rom 7.14.

entific understanding is the ordinance with power to save—or rather the Law is an ordinance based on scientific knowledge: for "the Word of God is power and wisdom."[754] (4) Again this same person, through whom "the Law was given" is an interpreter of laws, the first interpreter of the ordinances of God, the only Son, interpreting his Father's heart.

170(1) Next, those who show obedience to the Law and to the possession of any kind of true knowledge of it, cannot show faithlessness to or ignorance of the truth. Those who show such faithlessness and are obviously unwilling to be involved in its activities self-confessedly show a supreme ignorance of the truth. (2) So what form does the faithlessness shown by the Greeks take? It is an unwillingness to accede to the truth which asserts that the Law was given by God through Moses, while personally honoring Moses out of their own doctrines. (3) Plato, Aristotle, and Ephorus record that Minos received his laws from Zeus every ninth year, going to Zeus' cave; and that Lycurgus was educated in legislation on his frequent visits to Apollo at Delphi.[755] Chamaeleon of Heraclea in his work *On Drunkenness* and Aristotle in the *Constitution of Locri* record that Zaleucus of Locri got his laws from Athena.[756] (4) Those who go as far as possible in extolling the credibility of Greek legislation as divine, in the image of Mosaic prophecy, are inconsiderate in not admitting the source of the truth and archetype of their own records.

27

The Law Inflicts Penalties to Educate Us

171(1) No one should run down the Law as less than excellent because of its penalties. We must not say that the person who eliminates bodily disease is a clear benefactor, but the

---

754. 1 Cor 1.24.

755. Plato, *Laws* 1.624 A, 632 D; *Minos* 319 C; on Aristotle see nt. 611, fr. 535 R; on Ephorus see nt. 617, fr. 63; on Minos see nt. 386; on Lycurgus see nt. 388.

756. On Chamaeleon see nt. 287; Locri was a Dorian settlement in southwest Italy; on Zaleucus see nt. 386; Athena was the city goddess of Athens, patroness of skills.

one who tries to wean the soul from unrighteousness is less caring; the soul is of greater value than the body. (2) For physical health we submit to operations, cauteries and potions; the person who prescribes them is called healer[757] and doctor. He is not governed by jealousy or malice towards the patient. If he amputates limbs, he is following the rationale of his profession, to avoid the healthy parts being infected along with those. No one could charge medical science with evil practice.[758] (3) Similarly, when the soul is in question, shall we not submit to exile, the payment of fines, or prison, if only there is a chance of replacing unrighteousness with righteousness? (4) The Law cares for its subjects; it educates them in reverence for God; it tells them what they ought to do; it keeps them from offences; it sets a penalty for a modest offence; when it sees a person in a seemingly incurable state, plunged up to his neck in crime, then in concern that the others may be infected by him, as if it were amputating a limb of the body, it executes him for the greatest health of all.[759]

172(1) "When we are judged by the Lord," says the Apostle, "it is for our education, so that we may not be condemned along with the world."[760] (2) Earlier the prophet said, "The Lord has given me a stern lesson, but not handed me over to death."[761] Scripture says, "It is to teach you his righteousness that he taught you a lesson, tested you, and exposed you to hunger and thirst in a desolate land, for you to know in your heart all his statutes and judgments which I am laying on you today. The Lord your God will educate you just as a human will educate his son."[762] (3) Scripture again emphasizes the lesson taught by a good example: "It is a great education when a malefactor sees a criminal punished," for "the fear of the Lord breeds wisdom."[763]

173(1) The greatest, most fulfilling blessing of all is to be

---

757. Or "savior," omitting καὶ.
758. Except G. B. Shaw's *The Doctor's Dilemma!*
759. The image is from Plato, *Gorgias* 525 B–C.
760. 1 Cor 11.32. Some editors punctuate the original, "When we are judged, it is part of our education from the Lord"; but not Clement.
761. Ps 118.18.   762. Deut 8.2–3,11 freely.
763. Prov 22.36.

able to turn a person from wrongdoing to virtue and good deeds. The Law does this. (2) It follows also that when a person is taken prisoner by criminal greed for gain and falls into irreparable vice, one who kills him would be doing him a benefit. (3) The Law is a benefactor. It is able to turn criminals into good citizens if they are only willing to listen to its voice; it frees them from the evils which surround them. (4) It promises immortality to those who chose a life of disciplined righteousness. "Knowledge of the Law is the sign of a good intelligence."[764] And again, "Evil men do not understand the Law, but those who seek the Lord will have understanding in all that is good."[765] (5) The Providence that disposes all things cannot but be of authoritative excellence. Its power dispenses salvation in two ways: as our sovereign it brings us to our senses through punishment; as benefactress, it helps us by positive action for us. (6) It is possible not to be "a son of disobedience"[766] but "to transfer from darkness to light,"[767] to lend an ear to wisdom, to be under the Law first, as a slave to God, then to become a faithful member of his staff,[768] fearing God as his Lord, then, moving higher, to be enrolled among the sons.[769] Then, since "love covers a quantity of sins,"[770] the fulfillment of blessed hope is there to be received by anyone who[771] has been set down in the category of chosen sons called God's friends, who has grown in love, who is now chanting his prayer in the words "May my lord become my God!"[772]

174(1) The Apostle has shown the benefactions of the Law in this passage addressed to the Jews somewhat as follows: "But if you call yourself a Jew and rely on the Law and boast of your relation to God, and you know the will of God, and approve of things of excellence, since you are instructed in the Law, then you have confidence in yourself as a guide to the blind, as a light to those in darkness, as a corrector of the

---

764. Prov 9.10 adapted.   765. Prov 28.5.
766. Eph 2.2.
767. A free allusion to 1 John 3.14; John 1.4–5, 3.19.
768. Heb 3.5, citing Num 12.7.
769. Gal 3.26, 4.7.   770. 1 Pet 4.8.
771. Reading τὸν with Stählin for τοῦτον.
772. Gen 28.21; John 20.28.

foolish, as a teacher of the young, possessing in the Law the very pattern of truth and true knowledge."[773] (2) He is admitting that the Law has these powers, even if there are those who boast that they are living within law, though their society is not governed by law. "Happy is the man who has found wisdom, and the mortal who has known practical wisdom. From her mouth"—clearly Wisdom's—"emerges righteousness; on her tongue she carries law and mercy."[774] (3) The fact is that the Law and the gospel are the work of a single Lord who is "the power and wisdom of God."[775] The fear inbred by the Law is merciful and turns to salvation. "Do not let compassion, faithfulness and truth fall away from you; bind them about your neck."[776]

175(1) Like Paul, prophecy criticizes the people for not understanding the Law: "Destruction and trouble are on their roads, and they have not known the road of peace."[777] "There is no fear of God before their eyes."[778] (2) "Claiming to be wise, they became fools."[779] "We know that the Law is good, if anyone uses it lawfully. But those who desire to be teachers of the Law have no understanding," says the Apostle, "either of their own words or of the subjects of their assertions. The aim of our charge is love proceeding from a pure heart, a good conscience and a sincere faith."[780]

28

Moses Preferable to Plato in Dialectic

176(1) Moses' philosophy has four divisions: first, history; second, that which is properly called legislation (which would be properly classified under ethics); third, religious observances (a part of natural philosophy); (2) fourth, in general, the nature of the understanding of the divine, revelation,[781]

773. Rom 2.17–20.
774. Prov 3.13,16.
775. 1 Cor 1.24.
776. Prov 3.3.
777. Isa 59.7–8.
778. Ps 36.1.
779. Rom. 1.22.
780. 1 Tim 1.8,7,5.
781. The term for the culminating spectacle at Eleusis.

which Plato places among the really great mysteries.[782] Aristotle calls this form "metaphysics."[783] (3) Plato's dialectic, as he says in the *Statesman*, is a form of scientific knowledge which investigates the way of demonstrating reality.[784] It is accessible to the person of self-discipline, not as an instrument for speaking or acting in relation to human concerns, as our contemporary dialecticians practice it busily in their sophistry, but as an instrument[785] for being able to speak or act in ways approved by God, all with a view to power to act.

177(1) True dialectic is mixed with true philosophy. It considers events. It evaluates capacities and powers. It rises up to the supreme power of all. It dares to go beyond[786] to the God of the universe. It promises, not a practical experience of perishable objects, but a genuine knowledge of things to do with God and the heavens. The familiar use of[787] human skill in word and action goes along with it. (2) Scripture is certainly right to want us to become dialecticians of this kind when it encourages us to "Become reputable bankers,"[788] rejecting some coin but holding on firmly to the best. (3) This is real dialectic. It is practical wisdom. It makes choices among objects of intelligent thought. It shows genuinely and unambiguously what underlies each object. Perhaps it is a power that makes choices within classes of objects, going down to their peculiar characteristics, producing each object to be seen in its purity.

178(1) So this power is the only one guiding us to true wisdom, which is a divine faculty, with a true knowledge of real beings in their real states, possessing perfection, being free from passion of all sorts, not without the Savior who by

782. There is no clear reference: see Plato, *Phaedrus* 250 C; *Symposium* 209E–210E.
783. Really "first philosophy"; *Metaphysics*, 'After physics,' was the title of his advanced course on Physical Science.
784. Plato, *Statesman* 287 A.
785. Reading ⟨τοῦ⟩ with Mayor.
786. An allusion to Plato's Form of the Good, which is in another dimension "beyond" the reality of the other Forms (see Plato, *Republic* 6.509 E).
787. Omitting περὶ with Bywater.
788. This is not in our Bible (see Resch, *Agrapha* 43).

the word of God strips from us the ignorance that has swamped the soul's perception as a result of bad training, and who has given us the best faculty of perception,

> So that we can truly recognize both God and man.[789]

(2) It is he who has shown us in reality how[790] we are to know ourselves, he who reveals the Father of the universe to the person he wills, and so far as human nature can conceive him. "For no one knows the Son except the Father, and no one knows the Father except the Son and any person to whom the Son reveals him."[791]

179(1) The Apostle was certainly right in saying that he had come to know "the mystery through revelation, as I wrote briefly earlier. In accordance with this, as you read you are able to realize my understanding in the mystery of Christ."[792] (2) "In accordance with this you are able," he said, knowing that some have only taken milk, no solid food yet, and perhaps not milk in its pure state.[793] (3) There are four ways in which we can receive the meaning of the Law: It may present a type;[794] it may show a symbol; it may lay down a precept for right conduct; it may pronounce a prophecy. (4) I am well aware that to make these distinctions and expound them is the work of fully mature men. The whole of Scripture is not, in the proverbial saying, "a single Myconos."[795] If you wish to hunt down the whole process of God's teaching, you must approach Scripture with a more dialectical method to the best of your faculties.

---

789. Homer, *Iliad* 5.127; Apposite to the Christ who in Christian perception is both.

790. Omitting τε with Hiller; "Know yourself " was a Greek proverb associated with the Delphic Oracle and the Seven Sages (see nt. 279).

791. Matt 11.27.

792. Eph 3.3–4.

793. 1 Cor 3.2. Reading ἡ τάχα with Louth for αὐτίκα.

794. Supplied from the scholia to bring the number to four.

795. Myconos was an island of the Cyclades next to Delos where all the inhabitants were said to be bald: hence the proverb "It's all one."

29

The Greeks "all children" Compared to the Egyptians

180(1) So the Egyptian priest's words in Plato were absolutely splendid: "O Solon, Solon, you Greeks are all children.
You have in your souls no ideas from antiquity handed down
by tradition. There is not a single old man among the
Greeks."[796] (2) In speaking of old men, I imagine, he means
those who know matters of greater antiquity—that is, our tradition. *Vice versa*, youngsters are those who record more recent
matters—those the Greeks have made subjects of study, which
concern yesterday, or the day before, treating them as antique
and venerable. (3) So he added "a doctrine grown grey with
age";[797] we foreigners use rough and obscure metaphors! At
all events, sensible people approach the artificial business of
interpretation empirically.[798] (4) The priest is saying of the
Greeks that their thought processes are little different from
"children-stories."[799] We must not hear this as "childish stories" or "stories composed for children." (5) He was calling
the actual stories "children," on the grounds that those among
the Greeks who thought themselves sages would see only a
little way through them. By the "doctrine grown grey," he was
making a riddling allusion to the oldest truth of all, in the
hands of non-Greeks. To this phrase he opposed "child-story,"
exposing the storybook element in the approach of more recent generations, as having (like children) no element of antiquity, making it clear that their stories and philosophies are
both alike childlike.

181(1) So it was by divine inspiration that the power addressed Hermas in a revelation: "These visions and revelations are for the sake of those divided in mind, debating in
their hearts whether these things are true or not."[800] (2) Sim-

796. Plato, *Timaeus* 22 B.
797. Plato, *Timaeus* 22B.
798. I suggest ἀτέχνως rather than ἀτεχνῶς, see Plato, *Gorgias* 501 A.
799. Adding παίδων from Plato, *Timaeus* 23 B in view of what follows;
but Clement is wrong, Plato means "children's stories."
800. Hermas, *Shepherd*, Visions 3.4.3.

ilarly, too, demonstrations on the basis of an abundance of learning give a strong and powerful foundation to demonstrative arguments, insofar as their "minds are floating about"[801] still, like those of youngsters. (3) As Scripture says, "A sound precept is a torch, and the Law is a light on the road; for education shows the roads of life."[802]

(4) Law is sovereign of all,
     mortals and immortals,[803]

says Pindar. (5) Through these words I hear the institutor of the Law. I take Hesiod's words to have been spoken about the God of the universe, even though the poet spoke by guesswork rather than by a full grasp of what he was saying:

(6) The son of Cronus[804] established this law for human beings,
     for fish and wild animals and birds of the air
     to eat one another, since they have no sense of justice—
     to humans he gave justice, by far the best gift of all.[805]

182(1) So whether he is speaking of the innate law or the Law given on the second occasion—the law of nature and the Law of instruction are certainly from God, and one and the same.[806] Plato says in the *Statesman* that there is only one lawgiver, and in the *Laws* that there is only one person who will be capable of understanding cultural matters.[807] Through these passages he is teaching us that there is one Law and one God. (2) Moses clearly means the Lord when he speaks of a covenant, saying, "Look. I am my covenant at your side."[808] He had said "covenant" earlier, adding that he should not search for it in writing.[809] The covenant is the originator of

801. Homer, *Iliad* 3.108.
802. Prov 6.23.
803. Pindar, fr. 152 B.
804. Zeus.
805. Hesiod, *Works and Days* 276–9.
806. Reading ⟨ὤν⟩ with Wilamowitz.
807. Plato, *Statesman* 301 C, 309 C–D; *Laws* 2.658E–9A.
808. Gen 17.4.
809. Probably an allusion to Gen 17.2. Something has dropped out, but this is the general meaning.

the universe, who establishes its orderly disposition, and is called God because of its good order.[810] (3) In the *Preaching of Peter* you could find the Lord addressed as "Law and Word."[811] But at this point let me finish my first *Miscellany of Notes of Revealed Knowledge in Accordance with the True Philosophy.*

810. Similar word play (on *theos* and *thesis*) in the original.
811. On fr. 1 of the *Kerygma Petrou, the Preaching of Peter,* see E. Hennecke, *New Testament Apocrypha,* ed. W. Schneemelcher, tr. R. McL. Wilson (Philadelphia, 1964), 2.94–102.

BOOK TWO

1

Preface

1(1) The next point would be, since Scripture affirms the Greeks to be "thieves" of foreign[1] philosophy, to grasp how this is to be briefly demonstrated. We shall begin by establishing that in their writings they have copied the miracle stories of our history. We shall further prove that they plagiarized our most important doctrines and debased them—I have already demonstrated that our Scriptures are older than theirs—in matters concerning faith, wisdom, revealed knowledge, and scientific knowledge, hope and love, and concerning repentance, self-control, and above all fear of God (really a swarm[2] of the virtues of truth). (2) We shall embrace all that is demanded by my notes in relation to the proposed subject, and particularly the way in which those who have taken up the views of past generations in terms of practical philosophy have been eager to seize on the inner truths of the foreign philosophy, its use of symbols and enigmatic allusions—a method of considerable practical value, and in fact essential to the knowledge of truth.

2(1) In these terms I suppose it follows that in facing charges levelled against us by the Greeks we use a few passages of Scripture, and it may turn out that the Jew in listening to us could experience an easy conversion, on the basis of his beliefs, to the person in whom he has had no belief. (2) Take the best of the

---

1. John 10.8. "Foreign," i.e., Hebrew; cf. Tertullian, *Apology* 47.
2. Plato, *Meno* 72 A: The list is a curious and not altogether traditional one. Plato had singled out from a varied list current in Greek thought four virtues which Ambrose later called "cardinal"—wisdom, courage, self-control, justice. (See J. Ferguson, *Moral Values in the Ancient World* [London, 1958]); the Christian tradition added faith, hope, and love from 1 Cor. 13.

philosophers. A loving examination of their manner of living and the new doctrines they have come up with will naturally follow. We do not defend ourselves against our accusers. Far from it. We have learned to bless those who curse us,[3] even if they bring unfounded slanders against us. We work for their conversion. Perhaps in their omniscient wisdom they may learn discrimination and a sense of shame through exposure by foreigners. They may in the long run be able to discern the quality of the learning to which they are directing their overseas expeditions! (3) The things they have stolen must emphatically be defined by stripping them of their self-centered nature. The things which they boast of having discovered by "self-examination"[4] are exposed to refutation. It follows that we must move rapidly to matters concerning what they call the standard educational curriculum, showing the extent of its usefulness, and concerning astrology, mathematics, magic, and wizardry. (4) The whole of Greece prides itself on these as supreme sciences. "Anyone who speaks openly to refute error is a peacemaker."[5]

3(1) We have said several times already that we have no intention of playing the Greek and have made no preparation for doing so. That is quite enough to turn most people away from the truth. A truly philosophic approach will benefit its hearers in their understanding, not their language. (2) In my view, the person who cares for the truth must put his sentences together without deep thought and deliberation. He will simply do what he can in his effort to find a word for what he wants to say. The real world passes by those who concentrate on diction and busy themselves with that. (3) So it is the nurseryman's forte to grasp the rose growing among thorns without hurting himself. It is the specialist's forte to discover the pearl buried in the oyster's flesh. (4) It is said that birds have sweet-flavored flesh when they do not have an abundance of food ready to hand, and they have to make an effort to scratch with their

3. Luke 6.28.
4. Heraclitus (c. 500 B.C.) was an aphoristic thinker in Ephesus who influenced Stoic thought (see DK 22 B 101 and Plutarch, *Moralia* 1118 C).
5. Prov 10.10.

claws in order to secure their food. (5) So if anyone considers the analogy and has a passionate desire to know the truth which has been lost[6] in many persuasive arguments from the Greeks, like the true features behind horrific masks, he will make a major effort in his hunt. In Hermas' vision, the power appears and says to him, "Anything which may be revealed to you will be revealed to you."[7]

2

*That Faith Alone Allows Us to Know God and That
It Rests on a Solid Foundation*

4(1) "Do not preen yourself on your wisdom," says Proverbs. "In all your paths, look to know her, so that she may set your paths straight, and your foot will not stumble."[8] Through these maxims he wants to show that actions must follow the Word,[9] and to demonstrate further that we have to choose and cling to whatever is useful in any form of education. (2) The paths of wisdom are diverse, but they lead directly to the path of truth, and that path is faith. "Your foot is not to stumble," he says in relation to those who look like opposing the sole divine providential government. (3) He adds, "Do not be intelligent in your own eyes,"[10] following the godless reasonings of those who are in revolt against God's government, "but fear God," the sole possessor of power—from which it follows that nothing can stand in the way of God. (4) In particular, what follows teaches clearly that the fear of God is a movement away from evil.[11] He is really saying, "Turn away from all evil. This is the education offered by Wisdom." "The Lord educates those he loves," causing pain to induce understanding, and reestablishing them in peace and incorruption.

6. Reading διαλεληϑὸς εἰδέναι with Stählin.

7. Hermas, *Shepherd*, Visions 3.13.4.

8. Prov 3.5, 6.23 freely put together from memory.

9. The familiar wordplay, common in the *Protrepticus*, on the human and divine Logos.

10. Prov 3.7.

11. Prov 8.13 (cf. Job 28.28); *Paedagogus* 1.13.101; *Stromateis* 2.32; for a Stoic view, Chrysippus *SVF* 3.411.

5(1) So the foreign philosophy we follow is in actual fact complete and true. In Wisdom we find these words: "He has in person granted me a knowledge of reality free from error, for me to know the constitution of the universe" going on to "the qualities of roots."[12] The whole passage embraces the study of the natural world[13] extending to everything born into the world of our senses. (2) There follows an enigmatic allusion to spiritual beings in this addition: "I have known all that is hidden and all that is open to view; I was a pupil of Wisdom, who formed them all." There in a nutshell you have the profession of our philosophy. (3) The process of learning about these, if practiced under good government, leads upwards via Wisdom, who formed the whole universe, to the ruler of the universe, a being hard to catch, hard to hunt down, who always distances himself in retreat from his pursuer. (4) But this same ruler, distant as he is, has, marvellous to relate, drawn near. "I am God at hand,"[14] says the Lord. In his essential being he is distant—how ever could a creature subject to birth draw near to the unborn and uncreated?—but very close by the exercise of that power which has enfolded all things in its embrace. (5) It is written: "Can anyone act in secret without my seeing him?"[15] Yes, the power of God is always present, touching us with a power that is observant, beneficent, and educative.

6(1) As a result, Moses, convinced that God will never be known to human wisdom, says, "Reveal yourself to me,"[16] and finds himself forced to enter "into the darkness" where the voice of God was present; in other words, into the unapproachable, imageless, intellectual concepts relating to ultimate reality. For God does not exist in darkness. He is not in space at all. He is beyond space and time and anything belonging to created beings. (2) Similarly, he is not found in any section. He contains nothing. He is contained by nothing. He is not subject

---

12. Wis 7.17–20.
13. Camelot notes the derivation of the phrase from Aristotle, *On the Parts of Animals* 1.1.13.642 a 27; *Metaphysics* 5.1.8.1025 b 19, but that for Clement it is the first step on the ladder to the knowledge of God; Origen also saw it as a step in the same ascent.
14. Jer 23.23.   15. Jer 23.24.
16. Exod 33.13.

to limit or division. (3) "What sort of house will you build for me?"[17] says the Lord. He has not even built a house for himself! He has nothing to do with space. Even if it is written that "the heaven is his throne," he is not contained as the words suggest. He simply rests in the enjoyment of his handiwork. (4) So it is clear that truth has been hidden from us, as has already been shown by a single example, and as we shall a little later establish by several more.

7(1) Do not the people deserve acceptance who are willing to learn and, in Solomon's words, "are capable of knowing wisdom and education, setting the mind on the words of understanding, comprehending the subtle uses of language, and setting the mind on true justice" (recognizing that there is another justice which is taught by the laws of Greece and by all the rest of the philosophers but which does not accord with truth) (2) "and getting their judgments straight" (not forensic judgments, but meaning that we ought to have a sound and reliable standard of judgment within us) "so as to give power to the innocent to do anything, and perception and reflection to young men? On hearing this, the wise man"—the person who has been persuaded to obey the commandments—"will be wiser" with regard to knowledge. "The person of understanding will acquire the power of government and will understand proverbial sayings, obscure language, the sayings of the wise and their enigmas."[18] (3) For neither those inspired by God nor those equipped by them express sentiments that lead into error, still less into the traps in which the majority of sophists entangle the young without directing their studies to the truth at all. But those who possess the Holy Spirit search out "the deep places of God"[19]—in other words, they attain the hidden secrets that surround prophecy. (4) But it is forbidden to share holy things with dogs,[20] as long as they remain wild beasts. It is never appropriate to dilute the pure stream of divinity, the living water, for characters who are full of malice, disturbed, still without faith, or shameless in barking at the hunt.

17. Isa 66.1.   18. Prov 1.2–6.
19. 1 Cor 2.10.   20. Mark 7.27.

8(1) "Do not let the waters overflow beyond your spring or your waters spread into your streets."[21] "The majority do not turn their minds to the sort of things they encounter. If they are taught, they do not acquire knowledge, although they think they do." So says the admirable Heraclitus.[22] (2) Do you not realize that he is another critic of non-believers? "My just man shall live by faith," says the prophet.[23] One of the other prophets remarks, "If you do not believe, you emphatically will not understand either."[24] (3) How could a soul come to the study of these things, itself exceptional if, deep within, lack of faith over the teaching is fighting against it? (4) Faith, which the Greeks think alien and useless and which they consequently malign, is in fact preconception by the will, an act of consenting to religion and, as the divine Apostle puts it, "the assurance of things hoped for, the conviction of things not seen. For by it 'above all' the men of old received approval. Without faith it is impossible to please God."[25]

9(1) Others have defined faith as an act of consenting which unites us to an invisible object, rather as a demonstration forms an overt act of consenting to a matter previously unrecognized. (2) So, if it is an act of choice[26] desirous of some object, the desire is plainly an act of the intelligence; and since choice is the spring of action, faith is found to be the spring of action, being the foundation of an act of choice based on thought, a person giving through faith, in a preliminary way, the actual demonstration. (3) To follow freely what is best for you is the

21. Prov 5.16.
22. See DK 22 B 17 with Bergk's readings.
23. Hab 2.4.
24. Isa 7.9.
25. Heb 11.1–2,6, though few would attribute it to the "divine Apostle" today. The preceding language is of great interest. *Prolēpsis* is a term used by both Epicureans and Stoics: To the Epicureans it is a primary notion, previous to sense perception; to the Stoics it is a 'common idea' not coming from instruction or study, but inbred; *Synkatathesis*, 'act of consenting,' is an important Christian term (see below 2.27–8 and 5.1.3; Basil, *Against Eunomius* 3.5); for two forms of belief see 7.48.2 and 8.5.3 which may be paralleled with the two kinds of persuasion in Plato, *Gorgias* 454 E, although to Plato faith or belief is inferior to knowledge.
26. *Prohairesis*, 'act of choice,' another term of Hellenistic philosophy (see Epicurus, *Sententiae Vaticanae* 51; *SVF* 1.216, 3.173).

beginning of understanding. Choice, if it is inexorable, offers a strong impulse in the direction of knowledge. The practice of faith immediately becomes knowledge based on strong foundations. (4) The disciples of the philosophers define knowledge as a state which reason[27] cannot shake. So is there any other genuine firm establishment except[28] that of an actual religion whose sole instructor is the Word? Not in my view! (5) Theophrastus says that perception is the starting point of faith.[29] It is from perception that the first principles reach the reason and intelligence within us. (6) If a person has faith in the divine Scriptures and a firm judgment, then he receives as an irrefutable demonstration the voice of the God who has granted him those Scriptures. The faith no longer requires the confirmation of a demonstration. "Blessed are those who without seeing have believed."[30] (7) The seductive songs of the Sirens[31] demonstrated a superhuman power, putting all who passed into a state of shock, and inducing them almost despite themselves to accept their words.

3

In the Systems of Basilides and Valentinus Faith Is neither Free Choice nor Voluntary

10(1) Basilides' sect regards faith as a natural disposition, although they also make it a matter of election; faith to them discovers the subjects of learning by an intellectual apprehension without demonstration.[32] (2) Valentinus' followers attrib-

27. Or the Logos (as below); this is a Stoic definition (see Chrysippus *SVF* 2.93–5; cf. Philo, *On the Preliminary Studies* 140).
28. Added by Lowth; it makes no sense otherwise.
29. Fr. 13; Theophrastus was Aristotle's successor as head of the Lyceum.
30. John 20.29.
31. Reading ἐπικηλήσεις with Heyse for ἐπιτελέσεις; The Sirens were spirits of death, often portrayed as bird-women. Their song lured sailors onto the rocks. Odysseus escaped by shutting his men's ears with wax and having them bind him to the mast (see Homer, *Odyssey* 12.165–200).
32. Basilides (second century A.D.) was an Alexandrian Gnostic who brought together the Christian doctrine of salvation, Indian thought, and Greek linguistic philosophy, creating a complex myth of salvation. *Katalēpsis*, 'apprehension,' is another term of Hellenistic philosophy (see *SVF* 1.60,66,71, 2.70 etc.).

ute faith to us in our simplicity, but arrogate knowledge to themselves as saved by their nature. They want it to dwell in them in accordance with the superiority of the exceptional seed sown in them. They claim that it is very different from faith, as spirit is from the soul.[33] (3) Basilides' followers further say that faith and election are both particular to individual dispositions, and consequently, that faith on a world scale in every being follows from an election which lies beyond the world; further, they say that the gift of faith is proportionate to the hope of each individual.

11(1) In that case, faith is no longer the right action of a free choice, a natural superiority; the person without faith is not responsible and will not meet his just consequences; the person with faith is not responsible; the whole essential difference between faith and unfaith could not be a matter of praise or blame if you look at it rightly, being a foreordaining natural necessity determined by the universal power. We are like lifeless puppets controlled by natural forces. It is a predetermining necessity which forces willingness[34] and the lack of it. (2) In fact, I no longer can conceive of this living being whose impelling power has acquired a controlling necessity and is moved by an external cause.[35] What has happened to repentance for previous lack of faith, leading to remission of sins? The result is this: no baptismal boon from the Word,[36] no sealing of blessing, no Son, no Father. There is, I suppose, some divine power,

---

33. Valentinus (second century A.D.), the other great Gnostic leader, emphasized *gnosis*, 'knowledge,' as revealed, not acquired; he linked Greek, Egyptian, and Christian thought in a monumental system centering on the *pleroma* or 'fullness' of the godhead; See also F. M. Sagnard, *La gnose valentinienne* (Paris, 1947); and J. L. Kovacs, Clement of Alexandria and the Valentinian Gnostics, Ph.D. diss. (New York, Columbia University, 1978).

34. "Willingness and" added by Stählin.

35. Chrysippus, *SVF* 3.988.

36. The usual ambiguity with "baptism as a reasonable option." For baptism as a seal Camelot refers to Hermas, *Shepherd*, Similitudes 8.6, 9.16–17; Clement of Rome, *Second Epistle to the Romans* 7.6, 8.6; Irenaeus, *Demonstration of the Apostolic Teaching* 3; Tertullian, *On Baptism* 13; *Concerning Repentance* 5; *On the Writings of Heretics* 36; *Stromateis* 5.73; *Quis dives salvetur?* 39.42; see also F. J. Dölger, *Sphragis* (Paderborn, 1911).

consisting in the distribution of natural gifts to them, but without control of the foundation of salvation or faith springing from the will.

4

That There Is neither Knowledge nor Skill without an Act of Faith

12(1) We have received through the Scriptures the fact that human beings have been granted within their own power the choice of Yes or No by the Lord. Let us stick firmly to faith as to an infallible criterion. Let us display a "willing spirit."[37] We have chosen life. We have believed in God through his voice. Anyone who has faith in the Word knows that the thing is true, for the Word is truth. Anyone who has no faith in the one who speaks the word has no faith in God. (2) "By faith we understand that the universe was created by God's speaking so that the visible came into being out of the invisible," says the Apostle. "By faith, Abel presented a more acceptable sacrifice than Cain, and thereby was approved as righteous, with God granting approval on the basis of his offerings. Through his faith, even in death he still speaks to us." The passage goes on to the words: "than to enjoy the ephemeral delights of sin." These are the people whom, even before the Law existed, faith justified and established as heirs to God's promise.[38]

13(1) What is the point of presenting you with evidence of further examples of faith out of our history? "Time will fail me if I tell of Gideon, Barak, Samson, Jephtha, David, Samuel and the prophets,"[39] and so on. (2) There are four places where truth may be found: perception, intellection, scientific knowledge, and hypothesis. The primary in nature is the intelligence, but with us, and in relation to us, it is perception. The substance of scientific knowledge is constituted out of percep-

37. Matt 26.41.
38. Heb 6.12, 11.3–4,25; Gen 4.3–10.
39. Heb 11.32; the references in the Hebrew Scriptures are Judg 4–5, 6–8, 11–12, 13–16; 1 Sam 1–12, 15, 16–30; 2 Sam 1–24; 1 Kgs 1.1–2,11; Dan 6.

tion and intellection, and clarity is the common attribute of the last two. (3) Perception is the gateway to scientific knowledge. But faith travels through the world of perception, leaving hypothesis behind and speeding straight to the infallible and remaining firmly in the truth. (4) If anyone should suggest that scientific knowledge is provable by the help of reason, he must realize that the first principles are not able to be proved. They are not found by technical expertise, which is a matter of practical action rather than contemplation, or by practical thought, which is concerned with the mutable.

14(1) By faith alone is it possible[40] to arrive at the first principle of the universe. All scientific knowledge is the subject of teaching; things are taught on the basis of previous knowledge.[41] (2) The Greeks had no previous knowledge of the first principle of the universe, whether Thales,[42] who took water as the primary cause, or any of the other physical scientists who succeeded him. Anaxagoras may have been[43] the first to establish Mind in charge of material objects; yet not even he noted the cause[44] of creation, sketching in irrational vortices, leaving Mind mindlessly inactive. (3) So the Word says, "Do not call anyone your teacher on earth."[45] Scientific knowledge is a state resulting from demonstration. Faith is a grace which helps its possessor to climb from things which cannot be demonstrated to the ultimate simplicity, which is not matter, has no connection with matter, and is not subject to matter.

40. Reading οἷόν τε with Hiller for οἴονται.

41. Aristotle, *Metaphysics* 1.9.992 b 30; but Clement derived much of his philosophy secondhand from handbooks.

42. Thales of Miletus (early sixth century B.C.) asked new questions about the physical basis of the universe and the process of change: Water is the source of life, solidifies, and rarefies when frozen or boiled; others speculated on other elements, then a combination of them, until Leucippus and Democritus came up with an atomic theory.

43. Reading ἐπεὶ <εἰ> with Schwartz; Anaxagoras of Clazomenae (fifth century B.C.) was a leading philosopher and a friend of Pericles at Athens whom Socrates was excited to find exalting Mind; but to Anaxagoras Mind was the first cause only and played no part in subsequent dispositions (see Plato, *Phaedo* 97B–98C; DK 59 A 57).

44. Reading αἰτίαν with Bywater for ἀξίαν.

45. The closest parallel in the Gospels is Matt 23.8–10, but the words are so different that they must be taken from some lost source.

15(1) It looks as if those who have no faith, in Plato's words, "aim to drag everything down from the invisible heavens to earth, literally grasping at rocks and trees with their hands. They clutch everything of this sort and maintain that real existence attaches only to things subject to resistance and contact, defining existence as identical with body. . . . (2) But those who oppose them are on their guard making their defense from some invisible region, forcibly insisting that true reality resides in certain incorporeal forms which are the objects of thought."[46] (3) The Word says, "Look, I am doing something new, which no eye has seen, no ear heard, no human heart felt."[47] These are to be seen, heard, and grasped by a new eye, a new hearing, and a new heart, when the Lord's disciples speak, listen, and act in the Spirit. (4) There is an authentic coinage. There is also a spurious coinage, which nonetheless deceives ordinary people, though not of course the moneychangers, who know from experience how to distinguish and separate forgery from the real thing. So the moneychanger merely tells the man in the street that it is faked. How it is done, only the banker's intimates and the people trained to do so understand. (5) Aristotle says that faith is a judgment derived from scientific knowledge affirming a thing to be true.[48] So faith is more authoritative than science. Faith is the criterion of scientific knowledge.

16(1) Guesswork, an insubstantial hypothesis, simulates faith, rather as a flatterer acts the friend, or a wolf, the dog. We notice that the carpenter becomes a craftsman as the result of study, and the pilot will be able to pilot as a result of education in the skill. We have realized that the will to excellence is not enough; it is essential to study obediently. (2) Obedience to the Word whom we have named our instructor means faith in him without opposing him in anything. How could anyone oppose God? Knowledge is one with faith, and faith one with

46. Plato, *Sophist* 246 A–B, adding to Clement's MS <οἱ δὲ> with Mayor at the start of 15(2).
47. Isa 43.19, 64.4, 65.17; 1 Cor 2.9.
48. Not precisely in Aristotle's surviving work; this is borrowed from Clement in Theodoret, *Curatio* 1.90.

knowledge, through a mutual succession derived from God. (3) Even Epicurus, who set much more store on pleasure than on truth, supposed faith to be a preconception of intelligence.[49] He expounds "preconception" as a close attention directed to a clear object and a clear concept of the object. He said that it is impossible to conduct an investigation or pose a problem or even have an opinion, or even refute another, without this "preconception."

17(1) How could anyone who did not have a preconception of his aim learn anything about the object of his investigation? Anyone who learns immediately turns his preconception into an apprehension. (2) If the learner does not lack a preconception capable of grasping what is said in the course of his learning, then he is a person with ears open to the truth. "What happiness to speak to an audience which listens!"[50] The listener is quite happy too! (3) To hear properly is to comprehend. So if faith is simply an intellectual preconception over what is said, and that is called attention or comprehension or teachability, then clearly no one will learn without faith, since no one will learn without a preconception. (4) The prophet's dictum is demonstrably a supreme truth: "If you do not have faith, you cannot have understanding."[51] Heraclitus of Ephesus was paraphrasing this aphorism when he said, "If you do not expect the unexpected, you will never find it; it is hard to search out and discover."[52]

18(1) Furthermore, the philosopher Plato says in his *Laws*: "If a man is to know the happiness of bliss, he ought from the very outset to have a grasp of truth, so that he can live in truth as long as possible, since he is faithful. A person who is not faithful is a person who deliberately loves falsehood. If his love of falsehood is not deliberate, he is crazy; neither of these is enviable. No one who lacks faith or learning wins friends."[53]

---

49. Fr. 255; this is a common misconception of Epicurus: He did not advocate the naive pursuit of pleasure at all, and thought that pleasure was not attainable without morality; in fact, he set high store by truth.

50. Sir 25.9.

51. Isa 7.9.

52. On Heraclitus see DK 22 B 18 and nt. 4.

53. Plato, *Laws* 5.730 B–C: The text is corrected from meaningless words

(2) Perhaps it is this that he riddlingly calls "royal" wisdom in *Euthydemus*.[54] Certainly in the *Statesman* he says, "It follows that the knowledge held by the true king is a royal knowledge, and anyone who possesses it whether in public office or as a private individual will be totally justified in receiving the title of "royal" in the light of his actual expertise."[55] (3) Those who have shown faith in Christ as God are good in name and fact,[56] just as those of whom a king takes notice are rightly called royal. For just as "the wise are wise through wisdom, and the lawful lawful through law,"[57] so Christians are kings through Christ's kingship, and Christians through Christ.[58] (4) A little lower down he adds in clear language, "That which is right must accord with law, and right reason is law, being so by nature and not because enshrined in letters or elsewhere."[59] The stranger from Elea demonstrates that the man who is royal and statesmanlike is law incarnate.[60]

19(1) Such is the nature of the man who fulfills the Law, "doing the Father's will."[61] He is recorded in full view on a wooden board set high, standing as an example of divine virtue to any who have the power to see clearly. (2) The Greeks know

---

to the normally accepted text of Plato, but Clement is twisting Plato's meaning: in the original, the faithfulness is shown in friendship.

54. Plato, *Euthydemus* 291 D.

55. Plato, *Statesman* 259 A–B.

56. I have added "as God" to keep the Greek wordplay with "good" between *Christos* and *chrestos*, found also in Justin, *Apology* 1.4; Tertullian, Apology 3.5; Theophilus, *To Autolycus* 1.1 (Some people think that when Claudius expelled the Jews from Rome for a riot, *impulsore Chresto* [see Suetonius, *Claudius* 15], it was a Jewish-Christian conflict misunderstood by the authorities); the Christians were first so called at Antioch where they were nicknamed *chrestoi*, 'goodygoodies,' a name they disowned; however they accepted *Christianoi*, which is further complicated because *Chrestos* is also a name.

57. [Plato], *Minos* 314 C: In Plato's Theory of Forms it is through participation in or imitation of the Form of Wisdom that human wisdom acquires its quality; and Clement adapts this ingeniously.

58. This paragraph has a number of textual problems, but the general sense is clear; my reading is closer to the MS than most.

59. [Plato], *Minos* 317 B–C.

60. The stranger from Elea (the home of Parmenides and his school) appears in Plato, the *Statesman*, but the phrase "law incarnate" does not (although the idea does; see 295 E; 311 B–C); Camelot notes the derivation of the phrase from Philo, *Life of Moses* 1.162, 2.4.

61. Matt 7.21.

that the dispatches from the ephors at Sparta had legally to be recorded on wooden boards.[62] My law, as I have said already, is royal, incarnate, the true Logos.[63]

> Law is king of all,
> mortals and immortals,

as the Boeotian poet Pindar puts it.[64] (3) Speusippus in his first volume *To Cleophon* seems to write words closely similar to Plato: "If royalty is a thing of value, if the wise man is the only true king and ruler, then law, being right reason, is similarly valuable."[65] This is in fact so. (4) The Stoic philosophers hold doctrines which follow from these, attributing royalty, priesthood, prophecy, lawgiving, wealth, real beauty, nobility and freedom to the wise man and to no one else. This wise man, exceptionally hard to find, is actually recognized by them.

5

Faith, Source of Wisdom, Wealth, Liberty; Faith, the Mother of Virtue

20(1) All the doctrines I have been discussing seem to have been handed down to the Greeks by the towering figure of Moses. He teaches that the wise man possesses everything when he says, "Because God pitied me there is nothing I do not have."[66] (2) He notes that the wise man receives God's love when he says, "God of Abraham, God of Isaac, God of Jacob."[67] The wise man is found with the open title of "friend."[68] He is held before us with a change of name as "one who sees God."[69]

62. Plutarch, *The Life of Lysander* 19; Aulus Gellius, *Attic Nights* 17.9; but Clement garbles his facts, as Stählin points out.
63. Or "right reason," a Stoic phrase.
64. Pindar, fr. 49 quoted in Plato, *Gorgias* 484 B from which Clement presumably took it; Pindar (c. the beginning of the fifth century B.C.) was the greatest lyric poet of Greece; Boeotia is the region to the north of Athens and Attica.
65. Speusippus, fr. 193. Speusippus was Plato's successor at the Academy. But there is a problem: the attribution seems precise, but the sentiment is very Stoic (cf. *SVF* 3.619).
66. Gen 33.11.
67. Exod 3.6.
68. John 15.15; Jas 2.23 (alluding to Isa 41.8; cf. 2 Chr 20.7).
69. Gen 32.29–31; Philo, *On Abraham* 57.

He represented Isaac as a consecrated sacrifice and then chose him for himself to be for us a type of the ordering of salvation.[70] (3) Among the Greeks there are songs about Minos, as "a king who rules for nine years, an intimate of Zeus";[71] they had heard how God spoke with Moses "like a person chatting to a personal friend."[72]

21(1) Moses was a man of wisdom, a king, a legislator. But our Savior surpasses all human nature,[73] being beautiful to the point of being the sole object of our love in our yearning for true beauty,[74] "for he was the true light."[75] (2) Scripture presents him greeted as king by children in their innocence and by Jews without faith in him or knowledge of him, and proclaimed by the very prophets.[76] (3) He is rich to the point of scornfully rejecting the whole earth and all the gold above and below the earth, gifts offered him combined with all honor by the adversary.[77] (4) No need to say that he is the only high priest, the only one who understands the service of God, Melchizedek, king of peace.[78] He above any is capable of giving leadership to the human race. (5) He is our lawgiver, presenting us with the Law through the mouth of the prophets, and instructing[79] us in all that has to be done, not least when it is not clear.

22(1) Who is of higher birth, when his only father is God? Well, let us produce Plato to witness to his encounter with the same doctrines. In the *Phaedrus* he calls the wise man rich, using these words: "Beloved Pan, and all you other gods of this

70. Gen 22.1–19; the subject changes, without indication, to God.
71. Homer, *Odyssey* 19.179, cited in [Plato], *Minos* 319 D.
72. Exod 33.11.
73. The comparison derives from Heb 3.3.
74. Platonic, with reference to the *Symposium*, where Socrates in his speech tells how Diotima urged him on to seek the eternal unchanging Form of Beauty as the highest quest of love; but there love was *erōs*, 'passion,' here it is *agapē*, 'Christian love.'
75. John 1.9.
76. Luke 19.38; Zech 9.9.
77. Matt 4.8–10; Luke 4.5–8; Camelot notes that the language is Platonic.
78. Heb 6.20, 7.2; Gen 14.18; however Hebrews does not identify Jesus with Melchizedek.
79. I have used "instructing" to cover both commanding and teaching.

place, grant me inward beauty. May all my external possessions harmonize with my inward state. May I believe that wisdom is riches."[80] (2) The Athenian stranger speaks as follows in criticism of those who think that riches consist in a multitude of possessions: "It is impossible for those whom ordinary people account rich to be exceptionally rich and righteous at the same time. They apply the term to those who, among a small minority of human beings, have obtained material possessions of a high market value, and these could equally well be the possessions of a crook."[81] (3) "The man of faith possesses the whole world of wealth," says Solomon, "the man without faith does not even own an *obol*."[82] Far better to trust Scripture where it says that "a camel will pass through a needle's eye" sooner than a rich man will become a philosopher.[83] (4) Again, Scripture blesses the poor, as Plato realized when he said, "Poverty is to be regarded not as a diminution of possessions but as an increase in the desire to possess."[84] In fact, it is the desire for more, not the possession of less, that the man of virtue must abandon if he would be rich. (5) In the *Alcibiades* he calls vice "servile" and virtue "fit for the free."[85] "Lift the heavy yoke from yourselves," says Scripture, "and take up the easy one,"[86] just as the poets call the yoke "servile."[87] The words, "You were sold to your sins,"[88] harmonize with what I have just said. "Everyone who commits sin is a slave. (6) The slave does not continue in the house forever. If the Son frees you, you will be free, and the truth will free you."[89] (7) The Athenian stranger

80. Plato, *Phaedrus* 279 B–C; Socrates is speaking in a grove by the river Ilissus; Pan is a shepherds' god of the wildwood.

81. Plato, *Laws* 5.742 E.

82. Prov 17.6 (LXX); an *obol* is a small coin.

83. Luke 18.25; but Clement's twist is fascinating: To philosophize is to love wisdom; that is to love the Word, that is to be a Christian.

84. Plato, *Laws* 5.736 E; Luke 6.20; cf. 4.18; The thought was a cliché of Hellenistic philosophy (see H. Usener, *Epicurea* 135 [Leipzig, 1887] quoted by Seneca, *Epistles* 21.7).

85. Plato, *Alcibiades* 1.135 C.

86. Matt 11.29–30.

87. Aeschylus, *Seven against Thebes* 75; *Persians* 50.

88. Rom 7.14; but the words are not identical.

89. John 8.34–36.

alludes to the wise man's beauty in these words: "If anyone insists that just men, even if they are physically ugly, are wholly beautiful in regard to the justice of their character, practically speaking, no one who speaks in those terms would be thought to be speaking out of turn."[90] (8) Prophecy pronounces, "His looks fell below all the sons of men."[91] Plato in the *Statesman* says that the wise man is a king; the word is there.[92]

23(1) So much for this exposition; now to return to our discussion of faith. Plato uses a complete demonstration to show the universal need of faith, while at the same time exalting peace: (2) "It is impossible to become sound in faithfulness at moments of civil disturbance without complete virtue. Fighting men are prepared to die in war, very many of them mercenaries. A very large number of these grow wild, unjust, violent, irrational; the remainder are very few. If this is right, every legislator who has the slightest sense of what is needed will draw up his laws with his concentration fixed on the highest virtue." (3) This is the faithfulness we need on every occasion— in peace, always in war, and in the whole of the rest of our lives. It seems to gather together in its embrace all the other virtues. (4) "The best condition is not war or civil disturbance—abominable to seek for those!—rather mutual peace and benevolence count for most."[93] (5) From this it is clear that to Plato the highest prayer is for the possession of peace, and that faith is the supreme mother of the virtues.

24(1) It is reasonably said in Solomon, "Wisdom is in the mouth of the faithful."[94] Xenocrates too in his treatise *On Intelligence* says that wisdom consists in a scientific knowledge of the first causes and of intelligible being. He regards intelligence as twofold—practical and theoretical; the latter is human wisdom.[95] (2) That is why wisdom is a form of intelligence, but not every form of intelligence is wisdom. Scientific

90. Plato, *Laws* 9.859 D–E.
91. Isa 53.
92. Plato, *Statesman* 259 A–B.
93. Plato, *Laws* 630 B–C; the quotation is free.
94. Sir 34.8 (LXX).
95. Xenocrates, fr. 9; he was a disciple of Plato, kindly and austere, who headed the Academy 339–314 B.C.

knowledge of the first principle of the universe is demonstrably faith but cannot itself be demonstrated. (3) It is strange that the sectaries of Pythagoras of Samos, in calling for demonstrations of the objects of their investigation, found grounds for faith in "The Master has spoken," holding that in those words there was enough to establish all that they had heard,[96] while at the same time, "those who delight in the contemplation of truth"[97] should be prepared not to show faith in a teacher who merits faith, the only savior God, and should demand from him proofs of his words. (4) It is he who says, "Let anyone who has ears to hear hear."[98] Who is this? Let Epicharmus speak:

Mind sees, mind hears, all else is dumb and blind.[99]

(5) Heraclitus attacks people for "lack of faith," saying that "they do not know how to speak or listen."[100] No doubt he was helped by this text from Solomon: "If you like listening, you will learn. If you lend an ear, you will become wise."[101]

6

Connection between Faith and Repentance, Charity, and Gnosticism

25(1) "Lord, who has believed what we have heard?" says Isaiah.[102] "Faith comes from hearing, hearing comes from the utterance of God," says the Apostle. (2) "How shall they call on one in whom they have not shown faith? How shall they hear without a preacher? How shall they preach unless they are sent as apostles? As Scripture has it, 'How beautiful are

96. Pythagoras (sixth century B.C.) was a shadowy figure who emigrated from the island of Samos in the northeastern Aegean to Magna Graecia, where he founded a community dedicated to mathematics, mysticism, and political reform; for "The Master" (literally "He") "has spoken," see Diogenes Laertius 8.46 etc.

97. Plato, *Republic* 5.475 E.

98. Matt 11.15, 13.9, 43; Mark 4.23; Rev 2.7, 13.9.

99. Epicharmus (early fifth century B.C.) was a Sicilian writer of comedies, fr. 249 K.

100. On Heraclitus see DK 22 B 19 and nt. 4.

101. Sir 6.33.

102. Isa 53.1.

the feet of those who bring a gospel of good news.' "[103] (3) Do you see how he traces faith back through the act of hearing and the preaching of the apostles to the utterance of the Lord and to the Son of God? (4) Playing ball depends not only on a person using skill to project the ball, but needs another to catch it rhythmically, so that the exercise may give the players their fulfillment in accordance with the rules.[104] Similarly, instruction is a state worthy of faith, when the faith of the hearers, being a kind of natural skill, so to speak, conduces to learning.

26(1) So earth, when fertile, cooperates with the planting of seeds. There is no benefit in the best instruction if the learner is not ready to receive it, or prophecy for that matter, or preaching,[105] if the hearers are not open to persuasion. (2) Dry sticks are ready to receive the power of ignition and are easily kindled. The famous stone attracts iron through a common nature. Similarly, the resin from amber attracts sticks, and amber draws up a heap of chaff. The objects attracted respond to them being attracted by a mysterious spirit; they are not primary causes, but cooperating causes.[106] (3) Crime takes two forms, one using secrecy and deceit, the other actively operating with violence. So the divine Word has summoned everyone *en masse* in a loud voice, knowing perfectly well those who will not allow themselves to be convinced. Nonetheless, because we have the power to respond positively or negatively, and so that no one may produce the pretext of ignorance, he has made a summons full of righteousness, and demands of each only that of which each is capable. (4) There is one group for whom the capacity accompanies the will; they

103. Rom 10.14–17; Isa 52.7.

104. The ancients on the whole used cooperative rather than competitive play, and individual rather than team games; the exercise was for physical fitness and graceful movement; the ball was a large inflated skin: see Plutarch, *Moralia* 38 A, 582 F; Galen, *Minor Writings* 1.93; and for a modern treatment see E. Wegner, *Das Ballspiel der Römer* (1939).

105. ⟨κηρύξεως⟩ with Schwartz; some word has dropped out and this is a good guess.

106. Plato, *Ion* 533 D–E; Clement uses two different words for amber: it is not clear whether he intends a distinction.

have developed this by practice; they have purified themselves. There is another, who may not yet have the capacity,
but do already have the desire. Desire is the work of the soul,
practical action requires the body as well. (5) It must be said
that you do not measure actions solely by their outcome; you
also judge them by the motive in each case. Was the choice
easy? Was there repentance for past mistakes? Was there
understanding of the occasion of stumbling? Did he have af-
terthoughts, i.e., did he think straight, after the event? Repentance is a slow form of knowledge. Knowledge is the first
stage without sin.

27(1) Repentance is a good act performed by faith. If a
person does not faithfully see that it was a sin to which he was
previously prisoner, there will be no change of behavior at all.
If a person does not believe that wrong behavior involves punishment, whereas salvation is for those who live by the commandments, there will be no conversion either. Hope too is
constituted from faith. (2) Basilides' followers[107] define faith
as a disposition of the soul towards one of those things which,
not being present, do not affect the senses. Hope is an expectation of the acquisition of good;[108] but that expectation must
be governed by faith. Faithfulness consists in the infallible
protection of the things placed in our hands. What is being
placed in our hands? Affirmations about God, God's own
words, the commandments, and with them the practice of his
precepts. (3) This is the "faithful servant,"[109] the one who
receives his master's praise. The words "God is faithful"[110]
mean that there is value in having faith in his self-revelation.
His Word reveals himself and he is the God who is faithful.
(4) So if having faith is a matter of making hypotheses, how
is it that the philosophers think that their doctrines are firmly
established? The assent given willingly before a demonstration
is not a hypothetical conjecture; it is an act of assent to someone reliable.

107. On Basilides see nt. 32.
108. [Plato], *Definitions* 416.
109. Matt 24.45, 25.21, 23.
110. 1 Cor 1.9, 10.13; 2 Cor 1.18.

28(1) Who could be more potent than God? Lack of faith is a hypothetical conjecture of the opposite; it is weak and negative, just as the lack of faith is a state which finds faith hard to accept. Faith is a hypothesis made by the free will. It is a prejudgment made by a person of sound judgment before the actual apprehension. It is an expectation of something which is going to happen.[111] In other cases, expectation is an opinion about something which is uncertain. But when there is real faith it is a firm grasp of something. (2) That is why we have faith in the one in whom we have trusted, for the glory of God and his saving power. We have believed in the one and only God. We know that he will not fail to fulfill his high promises to us, and all that he has created because of those promises, and all that he has given us in his benevolence. (3) Benevolence consists in wishing blessings on another for his own sake.[112] God is in need of nothing.[113] It is on us that the beneficence and kindness of the Lord rests, a divine benevolence, a benevolence which is directed to practical blessings. (4) If "Abraham's faith was counted to him as righteousness,"[114] and we are, through what we have heard, the seed of Abraham, then we too must have faith. We are Israelites, not through physical marks, but because we have been open to persuasion through what we have heard. (5) So "Cheer up, barren woman with no child, break out in a shout, you who have not known birthpangs;" it is written: "The desolate woman shall have many children rather than the woman with a husband."[115] "You have lived to enter into the place marked out for the people; your children have found a blessing within the fathers' tents."[116] (6) If prophecy promises the same homes

111. Omitting δόξα with Schwartz and Stählin; but the right reading is uncertain.

112. Camelot notes the derivation of the definition from the Stoics via Philo, *On Noah's Work as a Planter* 106.

113. Philo, *The Worse Attacks the Better* 55; *On the Unchangeableness of God* 56.

114. Gen 15.6; Rom 4.3, 9, 22; Gal 3.6; Jas 2.23.

115. Isa 54.1; Gal 4.27.

116. The passage is not in Scripture and its source is unknown; but it is not out of harmony with the Isaiah passage.

for us and the patriarchs, then one single God is revealed in both the Testaments.[117]

29(1) There is a clearer addition: "You have received the testament of Israel as an inheritance,"[118] addressed to those who are called from among the gentiles, to the formerly barren woman of the husband who is the Word, the once desolate woman of her young bridegroom. (2) "The righteous man shall live by faith,"[119] faith which accords with the Testament and the commandments, since the Testaments, chronologically two, granted in the divine economy with an eye to the stage of progress, are one in power, Old and New, being presented by the one and only God through his Son. (3) In the same way, the Apostle says in his *Epistle to the Romans*: "The righteousness of God is there revealed to faith through faith,"[120] teaching a single process of salvation proceeding from prophecy to its fulfillment in the gospel, through one and the same Lord. (4) He also says, "I present you with the charge, Timothy my son, in agreement with the prophetic utterances pointing towards you, so that with them around you, you might fight a noble campaign, holding on to faith and a good conscience. There are those who have rejected this last and made shipwreck of their faith,"[121] because by their lack of faith they have polluted their conscience, and that came to them from God.

30(1) So it is no longer reasonable to attack faith as[122] common, easy, vulgar and, what is more, accidental. If the thing is merely human, as the Greeks supposed, then it would have been stifled. In fact it is spreading and[123] there is no place where it is not to be found. (2) I assert that faith, whether it

117. This is directed against Marcion (second century A.D.) and some of the Gnostics who set the God of the *Old Testament* in contrast with the God of the *New Testament*. On Marcion see now G. May, "Marcion in Contemporary Views," *Second Century* 6 (1987–88) 129–151, esp. 141, 147; and R. J. Hoffman, *Marcion: On the Restitution of Christianity* (Chico, California, 1984).

118. The passage is not in Scripture and its source is unknown.

119. Hab 2.4; Rom 1.17.   120. Rom 1.17.

121. 1 Tim 1.18–19.

122. Reading ⟨ὡς⟩ with Tengblad.

123. Reading ⟨καὶ⟩ with Schwartz.

is founded on love or, as those who malign it assert, on fear, comes from God, and is not torn apart by any other worldly affection or dissolved by any present fear. (3) For love creates faithfulness by its attraction to faith, while faith by the benefits it introduces is the foundation of love. And since fear is the tutor of the Law on the basis of faith, then the existence of fear is also a matter of faith.[124] (4) If existence is revealed in action, and fear, which threatens and deals with the future but does not act in the present, is a matter of faith, and its existence is a matter of faith, it is not itself creative of faith, seeing that it is precisely faith which makes it recognized as worthy of credence.

31(1) This great change, that a person passes from unfaith to faith and comes to faith through hope and fear, comes from God. This is important: faith appears to us as the first leaning towards salvation; fear, hope, and penitence develop in the wake of faith, in association with self-control and patience, and lead us to love and knowledge. (2) It was reasonable for the apostle Barnabas to say, "From what I have received I have been eager to send you a share, just a little one, so that in association with your faith you may also have knowledge in its fullness. Faith and patience are the supporters of our faith; longsuffering and self-discipline are our allies. As long as these qualities remain pure before the Lord, wisdom, understanding, scientific and revealed knowledge will join them in gladness."[125] (3) The virtues of which I have just been speaking are[126] the elements of knowledge. It follows that faith is a more fundamental element, as it is essential to the true Gnostic,[127] as essential as breath is to life for anyone living in this world. Without the four elements[128] it is not possible to live. Without faith, knowledge cannot follow. So faith is the foundation of truth.

---

124. The meaning is uncertain and the argument obscure.

125. *Epistle of Barnabas* 1.5, 2.2–3, slightly misquoted.

126. Reading ⟨οὐσῶν⟩ with Schwartz.

127. Clement contrasts the Christian revelation with those of Marcion, Basilides, and Valentinus.

128. Earth, air, fire, water.

7

Justification of the Fear of God

32(1) Those who attack fear[129] are running down the Law, and with the Law obviously the God who granted the Law as well. In[130] the subject before us there must be three factors: the governor, the government, and the governed. (2) At any rate, if, for the sake of hypothesis, anyone were to annul the Law, it would inevitably follow that all persons who are directed by desire would give themselves over to pleasure, neglecting all that is honorable, turning up their noses at religion, and combining immorality and impiety in their unfearing abandonment of truth. (3) "Yes," they say, "fear is an irrational avoidance, a pathological condition." What are you saying? How could you maintain this definition when the commandment, so far as I am concerned, was given by the Word? The commandment says No. It hangs fear over our heads for the instruction of those who are capable of receiving moral guidance. (4) So fear is not irrational; it obviously springs from the Word[131] enjoining, "You shall not commit murder, you shall not commit adultery, you shall not commit theft, you shall not bear false witness."[132] But if they want to be clever over words, let the philosophers call fear of the Law caution,[133] an avoidance governed by right reason.

33(1) Critolaus of Phaselis[134] used to call these people "word-soldiers"; he was not far from the mark. Those who are critical of us find the commandment refined and outstandingly good when they think of it under another name. (2) Caution is demonstrably reasonable when it means that a

129. The Stoics to whom fear was an irrational passion (see *SVF* 1.211, 3.378, 381) and the Epicureans who regarded fear and desire as the main obstacles to happiness (see e.g., Diogenes Oenoandensis, fr. 28).

130. Reading περὶ with Hiller for παρὰ.

131. Clement's favorite wordplay on *logos*.

132. Exod 20.13–16.

133. A Stoic term (see *SVF* 3.175,431; Cicero, *Tusculan Disputations* 4.6.13; Plutarch, *Moralia* 1037 F).

134. Critolaus of Phaselis (second century B.C.) was the head of the Peripatetics, somewhat influenced by the Stoics; he brought the school back to scientific studies.

wrongdoer is withdrawing from his ways—and that is the beginning of the growth of repentance from past offences. "The
fear of the Lord is the beginning of wisdom, and all who
practice it come to a sound understanding."[135] He is speaking
of the practice of wisdom, which means the fear of God leading to wisdom. (3) If the Law produces fear, then knowledge
of the Law is the beginning of wisdom, and there is no such
thing as a wise man without the Law. Those who deprecate
the Law are lacking in wisdom and consequently to be counted
as atheists. (4) Education is the beginning of wisdom. Scripture says, "They are irreligious people who will flout wisdom
and education."[136]

34(1) Let us consider what fearful things the Law proclaims.
If things which stand between virtue and vice—poverty, ill-
ness, lack of honors, low birth, and the like—are proffered
for praise by the civic laws, the Peripatetics, who believe in
three classes of good things and regard their opposites as bad,
find themselves in accord with that view.[137] (2) But for us, the
Law granted us teaches us to avoid the real evils—adultery,
shameless behavior, pederasty, ignorance, injustice, spiritual
sickness, death—not the death of separation of soul from
body, but the death of separation of the soul from truth. Here,
and in their results, lie the real evils, and they are awesomely
frightening. (3) As the oracles of God say, we should not
spread "nets unjustly before birds. Such people, sharing in
bloodshed, lay up a store of evils for themselves."[138] (4) Then
how is it that the Law is said to be less than good by some
heresies which attack the Apostle when he says, "Through the
Law comes knowledge of sin"?[139] To these people we say, "The
Law did not create sin, it revealed it." In laying down what
ought to be done, it condemned what ought not to be done.

---

135. Ps 110.10; cf. Prov 1.7.
136. Prov 1.7.
137. The Peripatetics were followers of Aristotle (384–322 B.C.) who identified as good things external goods, physical goods, and spiritual goods (*Nicomachaean Ethics* 1.8.1098 b 12).
138. Prov 1.17–18 (LXX).
139. Rom 3.20; Marcion (see nt. 117) condemned the law on the basis of
this text (see Origen, *Commentary on Romans* 3.6).

(5) It is a good instrument which teaches that which brings
health and salvation, advising its practice, and throwing a
spotlight on that which is pernicious with the injunction to
avoid it.

35(1) They have not understood the Apostle. What he was
saying was that the knowledge of sin was revealed through
the Law, not that it took its very being from the Law. (2) The
Law must be good if it educates us, given us to be "the tutor
leading us to Christ,"[140] so that, kept straight by the educational power of the Law, we might turn to the perfection found
through Christ. (3) Scripture says, "I do not want the death
of the sinner as much as a change in his attitude."[141] The
commandment produces a change of attitude by punishing
wrong behavior, and by prescribing actions beneficial to others. (4) I fancy that by death he means ignorance. "Anyone
who is close to the Lord is covered with lashes."[142] Clearly this
is the man who draws near to knowledge, who enjoys dangers, fears, afflictions or tortures in his yearning for truth. "A
properly educated son becomes wise, an intelligent son is
saved from the fire, an intelligent son will accept commandments."[143] (5) The apostle Barnabas, after quoting, "Woe to
those who have understanding in their own eyes and are
shrewd in their own sight,"[144] adds, "Let us become spiritual,
a perfect temple for God. So far as it rests with us, let us
practice the fear of God, and let us strive to keep his commandments, so that we may find joy in his acts of justification."[145] These are the grounds for the divine words: "The
fear of the Lord is the beginning of wisdom."[146]

8

Opinions of Basilides and Valentinus

36(1) At this point, Basilides and his followers, interpreting
this text, suggest that the Archon heard the words of the attendant Spirit. He was shaken by what he heard and saw, good

---

140. Gal 3.24.   141. Ezek 33.11; cf. 18.23, 32.
142. Jdt 8.27. Clement interprets in terms of the Christian Gnostic.
143. Prov 10.4–5. (LXX).   144. Isa 5.21.
145. *Epistle of Barnabas* 4.11.   146. See nt. 135.

news beyond his expectations. His shock was called fear, and became the beginning of a wisdom which classifies, distinguishes, perfects and restores human beings to their pristine state. It is not only the world but the chosen whom the Lord of all singles out and sends forth.[147] (2) Valentinus[148] seems to have had something similar in mind when in one of his letters he wrote in the following terms: "As if the angels felt fear because of this creation when it uttered words surpassing its created condition thanks to the one who planted a seed of the higher essence invisibly within it, speaking out openly, (3) so among the generations of cosmic humans, human actions became fears to those who performed them, statues, for example, and images, and all that human hands produce in the name of God. (4) Adam was created in the name of man, and inspired a fear of preexistent man, in that the latter was set within him. They were shaken to the core, and rapidly made their work vanish."

37(1) But there is only one first principle, as I shall presently show, and it will be clear that these men are fabricating meaningless nonsense. (2) Since God thought it best through the agency of the Lord to offer a preliminary education through the Law and the prophets, it was affirmed that "Fear is the beginning of wisdom"—"the fear of the Lord"[149]—a fear given by the Lord through Moses to those who are disobedient and hardhearted. Fear tames those whom the Lord does not choose. (3) The Word, our teacher, foresaw this from the first,[150] and provided an appropriate instrument for each approach, purifying it in a fit manner for honoring God. (4) Shock is a fear arising from an unfamiliar occurrence or at an unexpected occurrence, for instance, one associated with a message, and fear is an extreme sense of astonishment, at

147. On Basilides, see nt. 32. The Archon, or Ruler, is the dominant evil power, one with the god of the *Old Testament*; the reference is to the baptism of Jesus; the text from Psalms or Proverbs receives mythical personifications.

148. See nt. 33; a similar myth: The evil angels, representing the antigod, created man but, without their knowing, a spiritual seed was placed within man. The angels saw in the creation archetypal man and panicked (see Völker, fr. 1; Layton, fr. C).

149. Ps 110.10; Prov. 1.7.

150. Or "from heaven," a double meaning.

something which exists or has come into being.[151] (5) They do not realize that through this shock they are subjecting to passion the supreme God, whom they themselves hymn, and whom they place in ignorance before the shock. (6) If ignorance existed before the shock, and if shock and fear are the beginning of wisdom,[152] then it looks as if ignorance was a first cause preceding the wisdom of God and the whole creation of the universe, and the restoration of the elect as well.

38(1) Is this ignorance of good or of evil? If it is ignorance of good, why should a shock bring it to an end? The Ministry[153] makes preaching and baptism irrelevant to them. If it is ignorance of evil, how can evil be the cause of things that are very good? (2) If there had not been ignorance previously, the minister would not have come down from heaven, there would have been no shock to grip the Archon (I am following their picture), and he would not have received from fear the beginning of wisdom for the classification of the elect and the cosmic beings. (3) If the fear of the preexistent Man made the angels turn against their own creation, on the grounds that the essence from on high was invisibly implanted in their handiwork, then either they were jealous because of some groundless supposition (it really is beyond belief that angels should have been condemned to total ignorance of the work which they were trusted to produce, like a kind of child); (4) or alternatively they were gripped by foreknowledge and moved to action by it (but they would never have planned the means they used against an object which they knew in advance, and they would never have been so shaken by the work of their own hands if they had recognized the seed from on high by their foreknowledge); (5) or else finally it was their confidence in revealed knowledge which led them to this monstrous action, but that is quite impossible too, when they had learned

151. I have accepted, without any certainty, Mondésert's text οἷον (for ἅτε καὶ) ἀγγελίας, φόβος δὲ ὡς ⟨ἐπὶ⟩ γεγονότι ἢ ὄντι [ἢ] θαυμασιότης ὑπερβάλλουσα; the definition is Aristotelian (see *Topics* 4.5.126 b 17) and Stoic (see *SVF* 3.411).
152. Omitting, with Mayor, φόβος τοῦ θεοῦ, a patent gloss.
153. Gnostic term for the Spirit.

what an extraordinary thing it was to plot against the man in the *pleroma*, 'fullness,' and again against the man "made in the likeness," in whom, they had been led to understand, could be seen the archetype and—in accordance with the rest of the revelation—immortality.[154]

39(1) Against these and others, especially the Marcionites, Scripture cries out even though they do not listen: "Anyone who listens to me will rest securely at peace and will find quietness, without fear, free from all evil."[155] (2) So why do they want the Law? They will not call it both evil and just, making a distinction between goodness and justice. (3) The Lord in telling us to fear evil does not exchange one evil for another, but uses an opposite to annul its opposite. Evil is the opposite of good. Just is the opposite of unjust. (4) So if he has said that freedom[156] from evils comes from the absence of fear engendered by the fear of the Lord, then that fear is a good thing, and the fear that springs from the Law is more than just; it is good in disposing of evil. To produce absence of fear through fear is not the same as producing freedom from the passions through passion; it is more like implanting control of passion through education. (5) So when we hear "Honor the Lord and you will be strong. Fear none besides him,"[157] we accept the fact that it is the fear of sin, and obedience to the commandments given us by God, which constitute honor shown to God.

40(1) Awe is fear of the divine. But if fear is a passion, as some insist that fear is a passion, not every fear is a passion. Superstition is a passion, being the fear of spiritual powers which are themselves agitated by different passions. (2) On the other side, the fear of the God who is free from passions is itself free from passions. It is really not a fear of God but a fear of losing him. This fear is a fear of falling into evil; it

154. The meaning must be something like this, but the reading is uncertain at a number of points. The *pleroma* or 'fullness' is a well-known Gnostic term (see nt. 33).

155. Prov 1.33; On Marcion see nt. 117.

156. Reading ἀποχὴν with Stählin for MS ἀρχὴν (an excellent emendation).

157. Prov 7.1.

is a fear of evil. Fear of falling is a desire for incorruptibility and for freedom from the passions. (3) "A wise man in fearfulness turns away from evil, the fool confidently consorts with it," says Scripture, and again, "In the fear of the Lord lies the hope of strength."[158]

9

That Virtues Are Related to Each Other and
That All Are Related to Faith

41(1) Anyway, fear of this kind leads a person to a change of attitude and to hope. Hope is an expectation of good things which looks confidently to an absent good. You could also say that the inclination towards faith[159] moves in the direction of hope, and we have learned that hope is a guide in the direction of love. (2) Love must be harmony in things concerning reason, life, behavior,[160] or to put it in a nutshell, a sharing of life,[161] an outreach of mutual friendship and affection accompanied by right reason in intercourse with comrades. A comrade is a second self,[162] just as we address those who have been born again through the same Word as brothers. (3) Welcome to strangers is close to love; it is a form of *savoir-faire*[163] in dealing with strangers. "Strangers" means those to whom the things of this world are foreign. (4) "This world" is a phrase we are familiar with for those who set their hopes on the earth and on fleshly desires. "Do not conform with this world," says the Apostle, "but be transformed by the renewal of your mind, so that you may find by experience what is God's will, good, acceptable, perfect."[164] (5) Welcome to strangers is concerned

158. Prov 14.16, 26 (LXX).
159. The last two words are not in the Greek; Something has fallen out, and it is anyone's guess what—this is Schwartz's.
160. But Jesus is the Word, the Life, the Way, and the Truth (see John 1.1, 14.6).
161. A definition common to Aristotelians (see *Nicomachaean Ethics* 8.1159 B 31 etc.), Platonists (see *Definitions* 413 A) and Stoics (see *SVF* 3.292).
162. Aristotle, *Magna Moralia* 2.1213 A 23; Zeno in Diogenes Laertius 7.23 etc.
163. Mondésert's excellent phrase.
164. Rom 12.2.

with what is best for strangers. Strangers are guests, guests are friends, friends are brothers. "My friend, my brother," says Homer.[165] (6) Love of humankind,[166] through which affection emerges too, is a loving intercourse with human beings. Affection is a kind of *savoir-faire* shown in tenderness towards friends and family. Both are attendant upon love.

42(1) If the real human being within us is the spiritual man, then love of humankind is brotherly love for those who share in the same spirit. Tenderness is a means of guarding goodwill or a loving attitude. A loving attitude is one of total acceptance. To love[167] is to give pleasure by one's behavior, in whatever direction one is drawn. (2) Human beings are drawn to identity by concord, which is the knowledge of common goals. Likeness of judgment is a harmony of judgments. (3) "Let our love," he says, "be free from dissimulation. Let us grow to hate evil, attaching ourselves to good with brotherly love," and so on, ending, "If possible, as far as lies in you, live at peace with all human beings." Then he says, "Do not be overcome by evil, but overcome evil with good."[168] (4) To the Jews the same Apostle admits his evidence "that they have zeal for God, but their zeal is unenlightened. For in their ignorance of God's righteousness, seeking to establish a righteousness of their own, they failed to submit to God's righteousness."[169] (5) They did not understand the intention of the Law, and so failed to practice it. They made up their own version and thought that that was what the Law intended. They had no faith in the prophetic power of the Law. They followed the bare letter, not the inner meaning; fear not faith. "For everyone who has faith, the end of the Law, leading to righteousness, is Christ,"[170] the Christ who is prophesied by the Law.

43(1) This is the reason why he said to them through Moses, "I will make you jealous of those who are not a nation; I will

---

165. Homer, *Iliad* 4.155 etc.
166. This word appears at Titus 3.4; it was an important word throughout Greece after Alexander and later the Christians claimed it for their own (see J. Ferguson, *Clement of Alexandria* [London, 1958], 65–66).
167. Reading ἀγαπᾶν with Stählin.
168. Rom 12.9–21. 169. Rom 10.2–3.
170. Rom 10.4.

make you angry against a people without understanding,"[171] meaning of course a people who are ready to listen. (2) Through Isaiah he says, "I have been found by those who did not look for me, I have appeared to those who did not ask for me,"[172] obviously dealing with the times before the Savior's coming, after which Israel today appropriately hears these prophetic words addressed to them as well: "All day long I have reached out my hand to a disobedient and contrary people."[173] (3) Do you see the reason why the prophet calls them from the gentiles? He says clearly that it is the disobedience and contrariness of the people. God's goodness is shown in regard to them too. (4) The Apostle says, "Through their stumbling, salvation has come to the gentiles so as to provoke Israel to jealousy"[174] and the will to repentance. (5) The Shepherd quite simply, in speaking of the dead, knows that there were people of righteousness among gentiles and Jews, not just before the Lord's coming but before the time of the Law, people who pleased God, like Abel, Noah, and others, who were righteous.

44(1) Anyway, he says that the apostles and disciples who preached the name of God's Son, and have been laid to rest, have preached, in power and faith, to those who were laid to rest before their lifetime. (2) Then he goes on: "And they gave them the seal about which they were preaching. So with them they went down into the water and rose again. But these went down living and rose again living. The others who had died beforehand went down dead but rose up alive. (3) They were brought to life and knowledge of the name of God's Son through the apostles and disciples. That is why they rose up together with these, and found a fitting place together in the building of the tower, and together were built into the construction without need of knapping. They had gone to rest in righteousness and purity. All they lacked was the seal."[175] (4)

---

171. Rom 10.19 citing Deut 32.21.
172. Rom 10.20 citing Isa 65.1.
173. Rom 10.21 citing Isa 65.2.
174. Rom 11.11.
175. Hermas, *Shepherd*, Similitudes 9.16.5–7.

In the Apostle's words, "When gentiles, without possession of the Law, perform the requirements of the Law by nature, then they, without possession of the Law, are to themselves the Law."[176]

45(1) No need to say that the virtues are in train with one another, once it has been demonstrated that faith is exercised in relation to repentance and hope, caution in connection with faith, and that the patient practice of all these combines with a process of learning[177] to have its outcome in love, and love finds its fulfillment in knowledge. (2) But it is essential to note that we must attribute natural wisdom only to the divine. This is why the wisdom which instructs in truth is a power of God. Somewhere here is found the fulfillment of knowledge. (3) The philosopher has a love of truth and is a friend of truth; from being a servant he is now through love considered a true friend.[178] (4) Wonder at the world is the first step to knowledge, as Plato says in the *Theaetetus*,[179] and Matthias in his *Traditions*,[180] in suggesting, "Look with wonder at what is before you," establishes this as the first step to the knowledge which lies beyond. (5) Similarly, in the *Gospel according to the Hebrews*[181] it is written, "The man with a sense of wonder shall be king; the man who has become king will be at rest." (6) It is impossible for an ignorant person, as long as he remains ignorant, to be a philosopher. He has no notion of wisdom, and philosophy is the desire for true being and the studies which lead to it. (7) Even though there are people who have made a practice of noble action, they still need to make an

176. Rom 2.14.

177. On the need for practice and learning see Plato, *Protagoras* 323 D; *Republic* 7.536 B; *SVF* 13.225.278.

178. Allusion to John 15.15 (Jesus being the Truth: 14.6) and wordplay on *philosopher* = 'friend of wisdom.'

179. Plato, *Theaetetus* 155 D; cf. Aristotle, *Metaphysics* 1.982 B 12.

180. A Gnostic work. An apocryphal gospel is attributed to the same author, the name being taken from the apostle who replaced Judas (see Acts 1.26).

181. The most important of the lost early Gospels, written in Hebrew or Aramaic, related to Matthew, and used by a Jewish-Christian sect called the Nazaraeans; it was not obviously heretical, and contained material which may be authentic (see Hennecke-Schneemelcher, *New Testament Apocrypha* 1.164).

effort to understand how action ought to be taken and proper
use made of things, in accordance with the principle of likeness to God,[182] I mean the savior God, in honoring the God
of the universe through the mediation of the Word as high
priest,[183] who enables us to see clearly all that is genuinely
noble and just. Piety[184] is a practice of following God.

10

Christian "Philosophy"

46(1) Our philosopher holds firmly to these three things:
first, contemplation; second, fulfilling the commandments;
third, the formation of people of virtue. When these come
together they make the Gnostic Christian. If any one of them
is missing, the state of Gnostic knowledge is crippled. (2) That
is why Scripture, inspired by God, says, "And the Lord said
to Moses, 'Speak to the sons of Israel. You are to say to them,
I am the Lord your God. (3) You shall not follow the practices
of the land of Egypt, in which you lived. You shall not follow
the practices of the land of Canaan, into which I am bringing
you. (4) You shall not walk by their statutes. You shall perform
my decisions and keep my instructions and walk by them. I
am the Lord your God. (5) You shall keep all my instructions
and perform them. The person who performs them shall live
by them. I am the Lord your God.'"[185]

47(1) Whether Egypt and the land of Canaan symbolize the
world and misguidedness, or passions and vices, the text shows
us what we have to avoid, and the sorts of things we have to
practice, because they belong to God rather than to the world.
(2) When Scripture says, "The person who performs them
shall live by them,"[186] it is referring to the upbringing of the
Hebrews and of their neighbors, that is, us, to uprightness,

---

182. Plato, *Theaetetus* 176 A–B; A favorite passage with the Fathers and
many later mystics; Clement himself refers to it more than twenty times.
183. Heb 4.14, 5.10.
184. Some editors mark a lacuna here.
185. Lev 18.1–5; see also Philo, *On the Preliminary Studies* 86.
186. Lev 18.5; Gal 3.12.

which, combined with disciplined practice and progress, means life for them and us. (3) "For those who are dead through their falling away are brought to life with Christ,"[187] thanks to our covenant. (4) Scripture often takes up the words "I am the Lord your God." It is entreating us to turn around, teaching us to follow the God who has given us the commandments. It is gently reminding us to search for God, and as far as possible to make an effort to know him. This is the highest form of study, the supreme revelation,[188] real knowledge, not to be overthrown by reason. This has to be the only knowledge known to wisdom, and it is never separated from the practice of righteousness.

11

On Certitude in Faith

48(1) But the knowledge of those wise in their own opinion, Greek philosophers or foreign heretics, is, in the Apostle's words, "a knowledge which puffs up."[189] There is a trustworthy form of knowledge; one might call it a scientific demonstration of the traditions of true philosophy. We might say that it is a rational approach to providing, on the basis of accepted truths, an account in which we can put our faith in relation to matters in dispute. (2) Faith is of two kinds; one scientific, the other conjectural. Nothing prevents us from calling demonstration twofold; one scientific, the other conjectural, since we actually use two separate terms—knowledge and foreknowledge—one enjoying its own nature in its full and precise measure, the other incompletely. (3) Is there any reason to doubt that the demonstration we provide alone leads to truth, when it is provided out of divine Scripture, sacred writings, and the wisdom the Apostle describes as "God-taught"?[190] (4) Anyway, the process of learning consists in obedience to the commandments, or in other words, faith in God. And faith is a power of God, having the strength of truth.

187. Eph 2.5.
188. A technical term of the Mysteries.
189. 1 Cor 8.1.   190. 1 Thess 4.9.

49(1) Again it is written, "If you have as much faith as a grain of mustard seed you will shift the mountain,"[191] and again, "Let it be to you according to your faith."[192] One person receives healing through faith and is cured, another although dead rises again through the strength of the faith that he will rise again.[193] (2) Conjectural demonstration is a human matter; it is the product of rhetorical argument or even dialectical syllogisms. (3) The higher demonstration, which we have alluded to as scientific, instills faith by presenting the Scriptures and opening them up to the souls who are eager to learn, and this could hardly be other than knowledge. (4) In fact, if the arguments brought to a problem are accepted as true, on the grounds that they are derived from God and prophecy, then I imagine that it is clear that the conclusion derived from them will be true in consequence. We should be right in saying that knowledge is a form of demonstration.

50(1) Anyway, when the instruction is given to consecrate in a golden vessel the memorial of the food sent down by God from heaven, "the *gomor*," it is written, "is a tenth part of three measures."[194] For our purposes, "three measures" means three sources of judgment: perception of sensible objects; reason, for evaluating sentences, nouns, and verbs; and the intellect, for intelligible objects. (2) The Christian Gnostic will refrain from errors of reason, thought, perception, and action. He has heard that "anyone who looks with lust has committed adultery." He has taken it to heart that "Blessed are the pure in heart, for they shall see God." He knows that it is "not what goes into the mouth which defiles a person, but the things which emerge from his mouth which defile him. For out of the heart emerge intentions."[195] (3) This, in my view, is the true and just measure in God's eyes, by which measurements are made, the tenth part which holds a person together,

191. Matt 17.20.   192. Matt 9.29.
193. With reference to the raising of Lazarus (see John 11.21–2, 32, 40).
194. Exod 16.36; cf. Philo, *On the Preliminary Studies* 100. The *gomor* or *omer* is a dry measure, a tenth of an ephah, between six and one-half and seven pints.
195. Matt 5.8, 28, 15.11, 19: the last passage is cut short.

which the three measures mentioned earlier identified as of the highest importance. (4) We would be referring to: body, soul, the five senses, the power of speech, the power of procreation, and the intellectual or spiritual or whatever you want to call it.

51(1) We fairly clearly have to pass over everything else and pause at the intellect. In much the same way, in the universe we jumped over nine sections—the first which is formed of the four elements set in a single place owing to their identical treatment, and then the seven wandering planets, and the ninth of the fixed stars—and[196] with the tenth part we arrive at the knowledge of God, in a word, longing to pass behind the creation to the creator. (2) This is why the tenth part of the ephah and of the sacrificial victims was offered to God, the festival of the Passover started on the tenth day, marking the passing away from all passion and all things perceptible.[197] (3) The Christian Gnostic is rooted in faith. People wise in their own conceits use unstable, unfounded impulses and deliberately ignore the truth. (4) The Scripture makes good sense: "Cain left God's presence and went to live in the land of Naid, opposite Eden."[198] *Naid* means 'disturbance,' *Eden,* 'the good life.' (5) The good life from which the transgressor was expelled consisted in faith, knowledge, peace. Those wise in their own eyes do not want to hear even the first of God's commandments. They escape from the reins; they are self-taught; they are happy to transfer to the disturbance of a tossing sea; they drop from the knowledge of the one who knows no birth to the realm of birth and death; their opinions are constantly changing. (6) "Where there is no guidance, people fall like leaves."[199] Reasoned reflection, that is, the guiding

196. Most editors omit δὲ as ungrammatical; I suspect that in this long sentence Clement became ungrammatical.

197. Camelot points out that this is derived from Philo, *On the Preliminary Studies* 102–6; on the ephah see nt. 194; the Passover is the Jewish spring festival celebrating the deliverance from Egypt, and culminating in a sacrificial meal.

198. Gen 4.16; cf. Philo, *On the Posterity of Cain* 22; *Naid* or *Nod* in fact means 'exile' or 'wandering' and has no precise geographical location.

199. Prov 11.14.

power within us,[200] remains infallible as it takes charge of the soul, and is called its pilot. In fact, the inimitable guides us to the inimitable.

52(1) In the same way, "Abraham stood before the Lord, drew near, and spoke," and the Lord said to Moses, "You— stand here next to me."[201] (2) The followers of Simon want to conform their ways to the one who stands firm, the object of their worship.[202] (3) Faith and the knowledge of truth establish the soul which chooses them to remain the same and follow the same principles. (4) Change is related to falsehood; it is an alteration of a way of life; it is a form of rebellion; the Christian Gnostic is naturally related to quietude, rest, peace. (5) Pride and opinionatedness have corrupted philosophy. In the same way, false knowledge, though it bears the same name, has corrupted true knowledge. The Apostle writes of it, saying, "Timothy, guard what has been entrusted to you. Avoid the profane nonsense and contradictions of that which is falsely called knowledge. By professing it, some have missed their target in relation to faith."[203] (6) Because this verse exposes them, the heretics regard the letters to Timothy as unauthentic. (7) Well, if the Lord is "truth" and "the wisdom and power of God,"[204] as in fact he is, it would be demonstrated that the true Gnostic is the one who has come to know him and his Father through him. For he is also aware of these words, "The lips of the righteous know lofty truths."[205]

12

Double Object of Faith and Gnosticism

53(1) There are two forms of faith as there are two forms of time. We should be able to find two corresponding forms of virtue. Memory has to do with the part of time which is

200. The *hēgēmonikon* is the authoritative part of the soul (i.e., reason) in Stoic thought, placed in the heart (see e.g., *SVF* 1.202, 2.836–9).

201. Gen 18.22–3; Deut 5.31; cf. Philo, *On the Posterity of Cain* 27.

202. A Gnostic sect, deriving from Simon Magus (Acts 8.9–24) according to their own traditions, though perhaps from a later Simon of Gitta; according to their system the root of the universe is Unfathomable Silence.

203. 1 Tim 6.20.

204. John 4.16, 1 Cor 1.24.   205. Prov 10.21.

past, hope with the part to come. It is faith which tells us that the past has existed and that the future will do so. Further, we show love because we are convinced by faith that the past has existed and that the future will do so. Further, we show love because we are convinced by faith that the past is as it is, and because we accept the future at the hands of hope. (2) Throughout, love has been the companion of the Christian Gnostic, because he knows that there is one God. "And see, everything he had made was very good."[206] The Christian Gnostic knows that and is filled with wonder. Piety adds "length of life"[207] and "The fear of the Lord adds to our days."[208] (3) So just as the days are a part of our ongoing life, so fear is the beginning of love, and as it develops, turns into faith and then love. (4) My fear of a wild animal is different, being combined with hatred (remember that there are two kinds of fear). This is more like my fear of my father, where the fear is combined with love. Again, in my fear of chastisement, I am showing self-love, and choose to feel fear. And anyone who fears to offend his father is showing love towards him. (5) How blessed is the person who finds faith, being compounded of love and fear. Faith is a force leading to salvation, a power leading to eternal life.

54(1) Again, prophecy is foreknowledge; knowledge is the understanding of prophecy—knowledge, for example, of the things the prophets foreknew thanks to the Lord who reveals all things in advance.[209] (2) The knowledge of events which have been foretold reveals an outcome in three stages: one which has taken place in the past, one which is presently on us, and one which will occur in the future. (3) Next, the first and last, looking to a past and future fulfillment, fall under the rubric of faith; present actuality provides convincing confirmation of the other two. (4) Given a single prophecy, if one part is currently being fulfilled, and one has been accomplished, it follows that our future expectations are a matter for faith, and that the past is true. (5) For in the first place,

---

206. Gen 1.31.   207. Prov 3.16.
208. Prov 10.27.
209. The knowledge of the Christian Gnostic embraces the understanding of Scripture's hidden meanings.

something was present and later became past for us, so that faith in the past becomes a grasp of the past and hope of the future becomes a grasp of what will actually happen in the future. The followers of Plato and the Stoics alike say that our intellectual assent is within our own control.[210]

55(1) Every opinion, every judgment, every assumption, every process of learning—and we live by these and take our place in the company of human beings through them—is an intellectual assent. Clearly this is simply an act of faith. Lack of faith is a revolt against faith, and it shows that intellectual assent and faith are possible. You do not speak about the absence of something which does not exist! (2) Anyone who considers things as they really are will find that human beings are naturally reluctant to assent to falsehood, and have strong inclinations to faith in the truth. (3) "Faith is the virtue which holds the Church together," says the Shepherd, "and through it the elect of God find salvation. The virtue appropriate to males is self-control. In its train come simplicity, scientific knowledge, innocence, dignity, and love. All of these are daughters of faith."[211] (4) And again, "Faith takes the lead, fear builds the house, love brings everything to a conclusion." "We must fear the Lord for the process of building, not the devil who leads to destruction," he goes on, (5) and again, "We must love and perform the works of the Lord, that is, the commandments. We must fear and refrain from performing the works of the devil. The fear of God is a process of education and brings a person to love. Fear of the devil's works involves hatred."[212] (6) The same author says that repentance is "understanding in a big way. When you repent what you have done, you are no longer doing it or saying it. In testing your own soul in relation to wrong actions, you are doing good."[213] "Pardon for sins is different from repentance, but both show what is in our own hands."[214]

210. *SVF* 2.992; Certainly Plotinus as a Platonist uses the same thought (see *Stromateis* 1.14).
211. Hermas, *Shepherd,* Visions 3.8; what follows, however, is not in our present text of Hermas.
212. Hermas, *Shepherd,* Mandates 7.1–4.
213. Hermas, *Shepherd,* Mandates 4.2.2.
214. Hermas, *Shepherd,* Mandates 4.3, a vital passage for what follows.

13

Repentance and Responsibility

56(1) So a person who has received pardon for sins must refrain from future sin. For in the light of the first (and only) repentance of sins (which would be sins committed earlier in a person's first, pagan life, I mean a life led in ignorance), repentance is immediately available to those who are called, and it cleanses the region of the soul from anything discordant, to provide a foundation for faith. (2) The Lord, "having the knowledge of hearts"[215] and foreknowing all that is going to happen, has a foreknowledge from the very first of human instability and the devil's crooked villainy, and of how the latter is jealous of the forgiveness of human sins and by his mischievous calculations to induce them to share in his fall will introduce other occasions for God's servants to sin.

57(1) So in his great mercy he gave yet another chance of repentance to those who, despite their faith, fall into some form of disharmony, so that if anyone should after their calling fall into temptation, and be forced or tricked into sin, they may have one more chance of "a repentance which brings no regret."[216] (2) "For if we sin deliberately after receiving the knowledge of truth, there is no sacrifice for sins left anymore, but a fearful prospect of judgment and a fire zealous to consume the adversaries."[217] (3) Continual and repeated repentance for sins is no different from those who have once and for all turned away from faith, except alone in the consciousness of sin. I do not know which is worse: deliberate sin, or, after repentance for sin, offending again. (4) The sin appears by exposure on either side, one condemned in the moment of performance by the person acting contrary to the Law, the other as the act of a person who knows beforehand the crime he is going to commit, and nonetheless puts his hand to it. The one is indulging his temper or perhaps his pleasure without knowing what he is giving in to. The other repents of past

215. Acts 15.8.
216. 2 Cor 7.10.
217. Heb 10.25.

indulgences, then rushes back again to pleasure and joins the person who deliberately sinned in the first place. To repeat an action repented is a deliberate accomplishment of an action already condemned.

58(1) So the person who has made his journey to faith from his previous life among the gentiles has by that single act found remission of sins. Anyone who after that falls into sin, and repents again, even if he finds forgiveness, ought to be ashamed, since he can no longer enjoy baptism for the remission of sins. (2) The person reborn "not of blood nor of the will of the flesh"[218] but of the Spirit ought not merely to abandon the idols he once treated as gods but the actions of his previous life as well. (3) This would be repentance without falling into the same fault. To repent several times is simply the repeated practice of sins and a convenient reason for casual behavior out of lack of self-discipline.

59(1) To be repeatedly requesting forgiveness for offences repeatedly committed is not repentance, only its appearance. "The righteousness of the blameless keeps their way straight," proclaims Scripture, and again, "The righteousness of the innocent will set straight their way."[219] (2) It is certainly true that "As a father pities his sons, so the Lord has shown pity to those who fear him,"[220] as David writes. (3) So "those who sow in tears shall reap with joy";[221] this refers to people from among those who in penitence make full confession. "For blessed are all those who fear the Lord."[222] Do you see the similarity to the blessing in the gospel? (4) "Do not be afraid," says David, "when a man becomes rich and when the glory of his house increases. At his death he will not take all his possessions with him; his glory will not accompany him down below."[223] (5) "In your mercy, I will enter your house. I will offer worship towards your holy temple in fear of you. Lord, lead me in your righteousness."[224] (6) An impulse is a direc-

---

218. John 1.13.
219. Prov 11.5 in two different Greek versions.
220. Ps 103.13.   221. Ps 126.5.
222. Ps 128.1.   223. Ps 49.16–17.
224. Ps 5.7–8.

tion of the intelligence towards or away from some object. A passion is an overwhelming impulse, one that exceeds the bounds of reason, an impulse which is carried away and does not listen to reason. So the passions are an unnatural movement of the soul in disobedience to reason. This rebellion, this disaffection, this disobedience is in our control, just as obedience is in our control. This is why acts of the will are subject to judgment. If anyone were to pursue each of the passions individually, he would find them all irrational desires.[225]

14

Concerning an Involuntary Act

60(1) The involuntary does not come under judgment.[226] It is of two kinds, one arising from ignorance, the other from compulsion. How could one pass sentence on those who admittedly offended involuntarily? (2) In these circumstances a person does not know himself, like Cleomenes or Athamas in their madness;[227] (3) or else he does not know what he is doing, like Aeschylus revealing the mysteries in the theatre. When he was tried by the Areopagus and showed that he was not an initiate he was acquitted.[228] (4) Or perhaps a man does not realize what he is doing, like the one who releases his opponent and kills a friend instead of his enemy. (5) Or it may be a matter of the instrument employed, like the man practicing with javelins with buttoned points and killing someone with a spear which had lost its button. (6) Or a result unexpected from the method used, like the man who kills his opponent in the sports arena (his fight is directed to victory not death). (7) Or the reason for the action, as with the doctor who gives an antidote conducive to health which results in death. His object was a cure, not death.

225. A paragraph of Christian Stoicism (see *SVF* 3.377–8).

226. From Aristotle, *Nicomachaean Ethics* 3.2.1111 A.

227. Herodotus 6.75; Ovid, *Metamorphoses* 4.516; Cleomenes I was king of Sparta (c. 519–490 B.C.); Athamas was a mythical son of Aeolus and king of Orchomenus.

228. Passages were adduced from five plays: The story was told by Heraclides of Pontus.

61(1) In the past, the law gave rulings about the person who took life accidentally as with the man who had an unintended emission of semen, but they were not the same as for those who acted deliberately.[229] (2) And yet the former will be punished as for a deliberate act, if you interpret what happened to him with an eye to the real truth. For the person who has no control of the seminal word is suffering from a kind of irrational affection of the soul, close to talking nonsense. "The man of faith chooses to conceal things without breathing a word."[230] It is deliberate acts which come under judgment. (3) "The Lord tries the hearts and the kidneys."[231] The person who "looks with lust"[232] is under judgment. That is why it is said, "Do not lust,"[233] and, "This people honors me with their lips, but their heart is far from me."[234] (4) For God looks closely at the actual inner purpose, as when Lot's wife was the only one to turn of her own free will towards the wickedness of the world and he left her insensible, giving her the likeness of a pillar of salt, and leaving her without the power of forward movement, a statue, but not one without a useful message, but one intended to offer an astringent seasoning to the man capable of a spirited approach.[235]

15

Concerning a Voluntary Act and Concerning Repentance and Pardon

62(1) Voluntary action corresponds to desire, choice or an intellectual thought.[236] Certainly these three are very close to one another—going wrong, misfortune, crime. (2) Going wrong is roughly extravagant and debauched behavior; a misfortune is exemplified by shooting your friend in ignorance as if he were an enemy; a crime is tomb-robbing or violation of a sanctuary. (3) To go wrong is made up of ignorance in

229. Num 35.22–5; Deut 19.5; Lev 15.16, 22.4.
230. Prov 11.13.   231. Ps 7.9.
232. Matt 5.28.   233. Exod 20.17.
234. Isa 29.13; Matt 15.8.
235. Gen 19.26; Philo, *On Dreams* 1.247.
236. This is Aristotelian: Aristotle, *Eudemian Ethics* 2.7.1223 a 23; *Nicomachaean Ethics* 5.10.1135–6; *Rhetoric* 1.13.1374 b 5–10.

judging what ought to be done and the inability to do it, like falling into a ditch in ignorance or the incapacity to climb out because of physical weakness. (4) What is in our power is readiness for education and obedience to the commandments.

63(1) If we do not wish to have any part in these, but watch ourselves being given over to temper and lust, then we shall go wrong, or rather we shall be committing a crime against our own soul. (2) As Laius, with whom you are familiar, says in the tragedy:

> None of your advice escapes me.
> I have a mind, but Nature does me violence.[237]

In other words, he is given over to passion. (3) Medea similarly cries out on stage:

> I know the nature of the wrongs I intend to do,
> but my passion overpowers my judgment.[238]

(4) Ajax does not keep silent either but cries out when he is intending to kill himself with the sword. No trouble eats into the soul of a free man so much as dishonor.

> I have suffered. A profound corruption rises
> from the depths, keeps disturbing me, turning me over.
> I am assailed by the sharp goads of madness.[239]

64(1) These were made tragic by passion, countless others by lust: Phaedra, Anthea, Eriphyle,

> Who received precious gold for her dear husband.[240]

(2) A different stage applies these words to the famous comic character Thrasonides:

237. Euripides, *Chrysippus,* fr. 840.
238. Euripides, *Medea* 1078–9.
239. Reading συμφύρουσα ⟨ἀεὶ⟩ with Schwartz.
240. Homer, *Odyssey* 11.327; Phaedra, Theseus' wife, fell in love with her stepson Hippolytus: see Euripides, *Hippolytus*; Anthea is a title of Hera and Aphrodite; a girl of that name was one of fifty sisters bedded by Heracles under the impression that they were the same person: it is hard to see why one should be singled out (see Apollodorus 2.4.10; 2.7.8); Eriphyle was the wife of Amphiaraus, whom she betrayed for a necklace.

A cheap little slave has enslaved me.[241]

(3) A misfortune means going wrong without reason; to go wrong is to commit an unintended crime; a crime is a deliberate wrong act. So if I go wrong, it is my act but I do not intend it. (4) This is why Scripture says, "Sin will not lord it over you; you are not under Law but under grace,"[242] declaring to those who have faith "that we are healed with his stripes."[243] (5) Misfortune is an involuntary action committed by someone else against me. Crime also is found to be a deliberate action whether by myself or some other.

65(1) The Psalmist makes obscure allusion to these distinct methods of going wrong when he calls those blessed whose transgressions God has wiped out, and whose sins he has covered,[244] not counting the one and forgiving the others. (2) "For it is written, 'Blessed are those whose transgressions are forgiven, and whose sins are covered. Blessed is the man against whom the Lord reckons no score of sin, in whose mouth there is no deceit.' This blessing came upon those chosen by God through Jesus Christ our Lord."[245] (3) "Love covers a multitude of sins,"[246] and "the one who prefers the repentance to the death of a sinner"[247] wipes them out.

66(1) Offences which are not deliberately compounded are not counted. Scripture says, "The man who lusts has already committed adultery."[248] The Logos "who brings light"[249] remits our offences. (2) "At that time, says the Lord, they will seek crime in Israel, and there will be none; they will seek sins in Judah, and none are to be found,"[250] "for who is like me?

---

241. Menander, fr. 338 K; Menander (c. 342–290 B.C.), an Athenian, was the greatest writer of New Comedy.

242. Rom 6.14. The word for 'sin,' *hamartia,* is the same as that rendered 'going wrong' (earlier Clement used the cognate *hamartēma*); it means literally 'missing the target.'

243. Isa 53.5.

244. Ps 32.1.

245. Clement of Rome, *First Epistle to the Romans* 50.6–7, quoting Ps 32.1–2.

246. 1 Pet 4.8.

247. Ezek 18.23; cf. 18.32, 33.11.

248. Matt 5.28.   249. John 1.9.

250. Jer 50.20.

Who shall stand before my face?"[251] (3) You are seeing the proclamation of one single God, who is good, who rewards according to merit and remits offences. (4) It is clear that John in his longer letter is teaching the distinctive ways of going wrong in these words: "If anyone sees his brother committing what is a sin but not a mortal one, he is to make intercession, and God will grant him life for those whose sin is not mortal. (5) There is such a thing as mortal sin. I am not speaking about that as suitable for intercession. All crime is sin, and there is a sin which is not mortal."[252]

67(1) But David and Moses before David show their knowledge of these three doctrines in these words: "Blessed is the man who has not walked by the counsel of ungodly people"[253] like fishes moving in darkness in the deep. For those which do not possess scales, those which Moses decrees are not to be touched,[254] find their food below the sea. (2) "And has not stood in the path of sinners,"[255] like those who think that they fear the Lord, but go wrong like the pig. When he is hungry, he grunts, and when he has eaten his fill he does not recognize his master.[256] (3) "And has not sat in the seat of pestilence,"[257] like birds ready for their prey. Moses gave instructions: "Do not eat pig, eagle, hawk, crow, or any fish without scales."[258] That is Barnabas. (4) I personally heard a wise man[259] say something like this in interpretation: "The counsel of ungodly people refers to the gentiles; the way of sinners is the understanding of the Jews, and the seat of pestilence is the heretics."

68(1) Someone else has said more authoritatively that the first blessing was directed to those who never followed wicked opinions in revolt against God, the second to those who do not stick to the "wide and spacious road,"[260] or else to those who were brought up in the Law, those from among the gen-

251. Jer 49.19.   252. 1 John 5.16–7.
253. Ps 1.1.   254. Lev 11.10–12; Deut 14.10.
255. Ps 1.1.
256. *Epistle of Barnabas* 10.3.
257. Ps 1.1.
258. *Epistle of Barnabas* 10.1; cf. Lev 11.7–13; Deut 14.8–18.
259. Sometimes supposed to be Pantaenus.
260. Matt 7.13.

tiles who have repented. The seat of pestilence would be the theaters and lawcourts, or, rather, attachment to the powers of deadly wickedness and participation in their activities. (2) "But his will is in the Lord's Law," says Peter in the *Preaching*, calling the Lord "Law and Logos."[261] (3) It looks as if the lawgiver taught a different way of avoiding the three forms of sin. Verbal offences are represented by dumb fishes. There really is a situation where silence is superior to speech. "There is a reward without danger in silence."[262] Offences of action are represented by predatory carrion birds. . . .[263] A pig "enjoys mud"[264] and filth. And we must not have "a defiled conscience."[265]

69(1) The prophet is right to say, "It is not so with the impious. They are like the dust which the wind rips off the face of the earth. This is why the impious will not stand at the judgment."[266] They are already condemned, as "the person without faith is already judged,"[267] "or sinners in the assembly of the righteous" (those who are already condemned are not to be united to those who have lived without falling) "because the Lord knows the way of the righteous; the way of the impious will be destroyed." (2) Again the Lord shows us to our faces that our falls from grace and discordant acts are under our own control. He offers ways of healing appropriate to our different passions. He wants us to be put right by our pastors. He uses Ezekiel to charge some of them, I fancy, with situations where they have not kept the commandments: (3) From "you have not strengthened the weak" down to "there was no one to search for them or turn them back."[268] "For there is great joy with the Father over the rescue of one single

261. The *Kerygma Petrou*, *Preaching of Peter*, is a second-century apocryphal work probably deriving from Egypt; Clement is our chief source of knowledge of it (see Hennecke-Schneemelcher, *New Testament Apocrypha* 2.94–102).

262. Simonides (c. 556–468 B.C.) came from the island of Ceos, and rivalled Pindar as the leading poet of the time; see fr. 66.

263. Lacuna expounding the second and introducing offences of thought.

264. Heraclitus, fr. 13 DK (see nt. 4).

265. 1 Cor 8.7.   266. Ps 1.4–6.

267. John 3.18.   268. Ezek 34.4–6.

sinner," says our Lord.[269] (4) Abraham is the more praiseworthy in that "he went as the Lord told him."[270]

70(1) It was from here that one of the wise men of Greece drew the apophthegm "Follow God."[271] "The people of piety," says Isaiah, "have shown understanding in their deliberation."[272] (2) Deliberation is an investigation of the right means to pursue in present circumstances. Wise deliberation is the application of practical wisdom to deliberations. (3) Well? Does God, after Cain's forgiveness, consequently introduce the repentance of Enoch in demonstration that forgiveness naturally breeds repentance?[273] Pardon is not constituted for remission of penalty but for cure. The same applies to the making of the calf in the time of Aaron.[274] (4) This was the source of an apophthegm of one of the Greek sages, "Pardon is preferable to punishment," and similarly, "Take care, disaster is near,"[275] taken from Solomon. "My son, if you have become surety from your friend, you will be presenting your hand to your enemy. A man's own lips are a strong snare to him, and he is trapped in the speech of his own mouth."[276] (5) A little more mysterious is the sentence "Know yourself."[277] It comes from the text "You have seen your brother, you have seen your God."[278]

71(1) In this way I suppose we must take "You shall love the Lord your God with your whole heart and your neighbor

269. The sense is approximately found in Luke 15.7, 10; is Clement paraphrasing? or quoting from a lost gospel?

270. Gen 12.4.

271. Pythagoras (see nt. 96), cited in Diogenian 3.31.

272. Isa 32.8.

273. Gen 5.24; Philo, *On Abraham* 17.

274. Gen 32.

275. Pittacus (sixth century B.C.) was a politician and dictator in Mytilene as well as one of the legendary Seven Sages (see Diogenes Laertius, 1.76).

276. Prov 6.1–2.

277. Inscribed over the Temple of Apollo at Delphi, much quoted, and attributed to various sages including Bias, Chilon, and Thales.

278. Saying of Jesus not in the Gospels but also in Tertullian, *On Prayer* 26 (see Resch, *Agrapha* 65); Clement is eager to derive Greek philosophy from Jewish-Christian sources, but to derive an ancient Greek saying from the historic Jesus is to turn chronology on its head.

as yourself."[279] He says that the whole of the Law and the prophets depends on these commandments. (2) This matches the others: "I have spoken thus to you so that my joy may be made full. This is my commandment, that you love one another as I have loved you."[280] (3) "For the Lord is full of mercy and pity"[281] and "The Lord is good to all."[282] Moses, transmitting "Know yourself" with greater clarity, often says, "Keep an eye on yourself."[283] (4) "Sins are cleansed by acts of mercy and of faith; it is the fear of the Lord that turns everyone away from evil."[284] "The fear of the Lord is education and wisdom."[285]

16

We Are Not Able to Speak about God without a Certain Anthropomorphism

72(1) At this point, we become once again the victim of our parasitic accusers as they say that joy and sorrow are passions within the soul.[286] They describe joy as exaltation conformable to reason, and a state of delight, joy in worthy objects. They describe pity as sorrow for someone suffering unmerited evil. They say that experiences of this sort are affections of the soul; they are passions. (2) It seems that we continually think of the Scriptures in worldly terms in such respects, making analogies from our own passions, wrongly accepting our understanding of the will of God (who is impassible) by the analogy of the stirrings within us. (3) If we, who have a capacity for hearing, were to imagine a similar condition in the Almighty, we should be committing a godless error. (4) It is not possible to speak of the divine in its actual nature. But even though we are fettered to flesh, it is possible for us to

---

279. Matt 22.37–8; Mark 12.30–31; Luke 10.27; Deut 6.5; Lev 19.18.
280. John 15.11–12.   281. Ps 11.4.
282. Ps 145.9.
283. Gen 24.6; Exod 10.28, 23.21, 34.12; Deut 4.9, 6.12, 8.11, 11.16, 12.13,19,30, 15.9, 24.8.
284. Prov 15.27.
285. Prov 15.33; Sir 1.27.   286. Stoics.

hear the Lord, accommodating himself to human weakness for our salvation, in the words of the prophets.

73(1) Then, since it is God's will that those who obey the commandments or repent of their sins be saved, and since we have joy in our own salvation, the Lord who spoke through the prophets has set his own seal on our joy, as he says in the gospel in his love of humankind: "I was hungry and you gave me food. I was thirsty and you gave me drink. Anything you have done to a single one of the humblest of the humble, you have done to me."[287] (2) So just as he is nourished, without being nourished, through having nourished the person of his purpose, so he receives joy without having experienced outward change because the person of his purpose has found joy in repentance. (3) God is rich in mercy, and filled with goodness. Through the Law he gives us the commandments. Through the prophets he gives us warnings.[288] Today, more intimately, he saves us through the presence of his Son, having mercy on the objects of his mercy.[289] It is proper that the stronger show mercy to the weaker, and one human being, being born a human being, could hardly be stronger than another. But God is in every respect stronger than a human being. So if the stronger has mercy on the weaker, then it is God alone who will show us mercy. (4) Human beings learn to share as a result of justice; they pass on to others some of what they have received from God out of a natural attitude of kindliness and obedience to the commandments.

74(1) But God has no natural attitude towards us, as the founders of heresies like to think. It makes no difference whether we were formed from nothingness or from matter, since the former has no existence at all, and the latter is totally distinct from God—unless anyone is going to have the impertinence to say that we are a part of him and of the same substance as God.[290] (2) I do not know how anyone can bear

287. Matt 25.35,40.
288. Reading ⟨νουθετῶν τε⟩ with Schwartz; but something has dropped out.
289. Rom 9.15; Exod 33.19.
290. To the Gnostics man is an emanation from the divine nature, of the

to hear this if he has once known God and has turned his eyes upon our lives and the evils in which we are plunged. (3) On this assumption God would be partly at fault (an improper suggestion to make), that is, if the parts are parts of the whole which they make up (if they did not make up the whole, they would not be parts at all). (4) But God is naturally "rich in mercy"[291] and out of his goodness cares for us although we are not parts of him, and not his children by nature.

75(1) And the greatest indication of God's goodness is that although we are what we are, by nature "alienated"[292] from him, he nonetheless takes total care of us. (2) There is a natural love shown by animals towards their offspring, and a natural friendship which arises between like-minded people out of familiarity. But God's mercy is shown richly towards us even though we have nothing to do with him (in our essential being or nature, I mean, or in the peculiar power of our essential being; simply in the working out of his will). In fact, it is when a person freely rises to the knowledge of the truth by a process of self-discipline and learning that God calls him to the position of son, and that is the greatest progress of all. (3) "Iniquities trap a man; each person is bound in the ropes of his own sins."[293] "God is not responsible."[294] It is true that "a man is blessed if he always acts humbly and circumspectly."[295]

---

same substance therefore as God. (The word *homoousios* was later applied to the orthodox view of the Son's relation to the Father. For its Gnostic use, Camelot notes Ptolemaeus, *Letter to Flora* 8; Irenaeus, *Against Heresies* 1.5.1,5 and elsewhere; *Excerpta ex Theodoto* 42.3, 50.1, 58.1). Camelot rightly says that Clement emphasizes the *free* gift of grace.

291. Eph 2.4.   292. Eph 4.18.
293. Prov 5.22.
294. Plato, *Republic* 10.617 E.
295. Prov 28.14.

17

Knowledge and Will

76(1) Scientific knowledge is a disposition towards knowledge,[296] from which knowledge emerges; it results in a grasp of fact which a process of reasoning cannot overthrow. Ignorance is a representation of plausibility which a process of reasoning can overthrow. The matters overthrown or confirmed by reasoning are within our own powers. (2) Closely parallel to scientific knowledge are ἐμπειρία, 'experience,' εἴδησις, 'theoretical knowledge,' σύνεσις, 'understanding,' νόησις, 'ratiocination,' and γνῶσις 'revealed knowledge.' (3) Theoretical knowledge is a knowledge of the universe by species. Experience is a form of knowledge with comprehension of such a kind that it is possible to pay close attention to every object. Ratiocination is knowledge of what may be ratiocinated. Understanding is knowledge of possible relationships, or rather the firm identification of possible relationships, or the capacity to identify possible relationships in areas of practical or theoretical knowledge, alike of the individual constituents and the totality of those which fall within a single definition. Revealed knowledge is the knowledge of being itself, or a form of knowledge which accords with phenomena. Truth is the scientific knowledge of truth; the state of possessing truth is the knowledge of true things.

77(1) Scientific knowledge is constituted by reason and cannot be overthrown by any other form of reasoning. At this point it is constantly involved with revealed knowledge.[297] (2) When we refrain from an action, it is either through incapacity or the absence of will to do it, or both. (3) So we do not fly because we cannot and do not wish to. We do not swim (for the moment at least), although we can, because we do not wish to. We are not like the Lord because, although we would like to be, we cannot. (4) "No disciple is above his master; it is

296. *Epistētikē,* 'towards-knowledge,' is found nowhere else in ancient Greek.
297. Most editors omit these words.

enough if he is like his master."[298] Not in essential being; it is impossible for that which is secondary to be equal to that which is naturally primary in respect of essential being. Rather, by virtue of having become eternal, of having come to know the contemplation of reality, of being called sons,[299] of seeing the Father on his own on the basis of that which is related to him.[300] (5) In all this, the will leads the way; the powers of reason are naturally servants to the will. "Wish," says Scripture, "and you will have the power."[301] For the Gnostic Christian, will, judgment, and praxis are one and the same. (6) If a person's professions are the same, his doctrines and judgments will be the same, so that his words, his life, his behavior may accord with his commitment. "The heart that is right seeks knowledge"[302] and pays attention to it. "God has taught me wisdom and I have come to know the knowledge of holy things."[303]

18

Moral and Spiritual Excellence of the Law of Moses

78(1) It is evident that all the other virtues which are found in Moses' writings provided the Greeks with the starting point for their whole ethical material. I am speaking of courage, self-control, practical wisdom, justice, endurance, patience, propriety, continence, and above all, piety.[304] (2) I imagine everyone can see that it is piety which teaches us to worship and honor the highest and oldest cause of all.[305] (3) As to justice,[306] the Law itself brings it forward, training us in practical wisdom through abstention from visible idols, and by directing us, and it is from this source as from a spring that all

298. Matt 10.24–5.

299. John 1.12; Gal 3.26.

300. I.e., Jesus, John 14.9.

301. Reference unknown.

302. Prov 27.21 (LXX).

303. Prov 24.26 (LXX); cf. Wis 10.10.

304. Clement goes beyond Plato's analysis of virtue in the *Republic* as fourfold (see nt. 2).

305. Philo, *On Virtue* 34–5.

306. But the Greek *dikaiosyne*, Hebrew *tsedeq*, 'righteousness,' and Latin *iustitia*, 'obedience to law,' are not the same.

understanding grows. (4) "The sacrifices of the lawless are an abomination to the Lord, but the prayers of the upright are acceptable to him,"[307] since "righteousness is more acceptable to God than sacrifice."[308]

79(1) There is a similar text in Isaiah: "What is a multitude of sacrifices from you to me? says the Lord,"[309] and the whole passage: "Untie every bond of wickedness. For a sacrifice acceptable to God consists in a contrite heart, one that seeks its creator."[310] (2) "A false balance is an abomination in the Lord's eye, but a just weight is acceptable to him."[311] It is on the basis of this that Pythagoras warns people "not to step outside the beam of the balance."[312] (3) The message of the heretics is described as false righteousness, and "The tongue of the unrighteous will be destroyed, the mouth of the righteous distills wisdom."[313] But the former reckon "the wise people who have discernment"[314] as of no account. (4) It would be a long business to adduce the evidence concerning these virtues as the whole of Scripture sings their praises. (5) Courage is defined as the knowledge of what is to be feared, what is not, and what is intermediate between the two; self-control as a state of mind that preserves the judgments of practical wisdom in matters of choice and avoidance. It follows that patience, sometimes called endurance, is close to courage, being the knowledge of what is to be withstood and what not. So is superiority of spirit, the science which scorns the ephemeral. Caution, on the other hand, a rational process of avoidance of evil, is close to self-control.[315]

80(1) To keep the commandments, which means a faultless observance of them, is to defend our security in living. It is not possible to show endurance without courage, still less continence without self-control. (2) The virtues are closely linked

---

307. Prov 15.8.   308. Prov 16.7 (LXX).
309. Isa 1.11.
310. Isa 58.5–6 blended with Ps 51.19; Eccl. 12.1.
311. Prov 11.1.
312. Diogenes Laertius 8.18, where it is interpreted as observing equity (see nt. 96).
313. Prov 10.31.   314. Prov 16.21.
315. See *SVF* 3.175.

together, and a person who experiences them in their whole combination also experiences salvation, which preserves our well-being. (3) It is a reasonable conclusion about the whole sum of these virtues, if we have grasped the facts about them, that a person who holds one single virtue with revealed knowledge as a Christian Gnostic, holds them all because of their mutual links.[316] (4) Next, continence is a disposition which never goes beyond the conclusions of right reason. It is shown by the person who checks impulses which run contrary to right reason or the person who checks himself from acting impulsively contrary to right reason. (5) This is a form of self-control not without courage, since from the commandments spring practical wisdom which is obedient to the God who disposed . . . ,[317] and justice which copies the divine order. If we are continent, we follow justice in our journey in purity towards piety and in actions which consequently are obedient to God, so far as possible in the likeness of the Lord,[318] although in our nature remaining subject to death.

81(1) This is what it means to be "just and holy with practical wisdom." The divine is free alike from need and passion.[319] It is not properly to be called continent; it is never exposed to a passion to have to overcome it. Our nature is subject to passion, and needs continence, and uses it to practice reducing to needs in the effort to acquire a disposition not far from the nature of the divine. (2) The good man has few needs. He is on the boundary between a mortal and an immortal nature. His physical body and the process of birth leave him with needs, but he has been trained by continence under the guidance of reason[320] to keep them few. (3) What reason lies behind the law forbidding a male to wear female dress?[321] Presumably it wants us to be masculine and avoid femininity, whether in our physical appearance, our actions,

316. Christian version of a Socratic or Platonic paradox (see Plato, *Protagoras* 329 C ff.).

317. Something is missing.

318. See nt. 182.

319. Stählin notes the detailed derivation of this and the next 20 sections from Philo, *On Virtue*. The desire for passionlessness is Stoic (see *SVF* 3.201).

320. Or "the Word."   321. Deut 27.5.

or our thoughts and reasoning. (4) It wants the man who spends his time with truth to show himself masculine in patience and endurance—in his life, behavior, words, and practice—night and day, even if it should happen that he is overtaken by the necessity of a witness coming through blood.[322]

82(1) Again, the law in its humanity says that if a man has built a new house but has not yet moved in, or laid out a new vineyard but not yet enjoyed the fruit, or become betrothed to a girl but not yet married her, he is to be excused military service.[323] (2) This makes military sense, since we would be unenthusiastic in our military service if we were being pulled in the direction of the things we longed for (people expose themselves to danger without a second thought only if they are free in relation to natural impulses). (3) It is also humane, in the calculation that the outcome of war is uncertain and it is unjust for such a man not to benefit from his own labors, and for someone else (who has taken no trouble) to secure the property of those who have put in the work.

83(1) The law also seems to be pointing to spiritual courage, when it lays down that a person who plants should enjoy the harvest, one who builds should live in the house, one who is engaged should marry. It does not nullify the hopes of those who discipline themselves to live by reason and revealed knowledge. (2) For "a good man's hope does not perish in death"[324] or life. "I love those who love me," says Wisdom. "Those who seek me will find peace,"[325] and so on. (3) Well! Did not the women of the Midianites use their beauty to distract the Hebrews when they were at war, and lead them from self-control through debauchery to godlessness?[326] (4) They first became their mistresses and used their beauty to charm them away from honorable behavior to the pleasures of whoring. Then they maddened them to the point of giving themselves to idolatrous sacrifices and foreign women. Overpowered by women and pleasure at the same time, they re-

322. I.e., martyrdom.   323. Deut 20.5–7.
324. Prov 11.7.   325. Prov 8.17.
326. Num 25; Philo, *Life of Moses* 1.295; *On Virtue* 34 ff.

nounced God and the Law. Almost the whole people became subject to their enemies through female wiles, until fear made them aware of their danger and checked them.

84(1) Those who survived faced the danger, entered on the struggle for their religion and established themselves as masters of their enemies. "Worship is the beginning of wisdom, the understanding of holy things is insight, knowledge of the Law is the mark of a good intelligence."[327] (2) Those who suppose that the Law creates a fear which is a passion have not the virtue to understand, and have never really put their minds to the Law. "The fear of the Lord creates life. The person who goes astray suffers from pains which revealed knowledge never reviews."[328] (3) This is presumably the mystical sense of Barnabas' words: "May God, the ruler of the whole universe, grant you too wisdom and understanding, scientific knowledge, revealed knowledge of his acts of righteousness, patience. So be taught by God, seeking out what the Lord seeks from you, so that you may be finders at the day of judgment." By revealed knowledge, he calls those who meet with these qualities "children of love and peace."[329] (4) There is a great deal about sharing and exchanging, but it is enough to say that the Law forbids lending at interest to a brother.[330] By brother it means not merely one born of the same parents, but a member of the same tribe, or one of the same faith, who shares in the same Logos. The Law does not deem it right to collect interest on the capital; it seeks free giving to those in need, with hands and minds wide open. (5) God is the creator of this free gift: it is he who shares his goods, exacting only reasonable interest—the most precious things human beings possess: gentleness, goodness, high-mindedness, repute, glory.

85(1) Do you not see this injunction as equally springing from care for humanity: "Pay the poor man's wages on the day he earns them"?[331] Scripture teaches that we must pay

---

327. Prov 9.10.   328. Prov 19.23 (LXX).
329. *Epistle of Barnabas* 21.
330. Exod 22.24; Lev 25.36-7.
331. Deut 24.15.

without hesitation the wages for services rendered. I suppose
that when the poor man is hungry his enthusiasm for his task
is reduced. (2) Again, it says that a creditor should not go to
his debtor's house to exact his pledge forcibly, but should invite him to bring it out, and that the person with the pledge
should not be stripped of his clothes.[332] (3) During the harvest
it forbids owners to gather up the bits which fall from the
sheaves, and similarly advises that in harvesting something
should be left behind unreaped.[333] By this it gives excellent
teaching to owners in the practice of generous sharing by leaving some of their property for those in need, and providing
the poor with a chance of food.

86(1) Do you see how the legislation proclaims simultaneously the justice and goodness of the God who provides
food unstintingly for all? (2) Again, in the grape harvest the
harvesters are forbidden to go back and cut anything that has
been left over or to collect fallen grapes; the same rules are
applied to olive gatherers.[334] (3) In fact, the principle of tithing
crops and flocks was an education in honoring the divine; not
being totally absorbed by profit, but sharing humanely with
the neighbor as well. I suppose that the priests received their
sustenance from these firstfruits. (4) So do we now understand
how the Law educates us in piety, sharing, justice, and humanity? (5) Well? Does it not enjoin that the land lie fallow
through the seventh year, and invites the poor not to be afraid
to use any crops that grow by God's grace, nature acting as
farmer for any who will?[335] Is not[336] the Law excellent? Does
it not teach justice? (6) Again, it enjoins the same practice in
the fiftieth year as in the seventh, restoring to each person
their property, if in the meantime they have been deprived of
land through some circumstance, setting a boundary on the
cupidity of those who have set their heart on possessions by
measuring the time during which they may be enjoyed, and

---

332. Deut 24.10.
333. Lev 19.9, 23.22; Deut 24.19.
334. Lev 19.10; Deut 24.20–21.
335. Exod 23.10; Lev 25.3.
336. Reading ⟨οὐ⟩ with Hervet.

wanting those who have been subjected to a long period of poverty not to be punished all their life long. (7) "Alms and faithfulness are the protectors of the king." "A blessing is on the head of one who shares." "He who has pity on the poor will receive blessing"[337] because he shows towards his fellow the love he holds for the maker of humankind.

87(1) What I have just said has other quite natural consequences concerning rest and the acceptance of the inheritance but they are not appropriate to disclose at the present. (2) Love is thought of in various forms, in terms of gentleness, goodness, patience, freedom from jealousy or envy, freedom from hatred, no holding of grudges. It is always complete, indivisible, shared with all.[338] (3) Again there is a text: "If you see a draught animal of relatives or friends or anyone at all you know, wandering in the desert, take it and return it to the owner. And if the owner happens to be away for a long period, keep it with your own animals until he comes back and then return it."[339] Scripture teaches us by means of[340] natural fellowship to treat the object found as a trust, and not to hold hatred of an enemy.

88(1) "A precept of the Lord is a spring of life." Yes indeed. "It helps us to escape from the snare of death."[341] Well. Does it not tell us to love strangers not only as friends and relatives but in their own right, body and soul?[342] (2) Yes, and it has shown honor to gentiles too, and shows no hatred for those who act wrongly. At any rate it says openly, "You shall not loathe Egyptians, since you lived as strangers in Egypt."[343] By Egyptian it means gentile, in fact anyone from anywhere in the world. (3) It is further forbidden to think of enemies as enemies, even if they are presently besieging your walls in the effort to capture your city, until you have sent them an envoy

337. Prov 20.28, 11.26, 14.21.
338. Völker notes the intrusion of this explicitly Christian passage on love in a long section otherwise based on the Judaism of Philo (see nt. 319).
339. Deut 22.1–2; Exod 23.4.
340. Reading ⟨διὰ⟩ with Hiller.
341. Prov 14.27.
342. Exod 23.9; Lev 19.33–4.
343. Deut 23.7.

to invite them to peace.[344] (4) Yes, and the instruction is given
not to behave violently to a captive woman but "let her grieve
for thirty days for those whom she wishes, and after that equip
her with new clothes and consort with her legally as with a
bride."[345] Scripture does not authorize union by rape or mer-
cenary transactions as with prostitutes, but solely unions for
the production of children.

89(1) Do you see humanity linked to continence? If an
owner is gripped by a passionate desire for a captive woman,
he is not allowed to gratify his pleasure; his lust is cut down
by a prescribed interval of time; the captive's hair is cut to put
a violating passion out of countenance. For if mature reflection induces him to marry, he will stick by her if she becomes
unbeautiful. (2) Next, if anyone has sated his lust, and no
longer thinks the captive worth living with, he is told that he
is not allowed to sell her; he may not even continue to keep
her as a domestic servant. Scripture wants her to be free and
liberated from domestic service, so that she may not suffer
intolerable pangs of jealousy on the introduction of some
other woman.

90(1) Well. The Lord tells us to relieve and lighten the burdens of beasts of burden, even when they belong to our enemies. He is teaching us at a distance not to take pleasure in
the misfortunes of others, and not to laugh at our enemies.[346]
He wants to teach those who have exercised themselves in
these disciplines to pray for their enemies.[347] (2) It is not good
to be jealous and pained at the good fortune of our neighbor,
and certainly not to take pleasure in our neighbor's misfortune. Scripture says, "If you find an animal belonging to your
enemy wandering, abandon anything which might fuel the
fires of your disagreement, take it and return it to him."[348] A
reputation for nobility follows the refusal to remember ills,
and leads to the cessation of hostility. (3) From this we become
disposed to concord, and concord leads to happiness. If you
catch anyone you regard as a traditional enemy acting stupidly

344. Deut 20.10, though that passage deals with Israelite attacks on a city.
345. Deut 24.10–14.   346. Exod 23.5.
347. Luke 6.27–8.   348. Exod 23.4.

and irrationally out of desire or temper, turn him towards good behavior.

91(1) It has already been clearly shown that the Law is good and humane, "a tutor leading us to Christ."[349] The same God is just and good, naturally working from start to finish for the salvation of every people. (2) "Show pity," the Lord says, "so that you may receive pity. Forgive so that you may be forgiven. As you do, so will it be done to you. As you give, so you will receive. As you judge, so you will be judged. As you benefit others, so you will receive benefits. The measure you use will be used in relation to you."[350] (3) The Law goes on to prevent dishonor to those who undertake servile work for the sake of[351] something to eat, and grants to those enslaved as a result of debts total freedom every seventh year.[352] (4) It further prevents suppliants being handed over to punishment. Nothing is truer than this sentence: "As gold and silver are tried in the furnace, so the Lord selects from among the hearts of human beings."[353] (5) Again, "The man who shows pity is long-suffering. Wisdom resides in everyone who takes care. Care will assail a man of intelligence, and in his good sense he will seek life. The person who seeks God will find both knowledge and righteousness. Those who seek him rightly have found peace."[354]

92(1) I personally think that Pythagoras derived from the Law his gentle attitude to irrational animals.[355] For example, he declared that people should refrain from taking[356] new births out of their flocks of sheep or goats or herds of cattle

---

349. Gal 3.24.

350. A summarizing potpourri of texts. See Matt 5.7, 6.14–5, 7.1–2, 12; Luke 6.37–8; also Clement of Rome, *First Epistle to the Corinthians* 13.2.

351. Reading ⟨ἐπὶ⟩ with Mangey.

352. Exod 21.2; Lev 25.39–41; Deut 15.12.

353. Prov 17.3.

354. A potpourri of passages from Proverbs: 19.8 (LXX), 14.23, 17.12, 16.8.

355. Pythagoras (see nt. 96) believed in the transmigration of souls from humans to animals and *vice versa*, and was consequently a vegetarian (see Plutarch, *Moralia* 993 A).

356. Reading ⟨λαμβάνοντας, ἀπέχεσθαι⟩ from the text of Philo (cf. nt. 319).

for immediate profit or by reason of sacrifice. He did this alike for offspring and mothers, drawing human beings to gentleness, starting from below with irrational animals. (2) Scripture says, "At least grant the offspring to its mother for its first seven days."[357] For if nothing comes to be without reason, and milk flows in the mothers for the nourishment of the offspring, then in taking the offspring away from the providential endowment of the milk, a person is doing violence to nature. (3) So Greeks and anyone else who runs the Law down ought to blush for shame if the law is generous over irrational beasts, whereas they actually expose human offspring to die, and yet for a long time with prophetic authority the law has cut short their ferocity through the commandment of which we have been speaking. (4) For if the law refuses to allow the offspring of irrational creatures to be separated from their mother before taking milk, it is far more forceful in preparing human beings against that cruel, uncivilized view. If they ignore nature, at least they may not ignore the lessons of the law.

93(1) It is permitted to take one's fill of kids and lambs, and this might be a possible excuse for separating offspring from mother. But what justification is there for the exposure of a baby? A man who did not want to bring children into the world ought not to have married in the first place rather than become a murderer through his inability to control his lust. (2) Again, the law in its excellence does not permit the joint sacrifice of offspring and mother on the same day.[358] As a result, the Romans too, if a pregnant woman is condemned to death, do not allow the sentence to be carried out before she has given birth.[359] (3) Anyway, the law explicitly forbids the slaughter of pregnant female animals until they have given birth,[360] checking at a distance the inclination of those who might offend against a human being. (4) In this way the law

357. Exod 22.30; Lev 22.27.
358. Lev 22.28.
359. Ulpian 1, 3, 18 (rescript of Hadrian); *Martyrdom of Perpetua* 15; cf. Plutarch, *Moralia* 552 D.
360. Not in the books of the Law as we have them.

has extended equity actually as far as irrational animals, so that from practice towards creatures of a different species we may use love of our own kind to overflowing in relation to our fellow humans.

94(1) Those who kick the bellies of some animals before they give birth, purposing to dine off a mixture of flesh and milk, have turned a womb designed for the production of offspring into a tomb for the fetus, although the lawgiver explicitly says, "You shall not boil a kid in its mother's milk."[361] (2) Our physical nature rebels against the thought of making the nourishment of the living a garnish for the death, or the cause of life an accessory to the death of the body. (3) The same law decrees, "Do not muzzle the ox as it treads the grain." For it is an essential principle that "the worker deserves his food."[362] (4) It also forbids the yoking of an ox and a donkey together for ploughing the soil.[363] There it is perhaps guessing at the disparity between the animals. It is at the same time showing clearly that we must not wrong any of those from other races by bringing them under the same yoke, when we have nothing against them apart from their foreignness, for which they are not responsible, which is not an immoral trait and does not spring from one. (5) It is my view that this is an allegory, meaning that we should not share the cultivation of the Logos on equal terms between pure and impure, faithful and faithless, as the ox is accounted a clean animal, and the donkey unclean.[364]

95(1) The Logos in his goodness, richly equipped with love of humankind, teaches that it is not right to cut down cultivated trees, still less to cut crops for purposes of vandalism before harvest, and even less still to destroy root and branch cultivated fruit, whether of the land or of the soul. It does not even allow the razing of enemy land.[365] (2) Yes, and farmers find their profit from the law. It enjoins them to take care of their young trees right to their third year, pruning them to prevent them being oppressed by excessive weight and being

361. Exod 23.19; Deut 14.21.
362. Deut 25.4; Matt 10.10.   363. Deut 22.10.
364. Philo, *On Virtue* 145.   365. Deut 20.19–20.

weakened through shortage of a nourishment spread too thinly. It enjoins them to trench and dig round them, to prevent parasites from inhibiting their growth. (3) It does not allow the harvesting of immature fruit from immature trees. After three years, the firstfruits are to be consecrated to God after the tree has reached maturity.[366]

96(1) This analogy from agriculture might be a kind of lesson, teaching us that we must cut out sins like parasitic growths and all the useless intellectual vegetation which grows alongside productive fruit until the young shoot of faith has grown to mature strength. (2) Time is needed for strength in a catechumen. In the fourth year the four virtues are consecrated to God. The third stage touches the fourth place, where the Lord is.[367] (3) A sacrifice of praise is more worthy than holocausts.[368] Scripture says, "It is he who gives you strength to exercise your power."[369] (4) By these words it is showing clearly that it is God who grants us gifts of good things, and that we ought as servants of the grace of God to sow God's gracious gifts and enable our neighbors to become people of honor. The aim is for the man of self-control to enable the continent to find their fulfillment, the man of courage to do the same for the noble, the man of practical wisdom for the understanding, and the man of justice for the just.

19

How the Gnostic Is an Imitator of God

97(1) It is the Christian Gnostic who is "in the image and likeness," who imitates God so far as possible,[370] leaving out none of the things which lead to the possible likeness, dis-

366. Philo, *On Virtue* 165–7.
367. On the four virtues see nt. 2; the analogies are forced. The text in paragraph (2) is uncertain: Either we omit [τε] with Stählin or assume a lacuna with Schwartz—unless Clement was writing carelessly; but the last phrase remains puzzling. Clement speaks of the Lord's *hypostasis*; G. L. Prestige, *God in Patristic Thought* (London, 1952), argued that this means not 'essential being' but 'dwelling-place.'
368. Ps 50.23, 51.15–16.
369. Deut 8.18.
370. Gen 1.26 (see nt. 182); Philo, *On Virtue* 168.

playing continence, patience, righteous living, sovereignty over the passions, sharing his possessions so far as he can, doing good in word and deed. (2) "The man who performs and teaches these things shall be greatest in the kingdom," says Scripture,[371] imitating God by the generous offer of similar gifts. For God's gifts are available for the benefit of all. (3) "Anyone who tries to act high-handedly annoys God,"[372] says Scripture. For bombast is a spiritual vice. Scripture tells us to repent from it as from the other vices by turning from disharmony and linking ourselves to a change for the better through the three instruments of mouth, heart, and hands.[373]

98(1) These are evidently symbolic—hands, of action; heart, of deliberation; mouth, of speech. There is an excellent text on the subject of the penitent: "You have chosen God today to be your God, and the Lord has chosen you today to be his people."[374] God makes his own the person who is eager to serve true reality and comes as a suppliant. (2) Even if he is only one in number, he is honored on equal terms with the whole people. He is a part of the people; he becomes the complement of the people, once he is reestablished out of his previous position, and the whole in fact takes its name from the part. (3) This high birth is shown in excellence of choice and practice. What benefit did Adam receive from such high birth? He did not have a mortal father; he was the father of humankind and our process of birth. (4) He was ready to follow his wife in choosing a course which brought shame; he had no concern for goodness or truth. Those were the terms on which he exchanged immortality for a mortal life—though not to the very end.

99(1) Noah, whose coming into being was different from Adam, was rescued by divine Providence; he brought himself as an offering to God. Abraham fathered children on three women. This was not for pleasurable enjoyment but, in my view, originally in the hope of multiplying his race. Only one

---

371. Matt 5.19.
372. Num 15.30 (LXX).
373. See Deut 30.14; Philo, *On Virtue* 171.
374. Deut 26.17–19.

son was the heir and inheritor of his father's goods,[375] the rest of his progeny were scattered far and wide. (2) This son had twins, and the younger satisfied his father and received the inheritance, taking his father's blessing; the elder was subject to him.[376] The lack of independence was a great benefit to the one of lower character. (3) This disposition is prophetic and allegorical. Scripture shows clearly that there is nothing the wise man does not possess[377] in the words "Because God was gracious to me, there is nothing I do not possess."[378] It teaches that we must reach out for one thing only, through which everything came into being and the promised blessings are distributed among the meritorious.[379]

100(1) So Scripture writes that the good man is heir to the kingdom and fellow citizen with the righteous people of the past, who lived in obedience to the Law or in accordance with the Law before the time of the Law and whose actions have become laws for us. (2) Again it teaches that the wise man is king[380] and shows those of a different race saying to him, "You are among us as a king deriving from God."[381] The subjects by a free decision obey the good man in their enthusiasm for virtue. (3) The philosopher Plato puts forward happiness as the goal of life and says it consists in "the greatest possible likeness to God."[382] This may come from his going along with the general principles of the Law (Philo the Pythagorean says in expounding the text of Moses, "Great natures free from passion aim fairly successfully in the direction of truth").[383] Or it may come from his thirst for learning and readiness to be taught by writings of the period. (4) For the Law says,

375. Isaac.
376. Esau and Jacob; Philo, *On Virtue* 207–209.
377. A Stoic paradox.
378. Gen 33.11.
379. Clement's language is ambiguous between "one thing" and "one person"—he no doubt has Matt 6.33 in mind; but his insistence on the meritorious does not accord with all theologies, although it can be brought within the idea of "made meritorious by God's grace."
380. Another Stoic paradox (see *SVF* 3.589–603).
381. Gen 23.6.
382. Plato, *Theaetetus* 176 B (see nt. 182).
383. Philo, *Life of Moses* 1.22.

"Walk behind the Lord your God and keep my commandments."[384] The Law actually calls "likeness" "following." Following in this spirit is the greatest possible likeness. The Lord
says, "Be merciful and show pity, as your heavenly Father is
merciful."[385]

101(1) It was on this basis that the Stoics laid down their
doctrine that the goal is to live according to nature, using the
word "nature" improperly rather than "God," since nature
applies to plants, crops, trees and stones.[386] (2) At any rate,
there is the clear statement: "Scoundrels think nothing of the
Law, but those who love the Law set it in front of them like a
wall."[387] For "the wisdom of able men will understand the
paths of wisdom, but the folly of fools goes in the wrong direction."[388] Prophecy says, "To whom shall I look if not the
man who is gentle and tranquil and who trembles at my
words?"[389] (3) We have been taught that there are three forms
of friendship. The first and best of these is based on virtue,
since the love which proceeds from reason is firmly based.
The second stands between the others and is based on mu-
tuality. It involves mutual sharing and is beneficial to life.
Friendship on the basis of free giving is mutual. The third,
and last, comes, as we put it, from habit. Some say that it
chops and changes, being based on pleasure.[390]

102(1) I think that it was a splendid statement of Hippodamus the Pythagorean: "Friendships are of three kinds, one
group arising from knowledge of the gods, one from the service of human beings, and one from animal pleasures."[391]
These are respectively the friendships enjoyed by philoso-

---

384. Deut 13.4.
385. Luke 6.36, but to the Stoics pity was a vice, since it left our peace of
mind at the mercy of circumstances outside our control (see *SVF* 1.213;
3.452).
386. "Live according to nature" (see *SVF* 3.4–9).
387. Prov 28.4–5.   388. Prov 14.8.
389. Isa 66.2.
390. Analysis derived from Aristotle, *Nicomachaean Ethics* 8.3.1156 A 6 ff.
and taken up and modified by the Stoics (see *SVF* 3.723).
391. Hippodamus the Pythagorean (fifth century B.C.) was a famous town
planner, the implementer of the grid system.

phers, ordinary human beings, and animals. (2) The real image of God is a human being who does good to others, and in so doing receives benefit, rather as a pilot in keeping others safe keeps himself safe at the same time. That is why when a person makes a request which is met, he does not say to the granter "Thank you for giving," but, "Thank you for accepting." In this way, to give is to accept, to accept is to give. (3) "The righteous show mercy and pity." "The upright will inherit the land; the innocent will be left within it; wrongdoers will be eradicated from it."[392] (4) I think that Homer was foreshadowing the man of faith when he said, "Give to a friend."[393] You should share with a friend so that he may remain still more a friend;[394] you should help an enemy so that he may not remain an enemy. Goodwill is bound into helpfulness; hostility is abolished by helpfulness. (5) But "if a positive attitude is there, its acceptability is related to what a person has, not what he lacks. It is not a matter of others being eased at the cost of a burden to you, but of equal sharing at this present moment," and so on.[395] He has spread his resources, he has given to the poor, his righteousness lasts forever," says Scripture.[396] (6) For the words "after the image and likeness," as we have said before, are not directed to physical matters—it is not right to compare mortal and immortal—but to intellect and reason, whereby the Lord can stamp his seal appropriately on the likeness related to his beneficence and his authority. (7) Leadership is kept on the right path not by physical qualities but by intellectual discrimination.

> Cities are well-governed by the counsels of men;
> so is the home—[397]

provided that the men are saints.

---

392. Prov 21.26; 2.21–2.
393. Homer, *Odyssey* 17.415.
394. These words have to be supplied to make up the balance in an obvious lacuna.
395. 2 Cor 8.12–14.
396. 2 Cor 9.9; Ps 112.9.
397. Euripides, *Antiope,* fr. 200 N.

20

Indispensable Role of Asceticism

103(1) Fortitude strongly forces itself in the direction of the divine likeness by harvesting freedom from passions through a capacity for endurance, if anyone takes to himself the stories of Ananias and company,[398] amongst whom was Daniel the prophet, a man filled with faith in God.[399] (2) Daniel lived in Babylon, like Lot in Sodom, or Abraham who a little later became "God's friend,"[400] in the country of the Chaldaeans. (3) So the king of the Babylonians drove Daniel down into a pit full of wild animals, and the king of the universe, the faithful Lord, brought him up again unharmed.[401] This is the patience which the Christian Gnostic will gain *qua* Gnostic. Under trial he will give blessing like noble Job.[402]

104(1) Like Jonah, he will offer prayer even when swallowed down by a sea monster, and his faith will restore him as prophet to the people of Nineveh.[403] Even if he is imprisoned with lions, he will tame the wild beasts, and even if he is thrown into the fire he will be covered with dew and will not be burned up.[404] He will be a witness night and day. In his language, his life, his behavior, he will be a witness.[405] (2) Living with his Lord, he will remain his "associate"[406] and table-companion in the spirit, pure in body and heart, sanctified in this thought.[407] (3) "The world," says the Apostle, was crucified "to him, and he to the world."[408] It is he who, carrying the Savior's cross, follows the Lord[409] in his tracks as the tracks of God,"[410] having become a saint among saints.

398. Reading ⟨τῶν περὶ⟩ with Stählin.
399. Dan 1.
400. 2 Chr 20.7; Isa 41.8; Jas 2.23.
401. Dan 6.   402. Job 1.21.
403. Jonah 1.17–3.4.
404. Dan 3, 6: an encouragement to later Christian martyrs.
405. The word "martyr" is the same as 'witness.'
406. [Plato], *Minos* 319 A; Homer, *Odyssey* 19.179.
407. Or "word," or "in respect of the Logos."
408. Gal 6.14.
409. Mark 10.34; Matt 10.38; Luke 9.23, 14.27, but Clement, himself from North Africa, may also have in mind Simon of Cyrene (see Matt 27.32).
410. Plato, *Phaedrus* 266 B; Homer, *Odyssey* 2.406.

105(1) The divine Law bears all the virtues in mind. It particularly directs human beings to continence, establishing that as the foundation of the virtues. In fact, the Law gives us a preliminary education in the acquisition of continence starting from the use of animals, forbidding the consumption of animals which are naturally fat, like the pig family,[411] which is naturally fat. Use of such food is orchestrated for people of luxury. (2) Tradition declares that one of the philosophers[412] gave the etymology of *hys*, 'pig,' as *thys*, 'sacrifice,' suggesting that it is fit only for sacrifice and slaughter. Life was given to this animal simply for the extravagant enjoyment of its flesh. (3) Similarly, the Law, to restrict our appetites, forbids the consumption of those fish which lack fins or scales;[413] these surpass the rest of fish in fatness.

106(1) This, I imagine, was the source from which the originator[414] of the mysteries took the prohibition on touching various animals, and further the removal of some parts of the sacrifices from use for reasons which the initiates know.[415] (2) If we have to master the belly and all that lies below it, then it is clear that we have received from the Lord from the first, the injunction through the Law to cut out covetous desire.[416] We would achieve this completely if we were to give an unhypocritical condemnation of the power which kindles desire—I mean pleasure. (3) Some people say that the notion of pleasure is a gentle, agreeable movement accompanied by sense perception.[417] (4) Tradition says that Menelaus was a slave to this after the capture of Troy when he came to execute Helen for her responsibility for all those evils, but even so had not the strength to go through with it. He was overpowered by her beauty and was brought to the recollection of pleasure.

411. Lev 11.7; Deut 14.8.
412. Cleanthes, second head of the Stoics, a religious genius (see *SVF* 2.516).
413. Lev 11.9–12; Deut 14.9–10.
414. Reading ⟨τὸν εὑρόντα⟩ with Schwartz.
415. It is not known precisely to what Clement is referring, but he might be alluding to Lev 16.26–8 or Heb 13.11.
416. Exod 20.17.
417. Aristippus of Cyrene (Diogenes Laertius 2.85–6), founder of the hedonistic Cyrenaics; his grandfather had been an associate of Socrates.

107(1) The consequence was the gibes of the tragic poets with their cutting exclamations against him.

> But you had only to see her breast to drop your sword
> and receive her kiss, buttering up the treacherous bitch.[418]

And again,

> Is it her beauty which has blunted their swords?[419]

(2) Personally, I agree with Antisthenes when he says, "I would shoot Aphrodite down if I could get hold of her; she has corrupted many of our best women."[420] (3) He calls physical love a natural vice. The poor devils worsted by it call this disease a god. In these phrases he shows that it is the unlearned who suffer these defeats in ignorance of a pleasure which ought to be kept at a distance even if it is called a divinity, or rather even if it is actually a gift from God for the practical purpose of the production of children. (4) Xenophon expressly calls pleasure a vice in the words: "My poor woman, what do you know that is good? What do you look upon as beautiful? You do not even wait for the desire for pleasurable objects. You eat before you are hungry, and drink before you are thirsty. To take pleasure in eating you have to manipulate cooks; (5) to take pleasure in drinking you have to provide expensive wines. You go all over the place in search of snow in summer. In order to take pleasure in sleeping you have to provide soft beds, and supports for the beds as well."[421]

108(1) In consequence Ariston says, "To face the whole quartet—pleasure, pain, fear and desire—you need a deal of disciplined practice and fighting spirit."[422]

> These run deep within through our inmost
> being, and disturb the heart of humans.[423]

---

418. Euripides, *Andromache* 629.
419. Euripides, *Orestes* 1287.
420. Fr. 11.1; Antisthenes was a down-to-earth associate of Socrates, through whom the Cynics somewhat dubiously claimed a link.
421. Xenophon, *Memorabilia* 2.1.30.
422. *SVF* 1.85.
423. From an unknown tragic author.

(2) "Even when people think highly of themselves, pleasure can turn their hearts to wax," says Plato, because "every pleasure and every pain nail the soul to the body"[424]—at any rate with a person who has not separated himself from the passions by the frontier of the cross.[425] (3) "The man who has lost his own life," says the Lord, "shall save it,"[426] either by scorning danger to offer it for his Savior, as he did for us, or by releasing it from any part in our everyday life. (4) For if you are willing to release your life, to set it apart, to set up a boundary (which is what the cross means),[427] separating it from delight and pleasure in this life, you will keep it[428] in the expectant hope in a state of "discovery"[429] and repose.

109(1) "This would be practicing dying,"[430] if we were willing to be contented with desires limited by nature, and not bursting natural boundaries into excess or running contrary to nature (which is the seed of sin). (2) "So we must put on the whole armor of God to be able to stand against the wiles of the devil,"[431] since "the weapons of our warfare are not physical but have divine power to destroy strongholds. We destroy arguments, and all the exalted attitudes raised against the knowledge of God. We take every thought prisoner, bringing it into subjection to Christ."[432] So says the divine Apostle. (3) There is undoubtedly need of a man who will feel no attraction or confusion in treating the things from which the passions spring, like wealth and poverty, glory and ingloriousness, health and disease, life and death, trouble and pleasure. (4) To use indifferently things which are matters of ethical indifference,[433] we need considerable powers of discrimination, as we have been corrupted in advance by much weakness

424. Plato, *Laws* 1.633 D; *Phaedo* 83 D.
425. See Gal 5.24.
426. Mark 8.35.
427. Camelot rightly says that there are here allusions to Gnostic language; to Valentinus the cross was a frontier (see Irenaeus, *Against Heresies* 1.2.4, 1.3.5, 1.4.1).
428. *Psyche* covers what we understand by 'life' and what we understand by 'soul.'
429. Matt 10.39.
430. Plato, *Phaedrus* 81 A.
431. Eph 6.11.
432. 2 Cor 10.4.
433. Stoic formulations.

and have enjoyed in advance a previous misdirection from a combination of ignorance and damaging upbringing and nurture.

110(1) The simple message[434] of our philosophy says that all passions are imprints made in the soul when it is malleable and yielding, and like seal impressions of the "spiritual" powers against whom "we are wrestling."[435] (2) I suppose it is the job of the powers of wickedness to try to implant something of their own nature in each being with a view to wrestling down and securing power over those who say No to them. (3) It follows reasonably enough that some lose the bout, but all who undertake the contest with better equipment for it fight with all the weapons at their disposal and keep on until they have won the crown,[436] whereas the powers just mentioned eventually succumb among the pools of blood in admiration at the victors. (4) Creatures which move may move by an inner impulse and perception, like animals, or by impulsion from without, like inanimate things. Among inanimate objects some say that plants move by a transition which leads the growth—that is, if anyone is prepared to agree with them that plants are inanimate.

111(1) Stones are said to be in a particular state. Plants share in a process of growth. Animals, even though without reason, have an inner impulse and perception as well as the other two descriptions just mentioned. (2) The power of reasoning is peculiar to the human soul. It does not make obligatory the sorts of impulses experienced by creatures without reason, but obliges us to discriminate between our inner perceptions and not just to be carried along with them.[437] (3) The powers of which we have been speaking offer souls readily disposed to that sort of thing spectacles of beauty, fancies, adulterous acts, pleasures, and similar seductive appearances, rather as drovers wave branches in front of their animals.[438]

---

434. Or "single-minded Logos."   435. Eph 6.12.
436. The reading is slightly uncertain, but the meaning clear.
437. Stoic (see *SVF* 3.714), perhaps from Philo, *Allegorical Interpretation* 2.22.
438. Plato, *Phaedrus* 230 D.

They trick those who cannot distinguish true pleasure from false, or a beauty that is perishable and insolent from beauty of holiness; they enslave them and lead them on. (4) Each decision, continually impressed on the soul, leaves an inner perception stamped upon it. And the soul, without knowing, is carrying around the image of the passion. The cause lies in the act of seduction and our assent to it.

112(1) Basilides[439] and his followers used to call the passions adventitious occurrences. They say that they are in essence spirits attached to the rational soul in some primitive disturbance and confusion, and that there are other different, bastard spiritual natures which grow up in attachment to these— the natures of wolf, ape, lion, goat, for example. Their peculiar characteristics make their appearance in the region of the soul and bring the desires within the soul into a plausible likeness of animals. (2) People then imitate the actions of the animals whose characteristics they hold within them, and not only grow familiar with the impulses and inner perceptions of animals without reason, but are keen to emulate the movement and beauty of plants because they carry attached to them the characteristics of plants.

113(1) They even[440] have the characteristics of inanimate states, like the hardness of a diamond. (2) But we shall argue later against this theory when we debate on the soul.[441] At present it is enough to observe that Basilides' man perpetuates the image of a wooden horse in the poetic myth, enfolding in one body an army of so many different spirits.[442] (3) Basilides' own son Isidore in his treatise *On the Adventitious Soul* realized the nature of this dogma almost in self-accusation. I quote *verbatim*: (4) "If you offer anyone a persuasive argument to the effect that the soul is not simple but that the passions of the corrupt appear by the force of the adventitious elements,

---

439. See nt. 32.
440. Reading ἔτι with Stählin and Wilamowitz for MS ἔχει.
441. An intended but unwritten treatise.
442. The Trojan horse, which the Trojans took inside their walls not realizing that it contained Greek soldiers—the most familiar account is in Vergil, *Aeneid* 2.13–268 (see also Quintus of Smyrna 12).

then the scoundrels of humanity will have a marvellous excuse for saying, 'I was compelled, I was carried away, it was not my fault, I acted unwillingly,' even though it was they who took the initiative in setting their hearts on wrong, and who failed to fight against the force of the adventitious elements.

114(1) "We must use our greater strength through our possession of reason and be clearly seen to conquer the lower creation within us." (2) Isidore further postulates two souls within us, like the Pythagoreans,[443] of whom we shall have more to say later. (3) Valentinus is another who writes to some correspondents about the adventitious spirits; again I quote *verbatim*: "There is only one good being, whose freedom of expression lies in the manifestation through the Son. Through him alone can the heart become pure, when every evil spirit has been driven from the heart. (4) For a multitude of spirits living there do not permit its purification. Each of these sees to its own affairs, and they often do violence with their indecent lusts. (5) I suppose the heart's experience is like an inn. It too has holes bored in it and dug in it and is often filled with filth when people stay there and behave outrageously with no consideration for the place, as if it were nothing to do with them. (6) The heart also, unless it takes care in advance, experiences something similar, being unpurified and a home for many spiritual powers. But when the Father, the only good being, has visited it, it is sanctified and blazes with light. In this way, the man with a heart like that receives blessings because he will see God."

115(1) I wish they would tell us what is responsible for the fact that such a soul is without forethought in the first place. Perhaps it is not worthy; could forethought be joined to it as a kind of result of second thoughts? Perhaps it comes to be saved by nature, as Valentinus will have it, and it cannot be but that it receives forethought from the first owing to its

443. Not really, but a strong division of the soul into rational and irrational; see e.g., Iamblicus, *On the Pythagorean Life* 69, 111, 130, 174, 205, 224, 229; Galen, *On the Opinions of Hippocrates and Plato* 5; Aëtius, *Placita* 4.4.1, 4.5.20 in H. Diels, *Doxographi Graeci* (Berlin, 1929. Reprint 1958), 389–90, 432.

kinship, and so offers no point of entry to impure spirits, unless it is forced from outside and proved weak. (2) For if he grants the soul the power of repentance and choosing the better course, he will be saying unwillingly what our truth states as dogma, that salvation comes[444] not from nature but from a change of obedience.[445] (3) Just as exhalations arise from earth and marshes and gather into mists and thick clouds, so the outpourings from physical desires produce an evil character in the soul, scattering the images of pleasure in front of the soul.

116(1) At any rate, they cast a shadow on the light of the intellect, when the soul attracts the outpourings from physical desires, and makes thick the gathering together of the passions by the continual enjoyment of pleasures. (2) Gold is not taken out of the earth in the form of an ingot. It is heated and purified, and only when it has become unadulterated is it called gold or purified earth. "Ask and it shall be granted you"[446] are words spoken to those who are able of themselves to choose higher things. (3) I do not need lots of words to describe how we say the activities of the devil and the unpurified spirits flow[447] into the sinner's soul. I need merely call as witness the apostolic figure of Barnabas (one of the Seventy and a collaborator of Paul)[448] when he says something of the sort: (4) "Before we believed in God, the habitation of our heart was weak and corruptible, in very truth a temple built with hands. For it was filled with idolatry and a home for evil spirits, through acting contrary to God."[449]

117(1) He is saying that sinners perform actions comparable

444. We must add ⟨εἶναι⟩ (Wilamowitz) or ⟨γίγνεσθαι⟩ (Stählin, Schwartz).

445. As Camelot notes, Valentinus held that the spiritual soul, akin to the divine, is out of place in the material world, and is saved by its natural kinship with the divine; Clement, however, insists on free repentance.

446. Matt 7.7.

447. Reading ἐπεισορεῖν with Tengland and Stählin for ἐπισπείρειν, an exemplary emendation.

448. Barnabas came from Cyprus. He was with Paul at Antioch and on the first missionary journey (see Acts 13 ff.). We do not know on what grounds Clement thought him one of the Seventy (see Luke 10.1) but cf. Eusebius, *Ecclesiastical History* 2.1.4.

449. *Epistle of Barnabas* 16.7–9.

to those of evil spirits; he is not saying that the actual spirits live in the soul of the man without faith. (2) This is why he adds, "Pay attention to building a worthy temple to the Lord. How? Learn. Accept the forgiveness of sins, hope in the Name, be newborn, created again from the start." (3) He does not say that the evil spirits are driven away from us but that our sins are forgiven, those sins which we committed comparably to them, before we came to faith. (4) So he had reason in putting the following to the contrary: "This is why in the inmost part of our house God in reality is living within us. How? His Logos, object of our faith; his proclamation of promise to call us; the wisdom of his judgments; the commandments of his teaching." (5) I know that I have myself encountered a particular heresy[450] whose chief proponent claimed to conquer pleasure by practicing pleasure. He was a deserter to pleasure through a simulated battle. What a marvellous Gnostic! (6) (He said he was a Gnostic.) He did not even say that it was a major achievement to keep off pleasure if you had never experienced it; the difficulty is, once you are in the middle of it not to be overpowered by it, which is why he practiced living in it.

118(1) The poor fellow did not notice the fallacies and self-deceit of his hedonistic skill. (2) Of course Aristippus of Cyrene[451] too attached himself to this view of the sophist who boasts his possession of truth. When criticized for his long association with the courtesan from Corinth he replied, "Ah, but I possess Lais; I am not possessed by her."[452] (3) Similar too are those who claim to be followers of Nicolaus. They keep one of the man's dicta, forcing its meaning: "One must misuse the flesh."[453] (4) But this admirable man showed that we ought

450. Not to be precisely identified, but there were sects in which liberty became licence.

451. On Aristippus see nt. 417: He said that the way to master pleasure was not to avoid it but to enjoy it without being carried away by it in advance (see Stobaeus, *Florilegia* 17.18); but who is the sophist? Valentinus?

452. The anecdote, familiar enough (see Diogenes Laertius 2.75; Stobaeus, *Florilegia* 17.18), is an appalling piece of egotism; Lais was one of the most famous of all courtesans.

453. Nicolaus, a proselyte from Antioch, was one of the original seven

to curtail pleasures and desires, and use this discipline to weaken the impulses and onset of the flesh. (5) Those who wallow in pleasure like goats are (you might say) violating the body and are plunged in the delights of passion. They do not realize that the body, whose nature is fleeting, falls into rags, while the soul is buried in a slough of vice,[454] when they follow the instructions of pleasure rather than a man of apostolic faith. (6) How are they different from Sardanapallus?[455] There is an epigrammatic presentation of his life:

> I possess all I ate, all my violent acts, all the joys
> accompanying love. These many luxuries are all that are left.
> For I am now dust, I who was king of mighty Nineveh.[456]

(7) There is no absolute necessity for the passion of pleasure. It follows on certain natural needs—hunger, thirst, cold, marriage.[457]

119(1) At any rate, if it were possible to drink or take food or produce children without pleasure entering in, then it would be shown that there was no other need of it. (2) Pleasure is not an activity, not a disposition, certainly not a part of us. It entered our life as a support, just as salt is said to exist to help the digestion of food. (3) But when it is unleashed and dominates the home, it brings desire into being first, an irrational licence and yearning for that which satisfies pleasure.[458] This persuaded Epicurus to lay it down that pleasure

---

deacons (see Acts 6.5); whether the Nicolaitans were really his followers, or stole a prominent name we do not know, but they were advocates of sexual freedom in the first century A.D. in Ephesus and Pergamum (see Rev 2.6, 15).

454. Plato, *Republic* 7.533 D.

455. Sardanapallus (presumably Ashurbanipal), the last king of Assyria, who withstood a siege by rebels for two years, and then made a huge pyre on which he immolated himself, his concubines and his treasures in a scene depicted by Delacroix in a painting in the Louvre. The story, not to be reconciled with history—the last king, Sin-shar-ishkun, was in fact energetic and brave—was told by Ctesias (see Diodorus Siculus 2.23–7; Justin 1.1,3; Athenaeus 12.529–30).

456. Choerilus of Iasos, court poet of Alexander the Great, and epic writer, is supposed to have written these lines.

457. *SVF* 3.405.

458. *SVF* 3.391, 326, 436; the reading is uncertain.

was the philosopher's goal.[459] (4) At any rate, he attributes divinity to "a stable constitution of the flesh and firm confidence about the flesh."[460] (5) Sensuality is simply a form of voluptuous gluttony, an excessive superfluity on the part of those dedicated to the passion of pleasure. (6) Diogenes wrote revealingly in one of his tragedies:

> Those who are sated at heart by pleasures
> of abominably effeminate luxury
> are unwilling for hardships however small,[461]

and so on—shameful words and typical of pleasure-seekers.

120(1) And so it is in my view essential for the Law of God to hold fear over our heads;[462] for the philosopher to use all care and attention in securing and maintaining freedom from anxiety, remaining throughout free from stumbling or sin. (2) The only way for peace and freedom to survive is through a ceaseless, tireless resistance to the attacks of the passions against us.[463] (3) These weighty Olympic antagonists are (one might say) sharper than wasps; pleasure in particular, which plots against us with magic spells and gnaws at us, not just by day, but in our dreams at night. (4) So once again, how can the Greeks be right to run down the Law when they themselves have been taught by fear to be slaves to pleasure? (5) Anyway, Socrates warns us to be on our guard against the things that induce us to eat when we are not hungry and drink when we are not thirsty and against the glances and kisses of handsome youths as they are prone to inject a poison more dangerous than scorpions and tarantulas.[464]

459. See nt. 44. Reading ⟨ὃ⟩ with Mondésert.

460. Usener, *Epicurea*, fr. 68.

461. *TGF,* 808; Diogenes of Sinope (fourth century B.C.) founded the unconventional Cynics, who went to extremes in practicing "non-attachment"; it is unlikely that he wrote the plays attributed to him.

462. Damocles, a courtier of Dionysius I of Syracuse, praised the dictator's happiness, who rejoined by hanging a sword over him suspended by a single hair.

463. A word has dropped out; it is anyone's guess what, but the meaning is clear.

464. Xenophon, *Memorabilia* 1,3,6;12; Stobaeus, *Florilegia* 17.44, 101.20; Plutarch, *Moralia* 124 D, 513 D, 521 F, 661 F.

121(1) Antisthenes preferred madness to pleasure.[465] Crates of Thebes says,[466]

Be proud of beating them by the character of your soul.
Do not be a slave to gold, or to loves which melt you
with yearning, or to the delight in violence which goes with them.

He adds in general,

Those who are free from slavery to pleasure and
enjoy an immortality of kingship and liberty.

(2) Elsewhere he writes bluntly that the remedy for an insatiable drive to sex is a hunger—or else a noose. The comic poets, even in calumniating Zeno the Stoic, provide evidence of his teaching in words like these:

He is a philosopher with a new philosophy.
He teaches hunger, and attracts disciples.
One loaf, a dried fig for main course, water to drink.[467]

122(1) All these are not ashamed to make a clear admission of the value of caution. Wisdom which is true and not irrational does not trust in mere words and oracular pronouncements, but in invulnerable armor and effective defenses,[468] the commandments of God. It practices corporate exercises and discipline, and receives divine power in the part of it inspired by the Logos. (2) Anyway, here are the words describing Zeus' aegis in verse:

Formidable, surrounded all about as in a garland by Fear,
together with Strife, together with Strength, together with chilling
    Rout,

---

465. Fr. 65 (see nt. 420).
466. Crates (c. 365–285 B.C.), was a leading Cynic whose partnership with his wife Hipparchia became legendary, fr. 3, 8, 9, 17.
467. Philemon (c. 364–264 B.C.) was a leading playwright who came from Syracuse and settled in Athens (see *CAF* 2.502); Zeno of Citium (335–263 B.C.) was the founder of the Stoics, an austere moralist, who produced a complete philosophical system later developed by Chrysippus.
468. Reading ἀμυντηρίοις with Münzel for μυστηρίοις, an excellent emendation.

together with the head of the formidable monster Gorgon,
formidable, frightening, symbol of Zeus as bearer of the aegis.[469]

123(1) For those who are able to discern salvation rightly, I
do not know if anything lovelier will ever appear than the
majesty of the Law and its daughter Caution. (2) In fact, when
it is said to be sounding too high a note, as the Lord suggested
to some to prevent any of those eager to serve him from singing out of tune and discordantly, I understand the meaning
not as too high in an absolute sense, but too high for those
who are unwilling to take on them God's yoke. To those who
are weak and have no voice, a note of medium pitch sounds
too high. To the unjust, an ordinary obligation appears too
strict. (3) Those who need the access of pardon because of the
attractions of sin imagine that truth is severity, austerity, a
form of mutilation; and anyone who does not allow himself to
be dragged down into sin in their company, a pitiless brute.

124(1) Anyway, tragedy has some good lines on Hades:

I will be quick to tell you[470] to what power you will be going.
One who knows no equity, and no favor.
his one and only love is simple justice.[471]

(2) Yes, and if we are not yet capable of doing all that the Law
lays upon us,[472] we can at least take a general conspectus of
the marvelous examples available to us in it, and find the
power to nurture an increasing love of liberty. Liberty would
help if we showed all the enthusiasm of which we are capable
in allowing ourselves to be challenged or shamed or to be
emulators. (3) Righteous men of the past living in accordance
with the Law were not "born of an oak of ancient fame or of
a rock."[473] At all accounts, in their will to be true philosophers
they brought themselves as a complete offering to God, and
"it was counted to them as faith."[474]

---

469. Homer, *Iliad* 5.739–42.
470. Reading ἐξερῶ τάχα with Nauck for ὡς ἔρωτα.
471. Sophocles, fr. 703.
472. Reading ἡμῖν ... ἐσμεν with Münzel and Stählin for μὴ ... ἐστε.
473. Homer, *Odyssey* 19.163.
474. *SVF* 1.241 (see nt. 267).

125(1) Zeno used to say excellently of the Indians that he preferred to see one single Indian in the fire to mastering all the theoretical arguments about hardship.[475] (2) We have copious streams to contemplate every day before our eyes, of martyrs facing the fire, the stake, or the headsman. (3) It was fear of the Law, which as a tutor led these to Christ and disciplined them to show their care even through their own blood. (4) "God has taken his place in the council of the gods, in their midst he will hold judgment over the gods."[476] Who are these gods? Those who have mastered pleasure, those who keep themselves aloof from passions, those who understand all their actions, the Christian Gnostics, those who are superior to the world. (5) And again, "I said, you are gods, and all sons of the Most High."[477] To whom is the Lord saying this? To those who have so far as possible turned their backs on all that is human. (6) The Apostle further says, "You are no longer in the flesh but in the spirit."[478] And again, "Although we are living in the flesh, the weapons of our warfare are not those of the flesh."[479] For "flesh and blood cannot inherit the kingdom of God. The perishable does not inherit the imperishable."[480] "Look, you die as human beings," the Spirit has said in rebuttal of us.[481]

126(1) We must join in disciplining ourselves to beware of all that is subject to the passions. We must, like true philosophers, escape from any foods that arouse sexual desire, from a dissolute relaxation in bed, from luxury, and all the passions that make for luxury. We realize[482] that others find this a grievous struggle. It is no longer so for us, since self-discipline is God's greatest gift. (2) "He has said, 'I will never forsake you or abandon you,'"[483] who have judged you worthy by a decision that is wholly genuine. (3) In this way, as we carefully

---

475. Zeno, fr. 241.
476. Ps 82.1, somewhat adapted.
477. Ps 82.6.   478. Rom 8.9.
479. 2 Cor 10.3.   480. 1 Cor 15.50.
481. Ps 82.7.
482. Something is missing that these words syntactically fill out.
483. Heb 13.5; Deut 31.6, 8; Josh 1.5.

strive to go to him, the Lord's "easy yoke"[484] will receive us. The Lord is the one and only charioteer who conducts each of us "from faith to faith"[485] progressively to salvation, for us to enjoy the appropriate fruits of happiness. (4) There is, according to Hippocrates of Cos, a discipline of the soul as well as of the body, "a state of health which does not shrink from hardship and cannot have enough nourishment."[486]

21

Diverse Opinions of Philosophers on the End of Man

127(1) Epicurus placed happiness in freedom from hunger, thirst, and cold. He spoke with a voice to rival the gods, having the impiety to say that in this he would oppose even Father Zeus, as if his doctrine was the victory in bliss of dung-devouring pigs rather than rational philosophers. Among those who take pleasure as the first principle we recognize as most important[487] the Cyrenaics and Epicurus: (2) they state explicitly that the goal is the life of pleasure, and pleasure is the only ultimate good. Epicurus says that pleasure is the elimination of pain. He claims that the proper object of choice is that which proceeds from itself and is drawn back to itself, clearly on all grounds consisting in a process of movement.[488] (3) Deinomachus and Callipho said that the goal is to do everything within our scope to attain the enjoyment of pleasure.[489]

484. Matt 11.30.
485. Rom 1.17.
486. Hippocrates, *Epidemics* 6.4–18; Plutarch, *Moralia* 129 F; Galen, *Protrepticus* 11.16.2 K. Hippocrates (fifth century B.C.), from Cos off the coast of Turkey, was the founder of a school of medicine. The treatises attributed to him come from different periods; I have kept the MS ὑγίεια against the text of Hippocrates: Clement does not always quote precisely.
487. Something corresponding to these five words has dropped out.
488. Epicurus, *Principal Doctrines* 3; see also Usener, *Epicurea* 200, 406, 450, 502. Epicurus (341–270 B.C.) was the son of an Athenian, born in Samos, who made pleasure the goal of life, but believed that to attain the maximum pleasure we should live simply, in retirement, avoiding excess of pain, eliminating desire and fear by self-control and scientific knowledge; for his precursors the Cyrenaics, whose school did not last, see nts. 417, 451.
489. Deinomachus and Callipho seem to have tried to bridge the gulf

Hieronymus the Peripatetic declared the goal to be living without trouble, and happiness to be the only good worth treating as a goal. Diodorus, a member of the same sect, similarly declared that the goal was to live a noble, untroubled life.[490]

128(1) Epicurus and the Cyrenaics say that pleasure is the primary thing appropriate to us. Virtue, they say, comes in incidentally for the sake of pleasure, and instills pleasure.[491] (2) Callipho and his followers hold that virtue came in incidentally for the sake of pleasure, but that somewhat later virtue, observing the beauty surrounding pleasure, proposed itself as equal in rank to the first principle, pleasure.[492] (3) Aristotle's school maintains that the goal is a life in accordance with virtue.[493] But in their view not everyone who possesses virtue enjoys happiness or the goal. The wise man is liable to be tortured. He may fall in with disasters outside his control He may for these reasons be glad of the desire to escape from living. In this case he is not in a state of happiness or bliss. (4) Virtue in fact needs time. It does not come into existence in a single day; it is constituted only in a fully mature adult. A child, as they say, never enjoys full happiness. The fullness of time would be a human life. (5) Happiness then comprises the three kinds of good things.[494] So the poor, the obscene, the diseased, those who are in domestic service, in their view, cannot be happy.[495]

129(1) Next, Zeno the Stoic regards the goal as a life in

---

between Stoics and Epicureans, by coupling virtue and pleasure as the goal (see Cicero, *On the Highest Goods* 5.8.21; *On Duties* 3.33.119; *Tusculan Disputations* 5.30.85; *Academic Questions* 2.45.139).

490. Hieronymus of Rhodes (third century B.C.), in fact, left the Aristotelians to found an independent school; Diodorus of Tyre, whose goal was the combination of virtue with absence of pain, succeeded Critolaus as head of the Peripatetics in the second century B.C.

491. Usener, *Epicurea* 509 (see nt. 488).

492. On Callipho see nt. 489. Clement is drawing on more than one handbook!

493. Aristotle, *Nicomachaean Ethics* 1.6.1098 a 18, 1.10.1100 a 2, 7.14.1153 b 17; *Magna Moralia* 1.4.1184 b 35.

494. External, physical, pertaining to the soul.

495. Something has dropped out, the last three words are a guess.

accordance with virtue; Cleanthes, a life in agreement with
nature;[496] and Diogenes,[497] paying proper attention to reason,
which he defined as resting in the choice of things in accordance with nature. (2) His pupil Antipater offered the hypothesis that the goal lies in the continual and infallible choice
of things in accordance with nature and rejection of all that
is not.[498] (3) Archedemus again expounded in the same way
that the goal is to live by choosing[499] the most important and
vital things which are in accord with nature without the possibility of going beyond them.[500] (4) In addition, there is still
Panaetius. He demonstrated that the goal is a life in accordance with the impulses granted us by nature. On top of all
these, Posidonius says that it is a life in contemplation of the
truth and order of the universe and in the effort to establish
this to the best of our ability without allowing ourselves to be
dragged about by the irrational part of the soul in any way at
all.[501] (5) Some recent Stoics have similarly maintained that
the goal is to live in consonance with our human constitution.
(6) Why should[502] I add Ariston to the list for you? He says
that the goal is indifference, but he does not differentiate indifference![503] (7) Or should I introduce the views of Herillus?[504] Herillus asserts the goal to be a life in accordance with

496. *SVF* 1.186, 2.552 (see also nts. 412, 467).

497. Reading ⟨Διογένης δὲ⟩ with Stählin and von Arnim; Diogenes of
Babylon was head of the Stoa in the second century B.C. (see the fragments
in *SVF* 3).

498. Antipater of Tarsus succeeded Diogenes as head of the Stoa, taught
to Panaetius, and lived to a great age (see the fragments in *SVF* 3).

499. Reading ⟨ζῆν⟩ ἐκλεγόμενον with von Arnim for ἐκλεγομένους.

500. Archedemus of Tarsus was probably a pupil of Diogenes (see the
fragments in *SVF* 3).

501. Panaetius (c. 185–109 B.C.), born in Rhodes, came to Rome at the
age of about forty, and tried to modify the excesses of Stoicism for Roman
consumption by eclectically drawing on Plato and Aristotle; Posidonius (c.
135–50 B.C.), from Syria, studied with Panaetius, followed a scientific bent,
and settled in Rhodes, where he became a figure of immense authority, a
historian as well as a scientific philosopher.

502. Reading ⟨ἂν⟩ with Dindorf.

503. Ariston of Chios, a pupil of Zeno of Citium (see nt. 467) but inde-
pendent-minded, held that the goal of life was total indifference to everything
(see *SVF* 1.333–403).

504. Reading ⟨ἂν⟩ with Dindorf; Herillus of Carthage was another inde-

knowledge. (8) Some hold that recent Platonists define the goal as a safe suspension of judgment in face of our inward perceptions. (9) Yes, and Lycon the Peripatetic said that the goal was true joy of soul; Lyciscus[505] said that it was joy in things of beauty. (10) Critolaus, another Peripatetic, said that it was the culmination of a life which flowed properly in accordance with nature, meaning the triple perfection finding its fulfillment in the three types of good.[506]

130(1) We must not be satisfied with what we have done and come to a full stop. We must so far as possible show a healthy ambition to present the doctrines of the physical scientists on the subject before us. (2) Tradition attributes to Anaxagoras of Clazomenae the view that the goal of life is contemplation and the freedom which springs from it; to Heraclitus of Ephesus that it is contentment.[507] (3) Heraclides of Pontus records that Pythagoras taught that happiness is the scientific knowledge of the perfection of the numbers of the soul.[508] (4) Even the thinkers from Abdera teach that there is a goal. Democritus in his treatise *On the Goal* identifies it with contentment which he called well-being, often adding, "Delight and its opposite form the boundary between fortune and misfortune, and that is where the goal is set for the life of human beings whether young or advanced in years."[509] (5)

---

pendent-minded disciple of Zeno, who treated knowledge as the goal (see *SVF* 1.409–21).

505. Reading Λύκισκος with Stählin and Wilamowitz for MS Λεύκιμος; Lycon (third century B.C.), head of the Peripatetics for forty-four years, was a statesman rather than thinker; Lyciscus is unknown.

506. See nt. 494.

507. Anaxagoras (fifth century B.C.) was a friend of Pericles, a pluralist and a cosmologist (see DK 59 A 29); Heraclitus (c. 500 B.C.) was a dark and obscure thinker, who saw the world in flux but with a principle of balance and order (see DK 22 A 21).

508. Reading ἀριθμῶν with Potter for ἀρετῶν; on Pythagoras see nt. 96; Heraclides of Pontus (fourth century B.C.) was a Platonic philosopher of wide interests.

509. DK 68 B 4: Some of the quotation is lacking in our MS tradition and has to be supplied from Stobaeus; strictly it was Protagoras and Democritus who came from Abdera, but Clement is probably thinking of the shadowy Leucippus, with Democritus the founder of Atomism; Abdera was remote, in Thrace.

Hecataeus placed it in self-sufficiency; Apollodorus of Cyzi-cus, in the satisfaction of the soul; Nausiphanes, in imper-turbability (which, he said, Democritus called alarmlessness).[510] (6) In addition, Diotimus declared the goal to be a full com-plement of the things that are good, which he called well-being.[511] (7) Again, Antisthenes found it in arroganceless-ness.[512] The so-called Annicerians, in succession to the School of Cyrenaics, laid down that there was no defined goal for the whole of life, but that there was a particular goal for each action consisting in the pleasure derived from that action.[513] (8) These Cyrenaics disowned Epicurus' definition of plea-sure, i.e., the elimination of pain, calling it the state of a corpse. We take delight not just in pleasures but in compan-ionship and in achievements. (9) Epicurus thinks that every joy within the soul springs from a previous affection of the flesh.[514]

131(1) Metrodorus in his book, *The Responsibility for Happi-ness Rests More with Us than with Things External to Us* says, "The good of the soul is simply a stable condition of the body and a confident hope about the body."[515]

22

Supreme Good of Man according to Plato

(2) The philosopher Plato[516] says that the goal is twofold. One consists in participation in the Forms and originates in the

510. Hecataeus of Abdera (c. 300 B.C.) was a historian of Egypt (see *FGrH* 3.264); self-sufficiency was in different ways a hallmark of all the Hellenistic schools, an attempt to escape from political uncertainties; Apollodorus (for the MS Apollodotus) is mentioned in Diogenes Laertius 9.38, but otherwise unknown; Cyzicus was a colony of Miletus, an island in the sea of Marmara; Nausiphanes of Teos (fourth century B.C.) was a link in the atomic theory between Democritus and Epicurus (see DK 75 B 3); on Democritus see DK 68 B 4.

511. Diotimus the Stoic is mentioned in Diogenes Laertius 10.3 as anti-Epicurean, hence linking Aristotle with Stoicism.

512. See nt. 420.

513. Anniceris of Cyrene (early third century B.C.) was an unorthodox Cyrenaic.

514. Usener, *Epicurea* 451.

515. Metrodorus of Lampsacus (331–278 B.C.) was a friend of Epicurus and a leading member of the school, though not an original thinker, fr. 5 K.

516. As Camelot notes, this is a summary of Platonic doctrine as held at

actual Forms; he calls it the Good. The other consists in participation in the Good and the acceptance of a likeness derived from it, and this comes about for human beings who claim a share of virtue and true philosophy. (3) That is why Cleanthes in his second volume *On Pleasure* says that Socrates at all times and all places taught that the just man and the happy man were one and the same, and laid a curse on the person who first distinguished between justice and expediency, as a committer of sacrilege. It is really sacrilegious to separate expediency from legal justice.[517] (4) Plato personally defined spiritual happiness as keeping your Spirit happy, meaning by Spirit the ruling factor within the soul. He called happiness the ultimate and most complete good of all.[518] (5) Sometimes he calls happiness a life of consistent harmoniousness[519] and sometimes the highest perfection in accordance with virtue, and he places that in the scientific knowledge of the Good and in likeness to God, defining likeness as "justice and holiness combined with practical wisdom."[520] (6) Is not this the way in which some of our people accept the view that a human being has received "according to the image" at birth, but will secure "according to the likeness" later, as he attains perfection?

132(1) Next, Plato teaches that this likeness will be set in the man of virtue in conjunction with humility. This is, I fancy, a gloss on the Scripture: "Everyone who humbles himself shall be exalted."[521] (2) In the *Laws* he says, "God, as the old tradition has it, holds the beginning, middle, and end of all things, and follows a straight course as he completes the circuit due to nature. Justice is his constant companion, avenging

---

the end of the second century A.D. Plato held that true reality consisted not in the changeable world of matter perceived by the sense, but an eternal world of Forms, known to the mind: There is the perfect Table or Chair, and perfect Justice and Beauty, in which our imperfect world partially participates or imitates; the Form of the Good is the ultimate in this scheme: it lies beyond even the reality of the other Forms.

517. *SVF* 1.558; on Cleanthes see nt. 412.

518. Plato, *Timaeus* 90 C: *eudaemonia*, 'Happiness,' is having your *daemon*, 'guardian-spirit,' well.

519. Plato, *Laches* 188 D; I read ⟨ἔσθ'⟩ὅτε at the beginning.

520. Plato, *Theaetetus* 176 B.

521. Matt 23.12; Luke 14.11.

those who abandon the Law of God."[522] (3) Do you notice how even Plato introduces care for the Law of God? At any rate he proceeds: "The person who intends to be happy takes hold of Justice and accompanies her in humbleness and good order." (4) He adds the implications of this and a warning based on fear and goes on, "Then what conduct does God approve? What is conformable to him? There is only one, with one traditional phrase to describe it. Like cleaves to like, provided it keeps within bounds. When conduct knows no bounds, it finds itself at home neither with controlled nor with uncontrolled conduct. It is essential that the person who hopes to find God's approval should be so far as possible like God.

133(1) "According to this principle, the man among us who shows self-control wins God's approval, being like God. The man who lacks self-control is unlike God and at variance with him." (2) In describing this as a traditional doctrine he is alluding to the fact that the teaching came to him from the Law. (3) In the *Theaetetus,* after admitting that evils "inevitably flit around our mortal nature and this place in which we are," he adds, "For this reason we must make an effort to escape as quickly as possible from this world to the next. The means of escape is the greatest possible likeness to God, a likeness which consists in the combination of justice and holiness with practical wisdom."[523] (4) Plato's nephew Speusippus says that happiness is a state of perfection amongst those who live according to nature, or alternatively, the state of good people; it is a disposition for which all human beings yearn; good people aim at it in the form of freedom from perturbation. To secure this happiness, the virtues would be needed.[524] (5) Xenocrates of Chalcedon defines happiness as the acquisition of the appropriate virtue and the power needed to serve it. (6) Then, as if he wants to say where it resides, he clearly indicates the soul. For the originating causes he points to the virtues; for its component parts he points to noble actions,

522. Plato, *Laws* 4.715E–176A, slightly misquoted.
523. Plato, *Theaetetus* 176 B.
524. Speusippus (c. 407–339 B.C.) was Plato's nephew and successor as head of the Academy—logician, mathematician, and ethical philosopher.

and states, dispositions, motions and attitudes of high morality; for its necessary concomitants he points to physical and external circumstances.[525] (7) Xenocrates' student Polemo clearly wants happiness to consist in self-sufficiency in all that is good, or at least the majority and most important of good things. At any rate, he lays it down that happiness could never exist without virtue, whereas virtue is self-sufficient for happiness and has no need of physical or external benefits.[526]

134(1) So much for that. We shall narrate the counterarguments to the views we have outlined at the proper time. We have the promise of reaching a goal that never comes to an end if we obey the commandments (i.e., God) and live in their light faultlessly in full understanding derived from the revealed knowledge of God's will. (2) The greatest possible likeness to the true Logos, the hope of being established fully as adopted sons through the Son—this is our goal, a sonship which constantly glorifies the Father through the "great high priest" who deigned to call us "brothers" and "fellow heirs."[527] (3) The Apostle in his *Letter to the Romans* writes a summary sketch of our end or goal: "Now that you have been set free from sin, and have become God's slaves, you have your harvest in sanctification, and your end is eternal life."[528] (4) He knows that the hope is of two kinds—one presently experienced, one in the future. He teaches that the goal is presently the establishment for which we hope. "Patience," he says, "produces character; character produces hope. Hope does not bring disillusion, because the love of God has been poured out in our hearts through the Holy Spirit he has given to us."[529] Through this love we find ourselves established in hope, which Scripture says elsewhere is given to us as rest.[530]

135(1) You could find similar passages in Ezekiel too: "The soul that sins will die. If a man is righteous and does what is lawful and righteous, if he does not eat on the mountains, if

---

525. On Xenocrates of Chalcedon see nt. 95.
526. Polemo, a convert of Xenocrates and head of Academy 314–270 B.C., was a moralist rather than a dialectician.
527. Heb 4.14, 2.11; Eph 3.6.
528. Rom 6.22.
529. Rom 5.4–5.
530. Ps 95.11; Heb 3.7–4.11.

he has not raised his eyes to the idols of Israel's house, if he has not corrupted his neighbor's wife or approached a woman at the season of her impurity"—he does not want anyone's seed to be violated—"if," he goes on, "he does no damage to any man, if he restores a debtor's pledge, if he never commits robbery, if he gives his bread to the hungry, (2) clothes the naked, refrains from offering his money at interest and does not accept a larger return, if he turns his hand away from crime, if he executes true judgment between a man and his neighbor, if he walks in my ordinances and has kept my ordinances to deal truly, (3) then he is righteous, he will live fully, says the Lord Adonai."[531] Isaiah invites the man of faith to a life of true dignity, the man who has received revealed knowledge to stop and think. After establishing that the virtue of a human being is not the same as the virtue of God, he goes on as follows: (4) "Seek the Lord. In finding him, call on him. When he draws near to you, let the irreverent abandon his ways, let the lawless man abandon his ways and turn to the Lord, and he will find mercy," and so on as far as, "your thoughts are far from my thoughts."[532]

136(1) "We," according to the noble Apostle, "receive from faith the hope of righteousness, for in Christ neither circumcision nor uncircumcision has any power, only faith working in love."[533] (2) "We earnestly desire each of you to show the same zeal for the full realization of hope," and so on to, "having become a high priest forever, after the order of Melchizedek."[534] (3) Wisdom, full of every virtue, uses similar words to Paul's: "Anyone who listens to me will live safely, trusting in hope."[535] The establishment of hope and hope itself are spoken of interchangeably. (4) That is why she has done admirably to add the word "trusting" to "will live safely," showing that the sort of person who has hold of the hope he hoped for is at peace. This is why she adds, "And he will be tranquil,

---

531. Ezek 18.4–9: The first two clauses of paragraph (2) are added from the text of Ezekiel; *Adonai* is 'Lord,' a divine name substituted for YHVH, which is usually given the vowel-points of the substitute.

532. Isa 55.6–9.   533. Gal 5.5–6.
534. Heb 6.11–20.   535. Prov 1.33.

without fear, free from all evil." (5) The Apostle speaks openly in the *First Letter to the Corinthians* when he says expressly, "Be imitators of me, as I am of Christ,"[536] to bring this about. If you imitate me and I imitate Christ, then you are imitating Christ as he is representing God. (6) So he establishes a target for faith in "the likeness to God so far as possible in justice and holiness combined with practical wisdom,"[537] and the goal in the actualization of the promise on the basis of faith. So from these bubble up those springs, noted earlier, of dogmas about the goal. But enough of this.[538]

23

Goals and Laws of Marriage

137(1) Marriage, I suppose, falls under the head of pleasure and desire, and should be treated here. Marriage is a union between a man and a woman; it is the primary union; it is a legal transaction; it exists for the procreation of legitimate children. (2) The comic dramatist Menander says,

> I give you my own daughter
> for the sowing of true children.[539]

(3) We ask the question whether it is right to marry. This is one of those questions named after their relation to an end.[540] Who is to marry? In what situation? With what woman? What about her situation? It is not right for everyone to marry; it is not right at all times. There is a time when it is appropriate; there is a person for whom it is appropriate; there is an age up to which it is appropriate. (4) It is not right for every man to marry every woman, on every occasion, in absolutely all circumstances. It depends on the circumstances of the man, the character of the woman, the right time, the prospect of

536. 1 Cor 11.1.
537. Plato, *Theaetetus* 176 B.
538. It looks as if this was the real ending of Book Two; the next chapter, on marriage, anticipates Book Three, although his first words force it into the theme of pleasure.
539. Menander, fr. 720 (cf. nt. 241).
540. Reading κατὰ ⟨τὸ⟩ with Schwartz.

children, the total compatibility of the woman and the absence of any violence or compulsion to drive her to look after the man who loves her.

138(1) This is why Abraham says of his wife when he is passing her off as his sister, "She is my sister on my father's side but not on my mother's, and she became my wife too,"[541] teaching that it is not right for children of the same mother to join in marriage. (2) Let us enter on the story briefly. Plato places marriage among external goods, using it to fashion the immortality of our race and a kind of permanence handed on like a torch to children's children.[542] (3) Democritus disparages marriage and childbearing owing to the numerous unpleasantnesses coming in their train, and the distractions from more essential matters.[543] (4) Epicurus concurs with him, as do all those who place the ultimate good in pleasure, freedom from disturbance and absence of pain.[544] (5) Again, to the Stoics, marriage and childbearing are matters of indifference, whereas to the Peripatetics they are good things.[545] (6) In general, these people take their dogmas no further than their tongues. They are slaves to pleasures, some enjoying mistresses, some prostitutes, and the majority of them boys. The famous quartet in the garden with the courtesan, in all their wisdom, paid honor to pleasure by their actions.[546]

139(1) So those who do not reckon particular acts to their advantage but lay them on others to perform (or *vice versa*) would not fail to come under the curse of Buzyges.[547] (2) Scripture has shown this briefly in the words, "Do not do to anyone else a thing you abhor."[548] (3) Besides, there are those who

541. Gen 20.12.
542. Plato, *Laws* 6.773 E, 776 B; *Symposium* 207D–208B.
543. On Democritus see DK 68 A 170.
544. Usener, *Epicurea* 526.
545. *SVF* 3.163.
546. Diogenes Laertius 10.4; Athenaeus 13.588 B: "The Garden" was the Epicureans' retreat.
547. *Buzyges*, 'Ox-yoker,' was a legendary Athenian hero who laid down the rules of agriculture and cursed all transgressors.
548. Tob 4.15; for the positive side see Matt 7.12 and Luke 6.31; it was enunciated by the great rabbi Hillel.

value marriage, saying, "Nature has made us equipped for marriage,"[549] as if clear from the organization of the male and female bodies, and they continually blare at us, "Be fruitful and multiply."[550] (4) But even if this is so, they should think it shameful that human beings, created by God, are more licentious than irrational animals, which do not couple with all and sundry, but with a single party of the same family, like doves, pigeons, turtledoves and all similar creatures. (5) Besides, they say, the childless person is deprived of his natural completeness, not having established a successor in his house to take his place. The man who has produced of himself one like him has achieved fulfillment—even more when he sees the other having followed in his footsteps too, in other words, when he has established a child in the same natural place as the father.

140(1) So there is every reason to marry—for patriotic reasons, for the succession of children, for the fulfillment of the universe (insofar as it is our business). The poets regret a marriage which is "half-fulfilled" and childless, and bless the marriage which is "abundant in growth."[551] (2) Physical ailments demonstrate the necessity of marriage particularly well. A wife's care and her patient attention seem to surpass all the earnest devotion of other family and friends; she likes to excel all others in sympathy and present concern; she really and truly is, in the words of Scripture, a necessary "helper."[552]

141(1) Menander, the writer of comic drama, runs down marriage, but he also sets its advantages in the other scale in answering the man who says,

> (S) I am not well disposed to the matter.
> (B) Yes, you take it in left-handed style.

He goes on thus:

---

549. See Aristotle, *Politics* 7.1334 B 29 ff.
550. Gen 1.28.
551. Homer, *Iliad* 2.701, 22.496.
552. Gen 2.18. Clement is not always such a "male chauvinist pig."

You are seeing in it the problems, the things
you take exception to. You are not concentrating on
    the blessings.[553]

And so on. (2) Marriage helps those of advanced years too. It provides a wife to take care of them, and nurtures children from her to be supports of old age. (3) Children

Are the glory of the dead.
Like corks, they support the net
and preserve the flaxen cord from the depths,

as the tragic dramatist Sophocles puts it.[554] (4) The legislators do not permit the highest offices of state to pass to unmarried men. The legislator of the Spartans[555] went further than laying a penalty on the unmarried state; he extended it to improper marriages, late marriages, and celibacy. (5) Our good Plato enunciated that an unmarried man should hand over the equivalent of a wife's upkeep into the public treasury, paying the appropriate costs to the authorities. If they do not marry or produce children, they will be playing their part in reducing the population and undermining the cities and the world they compose.[556]

142(1) Such behavior is irreverent. It undermines generation, which is a gift of God. It is a sign of weakness and unmanliness to try to escape from a partnership in life with wife and children. (2) A state which it is wrong to reject must be totally right to procure. So with all the rest. In fact, they say the loss of children is one of the gravest evils. It follows that the acquisition of children is a good thing. If so, so is marriage. (3) The poet says,

Without a father there could be no children,
without a mother, not even conception of children.[557]

553. Menander, fr. 325 (cf. nt. 241).
554. A good example of Clement's quoting from memory. The (misquoted) text comes from Aeschylus, *Choephori* 505-7.
555. Lycurgus.
556. Plato, *Laws* 6.774.
557. Menander, fr. 1085 (cf. nt. 241).

Marriage makes a man a father, a husband makes a woman a mother.

143(1) It is a great prayer in Homer for "a husband and a home," and not only that, but "with the blessing of concord."[558] For the rest of humankind, marriage finds concord in the experience of pleasure, but the marriage of true lovers of wisdom[559] leads to a concord derived from the Logos. It tells women to beautify their character rather than their appearance; it enjoins husbands not to treat their wives as sex-objects, making their goal the violation of their bodies, but directing their marriage to support throughout life and to self-control at the highest level. (2) In my view, the seeds of wheat and barley which are sown at carefully chosen moments are less precious than the seed that is a human being for whose benefit all the others are sown; and the farmers are sober when they sow those seeds.[560] (3) So marriage should be purified of every coarse and tainted practice, to avoid the reproach that the union of irrational animals is more conformable to nature within the accepted definition than human union.

144(1) There are some animals which mount their females at the appointed season and immediately abandon them, leaving the work of creation to providence. (2) The tragic poets have written this of the execution of Polyxene: "in dying" she took great care even so to fall decorously

Hiding what should be hidden from the eyes of males.[561]

(3) For her, marriage was a disaster. So to yield in subjection to the passions is the lowest form of slavery, just as to conquer them is the only true freedom. (4) Anyway, holy Scripture says that those who break the commandments have been sold to

---

558. Homer, *Odyssey* 6.181.
559. Or "philosophers"; he means Christians.
560. Against Mondésert: I think Clement means that farmers take care that they are in control of themselves at the work, but men are often drunk when they go to bed with women.
561. Euripides, *Hecuba* 568–70.

foreigners, i.e., sins naturally alien, until they turn and repent.[562]

145(1) Marriage must be kept pure, like a sacred object to be preserved from all stain. We are with our Lord when we wake from sleep; we go to sleep with gratitude, praying

alike when you go to bed, and when the holy light appears.[563]

We witness to our Lord throughout our lives, with reverence held within our soul and applying self-control to our body as well. (2) God really does approve of seemliness escorted from tongue to action. Coarse language is the road to a loss of a sense of shame, and shameful behavior results from the combination. (3) Scripture advises us to marry. It tells us never to divorce the conjugal yoke. The law says expressly, "You shall not divorce your wife except by reason of unchastity,"[564] and regards remarriage while the other of the divorced pair is alive as adultery.

146(1) A wife is clearly exempt from all suspicion if she refrains from prettifying or adorning herself beyond the proper limit, if she applies herself consistently to prayers and intercessions, if she avoids going out all the time, if she shuts herself off as far as possible from seeing those she ought not to be gazing at, if she puts the care of the home as a more valuable pursuit than gossiping. (2) Scripture says, "The man who marries a divorcee is committing adultery," for "if a man divorces his wife, he is committing adultery against her"; in other words, he is forcing her into adultery.[565] (3) Guilt in this does not attach merely to the man who divorces her; it attaches to the man who takes her on, since he provides the starting point for the woman's sin. If he were not to accept her, she would return to her husband.

147(1) What does the Law say? To halt any inclination to give way to the passions, it authorizes the execution of an

562. See Judg 2.14.
563. Hesiod, *Works and Days* 339; Hesiod (eighth or seventh century B.C.) was a Boeotian who, with Homer, had shaped Greek religious traditions.
564. Matt 5.32; 19.9.
565. Matt 5.32; Mark 10.11–12; Luke 16.18.

adulterous wife if duly convicted on the charge. If she is a priest's daughter, it authorizes her burning at the stake. The adulterer too is stoned to death, but not at the same spot, so that they do not enjoy a common death.[566] (2) The Law does not in fact conflict with the gospel, but is in harmony with it: Of course, the one Lord directs both. A loose woman is alive to sin but dead to the commandments. One who repents experiences a kind of rebirth through her changed behavior and has a renewal of life. The old whore is dead, the new child of repentance has passed again into life. (3) The Spirit, speaking through Ezekiel, confirms what I have said: "I do not want the sinner's death, so much as a change in his attitude."[567] (4) The men become liable to stoning because through their hardness of heart they are dead to the Law which they have disobeyed. The whole business of punishment is extended to the priest's daughter because "where much has been given, much will be required."[568] (5) I have decided to end Book Two of our *Miscellanies of Notes of Revealed Knowledge in Accordance with the True Philosophy* here in view of the length and number of the chapter headings.

566. Lev 20.10; 21.9; Deut 22.22–4.
567. Ezra 33.11.
568. Luke 12.48.

BOOK THREE

1

Views of Valentinus and Basilides on Marriage

1(1) The sect of Valentinus justify physical union from heaven from divine emanations, and approve of marriage. The followers of Basilides say that when the apostles enquired whether it was not better to refrain from marriage, the Lord answered, "It is not everyone who can accept this saying: some are eunuchs from birth, others from necessity."[1] (2) They explain the saying something as follows. Some men have from birth a physical aversion in relation to women. They follow their physical make-up and do well not to marry. (3) These, they say, are the eunuchs from birth. Those who are eunuchs from necessity are those ascetics who like the limelight and exercise control over themselves in hope of being newsworthy. Those who have suffered castration accidentally have become eunuchs from necessity.[2] It follows that those who are eunuchs from necessity are not eunuchs for any rational cause. (4) But those who have made themselves eunuchs for the sake of the eternal kingdom are making a choice of reasoned principle in their view because of the incidentals of married life; they are afraid of the amount of time spent on the provision of necessities.

2(1) Their view is that the Apostle's words "It is better to marry than to burn"[3] mean "Do not hurl your soul into the fire, clinging on night and day in fear of falling away from abstinence. A soul directed towards clinging on is being cut off

1. See Matt 19.11, but Clement seems to be quoting from a different source. Valentinus and Basilides were the two great second-century A.D. Gnostic teachers; Basilides was certainly in Alexandria.
2. Some editors regard this as a gloss.
3. 1 Cor 7.9.

from hope." (2) "So, if you have a quarrelsome wife" (I am quoting Isidore's *Ethics*), "be patient with her, to avoid being wrenched violently out of God's grace; get rid of the fire with your semen; then go to prayer with a good conscience."[4] (3) "When your prayer of gratitude," he goes on, "sinks to a petition, and your petition is that in future you may not act wrongly, rather than that you may act rightly—get married. (4) A man may be young or poor or highly sexed and unwilling to follow the Apostle's advice and get married. He must not be cut off from his Christian brother. He should say, 'I have entered the temple; there is nothing I can suffer.' (5) If he has an inkling of what is happening to him, he should say, 'Brother, lend me a hand to save me from going wrong.' Then he will receive help, spiritually and physically. He has only to desire to achieve[5] the good, and he will attain it.

3(1) "But sometimes we say with our lips, 'We do not want to sin,' but our intention is disposed towards sin. Such a person refrains from doing what he wants to do out of fear of punishment being set to his account. (2) The human condition involves some things which are natural and necessary, others which are merely natural.[6] To wear clothes is natural and necessary; all this business of sexual intercourse is natural but not necessary."[7] (3) I have passed on these statements to expose those followers of Basilides who do not lead upright lives, claiming that they have the authority actually to commit sin because of their perfection, or that they will in any event be saved by nature, even if they do sin, because of their ingrained election; their predecessors in the sect do not allow anyone to do the same[8] as they are doing. (4) So they should not wear the name of Christ as a cloak, live more licentiously than the most intemperate of the pagans, and bring ill-repute upon the

4. This passage is difficult: The MS has ἀντέχου; I read ἀνέχου with Epiphanius; Chadwick and Oulton say they are following Epiphanius but translate ἀπέχου; the quarrelsome wife comes from Prov 21.19; Isidore was the son of Basilides.

5. Reading ἀπαρτίσαι with Epiphanius.

6. Added by Stählin as necessary to the sense.

7. The analysis is from Epicurus (see Usener, *Epicurea* 456).

8. Reading ταὐτά for ταῦτα after Epiphanius.

name. [The Scripture text is] "Such men are false apostles, crooked workers" down to "whose doom shall match their acts."[9]

4(1) Self-discipline means disdain of the body, following obedience[10] to God. Self-discipline applies, not just to sexual matters, but to everything else for which the soul lusts improperly, because it is not satisfied with the bare necessities. (2) Self-discipline applies to speech, possessions and their use, desire generally.[11] It is not just that it teaches us self-control. It offers us the gift of self-control, a divine power and grace of God.[12] (3) I must tell you our people's view of the matter. We bless abstention from sexual intercourse and those to whom it comes as a gift of God. We admire monogamy and respect for one marriage and one only. We say that we ought to share in suffering and "bear one another's burdens,"[13] for fear that anyone who thinks he is standing firmly should in fact fall.[14] It is about second marriages that the Apostle says, "If you are on fire, get married."[15]

2

Views of Carpocrates and Epiphanes on Marriage

5(1) The followers of Carpocrates and Epiphanes think that wives should be held in common.[16] It is through them that the greatest ill-repute has accrued to the name of Christ. (2) This

---

9. 2 Cor 11.13–15.

10. The Stoics believed in a life in accordance with nature—*homologia* was a technical term for this (see *SVF* 3.11, Cicero, *On the Highest Goods* 3.6.21); Clement uses the word in relation to God.

11. See Aristotle, *Nichomachaean Ethics* 7.4.1146 B 9 ff.

12. See Wis 8.21.   13. Galen 6.2.

14. 1 Cor 10.12.   15. 1 Cor 7.9.

16. This whole account is packed with difficulty: Celsus (c. 170 A.D.), a pagan philosopher attacking Christianity, wrote of "Harpocratians who follow Salome" (see Origen, *Against Celsus* 5.62–4); Carpocratians are mentioned in Hegesippus, *Memoirs* (see Eusebius, *Ecclesiastical History* 4.22.5); Irenaeus (*Against Heresies* 1.25) gives a summary of Carpocrates' doctrine: The world was created by lower angels. Jesus through "recollection" of the divine was able to evade their power and others can do the same by revealed knowledge. Once

Epiphanes, whose writings I actually possess, was Carpocrates' son. His mother's name was Alexandria. On his father's side he was an Alexandrian, on his mother's he was from Cephallenia. His life lasted only seventeen years. At Same in Cephallenia he has been honored as a god. A shrine of quarried blocks of stone was built and dedicated to him there, together with altars, sacred precincts, and a university. The inhabitants of Cephallenia gather at the shrine at the time of the new moon, and offer sacrifice to Epiphanes to celebrate his apotheosis as if it were his birthday. There are libations, feasts and the singing[17] of hymns. (3) He was educated by his father in the general curriculum and in Platonic philosophy, and taught the knowledge of the Monad,[18] the source of the heresy of the Carpocratians.

6(1) In his work *On Righteousness*[19] he says, "God's righteousness is a kind of social equity.[20] There is equity in the way the sky is stretched out in all directions and embraces the whole earth in a circle. The night is equitable in displaying all the stars. From above, God pours out the light of the sun, which is responsible for the day and father of the light, over the earth equally for all those with the power of sight. The gift of sight is common to all. (2) There is no distinction between rich and poor, ruler and ruled,[21] fools and wise, female and male, slave

---

they are saved they can live as they will, morality being a human convention (Irenaeus includes details of initiation, including branding on the ear, and mentions a woman leader named Marcellina). Harpocrates was the Egyptian god Horus; *Epiphanes* means 'god incarnate'; the festival on Cephallenia, one of the Ionian islands to the west of Greece, sounds like a new moon festival; Alexandria in Cephallenia could well be a divine figure named after the city, but Clement does seem to know of an Epiphanes who wrote a book and died at seventeen, although perhaps he has wrongly identified this lad with a divine figure in Same; the Greeks believed, as is found in Cynic and Stoic utopias, that community of wives was practiced by primitive peoples.

17. Reading ᾄδονται for λέγονται after Epiphanius.

18. The Monad alone existed but was lonely; an Idea emanated from it, and from their intercourse emerged the universe.

19. Henry Chadwick (*Alexandrian Christianity*, LCC 2.25) writes, "The work merely consists of the scribblings of an intelligent but nasty-minded adolescent of somewhat pornographic tendencies."

20. See Plato, *Definitions* 411 E.

21. Reading δῆμον ἤ with Stählin.

and free.[22] He treats even the irrational animals no differently; on all the beasts he pours out his sunlight equally from above; he ratifies his righteousness to good and bad, so that none can have more than their share or deprive their neighbors so as to have twice as much light as they.[23] (3) The sun draws up[24] from the ground food for all animals alike; his righteousness is shared by all and given to all equally. In this respect it is exactly the same for individual cows and cattle as a whole, individual pigs and pigs as a whole, individual sheep and sheep as a whole, and so on. (4) It is this common shared quality which is revealed as righteousness among them. The same principle of commonality applies to all the species of plants alike in their seeding. Food is available in common to all animals that pasture on the land, and to all equally. It is not regulated by any law, but is there for all, as it were, in unison, by the generous provision of the giver, the[25] one who has authorized it so. This is his righteousness.[26]

7(1) "Matters concerning the production of offspring do not involve any written law either (or it would have been handed down in writing). All beings sow their seeds and produce their offspring on equal terms, possessing an innate common disposition from the hands of righteousness. The author and Father of all gave to all alike on equal terms an eye to enable them to see. He made this dispensation out of his righteousness. He made no distinction between male and female, rational and irrational, no distinction of any kind. He dispensed sight by his grace to all alike by a single ordinance in accordance with the principle of equal sharing. (2) The laws," he goes on, "by their incapacity to punish human ignorance, actually taught illegal behavior. The individualism allowed by the laws cut damagingly at the roots of the universalism of God's Law." He does not understand the Apostle's dictum in the words: "It was

---

22. Note that these are divisions said by Paul to be done away with in Christ (see Gal 3.28; Col 3.11).
23. Compare Matt 5.45.
24. Reading ἀνατέλλει with Sylburg.
25. Adding καὶ with Hiller.
26. Some editors treat this as a gloss, perhaps rightly.

through the Law that I knew sin."[27] (3) He suggests that "mine" and "yours" came into existence through the laws, so that the earth and possessions were no longer put to common use.[28] The same applies to marriage. (4) "For God has made vines for all in common; they do not deny the sparrow or the thief. So too with corn and the other fruits of the earth. It is transgression of the principle of common sharing and equality which has produced the thief of fruits and domestic animals.

8(1) "So God created everything for humanity in common. He brings the female to the male in common,[29] and joined all animals together in a similar way. In this he showed that righteousness is a combination of community and equity. (2) But those who have been born in this way have denied the commonality that unites births, and say,[30] 'A man[31] should marry a single wife and stick to her.' Everyone can share her as the rest of the animals show." (3) After these words, which I quote precisely, he goes on in the same vein to add, in these very words: "With a view to the maintenance of the race he has implanted in the male strong and energetic sexual desire. Law cannot make this disappear, nor can social mores or anything else. It is God's decree." (4) How can this fellow still be listed in our church members' register when he openly does away with the Law and the Gospels alike by these words? The former says, "You shall not commit adultery," the latter, "Everyone who looks with lust has already committed adultery."[32] (5) The words found in the Law, "You shall not lust," show that it is one single God who makes his proclamations[33] through the Law, prophets and Gospels. He says, "You shall not lust for your neighbor's wife."[34] (6) The Jew's neighbor is not the Jew, who is a brother of the same spirit. The alternative is that the neighbor is one of another race. How can a person who shares in the

27. Rom 7.7.
28. Omitting χοινά τε γὰρ, which is out of place.
29. Epiphanes passes from the meaning "universal" to "as a common possession."
30. Reading φάσιν with Hilgenfeld.
31. Reading ὃ with Sylburg for εἰ.
32. Exod 20.13; Matt 5.28.   33. I take this to be middle.
34. Exod 20.17.

same spirit fail to be a neighbor? Abraham is father of Hebrews and gentiles alike.[35]

9(1) If the adulteress and her paramour are both punished with death, it is surely clear that the commandment "You shall not lust for your neighbor's wife" applies to the gentiles, so that anyone who follows the Law in keeping his hands off his neighbor's wife and his sister may hear directly from the Lord: "But I say to you, you shall not lust." The addition of the pronoun "I" shows that the application of the commandment is more rigidly binding, (2) and that Carpocrates and Epiphanes are battling against God. Epiphanes[36] in that notorious book, I mean[37] *On Righteousness,* goes on like this, and I quote: (3) "So you must hear the words 'You shall not lust' as a joke of the Lawgiver, to which he added the even more ludicrous words 'for your neighbor's property.' The very one who endows human beings with desire to sustain the processes of birth gives orders that it is to be suppressed, though he suppresses it in no other living creature! The words 'for your neighbor's wife' are even more ridiculous since he is forcing public property to become private property."

10(1) These are the doctrines of our noble Carpocratians. They say that these people and some other zealots for the same vicious practices gather for dinner (I could never call their congregation a Christian love–feast), men and women together, and after they have stuffed themselves ("The Cyprian goddess is there when you are full," they say.[38]), they knock over the lamps, put out the light that would expose their fornicating "righteousness," and couple as they will with any woman they fancy.[39] So in this love-feast they practice commonality. Then by daylight they demand any woman they want in obedience—

35. Gen 17.5; Rom 4.16.
36. Adding ὅς with Wilamowitz.
37. Reading λέγω with Sylburg for λέγων.
38. From Euripides, fr. 895 N (see Athenaeus, 6.270 C), reading accordingly τοι Κύπρις, ἢ; the Cyprian goddess is Aphrodite, the goddess of sexual love.

39. This was a charge brought against ordinary Christians (e.g., Origen, *Against Celsus* 6.40) who practiced remarkable fellowship between men and women, meeting together behind closed doors.

it would be wrong to say to the Law of God—to the law of Carpocrates. I guess that is the sort of legislation Carpocrates must have established for the copulation of dogs, pigs, and goats. (2) I fancy he has, in fact, misunderstood Plato's dictum in the *Republic* that wives are to be held in common by everyone. Plato really meant that before marriage they are to be available to any who intend to ask them to marry, just as the theatre is open to all spectators; but that once a woman has married she belongs to the particular man who secured her first and is no longer held in common by everyone.[40]

11(1) Xanthus in his book entitled the *Works of the Magi* says, "The Magi think[41] it right to have sexual union with their mothers, daughters and sisters. The women are held in common by mutual agreement, not forcibly or secretively, when one man wants to marry another's wife."[42] (2) I fancy Jude was speaking prophetically of these and similar sects in his letter when he wrote: "So too with these people caught up in their dreams" who do not set upon the truth with their eyes fully open, down to "pompous phrases pour from their mouth."[43]

3

Man Is Born into Pain and So Should Abstain from Marriage

12(1) If even Plato and the Pythagoreans, like the followers of Marcion later (though he was far from maintaining that wives should be held in common), regarded birth as something evil, Marcion's followers held natural processes as evil because they were derived from matter that was evil, and from an unrighteous creator.[44] (2) On this argument they have no wish to

40. Plato, *Republic* 5.457 D; Clement's version is a total misrepresentation taken from the Stoic Epictetus (2.4.8–10): In Plato the "communism" applies only to the ruling class where men and women have equal status, and neither possesses the other; there is sexual abstinence and no promiscuity; copulation is permitted at festivals with a partner allocated by lot.

41. Reading ἡγοῦνται with Stählin for μίγνυνται.

42. Xanthus of Lydia (fifth century B.C.) was a historian who wrote a history of Lydia (see *FGrH* 2 A 90, 3 C 765).

43. The *Epistle of Jude* 8–16.

44. Marcion was the greatest of the second-century heretics, a shipowner,

fill the cosmos the creator brought into being, and choose to abstain from marriage. They stand in opposition to their creator and make haste towards the one they call god, who is not (they say) god in another sense. As a result, they have no desire to leave anything of theirs behind them here on earth. So they are abstinent not by an act of will but through hatred of the creator and the refusal to use any of his productions. (3) But in their irreverent war with God they stand apart from natural reason. They despise God's generous goodness. Even if they choose not to marry, they still use the food he has produced, they still breathe the creator's air. They are themselves his works and live in his world. They say that they have received the gospel of an alien knowledge. In one respect they ought to recognize the grace of the Lord of the cosmos; it is here on earth that they have received the gospel.[45]

13(1) We shall present precise arguments against these people when we treat the doctrine of first principles.[46] The philosophers whom we have mentioned, from whom Marcion's followers derived their blasphemous doctrine that birth is evil, although they prance about as if it were their own, do not, in fact, hold that it is naturally evil, but evil only to the soul which has discerned the truth. (2) They regard the soul as divine, and dragged down here onto earth as to a place of punishment. In their view, souls that have become embodied need to be purified. (3) This doctrine does not belong to Marcion's followers, but to those who hold that souls are placed in bodies, change their integument[47] and transmigrate. There will be another opportunity to respond to them when we discourse on the soul.[48]

---

and perhaps the son of a bishop, who drew a sharp and absolute antithesis between Law and Love (or Spirit), the *Old Testament* and the *New Testament*, the Creator and the Redeemer. I do not understand how editors tolerate δικαίου contrary to Marcion's beliefs (see Book Two, nt. 117), but it is an obvious correction by an orthodox scribe who has not understood: I propose ἀδίκου.

45. Chadwick notes that Clement is using an argument used by pagans against Christians generally against Marcion's followers (see Origen, *Against Celsus* 6.53, 8.28).

46. A part of the *Stromateis* promised but never written.

47. Reading μετενδύεσθαι (cf. Timaeus Locrus 104 D) which seems better than μετενδεῖσθαι; the doctrine is that of the Platonists and Pythagoreans.

48. *Stromateis*, 5.88.

14(1) Heraclitus certainly deprecates birth when he says, "Once born they have a desire to live and have their dooms," or rather enjoy their rest, "and they leave behind children to become dooms."[49] (2) Empedocles is clearly of the same mind when he says,

I wept and wailed when I saw the unfamiliar face,

and again,

For out of living creatures he made corpses, changing their forms,

and once more,

Oh! Oh! Unhappy race of mortals, unblest!
Out of what strife, what groans were you born.[50]

(3) Further, the Sibyl says,

You are human, mortal, and fleshly, and are nothing.[51]

This is not far from the poet's words:

Earth nurtures nothing feebler than a human being.[52]

15(1) Yes, and Theognis too points to birth being evil when he speaks in the following terms:

For earth-dwellers, best of all is not to be born,
not to see the dazzling sunbeams, or, once born, to pass
through Hades' gates as soon as may be.[53]

(2) Euripides, the writer of tragic drama, writes lines that accord with these:

---

49. DK 22 B 20: Heraclitus of Ephesus (c. 500 B.C.) was a pessimist who seems to be anticipating the Freudian death wish; in leading up to the quotation I read ἐπειδὰν φῇ with Diels.

50. DK 31 B 118, 125, 124, reading εἶδε' with Sylburg for ἠδὲ in the second passage (quoted here only); Empedocles of Acragas in Sicily (c. 493–433 B.C.) was a strange combination of scientist and mystagogue; the quotations are from his poem *Purifications*.

51. *Sibylline Oracles*, fr. 1.1.

52. Homer, *Odyssey* 18.130: Note that Homer is simply "*the* poet."

53. Theognis 425–7 (sixth century B.C.) was an elegiac poet from Megara, some of whose poetry seems wrongly attributed.

We ought to gather when a man is born
to mourn the evils to which he is coming.
When a man is dead and free from troubles,
then we should rejoice and felicitate him as we send him away.[54]

(3) Elsewhere he says something similar:

Who knows if life is death,
death life?[55]

16(1) Herodotus is obviously making Solon say the same as
this: "Croesus, every human being is a disaster."[56] His story
about Cleobis and Biton has the clear purpose of attacking
birth and praising death.[57]

(2) The generation of men is like that of leaves,

says Homer.[58] (3) Plato in the *Cratylus* attributes to Orpheus the
doctrine that the soul is in the body as a punishment. Here are
his words: "Some people say that it is the burial place of the
soul, which is at the present time entombed in it. (4) Because
the soul uses the body to mention whatever it would mention,
the body is rightly called the soul's burial place. However, it is
the followers of Orpheus who seem to have established the
name above all others, saying that the soul is paying the penalty
for acts that have earned the penalty."[59]

17(1) It is also worth noting Philolaus' remark. The follower
of Pythagoras says, "The theologians and seers of old are witnesses that the soul is yoked to the body to undergo acts of

54. Euripides, fr. 449 N from *Cresphontes*; but this is designed to be dra-
matically appropriate, not the poet's view.
55. Euripides, fr. 638 N from *Polyidus*, a famous and much parodied sentence (e.g., Aristophanes, *Frogs* 1477–8).
56. Herodotus, 1.32 slightly misquoted.
57. Herodotus, 1.31; Plutarch, *Moralia* 58 E, 108 F; *Solon* 27: Cleobis and
Biton were from Argos; they took the place of the oxen which should have
pulled their mother's carriage to Hera's temple; she prayed for their felicity,
and they died in their sleep; their statues may be seen at Delphi.
58. Homer, *Iliad* 6.146.
59. Plato, *Cratylus* 400 B–C. The pun is Plato's: Orphism was a religious
movement centering on the legendary musician Orpheus. Its aim was to free
the soul from the prison of the body.

punishment and is buried in it as in a grave."[60] (2) Pindar, speaking of the Eleusinian mysteries, adds,

> Blessed is the man who has seen these things
> before passing beneath the hollow earth.
> He knows the end of life as he knows
> the beginning granted by God.[61]

(3) Accordingly, Plato in the *Phaedo* does not hesitate to write as follows: "These men who established our mysteries" in the same vein down to "he will live with the Gods." (4) What about when he says, "As long as we have the body, and our soul is compounded with such an evil thing, we shall never adequately grasp the object of our desire"? Is he not enigmatically suggesting that birth is the cause of the greatest evils? (5) In the *Phaedo* he adds his witness: "All those who apply themselves to philosophy in the right way run the risk of the rest failing to notice that they are simply practicing the state of dying and of death."[62]

18(1) And again, "So on earth too the soul of the philosopher particularly despises the body, tries to escape from it, and seeks to secure an existence on its own."[63] (2) This clearly harmonizes with the divine Apostle's words: "Wretch that I am, all too human, who shall rescue me from this body of death?"[64]—unless he is using the phrase "body of death" metaphorically of the common mind of those who have been seduced into vice. (3)

---

60. DK 44 B 14: Philolaus (fifth century B.C.) was a Pythagorean from southern Italy, an important figure in Pythagorean astronomy; the authenticity of the fragments is disputed.

61. Pindar, fr. 137 a S, omitting κοινά, from a dirge perhaps for Hippocrates (brother to Cleisthenes); the climax of the revelation was something seen, perhaps a golden ear of corn since the mysteries were associated with the Corn Mother or Earth Mother Demeter, and her daughter the Maid, with the growth of the crops, and with life after death; Pindar (fifth century B.C.) was a Boeotian, the greatest of the Greek choral lyric poets.

62. Plato, *Phaedo* 69 C, 66 B, 64 A: Did Clement assume that his readers would recall the first passage from memory, or know exactly where to look for it, or was it a memo to himself to fill in the gap in his final version?

63. Plato, *Phaedo* 65 C–D.

64. Rom 7.24.

Long before Marcion, Plato, in the first book of the *Republic*, clearly saw sexual intercourse as the origin of birth and rejected it accordingly. (4) In the course of his praise of old age he adds, "I would have you know that as the other pleasures, the physical ones, die down, my delight and pleasure in conversation correspondingly increases." (5) He remarks on the practice of sex: "Hush, my dear fellow. I took the greatest pleasure in escaping from it, as in escaping from a crazy fierce dictator."[65]

19(1) Again in the *Phaedo* he writes disparagingly of birth: "The secret teaching on this matter is that human beings are in a kind of prison." (2) And again, "Those who have a reputation for holy living that sets them apart from others are the people who are set free and liberated from these areas on earth as from a prison, and reach the pure home above."[66] (3) All the same, even in that condition he recognizes the excellence of the government of the world, saying, "A man ought not to release himself from that prison and run away."[67] (4) To sum up, he does not offer Marcion grounds for thinking[68] matter evil, when he himself speaks reverently about the world: (5) "All that is good is got from the supreme disposer. From its previous state all that is chaotic or corrupt in the sky comes into being; from that state the world has the same qualities and produces them in living things."[69]

20(1) He proceeds to add with even more clarity: "The physical element in its make-up was responsible for all this; this was at one time tied up with its primeval nature since it was a disorderly chaos before coming into its present state of order."[70] (2) With equal power in the *Laws* as well, he expresses grief at the state of humankind in these words: "The gods took pity on humankind, born to labor as they were, and established the

---

65. Plato, *Republic* 1.328 D, 329 C; the speaker is the elderly Cephalus quoting Sophocles.
66. Plato, *Phaedo* 62 B, 114 B–C.
67. Plato, *Phaedo* 62 B.
68. Adding τοῦ with Heyse.
69. Plato, *Statesman* 273 B–C.
70. Plato, *Statesman*, preceding the previous passage.

succession of festivals as a respite from their labors."[71] (3) In
the *Epinomis* he goes through the causes of this pitiful state and
says, "From the first, birth was difficult for every living creature, first in achieving the state of an embryo, then in the process of birth, and again in growing up and being educated. It
all takes place through countless difficulties. Everyone agrees
on that."[72]

21(1) Well! Doesn't Heraclitus call birth a death, in conformity with Pythagoras and with Socrates in the *Gorgias* in this passage: "Death is all that we see when awake, dreams all that we
see when asleep."?[73] But enough of this! When we discourse
about first principles we will consider[74] the contradictions between the obscure sayings of the philosophers and the dog-
matic assertions of Marcion's followers. Except that I think I
have shown clearly enough that Marcion took the impulse for
his "strange"[75] doctrines from Plato without acknowledgment
or understanding.

22(1) To proceed with our account of self-control. We were
maintaining that the Greeks were highly critical of childbirth,
looking askance at its inconveniences, and that Marcion's followers understand this in a godless sense and show no gratitude
to the creator. (2) Tragedy says,

> Better for mortals not to be born than to be born.
> It is with bitter pains that I bear
> children. I bear and those I bear lack sense.
> I groan—no use!—at seeing vicious children
> and losing good ones. Even if they survive
> my poor heart melts with fear.
> Then what is this goodness? One soul is
> Enough anxiety and effort to sustain.[76]

(3) More in the same vein he writes,

---

71. Plato, *Laws* 2.653 C–D.
72. [Plato] *Epinomis* 973 D; reading αὖ τὸ with Sylburg for αὐτο.
73. DK 22 B 21 (see nt. 49); Plato, *Gorgias* 492 E; reading Πυθαγόρᾳ τε
with Hervet: the exact reference is uncertain.
74. See nt. 46; reading ἐπισκεψόμενα with Sylburg for ἐπισκεψώμεθα.
75. A punning allusion to Marcion's true god called Stranger.
76. Euripides, fr. inc. 908 N; the context is unknown.

I have long thought and still think
that humans ought not to produce children,
seeing to what trials we engender them.[77]

(4) But in these lines he clearly attributes the cause of evils to
the primal beginnings with the words,

Born to disaster and ill fortune
you were born a human, and took a life
of disaster from the source from which this upper air
first gave to all humans the breezes that nourish life.
You are mortal: do not now begrudge your mortal state.[78]

23(1) Again he presents similar ideas in the following passage:

No mortal is blessed,
none happy;
none was yet born sorrow-free.[79]

(2) Again he writes,

Ah! Ah! how many the chances of sorrow for mortals!
How many its forms! None can tell its end.[80]

(3) Once more he writes similarly,

Of all that mortals enjoy
nothing is happy through to the end.[81]

24(1) On these grounds it is said that the Pythagoreans abstain from sex. My own view, on the contrary, is that they marry
to produce children, and after raising a family they want to
keep sexual pleasure under control. (2) This is why they place
a mystic ban on eating beans, not because they lead to belching,

---

77. *TGF*, fr. 111.
78. *TGF*, fr. 112; reading πεπραγέναι with Musgrave in 1.1, ὅδε with Potter
in 1.4, and, with Valckenaer, omitting τοί in 1.5; Clement seems to attribute
all the passages to Euripides.
79. Euripides, *Iphigenia at Aulis* 161–3.
80. Euripides, fr. 211 from *Antiope*.
81. Euripides, *Suppliants* 269–70 adding οὐδὲν from the received text, and
reading εὐδαιμονοῦν for -ῶν.

indigestion, and bad dreams,[82] or because a bean has the shape of a human head, as in the line

> To eat beans is like eating your parents' heads,[83]

but rather because eating beans produces sterility in women. (3) Anyway, Theophrastus in the fifth book of his *Causes of Plants*[84] records that bean-pods set around the roots of young trees cause the shoots to dry up, and that if birds that haunt houses eat bean-pods for any length of time they become infertile.

4

Heretics Use Several Pretexts in Order to Exercise Licentiousness

25(1) From the heretics we have spoken of Marcion from Pontus who deprecates the use of worldly things because of his antipathy to their creator. (2) The creator is thus actually responsible for his self-control, if you can call it self-control. This giant who battles with God and thinks he can withstand him is an unwilling ascetic who runs down the creation and the formation of human beings.[85] (3) If they quote the Lord's words addressed to Philip, "Let the dead bury their dead; for your part follow me,"[86] they should also reflect that Philip's flesh was of the same formation, and he was not endowed with a polluted corpse. (4) Then how could he have a body of flesh without having a corpse? Because when the Lord put his passions to death he rose from the grave and lived to Christ.[87] (5) We have spoken of the lawless communism in women held by Carpo-

82. See Plutarch, *Moralia* 286 D–E.
83. *FPG* 1.200.
84. Theophrastus, *Causes of Plants* 5.15.1, reading Φυτικῶν with Sylburg; but Clement is working secondhand from Apollonius, *Mirabilia* 46; Theophrastus (c. 370–285 B.C.) from Eresus in Lesbos was a great scholar and teacher, successor to Aristotle.
85. In Greek myth the giants attacked the gods, who were saved by Heracles. The conflict was portrayed on the Siphnian Treasury in Delphi, and the altar of Zeus at Pergamum (now in Berlin).
86. Matt 8.22; Luke 9.60, but Philip is mentioned in neither passage; perhaps then Clement has taken the same story from a lost gospel.
87. Col 3.1,5; Rom 14.8.

crates. But when we mentioned Nicolaus' remark we omitted one point. (6) They say that he had a pretty wife. After the Savior's resurrection he was accused of jealousy by the apostles. He brought his wife out into their midst and offered her to anyone who wanted her in marriage. (7) They say that his action was consistent with the saying "The flesh is to be treated with contempt."[88] Those who are members of his sect follow his word and act simply and uncritically, and indulge in unrestrained licence.

26(1) However, I learn that Nicolaus had relations with no woman other than his wedded wife, and of his children the girls grew to old age as virgins, and the son remained innocent. (2) In these circumstances it was a rejection of the passions to wheel[89] out the wife, over whom he was charged with jealousy, into the middle of the apostles; and his control of the generally acknowledged pleasures was a lesson in "treating the flesh with contempt." I suppose that, following the Savior's command, he did not want "to serve two masters,"[90] pleasure and God. (3) Anyway, they say that Matthias taught the lesson of fighting against the flesh, holding it in contempt, never giving in to its desire for unrestrained pleasure, and enabling the soul to grow through faith and revealed knowledge.[91]

27(1) Those who call Licentious Aphrodite a mystical communion insult the latter name.[92] (2) It is called an action alike whether you do something wrong or right. In the same way communion is a good thing[93] when it involves a sharing of money, food, or clothing. But they use the word irreligiously

---

88. See *Stromateis* 2.118.3.

89. ἐκκύκλημα, 'a wheeled platform,' was used in the theater to display an internal tableau (see B. Knox, *The Greek Theater* [New Jersey, 1985], 271–2).

90. Matt 6.24; Luke 16.13.

91. Matthias filled the place of Judas in the Twelve (see Acts 1.23–6); a gospel is attributed to him, which may be the same as the *Traditions of Matthias*, a work valued by Basilides and his followers.

92. For Licentious Aphrodite (physical rather than spiritual love) see Plato, *Symposium* 181 A, but he may be forcing the meaning of a universal goddess; there were cults in Erythrae, Cos, Megalopolis, and Thebes as well as Athens.

93. Reading μὲν with Hiller for δὲ καί.

in applying it to any kind of sexual intercourse. (3) Anyway, there is a story that one of them encountered one of our beautiful virgins and said, "It is written, 'Give yourself to anyone who asks.'"[94] She did not understand the fellow's impudence and replied with the height of propriety, "If the subject is marriage, speak to my mother." (4) What godlessness! These communists in sexual freedom, these brothers in lustfulness, actually pervert the Savior's words. They are a disgrace not just to philosophy but to the whole of human life. They deface the truth, or rather raze it to the ground insofar as they can. (5) The wretches make a religion out of physical union and sexual intercourse, and think that this will lead them into the kingdom of God.

28(1) It is to the brothels that that sort of communism leads. Pigs and goats should be their companions. It is the whores who preside over the bordello and indiscriminately receive all comers who have most to hope from them. (2) "That is not how you have learned Christ, if you have been told of him, if you have learned your lessons in him, as the truth is in Jesus Christ—to leave on one side your former way of life, to put off the old human nature, which is deluded by its lusts and on the road to destruction. (3) Be made new in mind and spirit. Put on the new human nature, created in God's way, in the righteousness and holiness which truth demands, following the likeness of the divine."[95] (4) "Become imitators of God, like dear children, and set your course in love, as Christ loved you and gave himself up for us as an offering and sacrifice to God producing a pleasing fragrance. (5) Fornication, indecency of any kind, the profit motive, coarseness, trivial talk should never even be mentioned among you as is right for God's people."[96] (6) Yes, and the Apostle teaches the practice of chastity in speech when he writes, "Know well that everyone who practices fornication" and so on down to "but rather show them up."[97]

94. Misquoting Luke 6.30; Matt 5.42.
95. Eph 4.20–4. 96. Eph 5.1–4.
97. Eph 5.5–11.

29(1) Their doctrine was derived from an apocryphal work.[98] In fact I will quote the passage which is the mother of their impropriety. Whether the actual authors of the book are responsible (see their senselessness if in their licentiousness they falsely impugn God), or whether they encountered some others, they heard sound doctrine and held distorted ideas about it. (2) This is how the passage runs: "All things were one. Since this Unity thought it right not to be left alone, a Spirit of Inspiration emerged from it. It had intercourse with this and produced the Beloved. From the Beloved emerged its own Spirit of Inspiration, with which it had intercourse, producing Powers, invisible and inaudible" down to "each by her own name." (3) If these people were speaking of spiritual unions, like Valentinus' followers, then one might perhaps accept[99] their assumption. But only a person who has renounced salvation could attribute to the holy spirit of prophecy a union consisting in sexual violence.

30(1) Similar doctrines are expressed by Prodicus' school,[100] who falsely claim the name of Gnostics for themselves, calling themselves natural sons of the primal god. They make wrong use of their high birth and freedom to live as they will. What they will is a life of pleasure-loving, having come to the conclusion that they are inferior to none, being lords of the sabbath, and born princes superior to all humankind. For a king, they say, there is no written law. (2) In the first place,[101] they do not do all they want; many things will stand in the way of their desires and efforts. Further, what they do do, they do not as kings but as slaves liable to flogging; they are in fear of discovery in their secret adulteries; they are evading condemnation; they are afraid of punishment. (3) How can a

---

98. Unknown except for this passage.

99. Reading ἐπεδέξατ' ἄν with Mayor for ἐπεδέξατο; Valentinus was, with Basilides, one of the two great Gnostic leaders of the second century A.D. (see nt. 1).

100. Little is known of Prodicus, who claimed secret revelations from Zoroaster. He denied the need for prayer (God being omniscient), and had a strong doctrine of election. It is less likely that he was involved with the nudist Adamites.

101. Reading οὖν with Stählin for ὅτι.

combination of immoderation and dirty language be freedom? "Everyone who sins is a slave," says the Apostle.[102]

31(1) How can the man who has given himself over to every
lust be a citizen according to the Law of God when the Lord
has declared, "I say, you shall not lust"?[103] (2) Is a person to
take a decision to sin deliberately, and to lay it down as a
principle to commit adultery, to waste his substance in high
living, and to break up other people's marriages, when we
actually pity the rest who fall involuntarily into sin? (3) Even
if they have arrived in an alien world, if they prove unfaithful
in what belongs to another,[104] they will have no hold on the
truth. (4) Does a foreigner insult the citizens? Do them wrong?
Does he not rather behave as a visitor[105] and live out his life
in conformity with the regulations without offending the citizens? (5) How can they say that they are the only people with
a knowledge of God when they behave in the same way as
those the gentiles hate for their failure to obey the laws' in-
junctions—criminals, immoralists, the avaricious, and adulterers? (6) They ought to be living virtuous lives in a foreign
land too, so as to show that they really are of royal blood.

32(1) As it is, they have taken the decision to live lawlessly,
and won the hatred alike of human legislators and of the Law
of God. At any rate, the man who speared through the for-
nicator in Numbers is shown to be blessed by God.[106] (2) "If
we say," says John in his letter, "that we have communion with
him"—that is, God—"and walk in darkness, we are lying and
not acting out the truth. If we walk in the light as he is in the
light, then we enjoy communion with him, and the blood of
his son Jesus cleanses us from sin."[107]

33(1) How then are those who behave in this manner superior to the worldly? They are like the dregs of the worldly.
Like acts reveal like natures, I suppose. (2) Those who claim

102. John 8.34, but Jesus is speaking, and Clement's memory is confused
with Rom 6.16.
103. Matt 5.28.   104. Luke 16.12.
105. 1 Pet 2.11.
106. Aaron's grandson Phinehas: Num 25.8; reading εὐλογούμενος with
Lowth for εὐλαβούμενος.
107. 1 John 1.6–7.

superiority of birth ought to show superiority of character, if they want to escape incarceration in prison.[108] (3) It really is as the Lord said: "If your righteousness does not exceed the righteousness of the scribes and Pharisees, you will not enter the kingdom of God."[109] (4) Scripture shows in Daniel the principle of abstinence in food.[110] To sum up, David in the Psalms speaks about obedience: "How shall a young man keep his path straight?" The answer comes immediately: "By keeping your Word with his whole heart."[111] (5) Jeremiah says, "These are the Lord's words: do not follow the paths of the gentiles."[112]

34(1) In consequence, some other worthless scoundrels[113] say that humanity was fashioned by different powers, the body down to the navel being the product of divine craftsmanship, and below that of inferior work; which is why human beings yearn for intercourse.[114] (2) They forget that the upper parts of the body call out for food, and in some people show lust. They contradict Christ's statement to the Pharisees that the same God made our outer and our inner man.[115] In addition, desire does not come from the body, even though it expresses itself through the body.[116] (3) There is another group whom we call the Opponents. They affirm that the God of the universe is our father by nature, and everything that he has made is good. But one of those who came into being from him sowed weeds,[117] and brought into being the growth of evil things. He has surrounded us all with these evils and so set us in opposition to the Father. (4) For this reason we set ourselves to vindicate the Father in opposition to him, counteracting the will of this second being. So, since it is the latter who said,

108. Probably the spiritual prison of 1 Pet 3.19.
109. Matt 5.20.
110. Dan 1.10.
111. Ps 119.9–10.　　　　　112. Jer 10.2.
113. Reading μιαροὶ with Stählin for μικροὶ, a palmary emendation.
114. Attributed by Epiphanius (*Panarion* 45.2) to the sect of the Severians; a similar view is found in *On Virginity* 7 attributed to Basil of Caesarea but perhaps by the Arian Basil of Ancyra.
115. Luke 11.40.
116. Plato, *Philebus* 35 C.
117. Matt 13.25.

"You shall not commit adultery,"[118] we should, they say, commit adultery[119] so as to annul his order.

35(1) To these people we would say that we have been taught to recognize false prophets and those who merely make a pretense of the truth by their actions.[120] Your actions are evidence against you. How can you say that you still adhere to the truth? (2) Either there is no such thing as evil, in which case the one you charge with opposition to God does not merit reproof, and has never created anything evil (the tree and the fruit are eliminated together), or else, if evil really does exist, they must tell us what is their view of the commandments ordained about righteousness, self-control, patience, forbearance and so on: are they bad or good? (3) If the commandment which bans the performance of the vast majority of disgraceful actions is not good, then vice will be legislating against itself to its own undoing—which is impossible. If it is good, then in opposing good directions they admit that they are opposing the good and acting wickedly.

36(1) The Savior himself, the only person they think warrants obedience, has set himself in the way of hatred and abusiveness,[121] and says, "When you go to court with an opponent, try and achieve an amicable reconciliation."[122] (2) So they will either reject Christ's recommendation and remain in opposition to their opponent, or they will become friends and drop their suit against him. (3) Well? Can't you see, good people (I want to speak as if you were here with me), that in fighting against these excellent commandments, you are in conflict[123] with your own salvation? It is not these admirable directions you are undermining. It is yourselves. (4) "Your good actions should shine out," the Lord said.[124] It is your immorality that you display. (5) Besides, if your aim is to undo the lawgiver's commandments, why on earth do you aim to undo by your immorality "You shall not commit adultery" and

118. Exod 20.14.
119. Reading μοιχεύσωμεν after Theodoret, *Compendium of Heretical Narratives* 1.16.
120. Matt 7.16.   121. Matt 5.44.
122. Matt 5.25.
123. Reading ἀνθίστασθε with Sylburg for ἀνθίστασθαι.
124. Matt 5.16.

"You shall not corrupt boys"[125] and all that bears on self-control? Why do you do away with winter—he made it!—to produce summer when it is still the middle of winter? Why do you not make the land navigable and enable people to walk on the sea as the compilers of history say that Xerxes, a non-Greek, wanted to do?[126]

37(1) Why do you not oppose all the commandments? He said, "Increase and multiply."[127] In your opposition to him you should have totally refrained from sexual intercourse. He said, "I gave you everything for food and delight."[128] You ought not to have had any delights. (2) Besides, he says, "An eye for an eye."[129] You ought never to have met opposition with opposition. He told the thief to make fourfold restitution.[130] You ought to have paid the thief something in addition. (3) Similarly with the command "You shall love the Lord":[131] You ought to have opposed it and to have shown no love towards the God of the universe. Again he said, "You shall not make an image by carving or by melting metal."[132] The logical conclusion was for you to offer worship to statues. (4) It is irreligious of you to oppose, on your own admission, the creator, and to try and rival prostitutes and adulterers in your behavior. (5) Can't you see that you are in fact exalting the very one you regard as weak, if it is his will that finds fulfillment rather than the will of the good God? The other side of this is that you yourselves[133] are demonstrating the weakness of the one you call your father.

38(1) These people also collect passages from extracts of the prophets, making an anthology and cobbling them together quite wrongly, taking literally[134] what was meant alle-

---

125. *Didache* 2.1; *Epistle of Barnabas* 19.4.
126. Adding φασίν with Stählin; Xerxes, king of Persia, seeking to subjugate Greece in 480 B.C. bridged the Hellespont so that his army could march over (Herodotus, 7.55); but both aims are attributed to Antiochus Epiphanes in 2 Macc 5.21.

127. Gen 1.28, 9.1.   128. Gen 1.29, 9.2.
129. Exod 21.24.   130. Exod 22.1.
131. Deut 6.5.   132. Deut 27.15.
133. Reading πρὸς with Sylburg for πῶς.
134. Reading εὐθείας with Victorius for εὐηθείας.

gorically. (2) They say that Scripture has this: "They opposed God and found salvation."[135] But they add, "the shameless God." They accept this saying as advice extended to them. They think that it is salvation to oppose the creator. (3) Scripture does not say, "the shameless god." And even if it did, you idiots, it would be talking of the one we call the devil as shameless, whether as the maligner of humanity, or as the prosecutor of sinners, or as an apostate. (4) At any rate, the people referred to in the passage objected to being disciplined for their sins; they protested and murmured at the passage quoted because the other nations were not being punished for their offenses while they alone were put down for every single offense. Even Jeremiah was led to say, "Why is the path of the wicked easy?"[136] The passage[137] from Malachi already quoted is to the same effect: "They opposed God and found salvation." (5) The prophets in their oracular utterances do not merely say that they have heard certain messages from God; they demonstrably report the popular conversations, replying to objections voiced, as if they were officially recording questions from human sources. The saying before us is an example of this.

39(1) It may be these people whom the Apostle is inveighing against in his *Epistle to the Romans* when he writes, "We are slanderously charged by some people with saying that we are to do evil things so that good consequences may follow. No! Such a view is justly condemned."[138] (2) These are the people who, when they read, twist the Scriptures by their tone of voice to serve their own pleasures. They alter some of the accents and punctuation marks in order to force wise and constructive precepts to support their taste for luxury.[139] (3) "You who have provoked God with your words," says Malachi, "have actually

135. Mal 3.15.
136. Jer 12.1.
137. Reading τò with Sylburg for τῶι.
138. Rom 3.8.
139. Archbishop Whately once said of a preacher who strained his text, "I should like to hear that young man preach on 'Hang all the Law and the prophets.'" A preacher inveighing against a current hairstyle used the text "Top-knot, come down" (see Matt 24.17).

said, 'In what have we provoked him?' You do this by saying,
'Everyone who acts immorally is good in the Lord's sight and
he approves of them,' and, 'Where is the God of righteousness?' "[140]

5
There Are Two Kinds of Heresies—Licentious or Ascetic

40(1) We have no intention of making a closer examination
of this topic or mentioning more implausible heresies. We
have no intention of being forced to an individual discussion
of each of them in all their scandalous nature or prolonging
these notes to a vast length. Let us answer them by dividing
all the heresies into two groups.[141] (2) Either they teach a way
of life which makes no distinction between right and wrong
or their hymn is too highly strung[142] and they acclaim asceticism out of a spirit of irreligious quarrelsomeness. (3) I must
first expound the former division. If it is legitimate to choose
any way of life, then clearly it is legitimate to choose the way
that involves asceticism. If there is no way of life which carries
danger for the elect, then clearly this is particularly true of
the life[143] of virtuous self-discipline. (4) If the Lord of the
sabbath[144] has been granted freedom from accountability for
a life of licentiousness, the man whose social life is orderly will
be far freer from accountability. (5) The Apostle says, "Everything is legitimate for me; not everything is expedient."[145] If
everything is legitimate, that obviously includes self-discipline.

41(1) So just as the person who uses his legitimate choice
to live a virtuous life is worthy of praise, so the one who gives
us this free and sovereign right of legitimate choice, allowing
us to live as we wish, is far more to be reverenced and honored
in not allowing our positive or negative choices to fall into

140. Mal 2.17.
141. Reading, with Sylburg, ἐπιμεμνώμεθα for ἐπιμεμνήμεθα, προάγωμεν
for προάγοιμεν, τάγματα for πράγματα.
142. Reading ἄδουσαι with Schwartz for ἄγουσαι.
143. Adding ὁ with Hiller.
144. Matt 12.8; Mark 2.28; Luke 6.5.
145. 1 Cor 6.12, 10.23.

inescapable slavery.[146] (2) Neither has occasion for fear from the choice of license or discipline; but they are not held in the same respect. The person who drifts into pleasures is gratifying his body; the ascetic is freeing his soul from passions, and the soul has authority over the body. (3) If they tell us that we are called to freedom, we are not, as the Apostle puts it, to present that "freedom as an opening for our lower selves."[147] (4) If we are to gratify lust, if we are to think a reprehensible way of living a matter of moral indifference, as they assert, either we ought to obey our lusts at all points and, if so, to engage in the most immoral and irreligious practices in conformity with our teachers, (5) or we shall turn away from some of our desires, no longer compelled to live by amoral standards, no longer in unbridled servitude to our least honorable parts—stomach and sex-organs—pampering our carcass to serve our desire. (6) Lust is nurtured and vitalized if we minister to its enjoyment; on the other hand, it fades away if it is kept in check.

42(1) How is it possible for a person who is overpowered by physical pleasures to grow like the Lord or have a true knowledge of God? Every pleasure has its origin in a desire. Desire is a form of pain, a care which yearns for something it lacks.[148] (2) Those who choose this way of life simply seem to me, in the familiar words,

To be suffering grief on top of shame[149]

and choosing an evil "they have brought on themselves"[150] for the present and the future. (3) So if everything were legitimate and there were no fear of missing out on the ultimate hope because of immoral actions, then they might have some excuse for their wretchedly vicious lives. (4) Through the commandments we have a demonstration of the blessed life. We all

146. The Greek is difficult; the word for "positive choice" also means "heresy."
147. Gal 5.13.
148. Stock definition: Andronicus, *On the Passions* 124 K.
149. Hesiod, *Works and Days* 211.
150. Homer, *Odyssey* 18.73.

ought to pursue it without misunderstanding any of the statements or neglecting any of the properties, even the slightest of them. We are to follow where the Word leads. But[151] if we do slip up, we cannot avoid falling into "undying evil."[152] (5) We must follow God's Scripture, the road taken by the faithful, and we will, so far as possible, become like the Lord.[153] We are not to live amorally. We are, so far as possible, to purify ourselves from pleasures and lusts, and take care of our soul which should continue to be engaged solely with the divine. (6) For if it is pure and freed from all vice, the mind is somehow capable of receiving the power of God, when the divine image is established within it. Scripture says, "Everyone who has this hope in the Lord is purifying himself as the Lord is pure."[154]

43(1) It is impossible for those who are still under the direction of their passions to receive true knowledge of God. It follows that if they have not achieved any knowledge of God, they do not have any experience of final hope either. The person who fails to attain this end looks liable to the charge of ignorance of God. Ignorance of God is displayed by one's way of living. (2) It is absolutely impossible to combine actual scientific knowledge with a failure[155] to show shame at giving in to the demands of the body. It is impossible to harmonize the view that the supreme good consists in pleasure with the view that beauty of character[156] is the only good: This is seen only in the Lord, God alone is good and the sole fit object of love. (3) "You have been circumcised in Christ with a circumcision not performed with hands in stripping yourselves of your fleshly body, that is, in Christ's circumcision." (4) "So if

151. Adding δὲ with Schwartz.
152. Homer, *Odyssey* 12.118.
153. Clement is echoing a famous phrase from Plato, *Theaetetus* 176 B, but replaces "God" with "the Lord."
154. 1 John 3.3.   155. Adding μὴ with Stählin.
156. A difficult word to translate: the adjective means 'admirable,' 'of beauty,' 'excellence,' or 'virtue'; Lovers are often called *kalos*, 'dishy,' hence the last phrase about God; the reading is uncertain just before: I follow Stählin's τὴν ἡδονὴν τῷ for τῆι ἡδονῆι ἤ, and ἀγαθὸν for ἀγαθῶι (partly from Lowth).

you are risen together with Christ, look for the things above, fix your mind on them, not on earthly things. For you are dead, and your life has been buried in God together with Christ"—this hardly applies to the sexual immorality which they practice! (5) "So mortify your earthly members—fornication, filthiness, passion, lust; through these the visitation of anger is on its way." So they too should put away "anger, temper, vice, slander, dirty talk from their mouths, stripping themselves of the old human nature with its lusts and putting on the new human nature, which is renewed for full knowledge in accordance with the likeness of its creator."[157]

44(1) The nature of a person's way of living shows up clearly those who have come to know the commandments, since the behavior follows the inward reason. (2) The tree is known by its fruits, not by its flowers and leaves.[158] True knowledge is discerned from the fruits of behavior, not from the flower of theory. (3) We do not call bare theory knowledge; knowledge is a kind of divine understanding; it is that light engendered in the soul from obedience to the commandments which makes everything clear and enables a person to know what is in a state of change, to know his own humanity, to know himself,[159] and teaches him to establish himself within reach of God. For knowledge stands to the mind as the eye to the body.[160] (4) They should not call enslavement to pleasure freedom any more than they should call bitter sweet. We have learned to call freedom the freedom with which the Lord alone endows us, delivering us from pleasures, lusts and the other passions. (5) "Anyone who says, 'I know the Lord,' and fails to keep his commandments, is a liar, and there is no truth in him," says John.[161]

---

157. Col 2.11, 3.1–3, 5–6, 8–10.
158. Matt 7.16, 12.33; Luke 6.44.
159. The famous Greek injunction; I have accepted the MS text against most editors.
160. Aristotle, *Nicomachaean Ethics* 1.4.1096 B 29 has "The mind stands to the soul as the eye to the body."
161. 1 John 2.4.

6

Heretics Who Exercise Restraint out of an Impious
Interpretation of the Gospel

45(1) What about those who use religious language for ir-religious practices involving abstinence against creation and the holy creator, the one and only almighty God, and teach that we ought not to accept marriage and childbearing or introduce yet more wretches in their turn into the world to provide fodder for death? This is what we must say to them; first, in the words of the apostle John: (2) "Now many anti-christs have come, from which we know that it is the last hour. They went out from us, but were not of our company: if they had been, they would have stayed with us."[162] (3) Next we must turn their statements on the grounds that they destroy the sense of their citations. Here is an example: When Salome asked, "How long will death maintain its power?" the Lord said, "As long as you women bear children."[163] He is not speaking of life as evil and the creation as rotten. He is giving instruction about the normal course of nature. Death is always following on the heels of birth.

46(1) The design of the Law is to divert us from extrava-gance and all forms of disorderly behavior; this is its object, to draw us from unrighteousness to righteousness, making us responsible in marriage, engendering children, and living well. (2) The Lord "comes to fulfill, not to destroy the Law."[164] Fulfillment does not mean that it was defective.[165] The proph-ecies which followed the Law were accomplished through his presence, since the qualities of an upright way of life were announced to people of righteous behavior before the coming of the Law by the Word.[166] (3) The majority know nothing of self-discipline. They live by the body, not by the spirit. Without

---

162. 1 John 2.18–19 reading ἀντίχριστοι for ἀντίχρηστοι.

163. From the lost *Gospel according to the Egyptians* (see Hennecke-Schnee-melcher, *New Testament Apocrypha*, 1.166–9), reading τίκτητε with Dindorf for τίκτετε. See also *Stromateis* 3.63–4; *Excerpta ex Theodoto* 67.

164. Matt 5.17.

165. Reading ἐνδεῆ with Sylburg for ἐνδεεῖ.

166. Or "reason."

the spirit the body is earth and dust.[167] (4) The Lord condemns adultery in thought.[168] Well? Is it not possible to practice self-discipline within marriage without trying to pull apart "that which God has joined"?[169] That is the sort of thing taught by the dissolvers of the marriage bond. Through them the name of Christian comes into bad repute. (5) These people say that sexual intercourse is polluted. Yet they owe their existence to sexual intercourse! Must they not be polluted? Personally, I think that the seed coming from consecrated people is sacred too.

47(1) So it is not just our spirit which ought to be consecrated. It is our character, our life, our body. What is the sense of the Apostle Paul's words that the wife is consecrated by her husband, and the husband by his wife?[170] (2) What was it that the Lord said to those who questioned him about divorce, asking whether it was permissible to get rid of one's wife on the authority of Moses? He said, "Moses wrote this with an eye to your hardheartedness. But have you not read what God said to the first–formed male: 'You two shall come into one single flesh'? So, anyone who disposes of his wife except by reason of sexual immorality is making an adulteress of her."[171] (3) But "after the resurrection," he says, "they do not marry and are not given in marriage."[172] Yes, and this is what is said about the stomach and food: "Food is for the stomach and the stomach for food, and God will put an end to both."[173] He is rebuking those who think to live like boars or goats, to stop them eating and copulating without any sense of respect.

48(1) If, as they claim, they have already attained the state of resurrection,[174] and for that reason repudiate marriage, they should stop eating and drinking. For the Apostle said[175] that the stomach and food would be dispensed with in the

---

167. Gen 18.27.   168. Matt 5.28.
169. Matt 19.6.   170. 1 Cor 7.14.
171. Matt 19.3–9; reading ἔσεσθε with Sylburg for ἔσεσθαι.
172. Matt 22.30.   173. 1 Cor 6.13.
174. Chadwick notes several references to the view that the celibate is living the life of an angel: Basil, *On Virginity* 51; Jerome, *Against Jovinian* 1.36; Augustine, *On the Good of Marriage* 8; *Holy Virginity* 4, 12.
175. Reading ἔφη with Sylburg for ἔφην.

resurrection. (2) Then how can they hunger and thirst and suffer the flesh and all the other things from which the person who has attained through Christ the fullness of the expected resurrection will be free? Even those who worship idols fast and practice sexual abstinence. (3) "The kingdom of God does not consist in eating and drinking," he says.[176] It is possible even for the Magi by a mental effort to abstain alike from wine, animal food, and sex, although they worship angels and spiritual beings.[177] Just as humility is a form of meekness and does not mean maltreating the body, so asceticism is a virtue of the soul practiced privately, not openly.

49(1) There are those who say openly that marriage is fornication. They lay it down as a dogma that it was instituted by the devil. They are arrogant and claim to be emulating the Lord who did not marry and had no worldly possessions. It is their boast to have a profounder understanding of the gospel than anyone else. (2) To them Scripture says, "God is against the proud and gives grace to the humble."[178] (3) Next, they do not know the reason why the Lord did not marry. In the first place, he had his own bride, the Church. Secondly, he was not a common man to need a physical partner.[179] Further, he did not have an obligation to produce children; he was born God's only Son and survives eternally. (4) It is this very Lord who says, "Let no human being part that which God has joined together."[180] And again, "The Son of Man's coming shall be as in the days of Noah, when they were marrying, giving in marriage, building, planting, and as in the days of Lot."[181] (5) Since he is not speaking in relation to the gentiles, he adds, "When the Son of Man comes, will he find

176. Rom 14.17.
177. The Magi were perhaps originally a tribe from Media. The term came to be applied somewhat loosely to priests and seers of the Zoroastrian religion of Persia, which did indeed hold that life was a battleground between the forces of order and chaos with hosts of intermediate spiritual powers on either side.
178. Jas 4.6; 1 Pet 5.5; Prov 3.34.
179. Gen 2.18.
180. Matt 19.6; Mark 10.9.
181. Matt 24.37–9; Luke 17.26–30.

faith on the earth?"[182] (6) Again, "It will be bad for women pregnant or with child at the breast in those days."[183] (But these words are an allegory.) There was a particular reason why he did not even define the times "that the Father has established within his own authority."[184] It is so that the world should continue generation after generation.

50(1) What about these words: "Not everyone can take this saying. There are some eunuchs born as eunuchs, and some who were made eunuchs by human action, and some who have made themselves eunuchs for the kingdom of heaven. Let anyone who can accept the words accept them."[185] (2) They do not recognize that it was after his words about divorce that some of them asked whether, if that is the position with regard to the wife, it is not better to refrain from marriage, and it was then that the Lord said, "Not everyone can take this saying, only those who have a gift." (3) Those asking the question wanted to find out whether, when a wife had been condemned for sexual misconduct and removed, there was any advantage in marrying another. (4) Tradition records that quite a number of athletes have abstained from sexual intercourse as part of the discipline of physical training. Examples are Astylus of Croton and Crison of Himera.[186] The lutenist Amoebeus, newly married as he was, did not touch his bride.[187] Aristotle of Cyrene was the only man to turn up his nose at Lais' love.[188]

182. Luke 18.8.
183. Matt 24.19; Mark 13.17; Luke 21.23.
184. Acts 1.7.
185. Matt 19.12.
186. Plato, *Laws* 8.840 A and scholia; Astylus from Croton (early fifth century B.C.), a friend of the dictator Hiero, who won races in three successive Olympics in southern Italy, merited an ode in his honor by Simonides; Crison from Himera in Sicily ran in the Olympics in 447 B.C. (see Plato, *Protagoras* 335 E).
187. Aelian, *On the Nature of Animals* 6.1; *Varying History* 3.30; Amoebeus (third century B.C.) was an Athenian who lived near the theater, won the approval of Zeno the Stoic, and received one talent per performance (see Athenaeus, 14.623 D; Plutarch, *Moralia* 443 A).
188. On Aristotle see Diogenes Laertius 5.35 who identifies him as "a native of Cyrene, who wrote upon the art of poetry." Cyrene was a Greek colony in North Africa; Lais was a famous beauty and courtesan; reading ὑπερεώρα with Stählin for ὑπεώρα.

51(1) He promised the courtesan on oath that he would take her back to his homeland, if she helped him against his antagonists in some matter. She did so, and he fulfilled his oath in an amusing way. He painted the closest possible likeness of her and set it up in Cyrene—the account will be found in the *Character of Sports* by Istrus.[189] It follows that celibacy is not particularly praiseworthy unless it arises through love of God. (2) The blessed Paul says of those who show a distaste for marriage: "In the last times people will abandon the faith, attaching themselves to deceitful spirits and the teachings of daemonic powers that they should abstain from food, at the same time forbidding marriage."[190] (3) Again he says, "Do not let anyone disqualify you in forced piety of self-mortification and severity to the body."[191] The same author writes these words: "Are you bound to a wife? Do not seek a dissolution. Have you been divorced? Do not go looking for a wife."[192] Again he says, "Every man should have his own wife to protect him from temptation by Satan."[193]

52(1) Well? Did not the righteous of past days share gratefully in God's creation? Some of them married and produced children without loss of self-control. The ravens brought bread and meat as food to Elijah.[194] The prophet Samuel brought the leftovers from the haunch which had provided him with a meal and gave it to Saul to eat.[195] (2) They claim to be their superiors in lifestyle, but they will never remotely be able to match their praxis. (3) So "if anyone refrains from eating, he is not to denigrate one who eats. If anyone eats, he is not to judge one who abstains, since God has accepted him."[196] (4) Furthermore, the Lord says of himself, "John came abstaining from food and drink, and they say, 'He is possessed.' The Son of Man came eating and drinking, and

189. Istrus or Ister of Cyrene (second half of the third century B.C.), historian and pupil of Callimachus, wrote on the early history of Attica among much else, being particularly interested in religion (see *FGrH* 3 B 334).

190. 1 Tim 4.1–3.   191. Col 2.18,23 freely cited.
192. 1 Cor 7.27.   193. 1 Cor 7.2–5.
194. 1 Kgs 17.6.
195. 1 Sam 9.24, omitting ἦν with Victorius.
196. Rom 14.3.

they say, 'Look at him, a greedy drunkard, a friend of tax officers, a sinner!'"[197] Are they not criticizing the apostles? Peter and Philip produced children, and Philip gave his daughters away in marriage.[198]

53(1) In one of his letters Paul has no hesitation in addressing his "yokefellow."[199] He did not take her around with him for the convenience of his ministry. (2) He says in one of his letters, "Do we not have the authority to take around a wife from the Church, like the other apostles?"[200] (3) But the apostles in conformity with their ministry concentrated on undistracted preaching, and took their wives around as Christian sisters rather than spouses, to be their fellow-ministers in relation to housewives, through whom the Lord's teaching penetrated into the women's quarters without scandal. (4) We know the dispositions made over women deacons by the admirable Paul in his second letter to Timothy.[201] Furthermore, this same writer said strongly that "the kingdom of God is not a matter of eating and drinking"—or abstinence from wine or meat—"but of righteousness, peace, and joy in the Holy Spirit."[202] (5) Which of them goes around like Elijah wearing a sheepskin and a leather belt? Which of them wears no shoes and nothing but a piece of sackcloth like Isaiah? Or with nothing on but a linen apron, like Jeremiah?[203] Which of them will imitate John's Gnostic way of life?[204] The blessed prophets lived like that and still gave thanks to the creator.

54(1) This is the way to undermine the "righteousness" of Carpocrates and those who match him in sharing in a fellow-

197. Matt 11.18–19; Luke 7.33–4 where the text is "friend of sinners."

198. Quoted in Eusebius, *Ecclesiastical History* 3.30.1; Peter was married (Mark 1.30; 1 Cor 9.5) but we know nothing about children or about Philip's marital status from the *New Testament,* and there may be confusion between Philip the apostle and Philip the evangelist who certainly had daughters.

199. Phil 4.3, which modern scholars take to refer to Epaphroditus, or a man called *Syzygos,* 'yokefellow,' or the Philippi church, or to some other reference.

200. 1 Cor 9.5.

201. 1 Tim 5.9–15; Clement slips.

202. Rom 14.17.

203. 1 Kgs 19.13; 2 Kgs 1.8; Isa 20.2; Jer 13.1.

204. Matt 3.4; Mark 1.6.

ship of immorality. In the moment of saying, "Give to anyone who asks," Scripture goes on, "and do not turn away anyone who wants a loan."[205] This is the sort of fellowship Scripture teaches, not fellowship in lust. (2) How can there be a person who asks, receives, and borrows if there is no one who possesses, grants, and lends? (3) What does the Lord say? "I was hungry and you gave me food. I was thirsty and you gave me drink. I was a stranger and you took me into your home. I was naked and you gave me clothes to wear." Then he adds, "Insofar as you have done so to one of the humblest of these, you have done so to me."[206] (4) The same law is established in the *Old Testament* in the words "Anyone who gives to a begger is making a loan to God" and "Do not evade doing good to one in need."[207]

55(1) And again it was written, "Do not drop almsgiving and positions of trust" and "Poverty brings a man low, but the hands of the vigorous become wealthy," adding, "Look! A man who has never let his money out on interest is accepted" and "A man's personal wealth is adjudged his soul's ransom" (a clear and open statement).[208] So as the universe is compounded of opposites, hot and cold, dry and wet,[209] so too it is compounded of those who give and those who receive. (2) Again when he says, "If you want to be perfect, sell your property and give the proceeds to the poor," he is showing up the man who boasts of "having kept all the commandments from his youth."[210] He had not fulfilled "You shall love your neighbor as yourself."[211] At that moment the Lord wanted to bring him to perfection and was teaching him to share out of love.

---

205. Matt 5.42.   206. Matt 25.35,40.

207. Prov 19.17, 3.27 reading ἐνδεῆ for ἐνδεεῖ.

208. Prov 3.3, 10.4, reading ἀνδρείων for ἀνδρῶν; Ps 15.5, reading ἰδοὺ ἀνήρ with Sylburg for ἠδ' ἄν; Prov 13.8.

209. Commonplace of Greek philosophy from early times: For different treatments see J. Ferguson, "The Opposites," *Apeiron* 3 (1969) 1–17, and G. E. R. Lloyd, "The Hot and the Cold, the Dry and the Wet in Greek Philosophy," *JHS* 84 (1964) 92 ff.

210. Matt 19.19–21; Mark 10.20–21; Luke 18.21–2.

211. Lev 19.18; Matt 5.43, 19.19, 22.39; Mark 12.31; Luke 10.27; Rom 13.9; Gal 5.14; Jas 2.8.

56(1) So he has not stopped the proper acquisition of wealth but its unjust and insatiable acquisition. For "possession illegally promoted is reduced."[212] For "there are some who sow more and reap more, and some who find their resources reduced by hoarding."[213] About these it is written, "He made distributions and gave to the poor: his righteousness endures to eternity."[214] (2) The one who "sows and gathers in more" is the one who, by sharing his earthly, temporal property, gains an eternal reward in heaven; the other is the one who refuses to share with anyone but vainly "lays up treasure on earth, where moth and rust eat it away."[215] It is written about such a person as this: "In collecting his money he put it into a purse with a hole in it."[216] (3) This is the man of whose land the Lord says in the gospel that it prospered, and when next he wanted to store the harvest, he proposed to build larger barns and said to himself in the words of the story, "You have many good things in store for you for many years. Eat, drink, enjoy yourself." So the Lord said, "You are a fool. This very night they are demanding your life from you. Then who is to possess the things you have laid ready?"[217]

7

The Christian Idea of Continence

57(1) Human self-control (I am referring to the views of the Greek philosophers) professes to counter desire rather than minister to it, with a view to praxis. Our idea of self-control is freedom from desire. It is not a matter of having desires and holding out against them, but actually of mastering desire by self-control. (2) It is not possible to acquire this form of self-control except by the grace of God. That is why he says, "Ask, and it shall be granted you."[218] (3) Moses, though the needs of his body were covered with clothing, re-

212. Prov 13.11.
213. Prov 11.24, reading οἳ for οἱ.
214. Ps 112.9.   215. Matt 6.19.
216. Hag 1.6.   217. Luke 12.16–20.
218. Matt 7.7.

ceived this grace and for forty days felt no hunger or thirst.[219]
(4) Better to be healthy than to be ill and talk about health.
Better for there to be light than to be chattering about light.
Better genuine self-control than the sort taught by the philosophers. (5) Where there is light, there is no darkness. But
where there is deep-seated desire, even if it is solitary, even if
it is actually physically quiescent, union with the absent object
takes place in memory.

58(1) In general, let our affirmation about marriage, food
and the rest proceed:[220] we should never act from desire; our
will should be concentrated on necessities. We are children of
will, not of desire.[221] (2) If a man marries in order to have
children he ought to practice self-control. He ought not to
have a sexual desire even for his wife, to whom he has a duty
to show Christian love.[222] He ought to produce children by a
reverent, disciplined act of will. We have learned not "to pay
attention to physical desires," "walking decorously as in the
light of day"—that is, in Christ and the shining conduct of
the Lord's way—"not in drunken carousing, sexual promiscuity, or jealous quarreling."[223]

59(1) Further, we ought to examine not merely one single
form of self-control in sexual matters, but the other objects
which our soul self-indulgently desires, not content with bare
necessities but making a fuss about luxury. (2) Self-control
means indifference to money, comfort, and property, a mind
above spectacles, control of the tongue, mastery of evil thoughts.[224]
It actually happened that some angels suffered a failure of
self-control, were overpowered by sexual desire, and fell from
heaven to earth.[225] (3) Valentinus in his letter to Agathopus

219. Exod 24.18.
220. Reading προίτω with Sylburg for προείτω.
221. 1 John 1.13.
222. Contrasting agapē, 'Christian love,' with erōs, 'sexual passion,' and
epithymia, 'sexual desire.' (See A. Nygren, Agape and Eros, tr. Philip S. Watson
[Philadelphia, 1953]; Nygren's thesis has been challenged, but this passage
shows the contrast.)
223. Rom 13.14,13.
224. Reading λογισμῶν with Stählin for λογισμῷ; in the previous phrase
καταμεγαλοφρονεῖν is not found in classical Greek.
225. Gen 6.2.

says, "Jesus showed his self-control in all that he endured. He lived in the practice of godhead. He ate and drank in a way individual to himself without excreting his food. Such was his power of self-control that the food was not corrupted within him, since he was not subject to corruption."[226] (4) So we embrace self-control out of the love we bear the Lord and out of its honorable status, consecrating the temple of the Spirit.[227] It is honorable "to emasculate oneself " of all desire "for the sake of the kingdom of heaven" and "to purify the conscience from works of death to the service of the living God."[228]

60(1) There are some who in their hatred of the flesh ungratefully yearn to be free from marital agreement and participation in decent food. They are ignorant and irreligious. Their self-control is irrational. It is so with most of the other peoples of the world. (2) For instance, the Brahmans[229] do not eat meat or drink wine. But some of them allow themselves food daily, as we do, others every other day, as Alexander Polyhistor says in his *History of India*.[230] They despise death and set no value on life, believing in reincarnation. (3) They worship Heracles and Pan as gods. The so-called Holy Men of India also live out their lives in a state of nudity. These also rigorously pursue truth and make predictions about the future. As divine beings[231] they honor a kind of pyramid under which they believe the bones of some god are resting.[232] (4)

---

226. On Valentinus see nt. 99; B. Layton, *The Gnostic Scriptures* (New York, 1987), fr. E pp. 238–9; Agathopus is unknown.

227. 1 Cor 3.16.

228. Matt 19.12; Heb 9.14.

229. The priestly upper caste of India, known to the Greeks from early times through contacts at Babylon, and, since Alexander the Great, directly.

230. Alexander Polyhistor (first century B.C.) was born in Miletus, came to Rome as a prisoner of war, was freed by Sulla and took the name L. Cornelius Alexander. His output was vast, industrious, and uncritical (see *FGrH* 3 A 99 fr. 18).

231. Reading δαιμόνια with Schwartz for ἅ which must be wrong, although what is right is anyone's guess; Heracles, the heroic son of Zeus who was admitted after death to Olympus, was identified with Krishna, or perhaps Indra; Pan was a shepherds' god who caused "panic" and, by accident of name, was the "universal" god identified with Brahma.

232. As Chadwick says, the pyramids are Buddhist stupas; but there is some garbling, as nakedness is repudiated by Buddhists, and sounds more

The Gymnosophists[233] and the so-called Holy Men do not have wives. They regard this as unnatural and illegal. This is why they keep themselves chaste. The Holy Women also live in virginity. The indications are that they observe the heavenly bodies and prophesy future events from their signs.

8

Scripture Passages Cited by Heretics Censuring Marriage

61(1) Those who drag in a doctrine of moral indifference do violence to some few passages of Scripture, thinking that they support their own love of pleasure; in particular, the passage "Sin shall have no authority over you; for you are not subject to sin but to grace."[234] But there are other such passages, which there is no good reason to record for these purposes, as I am not equipping a pirate ship! Let me quickly cut through their attempt. (2) The admirable Apostle in person will refute their charge in the words with which he continues the previous quotation: "Well then! Shall we sin because we are no longer under Law but under grace? God forbid!"[235] With these inspired prophetic words, at a single stroke he undoes the sophistical skill at the service of pleasure.

62(1) So they have not understood,[236] it seems, that "we must all appear before Christ's tribunal, where each must receive what is due to him for his physical conduct, good or bad,"[237] that is, where a person may receive recompense for what he has done by means of his body. (2) "So that, if a person is in Christ, he is recreated"[238] in a way no longer subject to sin. "The past is gone"—we have washed away the

---

like Jains: On Buddha see *Stromateis* 1.21, and E. Benz in *Abhandlungen der Akademie der Wissenschaften und der Literatur, Geistes- und sozialwissenschaftlichen Klasse* (Mainz, 1951) no. 3.

233. The *Gymnosophists* or 'naked philosophers,' fascinated the Greeks: Aristotle fr. 35; Strabo 16.2.39; Plutarch, *Life of Alexander* 64; Lucian, *Fugitives* 7; Porphyry, *On Abstinence* 4.17 etc.

234. Rom 6.14.
235. Rom 6.15.
236. Reading συνιᾶσιν with Dindorf for συνιεῖσιν.
237. 2 Cor 5.10.
238. 2 Cor 5.17.

old life. "Look, new things have emerged"—chastity instead
of sexual looseness, self-control instead of license, righteousness instead of unrighteousness. "What have righteousness
and lawlessness in common? What fellowship is there between
light and darkness? Can Christ agree with Beliar? (3) What
have the faithful to do with the faithless? Can there be a com-
pact between the Temple of God and idols?"[239] "These are the
promises made to us. Let us purify ourselves of anything that
can stain flesh or spirit, aiming at the goal of holiness in the
fear of God."[240]

9

Heretics Quote the Words Spoken to Salome to Censure Marriage

63(1) Those who attack God's creation under the pious
name of self-control quote the words spoken to Salome, which
we have mentioned previously.[241] I fancy the passage comes
from the *Gospel according to the Egyptians*. (2) They maintain
that the Savior personally said, "I am come to destroy the
works of the female." "Female" refers to sexual desire, and its
works are birth and decay. So what are they to say? Has this
world order been undone? They could never say so. The universe remains in the same condition. (3) But the Lord did not
speak falsely. In reality he brought to nothing the works of
desire—the love of money, or winning, or glory, craziness over
women, a passion for boys, gluttony, profligacy and the like.
The birth of these means decay in the soul, if we become
"dead in sins."[242] This is what is meant by "female" lack of
self-control. (4) Birth and decay in creation are bound to take
place in accordance with the divine principle[243] until the time
of total dissolution and the restoration of the elect, an event
through which the beings which are mixed up with the material world are also assigned to their true condition.

239. 2 Cor 6.14–16; Beliar or Belial: only here in the *New Testament* as a
name of Satan, originally "the place of swallowing up," the underworld.
240. 2 Cor 7.1.
241. *Stromateis* 3.45 (see nt. 163).
242. Eph 2.5.
243. A Stoic and Platonic technical term.

64(1) It follows, as the argument reveals,[244] that it is in relation to the final consummation that Salome says, "How long will human beings go on dying?" Scripture uses the word "human being" in two senses, the visible and the spiritual,[245] one subject to salvation and one not. Sin is called the death of the soul. That is why the Lord answers with circumspection, "As long as women give birth," that is to say, as long as sexual desire is still at work. (2) "Therefore as sin entered the world through one human being, and death penetrated to all human beings through sin in that all sinned, death also held dominion from Adam to Moses," says the Apostle.[246] By natural necessity of divine dispensation, death follows birth, and the union of soul and body is followed by their dissolution.[247] (3) The object of birth is learning and knowledge, the object of dissolution is restoration. Woman is regarded as the cause of death because of giving birth, but for the same reason she is also to be regarded as the cause of life.

65(1) The woman who initiated transgression was called "Life," because she was responsible[248] for the succession of those who came to birth and sinned, mother of righteous and unrighteous alike; each one of us shows himself just or renders himself disobedient. (2) As a result, I do not think that the Apostle is disparaging life in the flesh when he says, "I shall speak out. Christ will now and always be glorified in my body, whether through my life or through my death. For to me life is Christ, and death is gain. But if life in the flesh means for me some fruitful work, I do not know what to choose. I am torn two ways. I have a desire to weigh anchor and to be with Christ; that is far better. But I feel a deeper constraint to remain in the flesh for your sake."[249] (3) In these words he showed clearly that love of God is the crowning reason for leaving the body, whereas to remain behind graciously for

244. A phrase from Plato, *Phaedrus* 277 C.
245. 2 Cor 4.16. 246. Rom 5.12,14.
247. Plato, *Phaedrus* 67 D.
248. I.e., Eve (Gen 3.20); reading διότι ... αἰτία with Schwartz for διὰ τὴν ... αἰτίαν.
249. Phil 1.20–4.

those in need of salvation is the reason for being in the flesh.

66(1) These people do anything rather than walk by the canon of the gospel in conformity with truth. Why do they omit what follows in the words spoken to Salome?[250] She said, "Then would I have done better if I never had a child?" (2) suggesting that childbearing was not a necessary obligation. The Lord replied in the words, "Eat every plant but do not eat a plant whose content is bitter." (3) By these words he is indicating that the choice of celibacy or wedlock is in our power and not a matter of the absolute constraint of a commandment. He is also clarifying the point that marriage is cooperation with the work of creation.

67(1) So no one should ever think that marriage under the rule of the Logos[251] is a sin, if he does not find it bitter to bring up children; indeed, for many people, childlessness is the most grievous experience of all. At the same time, if he does not regard the production of children as bitter because it drags him away from the things of God, for which there is necessarily no time, but does not look favorably upon life as a bachelor, then he can look forward[252] to marriage, since there is no harm in disciplined pleasure, and each of us is in a position to make a decision over the engendering of children. (2) I realize that there are some people who have used the excuse of marriage to abstain from it[253] without following the principles of sacred knowledge and have fallen into hatred of humankind so that the spirit of Christian love has vanished from them; others have become embroiled in marriage and indulged their taste for pleasure within the authority of the Law,[254] and as the prophet says, "have become like cattle."[255]

---

250. See nt. 163.
251. Or (as often) *logos*, 'reason.'
252. Reading ἐπιθυμείτω with Schwartz for ἐπιθυμεῖ.
253. Reading ἀπεσχημένοι with Sylburg for ἀπισχημένοι.
254. *Oxyrhynchus Papyrus* 215 (from an Epicurean writer).
255. Ps 49.12,20.

10

Mystical Explication of Matthew 28.20

68(1) Who are the two or three who gather in the name of Christ with the Lord in their midst?[256] By three does he not mean husband, wife, and child?[257] A wife is united with her husband by God.[258] (2) But if a man wishes to be unencumbered, and prefers to avoid producing children because of the time it takes up, then, says the Apostle, "he had better stay unmarried like me."[259] (3) Their interpretation of the Lord's meaning is this. In relation to the plurality, he is speaking of the creator, who is responsible for all coming into being;[260] in relation to the one, he is speaking of the savior of the elect, naturally the son of a different god, of course, the good god. (4) This is wrong. God through his Son is with those who responsibly marry and produce children, and it is the same God who in the same way is with the man who shows self-control in the light of the Logos.[261] (5) Another interpretation would make the three temper, desire, and reason;[262] yet another flesh, soul, and spirit.[263]

69(1) Perhaps the group of three of which we have been speaking is first an allusion to those called; secondly, to the elect; and thirdly, to the class of beings ordained to the highest honor.[264] The power of God watching over all things is with them, indivisibly divided among them. (2) So a person who makes proper use of the natural powers of the soul has a desire for appropriate objects but hates all that would injure, as the commandments prescribe. Scripture says, "You shall

256. Matt 18.20.
257. A beautiful and characteristic interpretation; see also Origen, *Commentary on Matthew* 14.2.
258. Prov 19.14.
259. 1 Cor 7.8.
260. Used in Wis 13.5 of the author of existence, but the Gnostic ascetics interpreted this as the lord of the processes of sexual union and birth.
261. Or "rationally" (nt. 251).
262. The threefold division of the soul in Plato, *Republic* 4.435 B–441 C; *Phaedrus* 254 C–E.
263. 1 Thess 5.23; Cf. Origen, *Commentary on Matthew* 14.3.
264. Angels.

bless anyone who blesses you and curse anyone who curses you."[265] (3) But when a person has risen above temper and desire, when he shows an actual love for the creation, for the sake of God the maker of all things, then he will live a life of true knowledge,[266] effortlessly embracing the state of self-control following the likeness of the Savior, bringing knowledge, faith, and love into a single unity. (4) From that point he is single in judgment and genuinely spiritual. He is totally closed to thoughts which arise from temper or desire. He is being brought to perfection according to the image of the Lord by the actual craftsman, becoming a fully mature human being,[267] at last worthy to be called brother by the Lord.[268] He is at once friend and son to him.[269] In this way the two or three are gathered into the same point, the truly Gnostic human being.

70(1) The concord of several, counting on the basis of the three with whom the Lord is found, may refer to the one Church, the one human being, the one race. (2) Or perhaps the Lord in giving the Law was with the one people, the Jewish. When he was responsible for prophecy and sent Jeremiah to Babylon,[270] and further called people from the gentiles through prophecy, he gathered together the two peoples.[271] The third is surely the one who is formed out of the two into a new human being, in whom he walks and lives[272]—the very Church. (3) The Law and the prophets are brought together with the gospel too, in the name of Christ into one true knowledge. (4) So those who out of hatred refrain from marriage or misuse their physical being indiscriminately, out of desire, are not in the number of the saved with whom the Lord is found.

---

265. Gen 12.3, 27.29; but cf. Rom 12.14.
266. As a true Gnostic.   267. Eph 4.13.
268. Heb 2.11.
269. We must omit ἐστιν with Schwartz or add καὶ with Hiller or θ' with Wilamowitz (the simplest); John 15.14; Gal 4.7.
270. A false deduction from Jer 50–51, or a confusion with Jonah, or a record of the legend in *Seder Olam Rabba* 26.27.
271. Eph 2.15.   272. 2 Cor 6.16.

11

Mandate of the Law and Christ concerning Concupiscence

71(1) That concludes that demonstration. Now I propose to establish the Scriptures which refute these heretical sophists and expound the norm of self-discipline which we keep in following the Logos.[273] (2) The person of understanding will think out the passage of Scripture that is appropriate to challenge each[274] of the heresies and use it at the apposite moment to refute those who set their dogmas against the commandments. (3) From the very beginning, as I have already said, the Law laid down the injunction "You shall not desire your neighbor's wife"[275] in anticipation[276] of the Lord's closely connected dictum in accordance with the New Covenant with the same meaning from his own lips: "You have heard the injunction of the Law 'You shall not commit adultery.' I say, 'You shall not lust.'"[277] (4) The Law wished males to have responsible sexual relations with their marriage partners, solely for the production of children. This is clear when a bachelor is prevented from enjoying immediate sexual relations with a woman prisoner-of-war. If he once falls in love with her, he must let her cut her hair short and mourn for thirty days. If even so his desire has not faded away, then he may father children by her.[278] The fixed period of time enables the overpowering impulse to be scrutinized and to turn into a rational appetency.

72(1) On the same basis, you would not be able[279] to point to anyone of the past generations approaching a pregnant woman in the pages of Scripture. Only later, after the birth and weaning of the child, would you again find the wives in physical relations with their husbands. (2) You will find that Moses' father observed this point. He left a three-year gap

---

273. Or "reason" (nt. 251).
274. Reading ἑκάστῃ with Stählin for ἑκάστη.
275. Exod 20.17.
276. Reading προ- with Sylburg for προσ-.
277. Matt 5.27–8.   278. Deut 21.11–13.
279. Adding ἄν with Stählin.

after Aaron's birth before fathering Moses.[280] (3) Again, the tribe of Levi observed this natural law from God although they were fewer in number than the others when they entered the promised land. (4) It is not easy for a tribe to grow to large numbers if the males only father children within the bounds of legal wedlock, and wait beyond pregnancy through breast-feeding to do so.

73(1) So it was reasonable for Moses to move the Jews gradually towards self-discipline when he ordered them to abstain from sexual pleasure for three successive days before hearing the words of God.[281] (2) "So we are temples of God, as the prophet said, 'because I will live and move among them and I shall be their God, and they shall be my people' "—if we follow the commandments in our way of living, individually and corporately, as the Church. (3) " 'So come out from among them and put a barrier between you,' says the Lord. 'Do not touch impurity. I shall receive you. I shall be a father to you. You will be sons and daughters to me,' says the almighty Lord."[282] (4) He is prophetic in telling us to put up a barrier to separate us not from the married, as they assert, but from the gentiles who are still living immorally, and also from the heresies of which we have been speaking, which believe in neither chastity nor God.

74(1) That is why Paul too speaks strongly against a similar group to those mentioned in the words, "Beloved, you possess these promises. Let us purify our hearts from everything which might stain flesh or spirit, aiming at the goal of holiness in the fear of God."[283] "My zeal for you is God's zeal. I betrothed you to Christ, with a view to presenting a chaste virgin to her one and only husband."[284] (2) The Church has obtained her bridegroom; she cannot marry another. But each of us has the right to marry, within the law, the woman of our choice. I am speaking of first marriage. (3) "But as the serpent in his wicked cunning deceived Eve, I am afraid that your thoughts may be corrupted so that you lose your singlehearted

280. Exod 7.7.
281. Exod 19.15.
282. 2 Cor 6.16–18.
283. 2 Cor 7.1.
284. 2 Cor 11.2.

devotion to Christ."[285] The Apostle's words are very cautious and instructive.

75(1) So that admirable man Peter says, "Beloved, I urge you, as temporary residents in an alien land, to abstain from physical desires. They are marshalled against your soul. See that your behavior is such that the pagans can look up to you. (2) This is God's will. You are to muzzle the activity of those without understanding by the quality of your actions. Live as free people, not as though your freedom were a cover-up for vice, but as slaves in God's service."[286] (3) Similarly, in his *Epistle to the Romans*, Paul writes [of the Scripture text]: "We are dead to sin: how can we continue to live in it? Our old humanity was crucified with him, so as to destroy the very body of sin" down to "Do not present the parts of your body to sin to be instruments of vice."[287]

76(1) At this point, I think that I ought not to leave on one side without comment[288] the fact that the Apostle preaches the same God whether through the Law, the prophets, or the gospel. For in his letter to the Romans he attributes to the Law the words "You shall not lust" which in fact appear in the text of the gospel.[289] He does so in the knowledge that it is one single person who makes his decrees through the Law and the prophets, and is the subject of the gospel's proclamation. (2) He says, "What shall we say? Is the Law sin? Of course not. But I did not know sin except through the Law. I did not know lust, except that the Law said, 'You shall not lust.'"[290] (3) If the heretics who assail the creator suppose that Paul was speaking against him in the words that follow: "I know that nothing good lodges in me, in my flesh, that is to say," they had better read the words which precede and come after these. (4) He has just said, "Sin lodges in me," which

---

285. 2 Cor 11.3; Clement does not, with some authorities, have the words "priority and."

286. 1 Pet 2.11–12, 15–16.

287. Rom 6.2–13.

288. ἀνεπισημείωτον does not appear in classical Greek.

289. Matt 5.27; Rom 7.7.　　　290. Rom 7.7.

makes it appropriate to go on to, "Nothing good lodges in my flesh."[291]

77(1) On top of this[292] he continues, "If I act contrary to my will, the effect is not mine but the effect of sin lodging in me," which, he says, "is at war with" God's "Law and my own reason and takes me prisoner under the Law of sin which is in my very bones. What a wretched man I am. Who will rescue me from this body which is doomed to death?"[293] (2) Once again, since he never remotely gets tired of doing good, he does not hesitate to add, "The Law of the Spirit has freed me from the Law of sin and death," since through his Son "God has pronounced judgment upon sin in the flesh so that the Law's ordinance might find fulfillment in us, whose lives are governed by the Spirit not by the flesh."[294] (3) In addition to all this, he makes what he has already said even clearer by asserting at the top of his voice, "The body is a dead thing because of sin,"[295] showing that if it is not the soul's temple it remains the soul's tomb.[296] When it is consecrated to God, he is going to continue, "the Spirit of the one who raised Jesus from the dead lodges in you, and he will give life even to your mortal bodies through his indwelling Spirit."[297]

78(1) So again he attacks the hedonists and adds, "The object of the flesh is death, since those whose lives are governed by the flesh follow the flesh in their objectives; and the object of the flesh is hostility to God, for it is not subject to God's Law. Those who live on the level of flesh cannot please God" should not be understood as some people lay down, but as I have already argued. (2) Then in distinction from these people, he addresses the Church. "You are not living by the flesh but by the Spirit, if the Spirit of God is dwelling in you. Anyone without Christ's Spirit is not of him. But if Christ is in you, then your body is a dead thing because of sin, but the

---

291. Rom 7.17–18.
293. Rom 7.20, 23–4.
295. Rom 8.10.
296. 1 Cor 3.16; Plato, *Cratylus* 400 B–C.
297. Rom 8–11.

292. Adding οἷς with Schwartz.
294. Rom 8.2–4.

Spirit is life through righteousness. (3) So, brothers, we are in debt. Not to the flesh, to follow it in our lives; for if you follow the flesh in the way you live, you are on the way to death. But if by the Spirit you put to death the practices of the body, you will live. For all who are guided by God's Spirit are sons of God." (4) He goes on to speak against the high birth and freedom which the heretics adduce so abominably as they vaunt their licentiousness. "You have not received a spirit of slavery to drive you once again towards fear. You have received a Spirit that makes us sons and enables us to cry out, 'Abba,' 'Father.'"[298] (5) That is to say, we have received the Spirit to enable us to know the one to whom we pray, our real Father, the one and only Father of all that is, the one who like a Father educates us for salvation and does away with fear.[299]

12

An Explication of Some Scripture Passages on Marriage

79(1) It is a lesson in self-discipline if physical union "is given a rest by agreement to allow time for prayer."[300] He appends the words "by agreement" to prevent a dissolution of the marriage and "time for" to prevent the husband who is forced to practice celibacy from slipping into sin, falling in love elsewhere while refraining from his own wife. (2) By the same argument he said that the man who supposes that he is acting wrongly in bringing up his daughter as a virgin will properly give her away in marriage.[301] (3) One man may make himself celibate; another may join in marriage in order to have children. Both ought to have the end in view of remaining firmly opposed to any lower standard. (4) If a person is going to be capable of keeping his life strict he is going to achieve greater worth for himself in God's eyes since his self-control combines chastity and rationality. If he goes beyond the rule

---

298. Rom 8.5–15.
299. The MS ἀπειγεῖ gives no sense; whatever the reading this is the general sense.
300. 1 Cor 7.5.
301. 1 Cor 7.36.

to which he has committed himself with a view to greater renown, then he is liable to fall short in relation to his hopes.[302] (5) Celibacy and marriage have their distinctive services of the Lord, their different ministries. I am referring to the care of wife and children. The peculiar quality of the married state is the opportunity it gives for the man who seeks fulfillment through marriage to accept the overseeing of everything in the common home. (6) The Apostle says bishops should be appointed from those who have learned by practice in their own home the charge of the whole Church.[303] (7) So each person should fulfill his service by the work in which he was called, so that he may be free in Christ and receive the appropriate reward for that service.[304]

80(1) Yet again in speaking about the Law he makes use of an analogy. "The married woman," he says, "is tied to her husband by law during his lifetime," and so on.[305] And again, "The wife is under the marriage bond as long as her husband is alive. If he dies she is free to marry, provided it is in the Lord. But in my view her greatest blessing is to remain as she is."[306] (2) Now, in the former passage he says, "You have died to the Law"—not to marriage!—"with a view to becoming another's, one who belongs to him was raised from the dead," at once Bride and Church. The Bride and Church must be pure alike from inward thoughts contrary to truth and from outward tempters, that is, the adherents of heretical sects who try to persuade her to sexual unfaithfulness to her one and only husband almighty God. We must not be led, "as the snake seduced Eve,"[307] whose name means "Life,"[308] to transgress the commandments under the influence of the wicked lewdness of the factions. (3) The second passage established monogamy. We are not to suppose, in agreement with some people's exegesis,[309] that the bond tying the wife to the husband means the involvement of the flesh with decay. He is

302. Something has dropped out of the text: the general sense is clear.
303. 1 Tim 3.4–5.   304. Echoes of 1 Cor 7.22–4.
305. Rom 7.2.   306. 1 Cor 7.39–40.
307. 2 Cor 11.3.   308. Gen 3.20.
309. Probably Tatian (Epiphanius, *Panarion* 46.2–3) (see nt. 311).

assailing the view of those atheists who attribute the invention of marriage directly to the devil. This is a view[310] which comes dangerously near to a slander against the lawgiver.

81(1) The Syrian Tatian, as I see it, had the effrontery to make this sort of thing his creed.[311] Anyway, he writes in his work *On Training Following the Savior*,[312] and I quote, "Agreement[313] conduces to prayer. The common experience of corruption means an end to intercourse. At any rate, his acceptance of it is so grudging that he is really saying No to it altogether. (2) He agreed to their coming together again because of Satan and because of weakness of will, but he showed that anyone who is inclined to succumb is going to be serving two masters,[314] God when there is agreement, and weakness of will, sexual immorality, and the devil when there is not." (3) He says this in his exegesis of the Apostle. He is playing intellectual tricks with the truth in seeking to establish a false conclusion on the basis of truth. (4) We too agree that weakness of will and sexual immorality are passions inspired by the devil, but the harmony of responsible marriage occupies a middle position. When there is self-control it leads to prayer; when there is reverent bridal union, to childbearing. (5) At any rate, there is a proper time for the breeding of children, and Scripture calls it knowledge,[315] in the words, "Adam knew his wife Eve, and she conceived and bore a son, and called him by the name of Seth, 'for God has raised up for me another child in Abel's place.'"[316] (6) You see who is the target of the slanders of those who show their disgust at responsible

310. Reading καθ' ἥν with Heyse for καί.

311. Tatian was a well educated Assyrian who converted to Christianity some time after A.D. 150: author of a defense of Christianity, and of a harmony of the Gospels (*Diatessaron*), something of a freethinker and Gnostic, he may have been founder of the ascetic Encratites; the orthodox rejected him, but his memory was alive in Syria.

312. The title echoes Luke 6.40; Eph 4.12.

313. Reading συμφωνία with Maranus for συμφωνίαν.

314. Matt 6.24.

315. There is almost a triple meaning: knowledge, revealed knowledge (*gnosis*), and sexual intimacy. In *Stromateis* 3.94 (3) Clement suggests that Adam's sin lay in seeking physical union before the right time.

316. Gen 4.25.

marriage and attribute the processes of birth to the devil?
Scripture does not merely refer to "a god." By application of
the definite article it indicates the almighty ruler of the universe.

82(1) The Apostle's added reference to their "coming together again because of Satan" is designed to anticipate and
cut at the roots of any possibility of turning aside to other love
affairs.[317] The temporary agreement serves to negate natural
desires but does not cut them out root and branch. These[318]
are why he reintroduces the marriage bond, not for uncontrolled behavior or sexual immorality or the operations of the
devil, but to prevent him from falling under their sway. (2)
Tatian makes a distinction between the old humanity and the
new,[319] but it is not ours. We agree with him in that we too
say that the old humanity is the Law, the new is the gospel.
But we do not agree with his desire to abolish the Law as being
the work of a different god. (3) It is the same man, the same
Lord who makes old things new.[320] He no longer approves of
polygamy (at that time God[321] required it because of the need
for increased numbers). He introduces monogamy for the
production of children and the need to look after the home.
Woman was offered as a "partner" in this.[322] (4) And if a man
cannot control himself and is burning with passion so that the
Apostle "out of sympathy" offers him a second marriage,[323]
then[324] he is not committing sin according to the Covenant,
since it is not forbidden by the Law, but neither is he fulfilling
the highest pitch of the gospel ethic. (5) He is acquiring
heavenly glory for himself, if he remains single and keeps
immaculate the union which has been broken by death and
cheerfully obeys what God has in store for him, becoming
"undistracted" from the Lord's service.[325] (6) In the past, a

317. Adding το with Münzel.
318. Reading ἃς with Stählin for ἦν.
319. Rom 7.2.
320. 2 Cor 5.17; Rev 21.5.
321. It is tempting to alter the text with Münzel to read καιρός, 'the moment.'
322. Gen 2.18.   323. 1 Cor 7.9,36.
324. Omitting ἐπεὶ with Heyse.   325. 1 Cor 7.35.

man coming from marital intercourse was required to wash.[326]
It cannot be too strongly said that the Providence of God
revealed through the Lord no longer makes this demand. The
Lord eliminates washing after intercourse as unnecessary since
he has cleansed believers by one single baptism for every such
encounter, just as[327] he takes in the many washings prescribed
by Moses by one single baptism.

83(1) In the past, the Law prescribed washing after the
generative deposit[328] of seed in prophecy of our regeneration
through the analogy of physical birth. It did not do so from
distaste for the birth of a human being. The deposit of the
seed makes possible the thing which emerges as a human
being. (2) It is not frequent acts of intercourse which promise
birth; it is the acceptance of the seed by the womb. In nature's
studio the seed is molded into an embryo. (3) How can marriage in the past be a mere invention of the Law, and marriage
as ordained by our Lord be different, when it is the same God
whom we worship? (4) "Man must not pull apart that which
God has joined together."[329] That is reasonable. Far more so
that that Son will preserve the things which the Father has
ordained. If the Law and gospel come from the same being,
the Son cannot fight against himself. The Law is alive because
it is spiritual,[330] if we interpret it in the light of true knowledge. (5) But we "have died to the Law through Christ's body
with a view to belonging to another, the one who was raised
from the dead," the one who was prophesied by the Law, "so
that we may bear fruit for God."[331]

84(1) So "the Law is holy; the commandment is holy, righteous and good."[332] We died to the Law, that is to say, to the
sin exposed by the Law, which the Law does not engender but
reveals. It enjoins what we ought to do and bans what[333] we
ought not to do. It shows up the sin that is hidden, "so that

326. Lev 15.18.
327. Reading ὁ with Heyse for εἰ.
328. Adding καταβολῇ with Hiller.
329. Matt 19.6.   330. Rom 7.14.
331. Rom 7.4.   332. Rom 7.12.
333. Reading ὧν with Stählin for τῶν.

sin may be seen for what it is."[334] (2) But if legally constituted marriage is sin, I do not know how anyone can claim to know God while saying that God's commandment is sin. If the Law is holy, marriage is holy. Accordingly, the Apostle points this mystery in the direction of Christ and the Church.[335] (3) Just as "that which is born of the flesh is flesh, so that which is born of the Spirit is Spirit,"[336] not just in the process of birth but in its education. So "the children are holy,"[337] objects of delight, when the Lord's words have brought the soul to God as a bride. (4) Anyway, there is a distinction between fornication and marriage, as great as separates the devil from God. "So you too have died to the Law through Christ's body with a view to belonging to another, the one who was raised from the dead."[338] It is implied that you have become attentive[339] in your obedience, since it is actually congruent with the truth of the Law that we are servants of the same Lord who gives us his instructions at a distance.

85(1) No question but that it is reasonable for the Spirit to say explicitly of people like that "that in the last days people will abandon the faith and attach themselves to deceitful spirits and the teachings of demonic powers, under the influence of hypocritical liars who are corrupt in conscience and try to put an end to marriage. They teach abstinence from foods which God created to be gratefully enjoyed by believers who have acquired an inward knowledge of the truth. Everything created by God is good. None is to be rejected provided it is taken in a spirit of gratitude. It is sanctified by God's Word and by prayer."[340] (2) It follows of necessity that there is no ban on marriage, or eating meat, or drinking wine, for it is written, "It is good to refrain from eating meat and drinking wine," if a person might give offense by eating, and, "It is good to stay as I am."[341] But both the person who takes his food gratefully, and the one who equally gratefully abstains

334. Rom 7.14.
335. Eph 5.32.
336. John 3.6.
337. 1 Cor 7.14.
338. Rom 7.4.
339. Reading προσεχῶς with Heinsing for προσεχεῖς.
340. 1 Tim 4.1–5.
341. Rom 14.21; 1 Cor 7.8.

with an enjoyment marked by self-discipline must follow the Logos[342] in their lives.

86(1) In general, all the Apostle's letters teach responsible self-control. They embrace thousands of instructions about marriage, the production of children, and domestic life. Nowhere do they blackball marriage, provided that it is responsible. They preserve the connection between the Law and the gospel. They welcome the man who embarks responsibly on marriage with gratitude to God, and the man who takes celibacy as his life companion in accordance with the Lord's will, each, as he has been called, making his choice[343] in maturity and firmness. (2) "Jacob's land was praised above any other land," says the prophet, glorifying the instrument of the Spirit.[344] (3) But there is a man who runs down birth,[345] describing it as subject to decay and death, who forces things,[346] and suggests that the Savior was speaking about having children in saying that we should not store treasure on earth, where it grows rusty and moth-eaten, and who is not ashamed to set alongside these the prophet's words: "You shall all grow old like clothes, and the moth will feed on you."[347] (4) We do not contradict Scripture. Our bodies are subject to decay and are naturally unstable.[348] Perhaps he might be prophesying[349] decay to his audience because they were sinners. The Savior was not speaking about having children. He was encouraging sharing of resources in those who wanted only to amass vast amounts of wealth rather than offer help to those in need.

87(1) That is why he says, "Do not work for perishable food, but for the food which lasts into eternal life."[350] Similarly, they

---

342. Or "reason."

343. Reading ἑλόμενον with Schwartz for ἑλόμενος.

344. Quoted from the *Epistle of Barnabas* 11.9, but the source of the prophecy is unknown. Barnabas has αὐτοῦ, but the MS αὐτὸς may be a misquotation.

345. Reading τῆς with Mayor for τις; the man is not known for certain.

346. He does violence to birth, and to Scripture, and to the Kingdom (see Matt 11.12).

347. Isa 50.9, omitting the first ὡς with Victorius.

348. With allusion to the school of Heraclitus which held that everything is in a state of flux.

349. Reading προφητεύοι with Hiller for προφητεύει.

350. John 6.27.

cite the dictum "The children of this age do not marry and
are not given in marriage."[351] (2) But if anyone ponders over
this answer about the resurrection of the dead, he will find
that the Lord is not rejecting marriage, but is purging the
expectation of physical desire in the resurrection. (3) The
words "The children of this age" were not spoken in contrast
with the children of some other age. It is like saying, "Those
born in this generation," who are children by force of birth,
being born and engendering themselves, since without the
process of birth no one will pass into this life. But this process
of birth is balanced by a process of decay, and is no longer in
store for the person who has once been cut off from life here.
(4) "You have one single Father in heaven"—and he is also,
as creator, Father of all. "Do not call anyone on earth Father,"
he says.[352] That is like saying that you are not to think of the
man who sowed you by a physical process as responsible for
your existence, but as a fellow worker, or rather a subordinate,
in bringing you to birth.

88(1) In this way he wants us to turn back and become like
children again,[353] children who have come to know their real
Father, come to a new birth by means of water, a method of
birth quite different from that[354] in the material creation. (2)
"Yes," he says, "the man who is unmarried cares for the Lord's
business, the man who is married cares how to give his wife
pleasure."[355] Well? Is it impossible to give pleasure to one's
wife in ways acceptable to God and at the same time to show
gratitude to God? Is it impermissible for the married man to
have a partnership with his wife[356] in looking after the Lord's
business? (3) But just as "the unmarried woman is looking
after the Lord's business in seeking to be holy in body and
spirit,"[357] so the married woman cares in the Lord for her
husband's business and the Lord's business in seeking to be

---

351. Luke 20.35.   352. Matt 23.9.
353. Matt 18.3.
354. Adding ἢ τῆς with Schwartz.
355. 1 Cor 7.32–3.
356. Reading συζύγῳ with Stählin for συζυγία.
357. 1 Cor 7.34.

holy in body and spirit. Both are holy in the Lord, one as a wife, the other as a virgin. (4) But the Apostle fittingly pronounces humiliating opposition at full pitch to those who incline to second marriage. He is quick to say, "Every other sin is outside the body. Sexual promiscuity is a sin against one's own body."[358]

89(1) If anyone goes so far as to call marriage fornication, he is once more reverting to blasphemous slander upon the Law and the Lord. Avarice is called fornication because it is the opposite of self-sufficiency. Idolatry[359] is called fornication because it is a spreading out from one God to many gods. In the same way, fornication takes place when a person falls away from a single marriage to a plurality. As we have remarked, the Apostle employs the words fornication and adultery in three senses. (2) It is in relation to these matters that the prophet says, "It was through your own sins that you were sold," and again, "You experienced defilement in an alien land."[360] He[361] is applying the idea of defilement to a partnership involving an alien body rather than the body given away in marriage for the purpose of producing children. (3) This is why the Apostle says, "So it is my wish that younger women should marry, have children, and be mistresses of their homes, without giving any opponent an opportunity to criticize. There are some already who have taken the wrong course and followed Satan."[362]

90(1) In fact, he expresses approval of the man who is husband of a single wife, whether elder, deacon, or layman, if he gives no ground for criticism in his conduct of his marriage.[363] He "will find salvation in bringing children into the world."[364] (2) Once again the Savior calls the Jews "a wicked and adulterous generation."[365] He is teaching that they do not know the Law in the way the Law requires. By following the tradition of other generations and the commandments of human

---

358. 1 Cor 6.18.
359. Adding ἤ with Stählin.
360. Isa 50.1; Bar 3.10.
361. Omitting τε with Stählin.
362. 1 Tim 5.14–15.
363. Titus 1.6; 1 Tim 3.2,12.
364. 1 Tim 2.15 where the subject is female.
365. Matt 12.39.

beings[366] they were committing adultery against the Law, denying that it was given as lord and master of their virginity.[367] (3) Perhaps he also knew that they were slaves to strange desires, which led them into unswerving slavery to sins so that they were sold to foreigners. Among the Jews there were no publicly appointed prostitutes; adultery was in fact forbidden.[368] (4) The man who said, "I have married a wife and cannot come"[369] to the dinner offered by God was an example to expose those who were apostates to God's command for pleasures' sake; for on this argument neither those who were righteous before the coming of Christ nor those who have married after his coming will be saved, even if they are apostles. (5) If they again adduce the well-known words of the prophet, "I have grown old amongst all my enemies,"[370] by "enemies" they ought to understand "sins." There is one sin, and it is not marriage but fornication, or they would make a sin out of birth and birth's creator.

13

Response to the Arguments of the Heretic Julius Cassian

91(1) In such ways Julius Cassian, the founder of docetism, argues his case.[371] Anyway, in his book *On Self-Control* or *On Celibacy* he says, and I quote, "No one should say that because we have the parts of the body that we do, with the female shaped one way and the male another, one for receiving, the other for inseminating, sexual intercourse has God's approval.[372] (2) For if this disposition was from the God towards whom we are eagerly pressing, he would not have blessed

366. Matt 15.2,9.
367. Jer 3.4 (LXX), adding δεχομένους with Mayor.
368. Exod 20.14; Deut 5.18.
369. Luke 14.20.
370. Ps 6.8 (LXX) reading ἐπαλαιώθην with the text for ἐπαλαιώθη.
371. Not known outside Clement and statements from Jerome dependent on him (see *Stromateis* 1.101); Docetism, of which he was certainly not the founder, but was presumably a leading exponent, was the doctrine that the humanity and sufferings of Christ were seeming rather than real.
372. The MS reading mixes two constructions, but Julius (or Clement) may have done this.

eunuchs,[373] and the prophet would not have said that they are 'not an unfruitful tree,'[374] taking an analogy from the tree for the man who by deliberate choice emasculates himself from ideas of this sort."

92(1) In an effort to defend his godless opinion he adds, "How would it be unreasonable to bring a charge against the Savior if he malformed us and then freed us from his mistake and from partnership with our genitals, appendages and private parts?" In this view he is close to Tatian. But he left Valentinus' school. (2) That is why Cassian says, "When Salome asked when she would know the answer to her question the Lord replied, 'When you trample underfoot the integument of shame, and when the two become one and the male is one with the female, and there is no more male and female.'"[375]

93(1) First then, we do not find this saying in our four traditional Gospels, but in the *Gospel according to the Egyptians*.[376] Next, he does not seem to me to recognize that allusively the male impulse is temper, the female, desire.[377] When these are at work, repentance and shame follow. (2) So when a person refuses to indulge temper or desire, which in fact grow from bad character and bad nurture till they overshadow and conceal rational thought, when he strips off the darkness these produce, when he repents and out of repentance feels shame, when he integrates[378] soul and spirit in obedience to the Word, then, as Paul joins in affirming, "there is no male or female among you."[379] (3) The soul stands aside from the mere appearance of shape whereby male is distinguished from female, and is transformed into unity, being neither male nor female.

373. Matt 19.12.
374. Isa 56.3.
375. Clement of Rome, *Second Epistle to the Corinthians* 12.2 which includes the words "and the outside inside."
376. One of the apocryphal Gospels, a secondary work with Gnostic tendencies, criticized by Origen (see nt. 163).
377. The two inferior parts of the soul in Plato (see *Republic* 6.492 A, 495 A; *Phaedrus* 254 C–E), to be governed by reason.
378. Reading ἐνώσῃ with Stählin for ἐνώσει.
379. Gal 3.28.

But our brilliant friend must take a more Platonic view and imagine that the soul is divine in origin and has come to our world of birth and decay after being made effeminate by desire.[380]

14

Explication of Scripture Passages Relevant to Cassian's Arguments

94(1) Then he does violence to Paul, in suggesting that he says that birth was constituted out of deceit. He is interpreting the words "My fear is that, just as the snake deceived Eve, your thoughts may be corrupted and diverted from a simple commitment to Christ."[381] (2) Besides, the Lord by general agreement came for the wanderers,[382] but they had not wandered from above to be born on earth (for birth, itself a creator, is a creation of the almighty, who would never drive the soul down from a better home to a worse). (3) But the savior came for those who were wandering in thought, for us. Our thoughts were corrupted by our love of pleasure and our neglect of the commandments. Perhaps too the first-formed human anticipated the appropriate moment, coveted the grace of marriage before time, and so committed sin, since "everyone who looks at a woman with an eye to lust has already committed adultery with her"[383] in not waiting for the right moment of rational will.

95(1) It was the same Lord who at that time also gave judgment on the desire which anticipates marriage. So when the Apostle says, "Put on the new humanity created after God's way,"[384] he is addressing us; we were shaped as we are by the Almighty's will. When he speaks of "old" and "new,"[385] he is not referring to birth and rebirth, but to disobedient and obedient ways of living. (2) Cassian thinks the "tunics of skins"[386]

---

380. Plato, *Phaedo* 81 C; *Phaedrus* 248 C.
381. 2 Cor 11.3.   382. Matt 18.11.
383. Matt 5.28.   384. Eph 4.24.
385. Adding καὶ καινὸν with Hiller.
386. Gen 3.21, a common interpretation. See Philo, *Allegorical Interpreta-*

are our bodies. We shall demonstrate later that he and those who argue like him are wrong in this, when we put our hands to the exposition of the genesis of humankind after the essential prolegomena. He goes on to say, "Those who are ruled by earthly values are born and engender. Our citizenship is in heaven and we welcome our Savior from there."[387] (3) We know this is well said, since we have a duty to behave as "temporarily resident aliens";[388] if we were married, as if we were single; if we have possessions, as if dispossessed; if we produce children, doing so in the knowledge that they will die; ready to give up our property, live without a wife if need be; dispassionate in our approach to the created world, with a mind above these things and a deep gratitude.

15

Explication of Scripture Passages on Marriage and Celibacy

96(1) Again, when Paul says, "It is good for a man not to have contact with a woman, but to avoid immorality let each have his own wife," he offers a kind of exegesis by saying further, "to prevent Satan from tempting you." (2) In the words "by using your lack of self-control"[389] he is addressing not those who practice marriage through self-control solely for the production of children, but those with a passionate desire to go beyond the production of children. He does not want the Adversary to create a hurricane[390] so that the waves drive their yearnings to alien pleasure. (3) It may be that[391] Satan is jealous of those whose lives are morally upright, opposes them, and wants to master them. That is why he wishes to subject them to his command and aims to provide a jumping-off point by making self-control laborious.

97(1) So it is reasonable of Paul to say, "It is better to marry

---

tion 3.69; *On the Posterity and Exile of Cain* 137; Origen, *Against Celsus* 4.40; Porphyry, *On Abstinence* 1.31.
387. Matt 20.25, 24.38; Luke 17.27; John 18.36; Phil 3.20.
388. Heb 11.13.
389. 1 Cor 7.1–2,5.
390. Reading ἐπιπνεύσας with Bywater for ἐπινεύσας.
391. Reading ἐπεὶ with Hervet for ἐπὶ.

than to burn with passion."[392] He wants the husband to pay due attention to his wife and *vice versa*. He does not want them to deprive one another of the help offered towards childbirth through divine dispensation.[393] (2) They quote the words "Anyone who does not hate father or mother, wife or children, cannot be my disciple."[394] (3) This is not an exhortation to hate your family, since Scripture says, "Honor your father and mother, for it to be well with you."[395] What he is saying is, "Do not be led astray by irrational impulses, and do not get involved in ordinary worldly practices." A family constitutes a household, and secular communities are made up of households.[396] Paul says of those who find marriage a full-time occupation that they are "concerned to satisfy the world."[397] (4) Again the Lord says, "Anyone married should not seek divorce; anyone unmarried should not seek marriage"[398]—in other words, if a man has taken a public commitment to celibacy he should remain unmarried.

98(1) Anyway, the same Lord gives corresponding promises to both through the prophet Isaiah in saying, "The eunuch should not say, 'I am a barren tree.' This is what the Lord says to eunuchs: If you keep my sabbath and fulfill all my ordinances, I will give you a place which is preferable to sons and daughters."[399] (2) To be a eunuch does not of itself make a person righteous, still less the eunuch's keeping of the sabbath, unless he performs the commandments. (3) To the married he adds these words: "My elect shall not labor in vain or produce children to be under a curse, since their seed is blessed by the Lord."[400] (4) If a man produces children in

392. 1 Cor 7.9.
393. Adding οἰκονομίας with Sylburg.
394. Luke 14.26.
395. Exod 20.12.
396. Aristotle, *Politics* 1.1252 A–B; the Greek words that I have rendered 'ordinary,' 'worldly,' and 'secular communities' have to do with *polis*, the 'city-state,' which is the basis of politics.
397. 1 Cor 7.33.
398. Not in our Bible (see Resch, *Agrapha* 429) perhaps from the *Gospel according to the Egyptians* (see nt. 163, reflected in 1 Cor 7.27).
399. Isa 56.3–5.   400. Isa 65.23.

obedience to the Logos,[401] nurtures them, and educates them
in the Lord, as with the man who fathers children following
instruction in the truth, there is a reward in store for him, as
for the elect seed too. (5) Some people accept the view that
the production of children is a curse; they do not understand[402] that it is against these very people that Scripture is
speaking. The Lord's true elect do not dogmatize or produce
children to be under a curse; they leave that to the heretical
sects.

99(1) So "eunuch" does not mean the man who has been
physically emasculated, still less the unmarried man, but the
man who is sterile in relation to truth. Previously he was "a
barren tree."[403] Once he has obeyed the Word and observed
the sabbaths, put his sins to one side and fulfilled the commandments, he will be in greater honor than those whose
education is theoretical and lack a proper way of living. (2)
"Little children," says the Teacher, "I am with you only a little
longer."[404] That is why Paul says in his letter to Galatians, "My
little children, I am going through the pains of childbirth with
you a second time until Christ is formed in you."[405] (3) Yet
again in writing to the Corinthians he says, "You may have
thousands of tutors in Christ but only one father. I am your
father in Christ through the gospel."[406] (4) This is why "no
eunuch shall enter God's assembly,"[407] being unproductive
and unfruitful in behavior and speech. But "those who have
made themselves eunuchs"—free from every sin—"for the
kingdom of heaven's sake,"[408] in fasting from worldliness,[409]
find blessing.

---

401. Or "reason."
402. Reading συνιᾶσι with Stählin for συνιεῖσι.
403. Isa 56.3.   404. John 13.33.
405. Gal 4.19.   406. 1 Cor 4.15.
407. Deut 23.1.   408. Matt 19.12.
   409. An allusion to words attributed to Jesus (*Oxyrhynchus Papyrus* 1.3)
about those who fast to the world.

16

*Explication of Scripture Passages Claiming Birth as an Evil
or a Good*

100(1) "Accursed be the day on which I was born—may it
never be blessed," says Jeremiah.[410] He is not simply saying
that birth is an accursed thing; he has withdrawn in impa-
tience at the sinful disobedience of the people. (2) Anyway he
goes on, "Why was I born to see trouble and toil? Why have
my days come to fulfillment in shame?"[411] All those who
preached the truth were in danger of persecution through the
disobedience of their audience. (3) "Why did my mother's
womb not become my tomb, to prevent me from seeing Jacob's
trials and the troubles of the house of Israel?" says the prophet
Esdras.[412] (4) "No one is pure from stain," says Job, "not even
if his life is only of one day's duration."[413] (5) It is for them
to tell us how the newly born child could commit fornication
or in what way the child who has never done anything at all
has fallen under Adam's curse. (6) The only thing left for
them to say and still be consistent, I suppose, is that birth is
evil not just for the body but for the soul for which the body
exists. (7) When David says, "I was brought into being in sin;
my mother conceived me in disobedience to the Law,"[414] he is
speaking prophetically of Eve as his mother: "Eve became the
mother of all who live."[415] If he was brought into being in sin,
it does not follow that he himself is in sin, still less that he
himself is sin.

101(1) Is everyone who turns from sin to faith, turning
from sinful practices, as if from his mother, to life? I shall call
in evidence one of the twelve prophets who says, "Am I to
make an offering of my firstborn son for impiety, the fruit of
my womb for the sin of my soul?"[416] (2) This is no attack on

---

410. Jer 20.14.   411. Jer 20.18.
412. 2 Esd 5.35.
413. Job 14.4–5; the quotation appears in a closely similar form in Clement of Rome, *First Epistle to the Corinthians* 17.4.
414. Ps 51.5.   415. Gen 3.20.
416. Mic 6.7.

the words "Increase in numbers."[417] He is calling the first
impulses after birth, which do not help us to knowledge of
God, "impiety." (3) If anyone uses this as a basis for saying
that that birth is evil, he should also use it as a basis for saying
that it is good, in that in it[418] we come to know the truth.
"Come back to a sober and upright life and stop sinning.
There are some who know nothing of God"—plainly the sinners.[419] "Since we are not wrestling against flesh and blood,
but against spiritual beings, potent in temptation,[420] the rulers
of this dark world," there is forbearance. (4) This is why Paul
says, "I bruise my own body and treat it as a slave" because
"every athlete goes into total training" (instead of "total training" we understand not that he abstains from absolutely everything but that he shows self-control in those things he has
taken a deliberate decision to use). "They do it to win a crown
which dies, we for one which never dies,"[421] if we win the
contest. No effort, no crown! (5) Today there are some people
who place the widow above the virgin in self-control, on the
grounds that she has shown a high-minded rejection[422] of a
pleasure she has enjoyed.

17

Asserting That Birth Is an Evil Is a Condemnation of Creation and the Gospels

102(1) If birth is an evil, then the blasphemers must place
the Lord who went through birth and the virgin who gave
him birth in the category of evil. (2) Abominable people! In
attacking birth they are maligning the will of God and the
mystery of creation. (3) This is the basis of Cassian's docetism,

417. Gen 1.28.
418. Reading αὐτῇ with Stählin for αὐτῷ.
419. 1 Cor 15.34 reading ἐκνήψατε with Paul for ἐκνίψατε.
420. Eph 6.12.
421. 1 Cor 9.25–7.
422. On καταμεγαλοφρονεῖν see nt. 224. It is a kind of negative Aristo-
telianism: Chadwick notes the same thought in Tertullian, *To His Wife* 1.8,
and the opposite view in Augustine, *Holy Virginity* 46; reading προτιμῶσι with
Heyse for προτείνουσι.

Marcion's too, yes, and Valentinus' "semi-spiritual body."[423] It leads them to say, "Humanity became like cattle in coming to sexual intercourse." But it is when a man, swollen with lust, really and truly wants to go to bed with a woman not his own, that that sort of man actually becomes a wild beast. "They turned into stallions crazed for mares, each was whinnying for his neighbor's wife."[424] (4) And if it is really argued that the snake took the practice of sexual union[425] from the irrational animals, and prevailed on Adam to come to an agreement on sexual intercourse with Eve, and that the first created humans did not naturally practice this, this is another attack on creation for having made human beings weaker than the irrational beasts by nature, so that the people first created by God had to follow their example!

103(1) But if it was nature that guided them, like the animals without reason, to the production of children, and they were sexually aroused before they should have been, while they were still new and young because they were deceived and led astray, then God's judgment upon those who did not wait for his will was a just judgment. At the same time, birth is holy. It was through birth[426] that the universe was constituted; so too the substances, the creatures, the angels, the powers, the souls, the commandment, the Law, the gospel, the revealed knowledge of God. (2) And "all flesh is grass and all human glory is like the flower of grass. The grass dries up. The flower droops. But the Lord's word remains firm"[427] and anoints the soul and makes it one with the Spirit. (3) Without the body, how could[428] dispensation for us, the Church, achieve its end? It was here that he, the Church's head,[429] came

---

423. On Cassian and Docetism see nt. 371; on Marcion see nt. 44; on Valentinus see nt. 99; I have translated *psychikos* as 'semi-spiritual': it stands between the physical and the spiritual.

424. Jer 5.8.

425. Reading συνουσίας with Major for συμβουλίας, and τύχη with Stählin for λέγη.

426. A Platonic term for the process of creation; the first book of the Bible is called Genesis.

427. Isa 40.6–8.   428. Adding ἂν with Major.

429. Eph 5.23.

in the flesh but without beauty of form,[430] teaching us to fix our gaze on the formless incorporeality of the divine cause. (4) "A tree of life," says the prophet, "grows in the soil of a healthy desire,"[431] teaching that desires held in the living Lord are good and pure.

104(1) They now want that union of man and wife within marriage, which Scripture calls knowledge,[432] to be a sin. They claim that this is indicated by the eating from the tree of good and evil, and teaches the fact that the commandment was transgressed by the use of the phrase "he knew." (2) If so, then the revealed knowledge of the truth is also an eating from the Tree of Life.[433] So it is possible for responsible marriage to take from that tree. (3) We have previously said that it is possible to use marriage for good or evil, and this, if we do not transgress the commandment, is the tree of knowledge. (4) Well? Does not the Savior heal body and soul alike from passions? It could not be, if the flesh were at enmity with the soul, that he would have put up fortifications against the soul in the soul's own territory by strengthening[434] flesh, the enemy, with health. (5) "Brothers, I tell you that flesh and blood are not able to inherit the kingdom of God; the perishable will never inherit imperishability."[435] For sin, being perishable, cannot enjoy fellowship with imperishability (that is righteousness). "Are you such fools?" he asks. "You have made a start with the Spirit. Are you now going to reach perfection through the flesh?[436]

18

Extremes of Opinion Regarding Marriage Should Be Avoided

105(1) So there are some people who have tried to extend the scope of righteousness and the strong, sacred concord with the power of salvation, as we have demonstrated. They

---

430. Isa 53.2; reading ἀειδής with Sylburg for ἀηδής, and δὲ ἐλήλυθεν with Bywater for διελήλυθεν.
431. Prov 13.12.   432. Gen 2.9 (see nt. 315).
433. Gen 2.9, 3.22, note the equation of truth and life.
434. Reading ἐπισκευάζων with Hervet for ἐπισκιάζων.
435. 1 Cor 15.50.   436. Gal 3.3.

have a blasphemous acceptance of self-control combined with total atheism. It is proper to choose celibacy in accordance with the norm of health and to combine it with piety, in gratitude for God's gift of grace, without hatred of creation or denigration of married people. The universe is the product of creation; celibacy is the product of creation. Both should be grateful for their appointed condition, if they know what that is. (2) But there are some who have kicked over the traces and run riot. They really are "stallions crazed for mares, whinnying for their neighbors' wives."[437] They cling uncontrollably to pleasure.[438] They persuade their neighbors to hedonism. The miserable wretches listen to these words from Scripture: "Throw your lot in with us. Let us all have a common purse and a single bag for money."[439]

106(1) It is because of them that the same prophet gives us advice in these words: "Do not travel on the road with them; keep your steps clear of the paths they tread. It is not unjust for nets to be spread out for birds. By sharing in bloodshed they are laying up evils for themselves"[440]—that is to say, they are eager in pursuing immorality and are teaching their neighbors to do the same. "They are warriors," says the prophet, "beaten with their own tails"—or, as the Greeks put it, penises.[441] (2) Those to whom the prophecy alludes might well be lecherous, undisciplined fighters using their tails, children of darkness, "children of wrath,"[442] bloody assassins and murderers of their neighbors. (3) "Clean away the old leaven to become bread of a fresh baking," the Apostle calls loudly to us.[443] And again, in indignation at people like that, he instructs that "if any professed Christian practices fornication,

437. Jer 5.8.
438. Adding ἡδονῆς with Schwartz.
439. Prov 1.14, part of the tempting words of the wicked.
440. Prov 1.15–18.
441. The source of the quotation is unknown but there is a complexity of meaning: Both words are Greek and mean 'tail,' and both, like tail and penis (literally tail) are applied to the male sex organ; the second, *kerkos*, is also used of a bull's pizzle used as a whip in punishment (see also Rev 10.10 and 19 where the animals' tails are dangerous weapons); one suspects a double meaning in "warriors"; the idea of love as a battle is common enough.

442. Eph 2.3.   443. 1 Cor 5.7.

is governed by the hope of profit, worships idols, uses abusive language, gets drunk, or is a swindler, we should have no fellowship, not even at table, with him."[444] (4) "Through the Law," he says, "I am dead to the Law in order to live to God. I am crucified with Christ. It is no longer I who am alive"— in the way I used to live, lustfully—"but Christ who is alive in me," making me blessedly pure through obedience to the commandments. In consequence, whereas previously I was alive in the flesh following the ways of the flesh, "now my life in the flesh is lived by faith in God's Son."[445]

107(1) "Do not go off the road to gentile territory or visit a Samaritan town," says the Lord, to divert us from the opposite way of living, since "the lawless come to a dreadful fate. These are the paths of all those who achieve lawlessness."[446] (2) "Alas for that man," says the Lord. "It was good for him never to have been born rather than cause one of my elect to stumble. Better for him to have a millstone tied around his neck and be drowned in the sea rather than misdirect one of my elect."[447] "God's name is dishonored because of them."[448] (3) This is why the Apostle makes the lofty statement, "I wrote in my letter that you should have nothing to do with profligate living" down to "The body is not for sexual promiscuity but for the Lord, and the Lord for the body."[449] (4) To make sure that he is not identifying marriage with fornication he adds, "Or do you not realize that anyone who attaches himself to a prostitute becomes physically one with her?"[450] Will anyone call a virgin before marriage a prostitute? (5) "Do not deprive one another," he says, "except temporarily by mutual agreement."[451] By using the word "deprive" he is showing the due obligation of marrying, the production of children. He made a point of this earlier in the words, "The husband must give the wife what is her due, and *vice versa*."[452]

---

444. 1 Cor 5.11 reading ἤ for the first ἤ as in Paul.
445. Gal 2.19–20.
446. Prov 1.18–19.
447. Clement of Rome, *First Epistle to the Corinthians* 46.8, who is quoting Matt 26.24, 18.6–7; Mark 9.42; Luke 17.2.

448. Rom 2.24.   449. 1 Cor 5.9–6.13.
450. 1 Cor 6.16.   451. 1 Cor 7.5.
452. 1 Cor 7.3.

108(1) After making this contribution, she is a helpmate domestically and in the Christian faith. He goes on[453] to speak more clearly: "I have an order for the married. It is not from me but from the Lord. A wife is not to seek separation from her husband. If she does, she is to remain unmarried or come to reconciliation with her husband. The husband is not to divorce his wife. To the rest I speak in my own person not as representing the Lord. [From the Scripture text] 'If any Christian male' down to 'but now they are dedicated to God.'[454] (2) These people who run down the Law and marriage as if it were constituted merely by the Law and alien to the New Covenant—what do they say in face of this? Those who have such a loathing for sex and childbirth—what have they to say in answer to this legislation? For Paul also lays down that leadership in the Church should rest with "a bishop who presides successfully over his household" and that "marriage to one wife" constitutes a household with the Lord's blessing.[455]

109(1) "So to the pure, everything is pure," he says. "To the tainted minds of the faithless, nothing is pure; they are tainted in reason and conscience."[456] (2) As to illegitimate pleasure he says, "Make no mistake. The sexually immoral, worshippers of idols, adulterers, passive perverts, homosexuals, those who pursue profit, robbers, drunkards, people who use abusive language, and swindlers will not inherit the kingdom of God." We used to be such, but "have passed through the purifying waters."[457] But they purify themselves for this licentiousness. Their baptism is out of responsible self-control into sexual immorality. Their philosophy is the gratification of their pleasures and passions. They teach a change from self-discipline to indiscipline. The hope they offer is the titillation of their genitals.[458] They make themselves excluded from the kingdom of God instead of enrolled disciples.[459] Under the name of what they falsely call knowledge[460] they have embarked on the

---

453. Reading ἔτι with Sylburg for εἴ τι.
454. 1 Cor 7.10–14.   455. 1 Tim 3.2–4; Titus 1.6.
456. Titus 1.15.   457. 1 Cor 6.9–11.
458. Phil 3.19.   459. Rev 20.12,15; 21.27.
460. 1 Tim 6.20.

road to outer darkness.[461] (3) "For the rest, brothers, set your minds on all that is true, all that is holy, all that is righteous, all that is pure, all that is attractive, all that wins praise, whatever wins admiration for its moral excellence. Put into practice the lessons I taught, the[462] traditions I passed on, the words you heard from me, the actions you saw me perform. And the God of Peace will be with you."[463]

110(1) Peter in his letter says much the same: "In consequence, you have purified your souls in obedience to the truth, and your faith and hope are in God,"[464] (2) "as obedient children, not molded by the lustful desires of your former ignorance. The one who called you is holy. Be like him, holy in all your behavior, since it is written, 'You are to be holy, since I am holy.'"[465] (3) But our critique of the hypocritical pretenders to knowledge, however essential, has gone beyond what is necessary and stretched out our discourse to a considerable length. So this is the conclusion of Book Three of our *Miscellanies of Notes of Revealed Knowledge in Accordance with the True Philosophy*.

461. Matt 8.12, 22.13, 25.30.   462. Omitting ἃ with Stählin.
463. Phil 4.8–9.   464. 1 Pet 1.21–2.
465. 1 Pet 1.14–16 reading ἀγνοίᾳ for ἀγνείᾳ with the *New Testament* text; the quotation is from Lev 11.44, 19.2, 20.7.

INDICES

INDEX OF PROPER NAMES AND SUBJECTS

INDEX OF HOLY SCRIPTURE

Books of the Old Testament

Books of the New Testament